Atomic Dwelling

In the years of reconstruction and the economic boom that followed the Second World War, the domestic sphere encountered new expectations regarding social behavior, modes of living, and forms of dwelling. This book brings together an international group of scholars from architecture, design, urban planning, and interior design to reappraise mid-twentieth century modern life, offering a timely reassessment of culture and the economic and political effects on civilian life.

This collection includes essays that examine art, objects, and spaces in the context of practices of dwelling over the long span of the postwar period. The authors consider various postwar spaces and the ways in which the anxiety of the cold war era infiltrated the domestic sphere or, the ways in which various versions of "home" were conjured to ease broader outside political or cultural tensions. *Atomic Dwelling: Anxiety, Domesticity, and Postwar Architecture* asks what role material objects, interior spaces, and architecture played in quelling or fanning the anxieties of modernism's ordinary denizens, and how this role informs their legacy today.

Robin Schuldenfrei is Junior Professor of Art History at Humboldt-Universität zu Berlin.

Atomic Dwelling

Anxiety, Domesticity, and
Postwar Architecture

Edited by
Robin Schuldenfrei

LONDON AND NEW YORK

First published 2012
by Routledge
2 Park Square, Milton Park, Abingdon, Oxon OX14 4RN

Simultaneously published in the USA and Canada
by Routledge
711 Third Avenue, New York, NY 10017

Routledge is an imprint of the Taylor & Francis Group, an informa business

© 2012 selection and editorial material, Robin Schuldenfrei; individual chapters, the contributors

The right of the editor to be identified as the author of the editorial material, and of the authors for their individual chapters, has been asserted in accordance with sections 77 and 78 of the Copyright, Designs and Patents Act 1988.

All rights reserved. No part of this book may be reprinted or reproduced or utilised in any form or by any electronic, mechanical, or other means, now known or hereafter invented, including photocopying and recording, or in any information storage or retrieval system, without permission in writing from the publishers.

Trademark notice: Product or corporate names may be trademarks or registered trademarks, and are used only for identification and explanation without intent to infringe.

British Library Cataloguing in Publication Data
A catalogue record for this book is available from the British Library

Library of Congress Cataloging in Publication Data
Atomic dwelling: anxiety, domesticity, and postwar architecture / edited by Robin Schuldenfrei.
    p. cm.
    Includes bibliographical references and index.
    1. Architecture and society—History—20th century. 2. Domestic space—History—20th century. 3. Civilization, Modern—20th century—Psychological aspects. I. Schuldenfrei, Robin. II. Title: Anxiety, domesticity, and postwar architecture.
    NA2543.S6A86 2012
    720.1'03—dc23
    2011027447

ISBN: 978-0-415-67608-3 (hbk)
ISBN: 978-0-415-67609-0 (pbk)
ISBN: 978-0-203-14272-1 (ebk)

Typeset in Univers
by Florence Production Ltd, Stoodleigh, Devon

Contents

Notes on Contributors   vii
Acknowledgments   x

Introduction   xi
Robin Schuldenfrei

Part 1:
Psychological Constructions: Anxiety of Isolation and Exposure

1   Taking Comfort in The Age of Anxiety: Eero Saarinen's Womb Chair   3
Cammie McAtee

2   The Future is Possibly Past: The Anxious Spaces of Gaetano Pesce   26
Jane Pavitt

3   Scopophobia/Scopophilia: Electric Light and the Anxiety of the Gaze in American Postwar Domestic Architecture   45
Margaret Maile Petty

Part 2:
Ideological Objects: Design and Representation

4   The Allegory of the Socialist Lifestyle: The Czechoslovak Pavilion at the Brussels Expo, its Gold Medal and the Politburo   67
Ana Miljački

5   Assimilating Unease: Moholy-Nagy and the Wartime/Postwar Bauhaus in Chicago   87
Robin Schuldenfrei

6   The Anxieties of Autonomy: Peter Eisenman from Cambridge to House VI   127
Sean Keller

Contents

Part 3:
Societies of Consumers: Materialist Ideologies and Postwar Goods

7 "But a home is not a laboratory": The Anxieties of Designing for the Socialist Home in the German Democratic Republic 1950–1965 — 149
Katharina Pfützner

8 Architect-Designed Interiors for a Culturally Progressive Upper-Middle Class: The Implicit Political Presence of Knoll International in Belgium — 169
Fredie Floré

9 Domestic Environments: Italian Neo-Avant-Garde Design and the Politics of Post-Materialism — 186
Mary Louise Lobsinger

Part 4:
Class Concerns and Conflict: Dwelling and Politics

10 Dirt and Disorder: Taste and Anxiety in the Homes of the British Working Class — 207
Christine Atha

11 Upper West Side Stories: Race, Liberalism, and Narratives of Urban Renewal in Postwar New York — 227
Jennifer Hock

12 Pawns or Prophets? Postwar Architects and Utopian Designs for Southern Italy — 254
Anne Parmly Toxey

Coda

From Homelessness to Homelessness — 277
David Crowley

Illustration Credits — 291
Index — 295

Notes on Contributors

Christine Atha is Associate Professor of Design History at the School of the Art Institute of Chicago. Her current research is entitled "Doing Things by the Book: Discourses of Value and Improvement in British Design Culture," and is an examination of the relationship between politics, class and taste.

David Crowley is the Head of the Department of Critical Writing in Art and Design at the Royal College of Art in London. He has a long-standing interest in Eastern Europe and is the author of various books including *Warsaw* (Loncon: Reaktion, 2003) and *Pleasures in Socialism: Leisure and Luxury in the Eastern Blcc* (with Susan Reid, Northwestern University Press, 2010). He was co-curator of the 2008–2009 exhibition *Cold War Modern: Design 1945–1970* at the Victoria and Albert Museum.

Fredie Floré is a Lecturer in Architectural History at VU University Amsterdam and post-doctoral researcher at the Department of Architecture and Urban Planning, Ghent University. Her research focuses on the history of discourses on domestic architecture, home culture, interior, and design in Belgium and the Netherlands in the second half of the twentieth century.

Jennifer Hock is an architectural historian who specializes in the history and theory of modern American architecture and urbanism. Her research focuses on issues of community and identity and the politics of large-scale urban projects during the postwar period. Educated at Yale University, the University of London, and Harvard University, she currently teaches at Middlebury College in Middlebury, Vermont.

Sean Keller is Assistant Professor of architectural history and theory at the Illinois Institute of Technology. He received the 2009 Winterhouse Award for Design Writing and Criticism and is a frequent contributor to *Artforum*. His writing has also appeared in the anthology *Architecture and Authorship*, and the journals *Grey Room*, *Log*, *Perspecta*, *Constructs*, and *Art Journal*.

Mary Louise Lobsinger is Associate Professor of History and Theory of Architecture at the J.H. Daniels Faculty of Architecture at the University of Toronto. She has published on various topics in postwar architecture including Italian architectural discourse, Aldo Rossi, Cedric Price, and cybernetics. The materials discussed in her chapter in this collection are part of a longer book project.

Notes on Contributors

Cammie McAtee is a doctoral candidate in the History of Art and Architecture at Harvard University. She is currently completing her dissertation, "The Search for Form in Postwar American Architecture." She has published on Mies van der Rohe, Eero Saarinen, Hideo Sasaki, and her forthcoming publications include an essay on Philip Johnson and the Roofless Church in New Harmony, Indiana.

Ana Miljački is Assistant Professor of Architecture at MIT where she teaches core and option design studios and seminars in the history and theory of architecture. Her recent publications include essays for *Making Things Public*, *Handbook of Architectural Theory*, *Log*, *Perspecta*, *Centropa*, and *Praxis*. Her 2007 dissertation from Harvard University was titled "The Optimum Aesthetic: Environment, Lifestyle and Utopia in the Postwar Czech Architectural Discourse."

Jane Pavitt is the Dean of Humanities and Head of the History of Design Department at the Royal College of Art. She is a specialist in twentieth-century and contemporary design, with a particular area of expertise and interest in design curating. She worked as a research fellow and exhibition curator at the V&A museum for over ten years, curating a series of exhibitions which broadened the framework of understanding for design practice and history in the museum context. These included *Brand.New* (2000), an exploration of branding from a historical and contemporary perspective; and *Cold War Modern: Design 1945–1970* (2008). She is the co-curator (with Glenn Adamson) of the 2011 V&A exhibition entitled *Postmodernism: Style and Subversion 1970–1990*.

Margaret Maile Petty is a Senior Lecturer at the School of Design, Victoria University of Wellington, New Zealand. Her research broadly investigates the discourse, production, and representation of modern architecture and interiors, with a particular focus on the history and theorization of electric lighting. She has published her research in *The Journal of the Society of Architectural Historians*, *Interiors*, *PLAT*, *Scapes*, and elsewhere.

Katharina Pfützner is a Lecturer at the National College of Art and Design, Dublin, an associate researcher at the Graduate School of Creative Arts and Media, Dublin and a member of the editorial board of the visual and material culture journal *Artefact*. She is currently completing a doctoral dissertation that examines industrial design practice in the GDR.

Robin Schuldenfrei is Junior Professor of Art History at Humboldt University, Berlin. She received her Ph.D. from the Graduate School of Design, Harvard University. She is co-editor, with Jeffrey Saletnik, of *Bauhaus Construct: Fashioning Identity, Discourse, and Modernism* (2009). Her research focuses on the points of convergence between design, architecture, and interior architecture, with an emphasis on the history and theory of the object, particularly its status in society. She is currently working on a full-length study of luxury and modernism in architecture and design in early twentieth-century Germany.

Anne Parmly Toxey holds a Ph.D. in architectural history. She is Director of a design firm (Toxey/McMillan Design Associates), teaches architectural history and historic preservation, and directs the Arc Boutant Historic Preservation Program. This preservation field school conserves French and Italian monuments, including the Sassi of Matera. This site is the topic of her recent book, *Materan Contradictions: Architecture, Preservation, and Politics*.

Acknowledgments

This project's theme and the questions it poses have been with me for several years. For the opportunity to formulate its contours and for their thoughtful discussions, I would like to thank participants in graduate seminars taught at the University of Illinois at Chicago and at the Humboldt University, Berlin. Many of the essays in this volume were first presented in a session organized by the editor entitled "Anxious Dwelling / Postwar Spaces" at the Association of Art Historians (AAH) Annual Conference in April 2010 in Glasgow. For that opportunity to bring together an international group of scholars, I am extremely grateful to the organizers and to the contributing scholars and members of the audience for their engaged discussion of the material. At the University of Illinois at Chicago, I thank research assistant Erica Morawski, and at the Humboldt University, assistants Anja Seliger, and especially Kerstin Flasche, who entered the project at its latest stage and proved invaluable. At Routledge, I would like to express my appreciation to Georgina Johnson-Cook and Joanna Endell-Cooper for their thoughtful stewarding of this volume through various stages of editing and production. My deepest gratitude goes to the authors for their diligence and to John, Henry, and Theo Ackerman for their dedication in every way.

Introduction

Robin Schuldenfrei

Postwar dwelling was fraught with anxiety. In the years of reconstruction and economic boom that followed the Second World War, under modernism's visionary and watchful eyes, the domestic sphere engendered new expectations regarding social behavior, modes of living, and forms of dwelling. This was the case despite accelerated, if partial, liberalization of social mores and public and private roles, and often occurred precisely because of it; anxieties generated by and through changing behaviors and contained just below their surface helped to ensure that changes remained always reined in by norms in formation and transformation. The Cold War and the nuclear threat that cast its shadow over several decades of domestic life in North America, Western Europe, and the Eastern Bloc was a powerful source of anxiety, but hardly the only one. The essays collected in this volume bring together a varied set of circumstances, proposals, designs, plans, and social and material outcomes—involving architecture, objects, urban planning, and interior design—that illustrate this phenomenon and shed new light on the transformations it accompanied.

Though the subject matter under examination here is represented by widely diverging fields of inquiry and diverse examples with distinct "objects" across varying political spectrums, these studies describe a common historical and political world. Collectively this volume proposes to reappraise mid-twentieth-century modern life as it was ostensibly meant to be lived by its various protagonists against concurrent realities and practicalities, bringing forth new readings of modernism's demanding expectations and oft-desired controls as seen by promoters and detractors alike. Its contributions offer a series of reassessments of postwar commodity culture and the economic and political retooling of civilian life by variously examining the material of art, objects, and spaces in the context of practices of dwelling over the long span of the postwar period—tracing its first accounts prior to and during the Second World War and its last examples to the late 1970s onset of a nascent postmodern condition that began to disperse some of modernism's concentrated force. Throughout this period, the acquisition of domestic goods and their attendant spaces not only added to or abetted the unease felt between neighbors struggling to keep up, but between political systems, each with its own attendant ideologies surrounding the "domestic" realm. It was an era of the display of tremendous self-confidence on the part of various authorities—in government, in design fields, and in the arts—which propagated their expertise in ways that both emboldened and exerted pressure upon the individual, producing conceit and, alternatively, apprehension. This exuberance, which can be seen in goods and in ideologies alike, also manifested itself in patterns of living. This anthology examines the role of material objects, interior spaces, and architecture in fanning or quelling the anxieties of mid-century modernism's ordinary denizens, and seeks to contextualize this role in informing their contested legacy today. It investigates an expanded notion of "dwelling" as a means of developing critical insight into the *political stakes* of domestic culture and the *domestic culture* of politics. Seeking not just to excavate and explicate previously underexamined aspects of postwar spaces and cultural artifacts, it asks how we might interrogate them as discursive entities that give us greater insight into this period generally.

  Over the course of twelve chapters and a coda, scholars contend with various postwar spaces and the ways in which the anxiety of the cold war era infiltrated the "home" as widely defined or, in reverse, the ways in which various versions of the domestic sphere were conjured to palliate broader outside political or cultural tensions. They consider the primary importance of home as being constituted in a given community, and within that construct, a community's chosen domestic typology, rather than in individual circumstances or self-created environments—even as such typologies largely saw their primary unit, often more than ever, to consist in the atomic family. And while the postwar period is often positioned as following a rupture vis-à-vis the prewar period, constituted by the war, the relationship between wartime design efforts and postwar design is crucial to understanding the era; individual essays indicate how one Belgian firm sought to divest itself of its wartime, pro-German past by buying licenses from Knoll International to produce modern furniture, while in Chicago, members of the successor institution to the Bauhaus contributed to the war effort which, in turn, accelerated the assimilation of their designs and pedagogies in their new American context.

  These investigations foreground a wide range of respective themes—transparency, instability, comfort, assimilation, post-materialist consumption—via the examination of specific objects (art works, Italian hill towns, furniture forms, interior designs) and countries (including Czechoslovakia, East Germany, England, Italy, the United States). The breadth of approach runs from the focused study of a single object and type (such as Eero Saarinen's Womb Chair), to consideration of the ambiguous distinction between use-object and art-object (via the profoundly disturbing spaces of Gaetano Pesce), to the wider examination of period culture and its broad-scale impact on interiors and city planning alike (exemplified in the attempt to relocate the residents of a southern Italian town or of a section of the Upper West Side of New York City).

  The anxieties of the age have found a lasting representational resting place in the material evidence they left behind—whether an installation, exhibition pavilion, domestic interior, furniture type or prototype, or in the very notions of "materiality" evidenced by these works. In turn, the insecurity so prevalent in many spheres of life and art of this period reflects, reproduces, and reworks larger political tensions. Not just a period of outward conflict, however, the essays in this volume demonstrate the extent to which discord played out in inner realms as well. In doing so, they illuminate the degree to which particular objects hold the power to both mask and unmask broader ideologies, serving to reveal fears, bluster, and deeply ingrained cultural beliefs alike. Postwar promises to transform society were never fully delivered upon, but anxieties about the predicted changes kept the denizens of the postwar period on edge.

Essays in the first part of this volume, "Psychological Constructions: Anxiety of Isolation and Exposure," address the issue of "anxiety" most directly. Via Saarinen's Womb Chair, Cammie McAtee aptly demonstrates modern design's search to answer the perceived need for comfort. Jane Pavitt uses spaces designed by Gaetano Pesce to highlight the period's fear of isolation as one specific strand of postwar anxiety. The often anxiety-producing line between enclosure and exposure forms the basis of Margaret Maile Petty's discussion of glass and electric lighting in postwar architecture. While closely examining the material conditions of the specific objects and spaces under discussion, the authors in this section, crucially, highlight psychological aspects of the material engagement with these works. Together, they demonstrate that the anxiety so prevalent in the period had a profound effect on the design of spaces and objects, as well as on their dwellers and users.

Essays in the next section, "Ideological Objects: Design and Representation," explore the ways in which objects of architecture and design, beyond their intended use, were instilled with symbolic—often political—meaning. The Czechoslovak Pavilion at the 1958 Brussels Expo, as Ana Miljački argues, came to represent a vision of socialist architecture acceptable to the West. Robin Schuldenfrei posits that through their activities for the war effort, New Bauhaus protagonists sought to become assimilated and accepted in America, and it was these wartime activities that made it possible for them to reposition their design and teaching for a time and circumstance beyond war. Focusing on Peter Eisenman's work in the 1960s and early 1970s, Sean Keller traces the ways in which the architect's appeal to formal logic and process express a counter-desire for autonomy for architecture—that would deny design's potential to provide a comforting sense of cultural stability. Thus, essays in this section bring to light the ways in which objects were called upon to represent or resist the ideologies of the cultures that generated them.

In the third part, "Societies of Consumers: Materialist Ideologies and Postwar Goods," multiple facets of the symbolism of—and reaction to—postwar consumerism come to the fore. A specific anxiety was behind the design and mass-production of domestic objects in East Germany, as Katharina Pfützner shows: politicians' desire to shape explicitly socialist goods and the contested role of modernism in this cultural politics. Fredie Floré explores how the Belgium firm De Coene, which had been convicted of being an economic war collaborator for producing goods for the German military during the war, was able to rehabilitate itself through the production of another set of objects—modern office and home furnishings, the licenses for which it was able to purchase from Knoll International. Mary Louise Lobsinger demonstrates how the self-styled radical designers of the neo-avant-garde in Italy created expensive domestic objects even as they positioned themselves as critical of consumer culture, materialism, and conformity. Never quite at home in their cultural realms, the subjects of the essays in this section illustrate the fluid, symbolic qualities of consumer goods in the postwar period and the ways in which everyday, modern objects were freighted with meaning through the clash of economic systems.

In the fourth section, "Class Concerns and Conflict: Dwelling and Politics," issues related to the social organization of groups come to the fore as they intersect with the perceived need for change in postwar dwelling. Christine Atha uses texts aimed at working-class households in England by political agencies and design authorities to explore how modernism was again called on to assist in moral and social reform in the postwar period, with the goal of changing working-class interiors and social structures alike. Housing as a contested cultural product, specifically a neighborhood renewal project in New York's Upper West Side, is taken up by Jennifer Hock in order to problematize anxiety surrounding race perceptions and demonstrate the limits of attempts at racial integration in modern redevelopment projects. Anne Parmly Toxey explores similar efforts by authorities to modernize the domestic situation in the rural southern Italian town of Matera by relocating the residents to new, modern towns and, in the process, pressuring them to adopt modern ways of living. In each essay, the author demonstrates how latent and not-so-latent anxieties about the habits and modes of dwelling of particular social groups influenced the actions—albeit generally well-meaning—undertaken by those in power.

Taken together, the essays explore a world of design in which much was at stake. Competition and perceived inadequacies often fomented anxiety in the period in which postwar modernism and the Cold War were simultaneously most ascendant. However, anxiety not only derived from open contest divided along east / west lines, but—as the contributions to this volume amply illustrate—just as often between "friendly" countries such as Italy and the United States, or—in an era characterized also by large-scale migrations and halting decolonization, desegregation, and women's liberation—through policies that divided people within societies. Social and political dissonance also found less-public manifestations in the spaces and activities of domestic life, in anxieties that the sweeping programs of modernism sometimes sought to manage and that it, and the scores of new, modern objects, living spaces, and "conveniences" it generated, often also provoked. By deeply investigating a number of these objects and spaces, their protagonists and their discourses, the essays in this volume illuminate a myriad of competing concerns of the period which throw their subjects into sharper relief—a broad range of objects and spaces interrogated for their wider meaning across multiple political spectrums and cultural and economic contexts. The tensions of the age proved to be transmutable.

Part 1

Psychological Constructions

Anxiety of Isolation and Exposure

Chapter 1

Taking Comfort in The Age of Anxiety
Eero Saarinen's Womb Chair
Cammie McAtee

Almost immediately upon its debut on the home furnishings market in 1948, Knoll's chair no. 70, or "Womb Chair," as it was quickly dubbed, achieved cult status as a design object (Figure 1.1). Emerging at the beginning of the era of prosperity, the chair enjoyed consistent popularity from the 1940s into the 1960s, ironically becoming a "classic" in a period defined by planned obsolescence and the cult of the new. Arguably Knoll's signature piece of the first two decades of the postwar period, in recent years the Womb Chair has resurfaced as an icon of mid-century modernism.[1] Its well-known designer, the Finnish-American architect Eero Saarinen (1910–1961), was a leading protagonist among the group of American practitioners who would become known as the "form givers." Although he adhered to the tenets of modern architecture as defined by Mies van der Rohe and Le Corbusier, Saarinen sought to expand the vocabulary and range of expression of architectural form, a goal he achieved in such buildings as the Jefferson National Expansion Memorial in St. Louis (1947–1965), the David S. Ingalls Hockey Rink at Yale University (1956–1959), and the Trans World Airlines Terminal at John F. Kennedy Airport, Idlewild (New York) (1956–1962).

Designed between 1946 and 1948, the Womb Chair predates these feats of engineering and sculptural form.[2] Through this, Saarinen's interpretation of the American "easy" chair, the designer challenged the popular perception that modern design was cold and uncomfortable. The Womb Chair confronts the poles of style and comfort, of artwork and everyday object. Contrasting hardness and softness, rigidity and flexibility, mass and line, the chair was artfully assembled to bring a sense of drama to the postwar home.

The Womb Chair has most often been examined from the point of view of Saarinen's trajectory as an object designer and architect and for the technological innovation it brought to furniture design.[3] This essay opens up its interpretation to

1.1
Womb Chair (Knoll chair no. 70) with Ottoman, 1946–1948 (Unknown photographer)

consider the impact of America's emotional state on its design. I examine the Womb Chair within the context of the Age of Anxiety, as the postwar years were popularly known. Anxiety was a persistent subtext within American culture during the country's most optimistic years, pervading the domestic realm as well as other social, political, and cultural arenas. I explore what this "overtly anxious" culture, as one observer called it, contributed to both Saarinen's design and the reception of the chair, including Saarinen's own understanding of what he had created. I argue that the chair is testimony to Saarinen's intuitive manner of designing, one that ultimately sought to create affective forms that engaged their users—in this case, sitters—on deeply psychological as well as physical levels.[4] But I will first consider the form of the chair and its formal origins. As my argument is supported by the physical experience of the Womb Chair, its haptic as well as optic qualities will be referenced throughout.

Organic Chair

A seemingly simple construction, the Womb Chair is actually a complex, even complicated, assemblage.[5] Wider than it is tall and almost as deep, the chair consists of two main elements: a large curving fiberglass seating shell and a tubular steel frame that loops under the arms and beneath the seat, where it meets a shorter curved piece supporting the front of the chair. The rounded form of the shell is interrupted by a deep U-shaped well at its base; a void that breaks the profile into three angles. Padded with a layer of foam rubber on the upper "seat" side, the shell, including the opening at the back, is completely enveloped by a woven textile. Approached straight-on, the shell seems to almost levitate above the supporting structure, its curving form delicately cradled by, rather than attached to the thin

Taking Comfort in The Age of Anxiety

1.2
Charles Eames and Eero Saarinen with Don Albinson (fabricator), first full-scale prototype and small model of "Conversation" chair for the Museum of Modern Art's "Organic Design in Home Furnishings" exhibition, September 24–November 9, 1941 (Unknown photographer, March 1941)

structural members. The final components are two cushions, down-filled in the early years of the chair's production, which fit over the seat and the well.

The formal origins of the Womb Chair lie in part within a series of chairs co-designed by Saarinen and Charles Eames for the Museum of Modern Art's 1940 competition "Organic Design in Home Furnishings" (Figure 1.2). Taking first place in their category, the chairs catapulted Eames and Saarinen into the forefront of American design and went far towards launching their independent careers. The success the series of chairs and sofa found with the competition jury relied upon the careful negotiation of good design and contemporary art. The curvilinear shapes of the chairs represented significant new directions for both designers. While Saarinen's earlier forays into furniture design were closely tied to his father's work and had drawn on Art Deco and modern design of the 1920s and 1930s, Eames, for his part, had experimented with historicism as well as streamlined Moderne in his architectural and design work. Leaving behind Constructivist and Functionalist design of the 1920s and 1930s, they instead took their inspiration from biomorphic forms, which had been introduced into art in the mid-1910s and further developed in the 1930s in the paintings of Joan Miró and the three-dimensional constructions of Alexander Calder, and had found expression more recently in the decorative arts through the furniture of Alvar Aalto and Frederick Kiesler.[6] It was Saarinen who gave the chairs their strong sculptural quality.

1.3
Full-scale model of a Grasshopper Chair (Knoll chair no. 61), 1943–1946 (Photograph by Harvey Croze, December 1946)

As a first step towards putting them into commercial production, the Museum of Modern Art commissioned the Massachusetts-based furniture manufacturer Heywood-Wakefield and the Haskelite Manufacturing Corporation of Chicago to make prototypes of all the notable competition entries for an exhibition. Wartime material shortages, however, made large-scale production of Saarinen's and Eames's chairs impossible.[7] In the end, the long-term significance of the "Organic Design" chairs lay in the directions their designs took the two young designers. They encouraged Eames and his collaborator and wife, Ray Kaiser Eames, to further explore molded plywood resins, thus initiating a research project that stretched into the 1950s, culminating in their celebrated leather padded Lounge Chair and Ottoman (1956). And though he was increasingly occupied by the demands of the busy architectural practice he shared with his father Eliel, Saarinen, too, continued to work on furniture. In 1946, his Aalto-esque bentwood Grasshopper Chair (1943–1946) was brought out by Knoll Associates, the interior and furniture design company headed by Hans Knoll and Florence Schust Knoll (Figure 1.3).[8]

Chair No. 70

The commission of the Grasshopper Chair was part of Florence Knoll's larger project to put new furniture designs by American architects and designers into production alongside well-known pieces by Europeans.[9] She envisioned these works as functioning as sculptural elements within domestic environments and within the business interiors she created for some of the most powerful companies of the time. Florence Knoll herself designed the background pieces, or as she saw them, the

Taking Comfort in The Age of Anxiety

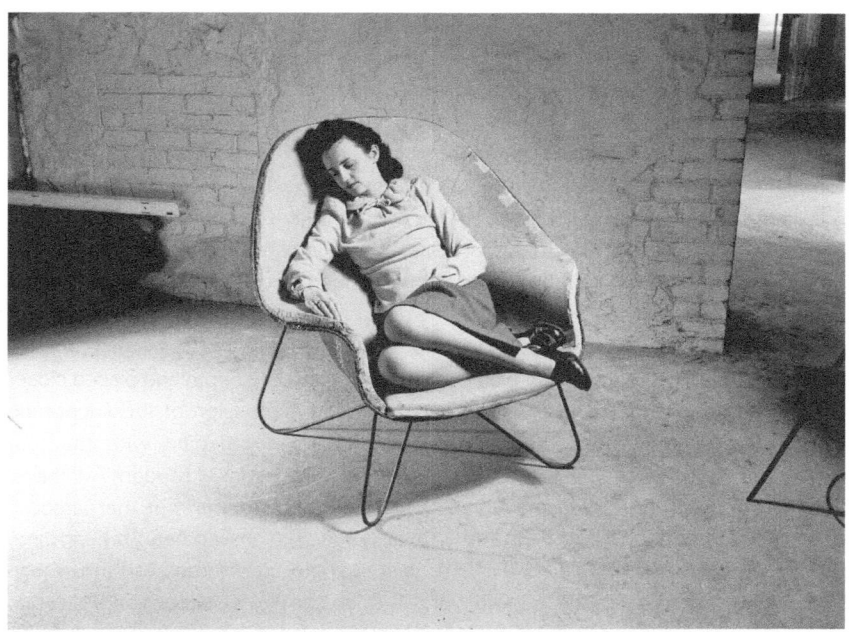

1.4
Above: Cranbrook student Agnes LaGrone Steen resting in Womb Chair prototype with "Butterfly" Chair base, 1946 (Photograph by Harvey Croze, December 1946)
Below: Eero Saarinen seated in Womb Chair prototype with exposed shell in the living room of his home in Bloomfield Hills, Michigan, 1947 (Photograph by Harvey Croze, 1947)

architecture.[10] She drew upon her friendships with several designers closely associated with the Cranbrook Academy of Art, where she had studied in the late 1930s.[11] She was especially close to Saarinen; the two had even been romantically involved for a brief period.

In 1946 Florence Knoll approached Saarinen to design another chair for the company. For this piece of furniture she had a specific program in mind, later recalling that she asked Saarinen to create a chair "like a big basket of pillows that I could curl up in."[12] As the story goes, Saarinen abandoned the two-dimensionality of the Grasshopper Chair and returned to the molded three-dimensional prototypes he had developed with Eames in 1940. The design of what would be officially known as Knoll's chair no. 70 loosely blended the "Conversation" and "Lounging shape" prototypes, but the seating shell was expanded in width and depth and placed closer to the ground, giving it a more informal quality. The expression of the supporting members proved to be a thornier problem. Clearly dissatisfied with the four conventional legs he and Eames had proposed for the Museum of Modern Art chairs, Saarinen experimented with many variations, even briefly trying out the parabolic base of Jorge Ferrari-Hardoy's Butterfly Chair (1938), which had been brought into production by Knoll in 1947–1948.[13] The sinuous line complemented rather than broke with the form of the shell (Figure 1.4). A compromise between the two structural systems was eventually adopted, likely to balance formal issues with those of stability. The desire for a clean, organic support initiated what Saarinen later called his mission to "clear up the slum of legs," which was achieved with the Pedestal Chair in the mid-1950s.[14]

Plastic Chair

Where the design most significantly departed from its predecessors was its use of plastic for the seating shell. Saarinen appears to have had plastic in mind from the very outset. It is not surprising that he was familiar with this new material at this early point. Even before the close of the Second World War, the plastics industry had begun to aggressively market its products for domestic use in the postwar period. In the spring of 1946, the same year Saarinen began working on the chair, the Society of the Plastics Industry organized the first public exhibition of their products. Held for a six-day period in New York, the exhibition attracted over 87,000 visitors. Alongside hundreds of other new materials, Fiberglas, a trade name that came to describe both polyester plastic reinforced with fiberglass and glass-reinforced plastic (both of which functioned as plastic not as glass), made its public debut.[15] Hans and Florence Knoll undoubtedly visited the exhibition, and it seems likely that Saarinen, with his well-known interest in new technologies, was also in attendance and saw first-hand the fiberglass fishing rods, skis, baby strollers, and one-piece boat frame on display. Moreover, through his work for the General Motors Corporation, Saarinen was well aware of the interest the material was generating in the automobile industry. In 1946 the first postwar prototype for a fiberglass automobile body came out.

Saarinen's and Florence Knoll's turn to plastic was more than timely; it was culturally significant. As historians of technology and popular culture have shown, the rise of plastic neatly segued with the greater affluence and corresponding consumer confidence that many Americans experienced in the postwar period. Plastic's malleability, its capacity to support bright, dense color and a variety of textures, its ease of production and relative cheapness all combined to make it the perfect material to express the ideals of a consumer society that privileged endless change, transformation, and newness. As well as enjoying the flexibility and functionality of Earl Tupper's standardized serving and storage containers (1947), the consumers who purchased them could also agree with Roland Barthes's prediction that "ultimately, objects will be invented for the sole pleasure of using them."[16] Saarinen's chair no. 70 thus anticipated the assimilation of a material that would develop a deep dialectical relationship with 1950s culture.[17] For Saarinen, however, the choice of a material that could be easily molded was based on its potential to express sculptural form, which he gradually came to believe was the chief concern of design.[18] With this issue in mind, he optimistically brought plastic forward as *the* material of postwar furniture design. In 1946, however, he was unconcerned with expressing the material's specific visual or tactile qualities; there were signs that he in fact was intent on hiding them. In this regard he was in conflict with Charles and Ray Eames, who espoused a "truth to materials" doctrine and accordingly prioritized the materiality of their furniture. The distance between their approaches at this time is illustrated by the Eameses' first fiberglass chair (1948–1950), which equally valorizes the material and the form of the seating shell.[19] It would only be in 1955 with the single pedestal Tulip Chair that Saarinen would acknowledge the aesthetics of the plastic shell. In 1958 he made comments deploring the technical limitations that forced the mixing of materials:

> For thousands of years, from Tutankhamen's chair through the Chippendale chairs, the chair was all wood. Now, because of technological and economic changes, plastic is a much more logical and desirable material. But the chair today is not all plastic—it is half plastic, half metal. I look forward to the day when the chair will become all one material again and that material will be plastic.[20]

Though these comments put Saarinen on record for wanting to use materials "honestly," his commitment to this ideal had its limits: when problems arose in the manufacture of the later Pedestal series pieces, Saarinen was willing to insert a metal support beneath the plastic base, thus privileging visual appearance over structural truth, a prioritization that was consistent with his approach to architectural form.

But whatever its promise, in 1946 fiberglass technology was still in its infancy and Saarinen and Florence Knoll struggled to find a manufacturer. They eventually succeeded in convincing the Winner Manufacturing Company of West Trenton, New Jersey, which was working with resin-bonded fibers, to construct prototypes for the seating shell.[21] However, even after he had found a way of producing the molded form of the shell, Saarinen seems to have harbored some doubts about hiding the chair's structure from view. Photographs document a highly finished prototype for a padded seat mounted on an exposed shell, possibly made of molded plywood (Figure 1.4). Given that this shell is in the same shape as the final fiberglass one and the curving chrome support is the same as the one chosen for the final version, the return to an exposed form came very late in the process. If the relationship between the shell and its padded "interior" is somewhat awkward here, it would provide a basis for the Pedestal series in which a cushion is fitted into the plastic shell.

Thus, although its shape comes from the material used to produce it, it is the concept of *plasticity* rather than the material *plastic* that animates the form of the Womb Chair. Built into the organic shape of the seating shell are associations of flexibility, growth, and transformation. Movement is conveyed in every fold. Felt beneath the layers of textile and rubber padding, the plastic shell recoils away from the outer edge, curling into itself, while the arms or "wings" of the chair curve outwards, undulating into space. A sense of forward motion is expressed in the folds of the arms, which can also be interpreted as physical imprints of the downward pressure of a body pushing up from the seat. As Barthes wrote in 1956, plastic "is less a thing than a trace of a movement."[22] The force of this pressure is underscored by the position of the legs, splayed backwards and forwards in anticipation of receiving the sitter's weight. The chair's plastic form reads as the frozen register of the very acts that define it: sitting and rising.

Returning to the photograph of the "Butterfly" prototype, we see tucked up into the chair a woman who appears to be sleeping. The chair's organic shape absorbs her body, providing a stable structure to rest upon, its padded rigidity configuring but not controlling her position.[23] While the reclining form gently holds the sitter's back, the wide seat and low arms encourage freedom of movement. As the initial view of the completed chair shows, the naturalness of its shape is enhanced by the extreme tactility of its fabric surface, which brings warmth to the form. The choice to encase the hard shell in layers of textile, padding, and down-filled cushions shows that Saarinen, unlike Eames, understood that for all its flexibility, plastic had a tactile downside, what Barthes identified as its "undoing": namely, "what best reveals it for what it is is the sound it gives, at once hollow and flat . . ."[24] The texture of the textile "skin," stretched flush with the molded form, emphasizes and further softens the hard edges. The values of light and shadow are complicated by the uneven surface of the woven fabric, which absorbs light, deepening the shadows of the folds.[25] The blurred geometries of the cushions—a rounded square and a trapezoid—subtly suggest archetypal forms and contribute to the overall organic quality, even harmony, of the ensemble of elements.

The result is an extremely "comfortable" chair, as the Womb Chair has been consistently described throughout the sixty-three years of its reception. In a post-design reflection, Saarinen claimed this was his goal:

> I designed the "womb" chair because there seemed to be a need for a large and really comfortable chair to take the place of the old overstuffed chair. . . . the need for such chairs has not passed. Today, more than ever before, we need to relax.[26]

But what do qualifiers like "comfortable" and "relaxing" actually mean? And what is their meaning in relation to the American home of the late 1940s and 1950s? We know these words are socially constructed, their meaning dependent upon the values held by the society that produces and receives material culture. Rather than taking Saarinen's claims at face value, I want to now consider what "comfort" signified in the context in which the Womb Chair was designed and why Saarinen was so emphatic that Americans needed to relax.

Anxious Chair

In contrast to the rosy picture often painted of America's postwar "affluent society," as we know well by now, there was a darker side to the years immediately following the War. Often referred to as the Age of Anxiety after the title of W.H. Auden's 1947 poem, the period was characterized for many by lingering depression over the deprivations of the 1930s and the trauma of both world wars, as well as by the new destabilizing threat of Communism fed by the Korean and Cold Wars and later by McCarthyism.[27] The overall sense of instability these threats created was accompanied by heightened anxiety and stress, two terms that not only rose to become catch words in the 1940s and 1950s, but came to characterize the prevailing mood of America. For example, in his influential 1949 book, *The Vital Center: The Politics of Freedom*, Arthur Schlesinger Jr. referred to "Politics in an Age of Anxiety" (though he positioned America as still resisting the descent of much of the world into a state of anxiety). In his groundbreaking 1950 study *The Meaning of Anxiety*, the existential psychologist Rollo May wrote that distressing new levels had been reached:

> [It] is a pervasive and profound phenomenon in the middle of the twentieth century. The alert citizen, we may assume, would be aware not only of the more obvious anxiety-creating situations in our day, such as the threats of war, of the uncontrolled atom bomb, and of radical political and economic upheaval; but also of the less obvious, deeper, and more personal sources of anxiety in himself as well as in his fellow-men—namely the inner confusion, psychological disorientation, and uncertainty with respect to values and acceptable standards of conduct.[28]

As May outlined, anxiety seemed to permeate American life. Writing somewhat later, another notable observer on anxiety's pervasiveness in contemporary society, the cultural anthropologist Margaret Mead, connected the popular parting phrase "take it easy" with the commonly held belief that Americans were under too much pressure.[29] In its turn, anxiety created "stress," a term that is largely a postwar construction especially in its psychological sense.[30] Chiefly through the research of the biologist Hans Selye, stress gained its popular definition as the physical *and* psychological "wear and tear caused by life."[31]

Not surprisingly, with anxiety and stress so foregrounded during this period, Americans, concerned about their wellbeing, searched for relief. The development of anti-anxiety agents in the early 1950s brought temporary release from these troubles.³² The first tranquilizer, Miltown, popularly known as the "peace" pill, "don't-give-a-damn" pill, or "Executive Excedrin," was enthusiastically embraced when it was introduced in 1955. A year later, no less than one in twenty Americans had tried it and Miltown was credited with keeping corporate America functioning.

The domestic sphere, too, had an especially important role as a space of refuge from the plethora of real and perceived threats and the resulting sense of fear and apprehension they created. Domesticity took center stage, the home reinvested with significance intended to keep dissolution and meaninglessness far away. Yet the home did not necessarily offer escape; reading it through Foucault's lens, Christopher Reed has noted that "The domestic, perpetually invoked in order to be denied, remains through the course of modernism a crucial site of anxiety and subversion."³³ Norman Rockwell's cover for the 1959 Easter weekend issue of the *Saturday Evening Post* shows exactly this Janus-face of modernity at work in the domestic context (Figure 1.5).³⁴ Often reproduced in literature on Saarinen as visual evidence of the Womb Chair's deep penetration into American popular culture, the content of Rockwell's painting *Easter Morning* (1959) has so far escaped closer examination for what it tell us about the reception of the chair. The image depicts the traditional ritual of the departure for morning church service, mother and children dressed in their Easter best, fitted with new hats, shoes brightly shined, and prayer books tightly clasped to chests. Their moral and physical rectitude is placed in stark contrast with the father slouching down into the chair; his descent into irreligion underscored by the sports page of the newspaper, cigarettes and coffee that are his attributes. Wisps of unkempt hair suggest horns, the prison-striped pajamas and bright red bathrobe presentiment of a dark fate possibly awaiting him. The storylines announced above the painting on the cover of the *Post*—"Our Gamble With Destiny" and "Warning To Young Men"—were obviously chosen to reinforce the visual message. But at the same time, the Womb Chair clearly serves as a shelter for the wayward husband and father, functioning as a buffer between the traditional values represented by his family and his own questionable, perhaps modern, choice to opt out of the ritual. The duality in Rockwell's characterization of the chair suggests that his critique was softened by sympathy for the desire to escape the anxiety and stress caused by domestic, work and moral responsibilities; perhaps the artist also understood the chair as a much-needed refuge from the family as well as wedge breaking its unity.

Not surprisingly, Rockwell himself was not a collector of modern design. His studio in Stockbridge, Massachusetts (the view from which is shown through the large picture window in the final painting) was mostly furnished with traditional American wood furniture.³⁵ While the presence of a rather Scandinavian wood chair with webbing in photographs of his studio around 1960 suggests that the artist was open to some forms of modern design, he did not own either the Womb Chair or the molded plastic Eames chair that appears at the edge of the final *Easter Sunday* painting. Study photographs of the chair and models were instead shot in Knoll's New York showroom at 575 Madison Avenue (Figure 1.5). Further photographic studies for the general scene were made back in Stockbridge. While views of other chairs

Taking Comfort in The Age of Anxiety

1.5
Above: Norman Rockwell, *Easter Morning*, 1959; cover of the *Saturday Evening Post*, May 16, 1959, Norman Rockwell Museum Archives, Stockbridge, MA
Below: Studio set-up for *Easter Morning* with mother and children models, Womb Chair, and Pedestal side table in Knoll Showroom, 575 Madison Avenue, New York, 1959 (Photograph by Robert Scott, 1959), Norman Rockwell Museum Archives, Stockbridge, MA

appear within these reference photographs, the formal qualities of the Womb Chair, especially its generous spatial presence, likely won Rockwell over to it. But in choosing the Womb Chair as the center and crucible of a painting that would become closely associated with mid-century American society, Rockwell succeeded in placing it at the heart of the revolution in family dynamics the country was entering.

Like the makers of Miltown and even Norman Rockwell, both the chair's designer and client understood that Americans needed relief from anxiety and stress. This shared understanding was rooted in their personal experience of domestic angst. By 1946, when he began to work on his second chair for Knoll, the edges of Saarinen's seven-year marriage to his wife, the sculptor Lily Swann Saarinen, were beginning to fray; they would divorce in 1953. Both Eero and Lily sought professional help—she for chronic depression, he largely for guidance on whether he should divorce her. During these years "home" was very much a contested territory for Saarinen. A few of his letters to his therapist Dr. "B" have survived.[36] Though they postdate the design of the Womb Chair by several years, the letters give insight into the many anxieties that plagued Saarinen, among them his excessive ambitions, fears that his eyesight would fail, concerns about not being "100 percent" American, his feelings about women and their role in his life, and his relationship with his famous father Eliel, about whom he expressed a sense of inferiority. They also reveal that much of Saarinen's anxiety centered on his domestic surroundings, with one of the chief complaints expressed about his wife being her disinterest in their home. Blaming himself as well as Lily for the failure to make their home a place of which he could be proud, Saarinen took stock of the situation in a letter to Dr. B:

> My habits are such that I do not spend any time at home[.] I have completely neglected my home—I have done nothing to create a beautiful atmosphere out of this—I have ceased to read and develop myself in related fields such as history, literature etc. These neglects are in complete contradiction to my father's life, which I seem to wish to pattern [my own on] and I have a great yearning for them . . .[37]

Saarinen then went on to express a desire to create a modern equivalent of Hvitträsk, the country home designed by Eliel in Finland, something that would be on par with the Eameses' "dream home" in Pacific Palisades, California (1945–1949).[38] He added: "my life would only be half lived if this does not happen."

The domestic realm of Hans and Florence Knoll was reputedly as fraught as that of the Saarinens, the happy images of the couple diffused in publicity photographs a mask for a tense home life.[39] The home, moreover, seems to have been a design context Florence Knoll deliberately kept at bay, focusing instead on business environments.[40] If on the one hand this is somewhat incongruous with the reality that much of her company's success came from the lucrative home furnishings market, on the other, Florence Knoll had understandable professional reasons for distancing herself from the domestic context as a design environment. Trained as an architect, she sought to disassociate her work from the feminized world of interior decoration, calling herself an interior designer and directing Knoll's corporate-oriented Planning Unit.[41]

In light of this ambivalence towards domesticity, Florence Knoll's request for a chair in which she could "curl up" no longer appears straightforward and requires closer scrutiny. Her concept for the chair might be interpreted as a longing for a retreat *within* the home, a desire with which Saarinen could certainly sympathize. Rockwell's painting certainly backs up this role for the chair as a sanctuary. But there may be another layer to this complex object. Perhaps Florence Knoll was looking for something beyond bodily comfort, something "deeper" than "a basket of pillows," and that it was in answer to this unconscious wish that Saarinen designed the chair.

"Don't Give a Damn" Chair

Americans clearly needed some kind of relief from the pressures weighing upon them. In her cultural history of tranquilizers, the historian of medicine Andrea Tone writes that mid-century anxiety, like neurasthenia in the nineteenth century, "signaled American achievement and advancement; unwanted and uncomfortable, it was the inevitable price of success."[42] Psychoanalysis first, tranquilizers later, arrived in what Tone characterizes as "a society preoccupied with anxiety and committed to its containment."[43] By 1940 the country had surpassed Vienna and London to become the world center of psychoanalysis, Freud's theories having their biggest impact in the United States.[44] A 1947 article in *Life* magazine told of an unprecedented "boom" in the demand for "talk" therapy as Americans searched for relief from what the journalist called "the alarming prevalence of mental and emotional disorders in the population today."[45] By 1955 *Newsweek* magazine estimated that 7 million, or 1 in 17 Americans suffered from psychoneurotic complaints. True or not, the general perception was that Americans needed help and psychoanalysis went mainstream in response (Figure 1.6).[46] Eero and Lily Saarinen were just two among the thousands of Americans who turned to the profession with their problems. It is through the lens of the containment and control of anxiety that I will now examine the Womb Chair.

The idea that Saarinen may have designed the chair in response to anxiety is not original within the history of modern architecture and design. As is well-known, modern architects and designers engaged science to promote good health and to cure illness, including neurasthenia, as in Josef Hoffmann's Purkersdorf Sanatorium (1904–1905). Another attempt by a modern architect to create a chair that would encourage medical recovery, moreover, one with which Saarinen was very familiar, is Aalto's celebrated Paimio Chair (1931–1932) designed for the lounge of his recently completed Tuberculosis Sanatorium, Paimio, Finland. If generally admired for its dramatic bentwood curves, the angle of the chair back was intended to position the patient's body in a manner that would make breathing easier. But what may be the first piece of furniture specifically designed to alter its occupant's psychological state is the American psychiatrist Dr. Benjamin Rush's 1811 "Tranquilizer" Chair (Figure 1.7). Presented as an alternative to the straitjacket, the chair was designed to pacify psychiatric patients by controlling their exposure to

1.6
Jack Kamen, cover of *Psychoanalysis*, no. 1 (EC Comics / New Directions, 1955)

external stimuli.⁴⁷ It is, however, the *chaise longue*, the modern chair *par excellence*, specifically designed to resolve health problems, mental as well as physical, that is most pertinent to the genealogy of the Womb Chair.⁴⁸ Certainly, the semi-reclining shape of the Womb Chair, especially when paired with its optional ottoman, has a close formal connection to these earlier "cure" chairs.

But at the same time the Womb Chair differs from these forebears in a very significant way, in that it is neither utopian nor idealistic. Unlike the first generation of modern architects and designers who worked towards solving society's health and hygiene problems, Saarinen accepts the situation. His chair is conceived as a palliative for mid-century anxiety. It is about coping with the anxieties of modern life, not curing them. Like the tranquilizers developed a few years later, the Womb Chair is about relaxing, about giving temporary respite from the stresses of everyday life. It might even be called the "don't give a damn" chair.

It is through its palliative nature that Saarinen's chair bears a striking relationship with perhaps the most famous non-architect designed chair of the

Taking Comfort in The Age of Anxiety

1.7
Left: Sigmund Freud's couch from Berggasse 19, Vienna, installed in his consulting room at 20 Maresfield Gardens, London (Unknown photographer, 1986)
Right: Dr. Benjamin Rush, "Tranquilizer" Chair, 1811

twentieth century: the *chaise longue* in Sigmund Freud's consultation room.[49] Covered by a Persian carpet, and carefully positioned in relation to the analyst's chair, the couch supported the body as the mind's neuroses were explored through free association (Figure 1.7). The Womb Chair relates to the Freudian couch as a similarly safe and secure place for long hours of talking. The way it encourages relaxation makes it an ideal setting for the release of the unconscious. Interestingly, in this it plays counterpart to Charles and Ray Eames's Lounge Chair, which was and is one of the most popular chairs for analysts.

So to return to the physical chair a final time, it is my contention that the Womb Chair operates on a distinctly psychological level, engaging the sitter mentally as well as physically. The open form is very compelling: upon approaching it, one is inexplicably drawn towards and into the chair. One is seized by an almost irresistible psychological urge, even longing, to physically engage with it, to be absorbed within its deep folds, to become one with the chair. Enclosed within this insulated nest, or "basket of pillows," the sitter is soothed, gaining a sense of reassurance and wellbeing from the protective shell. Not only *comfortable*; the chair is *comforting*.

Womb Chair

Having raised the specter of Freud, we now might be able to make sense of the renaming of Knoll chair no. 70 as the Womb Chair. According to one of several popular myths, it received its nickname at the press launch in May 1948. Almost nine months pregnant at the time, Martha Howard Blake, then wife of the architecture critic Peter Blake, sat in it "happily and comfortably."[50] Florence Knoll, who had first introduced it to the press as the "curling chair" in reference to the physical position it encouraged, proclaimed it the "Womb" Chair and the name stuck.[51] Hans Knoll, however, refused to accept the popular name, and requested something more conventional. Saarinen replied: "I have been thinking and thinking about a printable name for that chair, but my mind keeps turning to those which are more biological than less biological."[52]

While the name was never used in official publicity, Knoll nevertheless seems to have exploited these references in its promotional campaigns. It was often featured in Herbert Matter's publicity photographs upholstered in Knoll's signature bright red color, which paradoxically only served to reinforce the biological associations raised by the nickname. Even today, when other retailers advertise the Womb Chair, it is typically upholstered in brilliant red tones. Whatever Knoll's intention, the message was received, as a striking photograph by the fashion photographer John Rawlings shows in a 1957 article by George Nelson.[53] Surrounded by eleven other "key contemporary chairs," the Womb Chair takes center stage within the image with a nude woman stretching along its inner curves, her body a mirror of its sensuous shape. The caption beneath repeated the by-now familiar connection of body and chair: "'The Womb' by Eero Saarinen, a plastic-shelled lounge chair which invites prenatal posturing." Less erotic but no less biological associations were also made. A 1959 article in *Family Circle* about child-friendly home furnishing featured a photograph of two young boys cavorting upon the arms of a Womb Chair, their Knoll-red pajamas vividly contrasting with the bright turquoise upholstery of the chair.[54] The decision to decorate in a carefree manner was justified by the author as insurance that "our innocents make it to manhood without the aid of an analyst's couch."[55]

Deeper meaning may indeed lurk in the appellation, as Saarinen himself suggested in a 1949 letter to his client J. Irwin Miller: "I'm glad to hear that you like the big chair. You might be interested to know that its unofficial name is the 'Womb Chair,' because it was designed on the theory that a great number of people have never felt really comfortable and secure since they left the womb. The chair is an attempt to rectify this maladjustment in our civilization."[56] This equation uncannily restates Freud's famous observation in *Civilization and Its Discontents* that "the house a substitute for the womb—one's first dwelling place, probably still longed for, where one was safe and felt so comfortable."[57] If Saarinen's paraphrase is more a reflection of the deep penetration of Freudian theories into American popular culture than an indication of any direct knowledge of them, it nevertheless speaks to the architect's ability to intuit the mood of his times.[58] The spatial contexts into which he inserted the Womb Chair indicate that he believed the chair possessed soothing qualities. In addition to environments that were contemplative, such as libraries, Saarinen also envisioned placing Womb Chairs in spaces that could be stressful, like a waiting lounge at the TWA Airline Terminal.[59]

The chair also played an important role in the crafting of Saarinen's public image. In the 1956 feature article in *Time* magazine that made him a household name, a photograph appears of a smiling Saarinen with his second wife Aline at his side and their young son Eames crawling at his feet.[60] More than a stunningly successful architect, the image and text told, Saarinen the man was also in rare possession of domestic contentment. But interestingly, leaning awkwardly forward over his knees in the Womb Chair, his thick glasses uncharacteristically removed from his face, Saarinen looks anything but comfortable. He seems to be actively resisting the downward pull of the chair's form, perhaps determined to maintain the tension necessary to keep his career moving forward. The Womb Chair figures in countless other photographs of Saarinen and his new family, possibly acting as a stand in for the home he did not live to design. It may also have been a connection to his father Eliel, who died peacefully on July 1, 1950 sitting in a Womb Chair.[61]

While much has been made of Saarinen's creation of rich symbolic forms—the heroic St. Louis Arch and bird-like TWA Terminal chief among them—his Womb Chair demonstrates that he was also a master of "affective form," as Sylvia Lavin has characterized the work of Richard Neutra.[62] However, unlike Neutra, who was deeply influenced by psychoanalytic theories and directly applied them to his architectural designs, there is no evidence that Saarinen could or would claim inspiration from either Freud or his American followers. As the Womb Chair shows, he was a deeply intuitive designer who worked closely with his clients to come up with unique solutions to what he saw as unique design problems. While on the surface Saarinen's "one-off" approach could be (and was) interpreted as a disturbing sign of a lack of principles, it might be more positively read as an empathetic design method that strove to produce forms that touched the mind as well as the body.

With the Womb Chair Saarinen gave form to concerns about anxiety and control that permeated postwar American culture and in doing so he created an object that struck a deep chord within society. He created a *comforting* comfortable chair, a much-needed quality to keep "The Age of Anxiety" at bay. If this success was largely founded on an unconscious project that was rooted in the personal lives of Saarinen and his client, by 1956, when he began designing what are perhaps his most intriguing forms—the TWA Terminal and the Yale Hockey arena—Saarinen was completely cognizant of his intentions. Merging sculptural shape, technological innovation, and spatial and psychological experience based on empathetic associations, Saarinen created forms that have never ceased to touch the users of these objects and spaces in a profound way.

Notes

Acknowledgments: I wish to thank Laura Tatum, Architectural Records Archivist, and the reference staff of Manuscripts and Archives, Yale University Library; Robbie Terman, Archivist, Cranbrook Archives; and Corry Kanzenberg, Curator of Archives, Norman Rockwell Museum for their help with research and photography. I am especially grateful to Jehane Kuhn for kindly inviting me into her home to sit in her vintage Womb Chair, and to Yves Colombe and Aliki Economides for sharing the adventure of seeing their Womb Chair's move from naked to clothed. My interpretation greatly benefited from Jennifer Roberts's comments on an early version of this essay and those of the editor Robin Schuldenfrei. My adviser Neil Levine has inspired my consideration of Eero Saarinen's work in myriad ways. As ever, Réjean Legault offered stimulating and challenging criticism. My research has been

Cammie McAtee

supported by grants from the Social Sciences and Humanities Research Council of Canada, Harvard Graduate School of Arts and Sciences, and the Center for Advanced Study in the Visual Arts, National Gallery of Art, Washington DC. I dedicate this essay to my daughter Constance.

1. The Womb Chair's only serious rival for this title was the Pedestal or Tulip Chair of 1955–1957, also by Saarinen. (I exclude Mies van der Rohe's Barcelona Chair since it was a design that was put back into production by Knoll rather than a new and unquestionably Knoll-sponsored design.) More than ten years after its launch, the Womb Chair received a ranking of #13 among "100 'Best Designed' Products," a chair design surpassed only by Charles and Ray Eames's side chair (1947) ranked #2, and the Barcelona Chair (1929), which came in at #3. Saarinen's later Pedestal Chair with arms also made the list (#75). See "The 100 'Best Designed' Products," *Fortune* 59 (April 1959): 135–141.
2. While the end date of the chair's design—1948—is based on the patent drawings and the start of Knoll's production of the chair, the Womb Chair developed from studies begun in 1945 for what later became Knoll's series 70 chairs. On this, see Florence Knoll's comments quoted by Jayne Merkel, "American Moderns: Eero Saarinen and his Circle," *Architectural Design* 72, no. 4 (July 2002): 29; and a dated photograph of the early series 70 studies in Brian Lutz, "Furniture: Form and Innovation," in *Eero Saarinen: Shaping the Future*, ed. Eeva-Liisa Pelkonen and Donald Albrecht (New Haven, CT: Yale University Press, 2006), 252 Figure 8.
3. On Saarinen's furniture designs, in addition to Merkel and Lutz, see R. Craig Miller, "Interior Design and Furniture," in *Design in America: The Cranbrook Vision 1921–1950* (New York: Harry N. Abrams, in association with the Detroit Institute of Arts and the Metropolitan Museum of Art, 1983), 98–121, 302–313.
4. The idea that the Womb Chair possesses a distinct psychological dimension was raised but was otherwise undeveloped by Antonio Román in *Eero Saarinen: An Architecture of Multiplicity* (New York: Princeton University Press, 2003), 99ff.
5. Five Womb Chairs were consulted for this study: two chairs with matching ottomans produced before 1955 in the American Decorative Arts Collection, Yale University Art Gallery; a chair in a Cambridge home, probably produced in the 1960s; a recently manufactured chair and ottoman on display in the Knoll showroom in Boston; and a recovered chair of unknown date. The chair's dimensions are approximately 90.5 × 98.5 × 85.0 cm.
6. See Martin Eidelberg, *Design 1935–1965: What Modern Was: Selections from the Liliane and David M. Stewart Collection* (Montreal: Musée des Arts Décoratifs in association with Harry N. Abrams, 1991), 88–93; and George H. Marcus, *Design in the Fifties: When Everyone Went Modern* (Munich: Prestel, 1998), 95–107.
7. On this issue see Lutz, "Furniture: Form and Innovation," 249–250; and Pat Kirkham, *Charles and Ray Eames: Designers of the Twentieth Century* (Cambridge, MA: MIT Press, 1995), 210.
8. Chair no. 61 (Grasshopper Chair), was designed in 1943 and put into production by Knoll in 1946 (discontinued in 1965). The American manufacturer Modernica has recently made it available again. The chair's bentwood structure bears a close relationship with that used in the slightly earlier series of chairs designed by Saarinen's Cranbrook colleague Ralph Rapson for Knoll starting in 1944. The idea that Hans Knoll may have actively encouraged both Rapson and Saarinen to design chairs in the same Scandinavian aesthetic of those of Aalto and Bruno Mathsson is entirely plausible. Unlike his wife and partner Florence, Hans Knoll favored Scandinavian design; the Dane Jens Risom was his main designer until around 1943. He was also well aware of the popularity of Aalto's furniture; the Museum of Modern Art had presented a touring exhibition of his furniture and architecture in 1938 and Aalto's Finnish Pavilion at the 1939 New York World's Fair was furnished with his pieces. For his part, Saarinen, who knew Aalto well, owned one of his Paimio Sanatorium chairs (Miller, "Interior Design and Furniture," 305 note 55). Saarinen's admiration for Aalto's furniture designs led him to feature his cantilevered stacking side chair (1930) and a very Aalto-esque armchair in a project for an interior

designed for *Architectural Forum*. See "A Combined Living—Dining Room—Study," *Architectural Forum* 67, no. 4 (October 1937): 303–305.

9   On Florence Schust Knoll, see Bobbye Tigerman, "'I Am Not a Decorator': Florence Knoll, the Knoll Planning Unit and the Making of the Modern Office," *Journal of the History of Design* 20, no. 1 (2007): 61–74.

10 This foreground/background conceptualization of interior space strongly reflected Knoll's study with Mies van der Rohe at the Illinois Institute of Technology between 1940 and 1941 (degree granted June 1941).

11 Florence Schust began studying architecture and design with Eliel Saarinen while attending Cranbrook's Kingswood School. After graduating in 1934, she briefly attended the School of Architecture at Columbia University and the Architectural Association in London before returning to do advanced work at the Cranbrook Academy of Art (1937–1940) and then at IIT. She later recalled how her project began: "At that time [the mid-1940s] I started to collect all of the people I really admired, like Saarinen, [Harry] Bertoia, and Rapson, who were at Cranbrook when I was there. That's how the Knoll designers happened." She added a few comments about her feelings about the Scandinavian design aesthetic Hans Knoll had built the company upon: "[Jens] Risom was a very good designer and he was doing this Danish thing. Not that it wasn't good, but it was different from what was coming from the architectural world. I'd studied with Mies and was very interested in that form of design." From interview with Paul Makovsky, "Shu U," *Metropolis Magazine*, July 2001: 38.

12 Florence Knoll quoted by Rita Reif, "Pioneer in Modern Furniture is Charting Expansion Course," *New York Times*, June 17, 1959. A variation on this recollection—"I was sick and tired of those chairs that held you in one position . . . I wanted a chair that was like a basket full of pillows . . . I wanted something I could curl up in"—is included in Eric Larrabee and Massimo Vignelli, *Knoll Design* (New York: Harry N. Abrams, 1981), 56.

13 Photographs at Yale and Cranbrook Archives record various bases for the Series 70 chairs. The Butterfly Chair is also known as the Hardoy and BFK Chair, the latter crediting Hardoy's partners Antonio Bonet and Juan Kurchan. Though seen as a very modern chair, the basic structure dates back to the late nineteenth century. On its history, see especially Peter Blake and Jane Thompson, "More Than You May Want to Know About a Very Significant Chair," *Architecture Plus* 1, no. 4 (May 1973): 72–80. The Hardoy Chair was "scheduled for regular production" by Knoll in 1948. See Mary Roche, "New Chair Offers More Relaxation," *New York Times*, May 19, 1948. That Saarinen was familiar with the Butterfly Chair is documented in photographs showing him seated in a high-backed "Organic" chair next to Ralph Rapson, who is seated in a leather-slung Butterfly Chair (Eero Saarinen Collection, Yale University Library [hereafter cited as Saarinen Collection, Yale]).

14 Saarinen, speech, Schöner Wohnen Congress, Munich, Germany (unpublished manuscript, October 24, 1960), Saarinen Collection, Yale; cited in Aline B. Saarinen, ed., *Eero Saarinen On His Work: A Selection of Buildings Dating from 1947 to 1964 with Statements by the Architect*, rev. ed. (New Haven, CT: Yale University Press, 1968), 66. All subsequent citations refer to this edition.

15 Though the technology that would lead to the development of fiberglass dates back to the nineteenth century, it was substantially developed in the United States through a collaboration between Corning Glass and Owens-Illinois in the 1930s. Fiberglas was significantly developed during the Second World War for the US Air Force. On the history of fiberglass, see especially Jeffrey Meikle, *American Plastic: A Cultural History* (New Brunswick, NJ: Rutgers University Press, 1995), 168, 194–205.

16 Roland Barthes, "Plastic," *Mythologies*, trans. Annette Levers (New York: Hill and Wang, 1972), 99. Originally published as "Petite mythologie du mois: le plastique," in *Les Lettres nouvelles*, March 1956.

Cammie McAtee

17   Jeffrey Meikle has observed: "As we finally entered the Plastics Age, with synthetics all around us, we began to describe our culture itself with terms and metaphors formerly used to characterize plastics." See Meikle, "Materials and Metaphors: Plastics in American Culture," in *New Perspectives on Technology and American Culture*, ed. Bruce Sinclair (Philadelphia: American Philosophical Society, 1986), 34.

18   Twelve years after the chair went into production, Saarinen emphasized this quality: "Charles Eames and I believe strongly that the compound curved shell of plastic is the more appropriate material for twentieth-century furniture, if one takes all the factors into consideration. The problem becomes a sculptural one—not the cubist, constructivist one—and so the problem is to relate this sculptural shape to the box-like room" (Saarinen, Schöner Wohnen Congress address).

19   The Eameses' first proposal to use a shell of resin and fiberglass cloth formed part of their submission to the 1948 Museum of Modern Art competition for low-cost furniture. Although conceived as the support of a *chaise longue*—"La Chaise"—it was decided to bring out the designs of side and arm chairs, presented in the proposal constructed as stamped-metal, in fiberglass, thus launching the Eameses' most commercially successful designs. The armchair was first produced by Zenith Plastics for Herman Miller in 1950, but "La Chaise" was not put into production until 1990. On this subject, see Kirkham, *Charles and Ray Eames*, 234ff.

20   Saarinen quoted in "Furniture to Live With," *Monsanto Magazine*, April–May 1958: 9.

21   On the technical specifications of the seating shell, see Lutz, "Furniture: Form and Innovation," 253–254; and Miller, "Interior Design and Furniture," 120, 310 note 146. When Saarinen and Florence Knoll contacted Winner Manufacturing the company was working on developing fiberglass boats for the U.S. Navy. They may have learned about the company through the 1946 New York Boat Show exposition. The company had presented the first plastic boat ever shown at the Boat Show—a ten-foot dinghy constructed of polyester reinforced by sisal fibers—which was not well received by the wood-loving boating community. On the company's work at that time, see George H. Waltz, Jr., "Biggest Plastic Makes New Navy Boat," *Popular Science* 153, no. 4 (October 1948): 144–148. The company made another significant contribution to modern architecture as the supplier of the fiberglass panels used to construct Monsanto's House of the Future (1957).

22   Barthes, "Plastic," 97.

23   This close study of the body's relationship to the chair was a continuation of studies undertaken by Eames and Saarinen for the "Organic Design" chairs. Saarinen's then-wife Lily Swann Saarinen recalled that she and Ray Kaiser, who had very different body types, were asked to try the prototypes to ensure they were equally comfortable. Robert Brown, "Oral history interview with Lilian Swann Saarinen, 1976–1981," Archives of American Art, Smithsonian Institution. See below as well.

24   Barthes, "Plastic," 98.

25   In the early years before the company established its textiles division, Florence Knoll had turned to English haberdashers for the soft woven materials she wanted for Knoll's upholstery.

26   Saarinen quoted in *Eero Saarinen On His Work*, 66.

27   W.H. Auden, *The Age of Anxiety: A Baroque Eclogue* (New York: Random House, 1947). Although the setting of the poem was a bar in New York in the 1930s, the "age of anxiety" was applied to the period in which it was published. Auden's "age of anxiety" referred to past events—the trauma of the First and Second World Wars and the privations of the Depression. The poem inspired Leonard Bernstein's Second Symphony (1948) named after the poem, and Jerome Robbins's ballet (1950), both of which Auden reputedly detested. See Humphrey Carpenter, *W.H. Auden: A Biography* (London: George Allen & Unwin, 1981), 348.

28   Rollo May, *The Meaning of Anxiety* (New York: The Ronald Press Company, 1950), 3. Analyzing writing on anxiety by such writers as Kierkegaard and Freud, May intended his study to provide a comprehensive theory of the malady that could be used in psychological analysis.

29 Margaret Mead, "One Vote for This Age of Anxiety," *New York Times*, May 20, 1956. Interestingly, Mead was one of the few observers of the phenomenon to give "anxiety" in American culture a positive reading. In the *Times* article she commented that the widespread feeling of anxiety in American society denoted a milestone in human development. Contrasting the lives of contemporary Americans to those of "primitive" peoples and "peasants," she placed anxiety in opposition to fear, terror and despair. "Anxiety," she noted, only existed in societies that were relatively safe. "For most Americans," she wrote, "there remains only anxiety over what may happen, might happen, could happen." She interpreted its presence as a sign of "hope for the first time in society where there will be freedom from want and freedom from fear. Our very anxiety is born of our knowledge of what is now possible for each and for all" (ibid.).

30 For the history of twentieth-century discourse on "stress," see Tim Newton, "Knowing Stress: From Eugenics to Work Reform," in *"Managing" Stress: Emotion and Power at Work* (London: Sage Publications, 1995), 18–57.

31 Though Selye had begun to explore "stress" as early as 1926, he only began to theorize it following the Second World War when interest in the psychology of stress grew. Among Selye's many works on the subject, see *The Stress of Life* (New York: McGraw-Hill, 1956).

32 Barbiturates developed in the early years of the twentieth century offered a pharmaceutical answer to the problem of mid-century neurasthenia, but they were highly addictive and even deadly. On the cultural and pharmaceutical history of anti-anxiety agents, see Andrea Tone, *The Age of Anxiety: A History of America's Turbulent Affair with Tranquilizers* (New York: Basic Books, 2009). Except where otherwise noted, statistics on the use of anti-anxiety drugs are drawn from this excellent study.

33 Christopher Reed, "Introduction," in *Not At Home: The Suppression of Domesticity in Modern Art and Architecture*, ed. Christopher Reed (New York: Thames and Hudson, 1996), 16.

34 The painting was featured on the cover of the May 16, 1959 issue of the *Saturday Evening Post*.

35 I am grateful to Corry Kanzenberg for sharing her knowledge about Rockwell's studio set-up for the preparatory work for *Easter Morning*. The view through the window is that of Rockwell's backyard in Stockbridge and shows the artist's own icehouse and his neighbor's house.

36 Saarinen, "Letters to Psychiatrist (Dr. B), 1952–1953," Aline and Eero Saarinen Personal Papers, Archives of American Art, Smithsonian Institution (hereafter Saarinen Personal Papers, AAA). The letters are undated with the exception of three: April 1952, September 1, [1952], and January 12, 1953. References in letters to Aline Louchheim indicate that Saarinen's therapy continued at least until the end of 1953. The letters identify Dr. "B" as "Bartameyer" and "Bartemeyer," which are likely misspellings of "Bartemeier." (Saarinen was a notoriously bad speller.) Leo H. Bartemeier was a highly regarded psychiatrist and psychoanalyst. He taught at Wayne State University and the University of Michigan, and practiced privately in Detroit between 1926 and 1954. He was president of the American Psychiatric Association in 1951–1952, a close friend of Karl A. Menninger, and considered "one of the world's leading psychoanalysts." See Walter E. Barton, *The History and Influence of the American Psychiatric Association* (Washington, DC: American Psychiatric Press, 1987), 240. Lily Saarinen had begun therapy around 1948 with Dr. J. Clark Moloney, a Detroit psychoanalyst described by a colleague as a dyed-in-the-wool Freudian. Letters about the Saarinens' divorce agreement indicate that her analysis was expected to finish in late 1953. The change in her identity from artist—she was a sculptor—to primarily a wife and mother to the couple's two children, a bout of tuberculosis, in addition to her husband's absolute devotion to his architectural practice likely contributed to her psychological problems. In the letters to his therapist Saarinen chronicles problems in their marriage that began ten years earlier.

37 Saarinen to Dr. "B," n.d., c. 1952, Saarinen Personal Papers, AAA.

38 "I feel a great need to create my own Hvitträsk, molded in size etc. to the economies of our time. I feel however that my life would only be half lived if this does not happen. Such a home should be radical beautiful—one of the 5 or 6 best in the country—the prototype I think of is what Charlie & Ray [Eames] have created—an oasis of culture and taste in this cultural poverty. It should be in a sense an exhibition of what I stand for in architecture and interior design" (ibid.). His statement here clearly reveals his admiration for what the couple created together. It would only be near the end of his own life that Saarinen, happily married to the art critic Aline Louchheim, would start work on his own ideal home, which he described in the Schöner Wohnen address in 1960. On this home, see Alexandra Lange and Sean Khorsandi, "Houses and Housing," in *Eero Saarinen: Shaping the Future*, 259–260.

39 Saarinen warned Florence Knoll not to marry Hans on account of his reputation as a "ladies man." Letters between Saarinen and Aline Louchheim indicate that Florence Knoll was considering divorce as early as the summer of 1953. As part of his project to find a more suitable second wife, Saarinen rated marriages among his family and friends. Of them, his parents and Ray and Charles Eames received the highest grades (95 percent), while the Knolls received a low grade of 40 percent, just slightly higher than his own marriage (Saarinen to Aline Louchheim, n.d., c. July 1953, Saarinen Personal Papers, AAA). On the issue of marriage with the creative context of the Knolls, Eameses, and (Eero) Saarinens more generally, see Alexandra Lange, "This Year's Model: Representing Modernism to the Post-war American Corporation," *Journal of Design History* 19, no. 3 (2006): 242–244.

40 This being said, Florence Knoll's home did play a major role in her work for Knoll. For example, she apparently discovered the answer to Harry Bertoia's technical problems with his wire seating—a rubber-sprayed dish drainer—in her kitchen (Reif, "Pioneer in Modern Furniture"). Reif also described a roasting pan filled with flowers on Florence Knoll's coffee table as a proportional model for a vase she wanted to design.

41 On this issue see Tigerman, "'I Am Not a Decorator'."

42 Tone, *The Age of Anxiety*, 108–109.

43 Ibid., 100.

44 In the vast bibliography of this subject see especially John C. Burnham, "The Influence of Psychoanalysis Upon American Culture," in *American Psychoanalysis: Origins and Development*, ed. Jacques M. Quen (New York: Brunner/Mazel, 1978), 52–72; and several articles and books by Nathan G. Hale Jr.: "American Psychoanalysis Since the Second World War," in *American Psychiatry After World War II (1944–1994)*, ed. Roy W. Menninger and John C. Nemiah (Washington: American Psychiatric Press, 2000), 77–102; "From Berggasse to Central Park West: The Americanization of Psychoanalysis," *Journal of the History of the Behavioral Sciences* 14 (1979): 299–315; *The Rise and Crisis of Psychoanalysis in the United States: Freud and the Americans, 1917–1985* (New York: Oxford University Press, 1995).

45 F.S. Wickware, "Psychoanalysis," *Life*, February 3, 1947: 98.

46 As one commentator of the time remarked, psychoanalysis was about "as controversial as the American flag" (cited by Tone, *The Age of Anxiety*, 47). Saarinen's discussions about therapy with Aline Louchheim testify to the mainstreaming of analysis (Saarinen Personal Papers, AAA).

47 Often called the "father of American psychiatry," Dr. Benjamin Rush described his invention in his book *Medical Inquiries and Observations Upon the Diseases of the Mind* (Philadelphia, 1812), 181–182. An engraving of the chair was reproduced in *The Philadelphia Medical Museum*, new ser., I (Philadelphia: John Redman Coxe, 1810/1811). One chair was constructed and used at the Pennsylvanian Hospital, but as it was not considered particularly successful in the treatment of psychiatric patients, no further exemplars were made.

48 On this coupling, see Margaret Campbell, "From Cure Chair to Chaise Longue: Medical Treatment and the Form of the Modern Recliner," *Journal of Design History* 12, no. 4 (1999): 327–343; and Robin Schuldenfrei, *Design~Recline: Modern Architecture and the Mid-Century Chaise Longue*, Harvard University Art Museums Gallery Series, no.40, 2004.

49 There is some debate about whether the patient couch in Freud's office is a *chaise longue à la lettre*. To add my thoughts, given Freud's fascination with antiquity—his office was filled with fragments—the inclined form he selected for his patients to rest upon might be read as an ancient Roman couch, which was a forerunner to the *chaise longue*. On Freud's couch see Lydia Marinelli, ed., *Die Couch: Vom Denken im Liegen* (Munich: Sigmund Freud Privatstiftung/Prestel, 2006).

50 Peter Blake, *No Place Like Utopia: Modern Architecture and the Company We Kept* (New York: Alfred A. Knopf, 1993), 173–174.

51 Mary Roche, "New Chair Offers More Relaxation," *New York Times,* May 19, 1948.

52 Quoted in Walter McQuade, "Eero Saarinen, A Complete Architect [obituary]," *Architectural Forum* 116, no. 4 (April 1962): 113.

53 George Nelson, "Chairs," *Holiday* 22 (November 1957): 137–142.

54 Evan Frances, "How to Furnish with Children at Heart," *Family Circle*, February 1959: 46–47, 78.

55 Ibid., 46.

56 Saarinen to Irwin Miller, July 14, 1949, Saarinen Collection, Yale.

57 Sigmund Freud, *Civilization and Its Discontents*, trans. David McLintock (London: Penguin Books, 2002), 28. Originally published as *Das Unbehagen in der Kultur* (Vienna: Internationaler Psychoanalytischer Verlag, 1930).

58 On Freud and American popular culture, see chapter "The 'Golden Age' of Popularization, 1945–1965," in Hale, *The Rise and Crisis of Psychoanalysis*, 276–299; and Burnham, "The Influence of Psychoanalysis," 52–72.

59 Several Womb Chairs appear in a presentation drawing for the Ambassador Club, Trans World Airlines Terminal; drawing reproduced in *Eero Saarinen: Shaping the Future*, 204. Though the realized lounge did not include any Womb Chairs, the curves that define the chair were also expressed in the built-in seating banks in both the lounge and the main waiting room.

60 "The Maturing Modern [Architect Eero Saarinen]," *Time* 68 (July 2, 1956): cover, 50–57. The chair that appears in the photograph was the object of a tug-of-war during Saarinen's divorce from Lily Saarinen. In a letter written while the Saarinens were outlining the terms of their separation, Aline Louchheim wrote: "Lily will want everything you have—but NOT the womb-chair. I want that . . . " (Aline Louchheim to Saarinen, n.d., c. June 1953, Saarinen Personal Papers, AAA).

61 According to Albert Christ-Janer, Eliel Saarinen died sitting in "Eero's 'womb' chair" on July 1, 1950. Albert Christ-Janer, *Eliel Saarinen: Finnish-American Architect and Educator* (Chicago: The University of Chicago Press, 1979), 21.

62 Sylvia Lavin, *Form Follows Libido: Architecture and Richard Neutra in a Psychoanalytic Culture* (Cambridge, MA: MIT Press, 2004).

Chapter 2

The Future is Possibly Past
The Anxious Spaces of Gaetano Pesce

Jane Pavitt

Dwelling in the Age of Great Contaminations

At the landmark exhibition *Italy: The New Domestic Landscape, Achievements and Problems of Italian Design*, held at New York's Museum of Modern Art in 1972 (May 26–September 11), the architect and designer Gaetano Pesce (1939–) staged an installation of a subterranean dwelling, which supposedly formed part of a small underground city. The city, located in the Alpine region of Southern Europe and dated to around 2000 AD, had been excavated by an archaeologist of the future to unearth evidence of a communal dwelling for twelve people, as well as a smaller dwelling for two (Figure 2.1). This is all that remains of a disappeared community, who had lived their last days in a series of underground caverns, which they had built first for the purpose of extracting water and mineral resources. Once hollowed out, these caverns were then inhabited by their creators, who closed themselves in from the world above ground, "hermetically sealing off the interior from the outside world" with a huge stone. Once enclosed, the community had pushed further underground, expanding their habitat with further excavation. The archaeological evidence leads to speculation on the anxious condition of twentieth-century society: although the reasons for retreat were left oblique, the site is described as belonging to "The Period of Great Contaminations," implying, it seems, ecological disaster or nuclear apocalypse. Pesce's analysis of his imagined site is presented in the accompanying catalogue and display notes in the form of an archaeologist's report—field notes on the end of a civilization, projected into the future. The suggestion of a contaminated world, combined with his remark that "further study might throw additional light on the psychological effect that the term 'the year 2000' had on those living both before and after that date," helps us to conclude that here was the site of a traumatic, exhausted end to a modern age, yet to come.[1]

2.1
Gaetano Pesce, "The Period of Great Contaminations," Habitat for 2 Persons, 1971, gouache, watercolour and graphite on paper

Pesce's installation, conceived as the entrance to a series of designed environments created by participants to the MoMA exhibition, was comprised of models, drawings, and full-scale reconstructed spaces based on the imagined archaeological evidence. The communal dwelling supposedly discovered at the site measured 13 × 6 meters in plan and five meters in height, and was a two-tier space comprised of upper spaces which may have marked the route to the outside world, or perhaps defense posts guarding against attack. Other interior spaces were a combination of natural caves and man-made excavations, containing evidence that suggested their various use for water storage, living, bathing, work, leisure, and social rites. Evidence included a large fragment of a gate or doorway to the city (six meters in height), and a seat. The walls were made from blocks of rigid polyurethane fixed to a stone floor, in order to insulate the inhabitants from the damp underground conditions. Furnishings and interior elements were also made from rigid polyurethane, except for some soft plastic seating. There were no windows or openings in the plastic walls, except for the single entrance and some drainage holes. All the

2.2
Gaetano Pesce, "The Period of Great Contaminations," Habitat for 2 Persons, exhibition installation, 1972

material evidence at the excavation site, except the masonry and the cave walls, had however disintegrated—"the structures in wood, ABS plastic, melamine, polyurethane etc., [were] irreparably lost or damaged by heat and humidity."[2] The MoMA installation showed the reconstructed dwelling spaces made from polyurethane—a kind of reverse Pompeii in plastic (Figure 2.2).

The imaginary archaeologists were helped in their decoding of the space by the fortuitous discovery of several other documents at the site: some "fragments of a volume," pictorial records, and a short film documenting "some scenes of family life . . . probably shot by some member of the family concerned."[3] In reality, of course, the film (entitled *Paessagio Domestico*) was made by Pesce in collaboration with the photographer Klaus Zaugg, and was shown alongside the installation in the MoMA exhibition (Figure 2.3).This documentary evidence was used to evoke the levels of disturbance and alienation experienced by the inhabitants. In the text, Pesce suggests a strong degree of ritualistic significance in the forms and plan of the space

2.3
Gaetano Pesce, "The Period of Great Contaminations," Habitat for 2 Persons, exhibition installation, 1972

(such as a cruciform table): "the house in itself is not only a mass of blocks arranged for a precise purpose, but it nurtures and conceals an interior pregnant with symbols that are unequivocally related to the mode of representation of that time . . ."[4] In extracts from the fictional archaeologists' report, Pesce describes evidence for an "urban hypothesis" based on the underground spatial organization, its means of defense, circulation, and its relationship to its natural environment and resources. He hypothesizes the effects upon human behavior of this underground existence: first, the need for isolation and the resulting lack of human contact and communication, and second, the development of social rituals and taboos. The resulting mindset of the inhabitants is conjectured as being like that of pre-modern or primitive cultures, based upon the "decline of the technological dream" and "insecurity as the prospect of the future."[5]

How did Pesce's bleak and dystopian vision of the future fit within an exhibition that, on first view, set out to showcase the achievements of contemporary

Italian design? *The New Domestic Landscape* marked a critical point in the development of Italian design, as it emerged from its increasingly ideological engagement with the forces and consequences of production and consumption in the mid- to late 1960s. Its organizer, the Argentinian-born designer and MoMA curator Emilio Ambasz, had initiated a project that intended not only to examine the formal, technical, and aesthetic aspects of design, but also to explore its social, economic, and political implications. Felicity Scott, in her recent analysis of the exhibition, argues that the "remarkable presence, even excessiveness" of discourse in the exhibition pointed to Ambasz's own highly theorized understanding of the role of design.[6] Ambasz was at pains to stress the high levels of criticality evident in the exhibited work and in his curatorial approach at all times. In his opening statement to the catalogue, he stated: "If, at the beginning of research for the exhibition, Italian design seemed so dazzling that it was momentarily possible to assume that transplanting its most outstanding examples would be sufficient to recall the luminosity of their original breeding ground, deeper examination made it increasingly evident that the problem was far from simple."[7] The identification of the problems as well as the achievements of Italian design (as referenced in the exhibition title) led him to direct a project that was intended not only to elucidate the state of contemporary Italian design, but also to showcase techniques of provocation, resulting "in an exhibition revealing the contradictions and conflicts underlying a production of objects, which are constantly generated by designers, and which in turn generate a state of doubt amongst them as to the ultimate significance of their activity."[8]

The conceptual and display strategies employed to achieve this included a complex typology of recent objects and prototypes, as well as a set of specially commissioned environments, accompanied by films and other textual layers of explication. In placing this emphasis on environments, both designers and the visiting public were directed to explore the exhibits as a form of commentary on social practices, meanings and rituals. Whilst these conditions were not seen as particular to the Italian example, but rather applicable to all late capitalist societies (an important point given its American audience), Ambasz was at pains to stress that Italy offered a vital testing-ground for the critical and discursive understanding of design. Whilst the accompanying catalogue offered essays which gave critical perspective to twentieth-century histories of Italian style, design, and social/urban planning, the exhibition content was restricted to design developments which roughly spanned the period 1965–1972, focusing attention on what was known as Radical Design in Italy, after Germano Celant's formulation of "architettura radicale."[9]

Within this complex framework, Ambasz then set about subjecting Italian practice to an even greater level of taxonomic analysis. The exhibition was split into two sections: the first (displayed in giant containers in the museum's garden), grouped objects according to their formal and technical means, their socio-cultural implications, and their propensity for demonstrating more flexible patterns of use. The second section, comprised of eleven environments, was divided according to two categories: broadly "pro-design" and "counter-design" (as well as a competition section for "young" design groups). Only Pesce's installation was set apart from this framework and given its own category of "design as commentary."

The exhibition reflected the high degree of technological experimentation in Italian design, together with an intellectual engagement with its social and economic constraints and possibilities. In the late 1960s, these tendencies coalesced to form a highly nuanced position in relation to late modernist utopian thinking—a set of critical, or post-utopian positions. The subject of utopia was key to the exhibition's formulation—by focusing on design's postulations about the future (and involving a high degree of speculative technological thinking), the curators and exhibitors could not avoid formulating utopian scenarios, but did so within a critical framework which acknowledged the divisive as well as the liberating effects of technology. As Scott has succinctly put it: "What form could this utopia without utopianism take?"[10]

Pesce's installation seemingly avoided such contradictions. Positioned as the prologue to the "environment" section of the exhibition that would explore these postulations, it appeared to present the reverse view: the underground city of the period of "great contaminations" was an essay in failure. Whatever social or ecological conditions had brought about the withdrawal underground, it had resulted in a retreat to primitive and base forms of social operation. In this way, Pesce was able to present a social hypothesis removed from contemporary conditions, which privileged the conditions for living as refuge and subsistence, whilst suggesting the heightened importance of ritual and symbolism in human behaviors. As we shall see later in this essay, these were themes that Pesce was to develop in his work over the coming decade. In terms of *The New Domestic Landscape*, however, Pesce's installation was not simply a curious oddity out of synch with the tenor of the rest of the exhibition. The importance of the exhibition has been explored in numerous contexts, but little attention has been paid to Pesce's contribution.[11] Ambasz's formulation of the "environment" section of the exhibition divided the exhibitionary tendencies in two:

> The first attitude involved a commitment to design as a problem-solving activity, capable of formulating, in physical terms, solutions to problems encountered in the natural and sociocultural milieu. The opposite attitude, which we may call one of counterdesign, chooses instead to emphasize the need for a renewal of philosophical discourse and for social and political involvement as a way of bringing about structural changes in our society.[12]

The first group comprised environments by Gae Aulenti, Ettore Sottsass, Joe Colombo, Alberto Rosselli, Marco Zanuso and Richard Sapper, and Mario Bellini; the second by Ugo la Pietra, Archizoom, Superstudio, Gruppo Strum, and Enzo Mari. Whilst space in this essay precludes a detailed discussion of each installation, the first section included a series of fixed and mobile dwellings which functioned as adaptable containers (Aulenti, Sottsass, and Bellini for example). The second set of environments had less to do with flexible dwelling space, and more with the unsettling and transformative effects of a highly technologized and mediatized world. These installations privileged new media solutions that, in Superstudio's terms, suggested "a life without objects."[13] As previously stated, Pesce's installation was set apart from both groups. But it nevertheless addressed the criteria described by Ambasz in his summary of the "environment" priorities:

> It becomes evident that neither the experiences of today nor the visions of tomorrow can be emphasized at the expense of one another, and that the search for quality in daily existence cannot afford to ignore the concomitant problems of pollution, the deterioration of our cities and institutions, and poverty.[14]

Pesce met Ambasz's intentions on various fronts: the "search for the long-range meanings of the rituals and ceremonies of the twenty-four hours of the day" as well as "evolving notions of privacy and territoriality" and "the ceremonies and behaviors that assign [spaces and artifacts] meaning.[15] Both object displays and environments were prepared in close collaboration with Italian manufacturers. The environments were produced with companies who were close supporters of the represented designers. In Pesce's case, three companies supported his installation financially: Cassina and its sister business C&B Italia, and Sleeping International Systems Italia. Cassina and Sleeping International Systems manufactured the installation components. Pesce had worked commercially with C&B Italia since its production of his UP chair in 1969, and his relationship with Cassina throughout the 1970s was to be the most significant of his career. Indeed, he named Cassina's creative director, Francesco Binfaré, as vital to the development of his hypothesis for *The New Domestic Landscape*.[16]

The displays were also overlaid with text and media supplied by the curators and designers.[17] The accompanying film to Pesce's installation reinforced its post-apocalyptic setting. In the film, which is largely silent save for the constant dripping sound of the watery caves, the camera pushes through the underground spaces, encountering naked figures crouching, sitting or lying in isolation. Even when two figures sit together, their heads in their hands or resting on a table in front of them, there is no contact between them. They are filmed in a half-light, moving through the cavernous spaces and molten plastic interiors in a somnolent way, listless and exhausted. But the film is punctuated by brief snatches of a more restless activity, bodies suddenly moving in dense packs, hints of orgiastic scenes or ritual sacrifice. The narrative format of Pesce's environment set it apart from the other scenarios on display. Whilst each environment also employed spectacular effects (including film and sound) to deliver a thesis on the future social conditions for design (or the designed conditions for future society), Pesce chose to attack his concept of the future retrospectively—as an anterior future; the future as it will have been. By adopting the fictional position of archaeologist as commentator, Pesce positioned himself as outside a narrative of possibilities and solutions, preferring the role of apocalyptic soothsayer, postulating on a future of collapse and impossibility.

Pesce's installation explored many of the preoccupations that would run through his work in the 1970s: the idea of the symbolic habitat; of death and the body; the mixing of sacred, sexual and scatological references; and a fascination with the mutability of plastic. Like many of the environments presented at MoMA in 1972, his marked a critical turning point in the development of late modernism and the rethinking/unthinking of utopia. To theatrical effect, Pesce engaged with prevalent anxieties concerning the future of society: the threat of conflict, the possibility for ecocide or nuclear destruction, human insecurities and the instability of human relationships in the face of such disquiet.

Subterranean Homesick Blues

Two years after the MoMA exhibition, Pesce imagined another project for New York—an unbuilt proposal for an underground church on an empty Manhattan parking lot (Figure 2.4). The "Church of Solitude" project of 1974–1977 revisited the themes of his "Great Contaminations" environment. If his 1972 subterranean dwelling was a place of post-apocalyptic horror, then the project for a church might be perceived as an opportunity to explore the idea of peace and sanctuary, underneath the noise and turbulence of the modern metropolis. This prism-shaped cavern could serve as a retreat from the chaos and congestion of the city. The site above ground was left open, save for earthworks in the suggested form of a face forming the entrance to the church (through the eyes and nose, down stairs or elevator). This rough ground was also littered with elements of a previous ruined architecture suggesting a church or basilica—columns, and the fragment of a gothic arch. But underground, the space seemed unstable, with tilting floors and walls, through which the rocky substructure of the city has penetrated. The regular drip of water into a limestone basin (like the dripping on the 1972 film) accentuated a feeling of insecurity and isolation. The Church of Solitude was not a place of solace, rather a place invested with what Pesce referred to as "fraught significances."[18] Its mixing of classical ruins with the signage of the parking lot is perhaps a conscious nod to the post-modern (we could think of Robert Venturi and Denise Scott Brown's twinning of Rome and Las Vegas, perhaps). The pre-ruined nature of the building also brings to mind the work of SITE architects who used the language of destruction—falling brickwork and cracking facades—to clad a series of chain stores for the US company BEST Products. But despite these comparisons with the visual language of postmodernism (which Pesce would distance himself from), his work did appear concerned with a sense of indeterminacy and placelessness that might be termed the condition of post-modernity, rather than its visual rhetoric.

Late modern architecture, in the formulation proposed by Sarah Williams Goldhagen and Réjean Legault, was often "anxious."[19] Just as the Italian radicals recognized that the fraught conditions of contemporary society made an impossibility of utopia, so others of the postwar generation sought to negotiate a path through the anxieties and psychological effects brought about by postwar, Cold War conditions. The development of a heavily militarized yet technologically experimental society had found many outlets in experimental architecture, which both embraced the possibilities of technical advancement whilst shadowing its negative implications.[20] Postwar modern architecture was bisected by Cold War anxieties at regular intervals. In built and imaginary form, there appeared numerous variations on the theme of anxious or atomic dwelling: from Buckminster Fuller's geodesic domes to

Jane Pavitt

2.4
Gaetano Pesce, "Church of Solitude" project, 1974–1977, watercolor, colored ink, pencil on paper

the sheltering forms of Frederick Kiesler, Isamu Noguchi, and Paolo Soleri. For every glass-walled home exuding transparency and openness—Mies's Farnsworth House (1949–1951) or Philip Johnson's Glass House (also 1949)—there were bomb-proof and shatter-proof structures made from hard concrete or plastic shells (like the famously indestructible 1957 Monsanto House at Disneyland California, made from fiberglass, which initially proved to be resistant to the wrecking-ball when it was finally demolished). Postwar architects such as Antii Lovag, Jean-Louis Chanéac, Georges Emmerich, Pascal Häusermann, and Ricardo Porro demonstrated a fascination for concrete or plastic cellular habitats with the womb-like appeal of caves and all seemed to reference Kiesler's concept of the Endless House (1950–1960). These prefab forms, as well as later concepts for mobile, self-assembly, or inflatable habitats such as those by Archigram and Coop Himmelb(l)au, could, by virtue of their adaptability, be suggested for use as festival accommodation, nomadic tents, or shelter for disaster victims. As well as structures intended to be worn like protective clothing, architects also designed defensive spaces underground.

Aside from the popularized concept of the shelter-home (regularly featured in the pages of *Life* magazine), underground sanctuaries were proposed for churches or cathedrals, such as Le Corbusier and Eduoard Trouin's Saint Baume Basilica, 1948, and Claude Parent and Paul Virilio's church of Saint-Bernadette-du Banlay, 1966 (both unbuilt) as well as Pesce's Church of Solitude.[21] Militarized architecture was sometimes the explicit source for these: Virilio had pursued a long-term fascination with the bunkers of the Atlantic Wall, photographing them from 1958 to 1965.[22] Whilst underground city complexes were usually the stuff of sci-fi comics and James Bond films, bunker complexes had been developed to protect military facilities in the 1950s. Discussing the pros and cons of underground cities for civilian life, historian of urbanism and technology, Lewis Mumford, conceded that, despite their protective benefits, "those in the underground city . . . are the prey of compulsive fears and corrupt fantasies . . . the underground city threatens in consequence to become the ultimate burial chamber of our incinerated civilization."[23]

Pesce experimented with a surprising number of subterranean buildings: not only the dwelling in the age of Great Contaminations, or the Church of Solitude.[24] A commission for the restoration of a nineteenth-century cliff-top villa in Sorrento, Italy (1973), for example, resulted in his proposal for the gutting of the existing house to leave only the exterior walls, which would be uninhabited but would act as the entrance hall to a newly excavated house deep inside the cliff, nine meters below the old floor level (the project was never built, due to objections from the architectural heritage authorities). Two ambitious urban planning developments of the 1970s also featured underground caverns: his competition projects for the Pahlavi National Library in Tehran (1977) and the Les Halles district of Paris (1979). Both proposals were intended as protests: the first flouted the competition rules whilst raising human rights issues by representing the oppressed minorities of Iran in symbolic form. The second was embedded, rather obscurely, with a critical commentary on French bureaucratic centralization (Pesce was living in Paris at the time). Whatever their political intention, what is of interest here is the symbolic use of underground space. Like the Church of Solitude, the use of dereliction or shattered urban fabric was disquieting. But the latter two projects employed subterranean space for its bodily or erotic symbolic potential also. Each project, viewed in plan, showed the form of a prone body rising up from the ground. The Iran project is clearly male: "a crucified, downtrodden man."[25] The Les Halles project is modeled on a woman, lying legs apart, whose form is mapped out across gardens and structures, and whose body is penetrated by the entrance to an underground series of chambers. Clearly for Pesce, underground space could be anxious (a place of entombment) as well as defensive; it was also uncannily intrauterine.[26]

The idea of the house or city of the future as defensive space has been explored most completely by Beatriz Colomina, in her reading of the 1956 House of the Future by Alison and Peter Smithson, the temporary exhibition house made for the Daily Mail *Ideal Homes* exhibition of that year in London.[27] Colomina argues that the Smithsons' house was not only a space age vision of a plugged-in, prefabricated, and expendable architecture, a futuristic showcase for moldable materials, but also "an architecture of paranoia . . . relentlessly on exhibit."[28] The House of the Future was peep show and bunker combined: a place of privacy and intimacy designed to be viewed by visitors through cuts made in its exterior walls, which were intended as a curvaceous skin of plastic (in fact fabricated from plywood, plaster, and paint). Apart from the viewing slots, and the automatic steel door, there was no relationship between the house and its exterior setting. It could feasibly be in space or underground—indeed, Colomina notes that the Smithsons' cited the Caves Les Baux de Provence in France as inspiration: "cave dwelling, like bomb shelters, submarines, and spaceships, corresponds to a time of extreme danger outside. Caves are all interiorized spaces, the first bunkers."[29] The house of the future was a bunker "full of defenses"—irradiated food, filtered air, artificial light, dust extraction, and a hermetically sealed entrance. In Colomina's reading, the Smithsons' house is a Cold

War ideal home *par excellence*, a fusion of modernist utopian dwelling with the kinds of atomic shelter-homes featured in the pages of *Life* magazine or displayed at World's Fairs.[30] Perhaps, then, Pesce's 1972 subterranean dwelling was the primeval or hippyish equivalent of the Smithsons' house: interiorized, defensive, a theatrical stage for the acting out of domestic and social rituals.[31]

Fossilized Plastic

In 1975, a one-man exhibition of Pesce's work, organized by the French Centre de Création Industrielle, based at the Centre Georges Pompidou, opened at the Musée des Arts Décoratifs in Paris (Figure 2.5). It was entitled *Le Futur est peut-être passé* (The Future is Possibly Past). The catalogue contained an essay (reprinted for an Italian audience in *Casabella* magazine), by the designer and *Casabella* editor, Alessandro Mendini, who writes in breathless and baroque terms about his friend:

> Gaetano never gives up. He hits us in the face with a limbo, a disgusting universe, the static scenario of a man when he penetrates alone into the other world, when he enters into "cadaverous" contact with the absolute. Immense rivers of blood, very slow, dense, dark currents, seas of blood. We are right in the middle of the Problem of Death. Death,

2.5
Gaetano Pesce, "Le Futur est peut-être passé," exhibition installation, Musée des Arts Décoratifs, Paris, 1975

agonized, stained, pantheistic, definitive, irreligious, decadent, voluminous, lugubrious, sick, tiresome, bourgeois, archaeological, inflated, leprous, primordial, Byzantine death, death without illusions, a slaughter-house. Death as environment, death as a habitat, death as a habit; fear, pain, loneliness as a habit. Interpenetration between death and life, the presence of death in the living, the presence of life in the dead, death during life, genesis as the prehistory of death, dialectic with death, the experience of the time and space of death, etc. Gaetano gets inside all this physically, goes and comes as he wishes, intervenes personally, treats death as an everyday personal occurrence, performs a kind of sacrifice upon himself, because his large plastic objects are nothing but enlarged casts of his own de-composed body, dissected and analyzed piece by piece, like an immense corpse on the surgeon's table, an "enormous" symbolization of death.[32]

The exhibition brought together Pesce's anxious concerns expressed in his architectural postulations of the early 1970s with a more visceral and sensuous engagement with both material and the body. So what did the visitor to the exhibition encounter? Dismembered body casts—ears, eyes, faces, hands, and feet—produced on the scale of furniture or embedded into architectural facades and interior spaces. Objects made from hardened plastic that showed the imprint of the human body, distorted and fragmented. Even objects made from meat, displayed in stages of on-going putrefaction. But above all, plastic—Pesce's signature material—with its softness and pliability, its capacity to buckle, bend, distort, rupture, blister, crack, and sag.

In Pesce's own words, in 1973, "The time has come to fill our spaces with fraught significances (anything capable of evoking an unconscious emotion like fear, insecurity, isolation, anxiety or death, above and beyond its immediate meaning, qualifies as significant)."[33] Objects could be the means to achieve this, and therefore must be double-coded, capable of bearing legible symbolic and emotional meaning. Pesce's objects often either imitate or allude to the body, or suggest a high degree of instability in their material or construction, in order to achieve this. They are also highly theatrical, often "acting out" their own coming-into-being as well as their own demise.

Pesce's experiments with furniture had begun in the late 1960s, in collaboration with the C&B Company (later B&B Italia), run by his friend Cesare Cassina. Exploiting the possibilities of expanded polyurethane foam, he developed a method for vacuum-packaging circular foam seats, which would resume their full shape once unzipped from the packaging by the purchaser at home. The UP series was a considerable success, as a bright and breezy form of Pop design. Its innovative technical nature characterized the collaboration between Pesce and Cassina, and the latter's various companies.

In the early 1970s, the Cassina company attempted, partly on the instigation of Pesce and Mendini, to establish an experimental division that would allow them to explore the more experimental end of furniture production under a

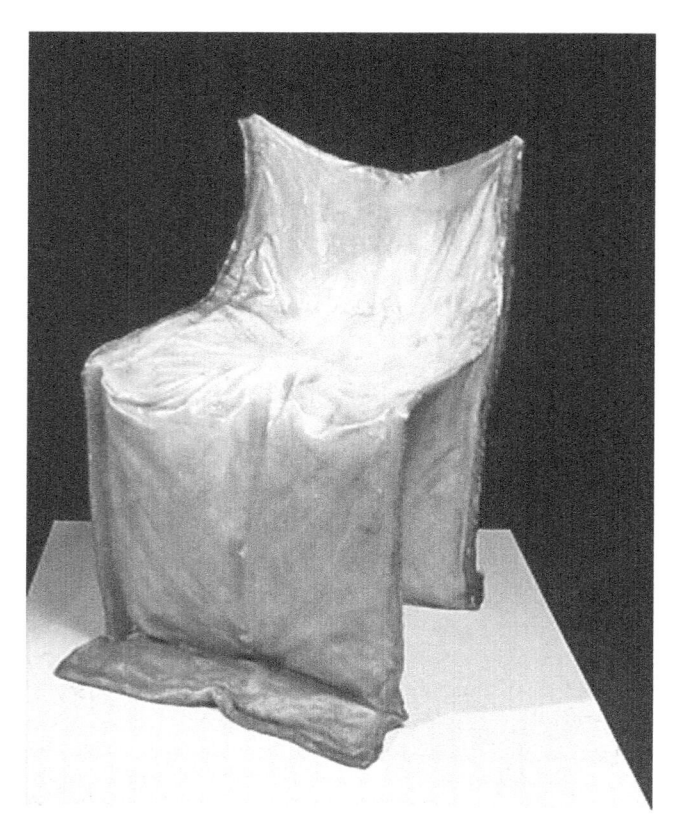

2.6
Gaetano Pesce, Golgotha Chair, 1972, Dacron-filled and resin-soaked fiberglass cloth, manufactured by Bracciodiferro S.r.L., Italy

different brand label. Bracciodiferro (which means "arm wrestle") became the label for a series of limited edition pieces, designed by Pesce and Mendini as well as by their close collaborators, such as Cuban designer Ricardo Porro. One of the first objects to be produced was Pesce's Golgotha chair, handmade from Dacron Fiberfill, a padded fiberglass cloth. Long sheets of the cloth were first soaked in polyester resin then draped across poles to create the form of a chair. When wet, it would be sat upon briefly, so it assumed the imprint of a figure, then left to harden. Made in this way, it needed no internal structural support, and each one was unique. In terms of its manufacture, it was decidedly low-tech. Its appearance was at odds with that of most furniture made from synthetic materials—instead of an object which celebrates its radical method of production, the Golgotha chair is abject—shriveled, as if recorded in the process of its own decay, a discarded shroud (Figure 2.6).

The Golgotha chair went into limited production, although a table, made to complete the suite of furniture, was really only featured in publicity material. The table was made from a honeycomb of glued-together glass foam blocks, gel-coated in red polyester resin to produce a surface like coagulating blood. The accompanying publicity shots were striking, like a piece of theatre in mid-performance (Figure 2.7). Barbara Lehman, Cassina archivist, has described them well:

2.7
Promotional Image for Golgotha Chair, 1972, Bracciodiferro S.r.L., Italy

In a biblical and prophetic atmosphere, a company of hippyish thespians portray tragedy and existential angst. These chairs depict Pesce's philosophy, which aspires to a self-determination of taste: Death alone makes us equal. Being alive means, among other things, being different. The objects that surround us should also be able to enjoy this prerogative, they should also be different.[34]

The characters from the Golgotha publicity shots could feasibly be the inhabitants of the dwelling from the age of Great Contaminations, acting out some biblical scenes of torment in their final days. It was quite some way to sell furniture. But theatricality and performance had been part of Pesce's repertoire since the 1960s, when as a young architecture graduate from UAUV in Venice he had become involved in the Arte Programmata movement in Italy. Arte Programmata, a loose affiliation of various groups, included Gruppo N from Padua, the German Gruppo Zero, the Milan-based Gruppo T, and the Paris-based Groupe de Recherche d'Art Visuelle or GRAV. Arte Programmata, as the name implies, reflected their interest in kinetic and light-based work, incorporating mechanical and electrical equipment. One of their concerns was the design of environments that would include the spectator in the production of the artistic experience, to provoke feelings of liberation or excitement, or perhaps disorientation and alienation, often by the use of illusory effects. In 1967, Pesce staged an event at a temporary theatre in Padua entitled "Piece per una fucilazione" ("Piece for an Execution") in which the audience were subjected to the scene of a firing squad: "For 27 minutes they watched a naked man bleed to death, his blood—500 gallons of hot red paint—oozing across the performance space and lapping against their chairs."[35]

Arte Programmata was also interested in art as a form of scientific and systematic research, using processes and technologies drawn from manufacturing. They employed the idea of the multiple as a means to avoid the "sacred aura" of the unique artwork, challenging its fetishized status. The use of industrial materials and processes was another way of achieving this. A manifesto on the subject of multiples, produced by GRAV in 1966, argued that "As long as multiplication allows us to question—even half-heartedly—the usual relationship between art and the spectator, we are for it. But this is only a first stage. A second stage could be, for example, the multiplication not only of works of art, but of ensembles that act as social stimuli, while at the same time liberating the viewer from the obsession of ownership."[36] The non-standardized series of objects developed by Pesce in the early 1970s conformed to this view, by occupying the space between a uniform mass production of objects and the unique, hand-made craft object. The Golgotha chair, its offer of a diversity of type and a certain kind of randomness in its production, was seen by Pesce to open up the possibility for the user to invest the object with personal, symbolic significance, just as the UP chair allowed the user to participate in its final stage of production, by releasing the object from its packaged state. These ideas can also be read in close connection to Jean Baudrillard's exploration of the symbolic value of objects and their place within a system of value, published as *The System of Objects* in France in 1968 (at a time when Pesce was living in Paris).

Pesce continued his exploration of material instability and the symbolic function of objects in projects for Cassina through the 1970s and 1980s. His chosen materials were plastic, particularly soft processes (thermoset plastics) using injected polyurethane foam, resins, and polyester, as well as felt and upholstery. Although the objects, given their limited production runs and high investment in experimental techniques, were expensive to produce, they nevertheless reflected his concern for so-called "poor materials." His fascination with plastics emphasized their malleability—so that objects carried the marks and effects of their production, suggesting that they are one step away from reverting to their raw state, or disintegrating under their conditions of use. In 1985, for example, Pesce produced a series of nine chairs at the Pratt Institute in New York. The Pratt chairs are made from polyurethane—molded forms that (like the Golgotha chair) have no other means of structural support other than their material. The sequence of nine is ordered according to their removal from the process of molding and hardening (Figure 2.8). The first in the series is soft and yielding so that it collapses uselessly on the floor. The second is slightly more hardened, and so on, until the third can bear the weight of a child, but no more. Subsequent chairs in the series can support an adult weight, whilst retaining a degree of flexibility and comfort. The last is so rigid as to be uncomfortable.

Pesce's use of malleable synthetic materials was not simply an exercise in technical possibilities and limitations. By emphasizing the molded forms of plastic

Gaetano Pesce's Anxious Spaces

2.8
Gaetano Pesce,
Pratt Chair, 1984,
urethane resin

and the relationship of seating to the human body (yielding, rather than resistant), he extended his interest in the time-bound properties of objects. Plastic is a material that tends to be celebrated for its newness and modernity (e.g. Roland Barthes), but Pesce's plastics emphasize their fleeting existence and potential decay, as if they are organic, synthetic materials made flesh. The excavation of the dwelling of the Period of Great Contaminations recorded only the disappearance of synthetic materials, leaving just their imprint in stone. Ironically, given the more contemporary concern for the persistent effects of plastics on the environment, Pesce nevertheless saw plastic as a transient and unstable material. But by the 1970s, the celebrated modernity and permanence of oil-based synthetics had been placed under threat by the ensuing oil crisis of the early part of that decade.

For Pesce, plastic was design made flesh. His material explorations were rooted in an interest in the visceral and sensual power of objects. Pesce's objects had life-cycles—they reflected and recorded the process of aging and decay of the human body. His treatment of materials is anxious and unstable. Their connection to bodily functions strengthened his sense that objects should heighten the narrative, personal, and even sacred connections with our surroundings. Only by acknowledging this could design move beyond its pragmatic and commercial constraints and explore the symbolic realm.

At the time of Pesce's exhibition *Le Futur est peut-être passé* at the Musée des Arts Décoratifs in 1975, Jean Baudrillard published an article in the Pompidou magazine *Traverses*, coinciding with the exhibition. The article, entitled "Le crépuscule des signes" ("The Twilight of Signs"), explored the function and symbolism of death in society. His ideas were published the following year as the influential work *Symbolic Exchange and Death*. For Baudrillard, and Pesce, too, death and the life-cycle of objects were an important part of understanding the symbolic order:

> The function of destruction, the function of death, is fundamental and our society has forgotten them. It is not sufficient to produce objects that only serve, we must produce objects that know death in order to reestablish the symbolic order. All discipline only fulfils itself if it desists from its object and places its own death in play. It is in this flight that, paradoxically, design can find itself a sense of the symbolic.[37]

Through a similar route to that suggested by Baudrillard, Pesce had repurposed design as a symbolic as opposed to a utilitarian act, and its products as poetic and communicative. Pesce's use of design as a site of philosophical speculation, his exploitation of material and process as a means of breaking free of the constraints of the "rational" object, and his speculations on the relationship between human ritual and objects in use arise from his deliberations on the anxious state of modernity. As with many radical designers, this direction emerged from a state of *impasse* in the late 1960s and early 1970s. By pursuing this negative and critical position through experimental works that attempted to inscribe objects with a condition of instability and insecurity, and to literally capture them in material form, Pesce managed to establish a highly personal and distinctive symbolic order in his work. But this attitude did not constitute a retreat from design. Given his close and successful relationship with manufacturers (namely Cassina), he was able to channel these ideas into commercial projects. The economic and intellectual power of Italian design in the 1980s and 1990s, having been through crisis in the 1970s, was built upon this kind of strategic thinking.

Notes

Acknowledgments: I would like to thank the studio of Gaetano Pesce for providing images for this essay, and other relevant source material. Comments on an early draft of this paper were gratefully received from Catharine Rossi and from Glenn Adamson, who also provided the translation of the quotation by Jean Baudrillard (note 37).

1. Gaetano Pesce, "Explanatory Notes," in *Italy: The New Domestic Landscape, Achievements and Problems of Italian Design,* ed. Emilio Ambasz (New York: The Museum of Modern Art, New York, in collaboration with Centro Di, Florence, 1972), 214–216.
2. Ibid., 215.
3. Ibid.
4. Ibid.
5. Ibid., 215–216.
6. Felicity Scott, *Architecture or Utopia: Politics after Modernism* (Cambridge, MA: MIT Press, 2007), 149.
7. Ambasz, 12.
8. Ibid.
9. The historical articles included essays on Italian Art Nouveau (Paolo Portoghesi), Futurism (Maurizio Fagiolo dell'Arco) and the postwar development of design (Vittorio Gregori). Other critical articles reviewed social planning and housing policy (Ruggero Cominotti and Guilio Carlo Argan) and different perspectives on the ideological contexts for Italian design (Alessandro Mendini, Germano Celant and Manfredo Tafuri). See Ambasz.
10. Scott, 145.
11. See, for example, Andrea Branzi, *The Hothouse: Italian New Wave Design* (London: Thames & Hudson, 1984).
12. Ambasz, 137.
13. Scott, 129–130 and Ambasz, 149–210.
14. Ambasz, 137.
15. Ibid.
16. Pesce names Cesare Cassina, the company director, for his support in its execution, and Francesco Binfaré, who "participated in the formulation of its hypothesis from the outset," see Pesce, in Ambasz, 212.
17. Scott, "Italian Design and the New Political Landscape," *Architecture or Utopia*, 119–149.
18. Pesce, quoted by Barbara Lehman, "Bracciodiferro: the Reconnoitring Workshop," in *Made in Cassina,* ed. Giampero Bosoni (Milan: Skira, 2008), 240.
19. Sarah Williams Goldhagen and Réjean Legault, eds. *Anxious Modernisms: Experimentation in Postwar Architectural Culture* (Cambridge, MA: MIT Press, 2001).
20. See, for example, David Crowley and Jane Pavitt, eds., *Cold War Modern: Design 1945–70* (London: V&A Publishing, 2008).
21. For a history of shelter-homes, see Kenneth D. Rose, *One Nation Underground: A History of the Fallout Shelter* (New York: New York University Press, 2001) and Sarah A. Lichtman, "Do-It-Yourself Security: Safety, Gender and the Home Fallout Shelter in Cold War America," *Journal of Design History* 19, no. 1 (Spring 2006): 39–55. In their typology of Fantastic Architecture, Conrads and Sperlich apply the category of "sheltering cave" to experimental architecture which also suggests the defensive or protective. See Ulrich Conrads and Hans G. Sperlich, *Fantastic Architecture* (London: The Architectural Press, 1963).
22. Paul Virilio, photographs first presented as an exhibition at the Musée des Arts Décoratifs, Paris, and published as *Bunker Archeologie* (Paris: Centres George Pompidou, 1976), translated into English as *Bunker Archaeology* (New York: Princeton Architectural Press, 1994).
23. Lewis Mumford, *The City in History* (New York: Harcourt, Brace and World, 1961), 481.

24 For further details on all of Pesce's architectural projects, see France Vanlaethem, *Gaetano Pesce: Architecture, Design, Art* (London: Thames and Hudson, 1989).
25 Vanlaethem, 70.
26 See Freud's formulation of the uncanny associations between womb, cave and grave in Sigmund Freud, "The Uncanny" (1919) in *Art and Literature,* ed. Albert Dickson (Harmondsworth: Penguin, 1985), 336.
27 Beatriz Colomina, "Unbreathed Air," in *Domesticity at War* (Cambridge, MA: MIT Press, 2007), 193–238.
28 Ibid., 227.
29 Ibid., 228.
30 Ibid., 228–229.
31 Of course, the Smithsons built their own primitive hut equivalent to the House of the Future: their installation Patio+Pavilion, included in the 1956 ICA exhibition *This is Tomorrow*. Richard Hamilton referred to this as a "garden shed . . . excavated after an atomic holocaust." Quoted in Ben Highmore, "Rough Poetry: Patio + Pavilion Revisited," *Oxford Art Journal* 29, no. 2 (2006): 287.
32 Alessandro Mendini, "Il concetto dell morte/The Concept of Death," *Casabella* 397 (1975): 42–43.
33 Pesce, quoted by Barbara Lehman, "Bracciodiferro: the Reconnoitring Workshop," in *Made in Cassina*, ed. Giampero Bosoni (Milan: Skira, 2008), 240.
34 Lehman, in Bosoni, 241.
35 Deyan Sudjic, "The Sweet Smell of Excess," *Blueprint*, October 1994: 23.
36 GRAV, *Multiples*, Paris, October 1966. A collection of GRAV texts in English can be found at the website www.julioleparc.org, including the 1966 *Multiples* text.
37 "La fonction de destruction, la fonction de mort, sont fondamentales et notre société l'a oublié. Il ne suffit pas de produire des objets qui servent, il faut produire des objets qui sachent mourir, pour rétablir l'ordre symbolique. Toute discipline ne s'accomplit que si elle se dessaisit de son objet et met en jeu sa propre mort. C'est dans cette voie que, paradoxalement, le design peut trouver le sens du symbolique." Jean Baudrillard, "Le crépuscule des signes," *Traverses*, no. 2 (November 1975): 37. English translation by Glenn Adamson.

Chapter 3

Scopophobia/ Scopophilia
Electric Light and the Anxiety of the Gaze in American Postwar Domestic Architecture

Margaret Maile Petty

In her investigation of Adolf Loos's European interiors from the 1920s and 1930s, Beatriz Colomina invokes Walter Benjamin's classic discussion of the interior of the detective novel, asking "can there be a detective story of the interior itself, of the hidden mechanisms by which space is constructed as interior? Which may be to say, a detective story of detection itself, of the controlling look, the look of control, the controlled look. But where would the traces of the look be imprinted? What do we have to go on? What clues?"[1] As both writer and detective, Colomina identifies and follows a series of traces and mechanisms to reveal a Loosian plot of gaze, body, representation and performance. In this narrative, the interior is exposed as a highly controlled space of "physical separation and visual connection" framing the "scene of domestic life."[2] In Loos's interiors these mechanisms largely function to direct the gaze inward, turning away from "the outside world."[3]

In the early postwar period in the United States, with its culture of celebratory consumerism and embrace of the new materials and techniques of modern architecture, a different but importantly related narrative can be culled from the domestic interior. Through the introduction of glass architecture and the visual opening and exposure of the domestic environment, the interior, rather than "detective story," becomes "film noir"; the scenography of the nineteenth century, cinematography. The increasing visuality of the postwar domestic environment, witnessed in both the popular representation and scopic organization of the interior, intensified gendered binaries of inside and outside. Furthermore, within the discursive construction of the postwar American domestic interior, the visual and psychological opening up of the private realm manifested in the potent subthemes of invasion, perversion, control, and deception. These are also central elements of the film noir genre.

In the postwar era, the glass curtain wall increasingly eroded the traditional domestic enclosure and the "turning away" of the gaze was reversed as the glowing scene of the private interior animated these new widescreen glass frames. This reversal was widely promoted in popular architectural magazines and journals through the emerging discipline of architectural photography, which appropriated many of the aesthetic conventions of Hollywood cinema. Indeed, the use of chiaroscuro black-and-white architectural photography as a means of representing modern domestic interiors in the early mid-century situates these spaces aesthetically within a *mise-en-scène* characteristic of American film noir (Figure 3.1). These images were published across a variety of popular media representing modern standards of "good living" and the idealized postwar middle-class American lifestyle. As such, these were politically and culturally charged images. To no small extent, the United States' involvement in the Second World War had been predicated ideologically upon the protection of the American family and way of life. In the postwar era, the domestic environment assumed a propagandistic role as evidence of the benefits of "freedom."[4] An advertisement for Thermopane picture windows appearing in *Architectural Forum* in 1949 claimed that in the popular postwar housing project Levittown, 3,000 returning war veterans "stood in line," to buy new houses with large picture windows (Figure 3.2).[5]

While the nineteenth-century European bourgeois interior turned inward, deflecting the gaze and insulating the individual and the family, the mid-twentieth-century American middle-class domestic interior opened itself up for display and inspection through the unmistakably cinematic frame of the window wall. Indeed, the postwar period is largely characterized by the rise of suburban American culture. The bourgeois European condition was largely urban and therefore held in tension with the city itself. In the United States the suburban development placed domestic architecture in an ambivalent context defined by generally agreed upon notions of family life and gender roles. The supposed sameness was intended to guarantee a kind of safety and therefore openness. However this is the origin of many of the tensions and anxieties regarding the mid-century suburban domestic environment.

As "openness" and transparency became increasingly essential components of "good living," significant challenges were raised for the occupation of domestic spaces, most notably the psychic dislocation caused by extensive visual exposure and the unrelenting presence of the gaze. The pregnant, shadowy depths so familiar from the contemporary film noir became the night-time setting for the glass-walled suburban house (Figure 3.3). However, the very tools of Hollywood— dramatic lighting and glamorized photography—were also used to mitigate anxieties of exposure and to provide the perception of control over the visual conditions of the private dwelling. The articulation of visual regimes within these spaces through electric lighting and the condition of the glass frame provide important entry points for the exploration of both scopophilic and scopophobic tensions. In the following essay I will pursue my own investigation of the American postwar domestic interior as a physical, textual, and psychological construction, probing some of the anxieties

Scopophobia/Scopophilia

This house was planned around the family of a man, his wife, and three children. It has been built in a suburb of The Hague, in Holland, in an area of dunes. The plan has carefully separated the living section from the bedrooms and kitchen in order to provide privacy for the social and the more intimate living functions of the house. All wood work is in light gray, the interior and exterior walls are white; all moving elements such as doors and windows are dark gray; the walls are of hollow brick; ceilings of Oregon pine; windows are steel; the heating elements are constructed in the floor for a convector heating system.

3.1
A. Fokke van Duijn (architect), private residence published as "A House in Holland,"
Arts & Architecture (January 1954)

3.2
"They Stood in Line," Thermopane advertisement, *Architectural Forum* (August 1949)

resulting from the increasing use of glass as well as the mechanisms put in place to respond to and mediate these points of rupture. Looking through the glass apertures of postwar houses (and the cameras that photographed them), I will argue that it is within this context that electric lighting became a powerful tool in the visual and psychic modulation of a domestic environment staged as interior within an architecture of windows.

Invasion

The phenomenon of glass walls in domestic architecture has wide-reaching social and cultural implications, particularly with respect to gendered scopic regimes and the long-standing binary tensions of the domestic and public realms. Certainly there is significant evidence that the window, as a transparent membrane between the interior and the exterior, was a key site of such tensions.[6] In mid-century psychoanalytic theory, the window was cast as a central location within the domestic

3.3
Richard Neutra, Chuey Residence, Los Angeles, 1956 (Photograph by Julius Shulman)

environment, mediating binaries of female and male, modesty and exhibitionism, narcissism and voyeurism. This perspective infiltrated architectural theory and discourse throughout the twentieth century.[7] In the 1966 essay, "From a Set of Forces to a Form," the architect Christopher Alexander argues for the recognition of "forces" as generative elements that summarize "recurrent and inexorable" tendencies in nature. Alexander provides a range of specific examples of generative forces at work in the physical environment, from gravity to thermodynamic heat flow. Yet when addressing the human environment Alexander singles out a woman's perceived vulnerability in relation to the window. He writes, "When we speak of a woman's need to protect herself symbolically against invasion, we mean to summarize the fact that she tends to enclose herself—for instance, with elaborate window curtains."[8] Substantiating this claim, Alexander cites Theodor Reik's *Of Love and Lust: On the Psychoanalysis of Romantic and Sexual Emotions*, in which the psychoanalyst argues that the domestic environment is a psychic continuation of the woman's own body and that she recognizes this space *as herself* as she moves within it.[9] Reik proposes that, "windows often have in this language the significance of an opening in the body, of the vulva of the woman."[10] Curtains, accorcing to Reik, function to express a socially conditioned feminine modesty and therefore are assigned all the usual frivolities of decoration and femininity:

> The curtains on the window take the place of the underwear covering and hiding female genitals. This unconscious significance of curtains for women explains not only the special attention paid to them in their thoughts, to their style and fabric, their color and material, but also the importance curtains have for women with regard to the ensemble for the room . . . Above all, the necessity of curtains at the windows finds its secret justification in that concealed emotional factor which is akin psychologically to modesty.[11]

In Reik's mid-century psychoanalytic theory, the window serves as both a specular surface for the narcissistic/female gaze and a frame for the scopophilic/male gaze, which ultimately the woman, as interior, can choose to allow or deny. The relationship between the symbolic modesty carried in the curtain and the intrinsically penetrating scopophillic gaze is exploited in a series of advertisements for Anton Maix fabrics that ran in *Interiors* magazine in the mid-1950s (Figure 3.4). In these advertisements, each one different, a woman is posed behind sheer draperies, looking out through the fabric at the reader. Here the "modesty" signaled by the curtains is challenged by the woman's direct gaze. In both Reik's text and in such popular mid-century imagery, curtains came to represent a central element in the eroticized tensions between "modesty" and a purposeful self-exposure that played out within the domestic interior.

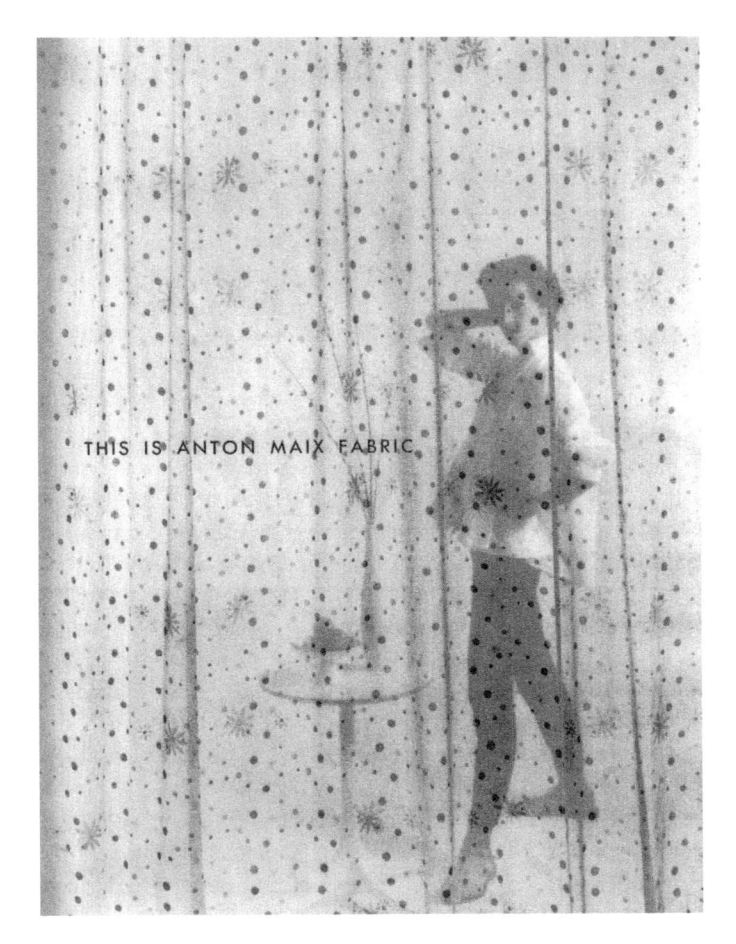

3.4
Anton Maix advertisement, *Interiors* (September 1955)

Perversion

In *Three Contributions to the Theory of Sex*, Sigmund Freud identifies the role of deviation in the "sexual instinct." Among the principal deviations Freud names "touching and looking" and argues for the primacy of the look in the formation of the sexual aim. He argues,

> In the perversion which consists in striving to look and be looked at, we are confronted with a very remarkable peculiarity. ... The sexual aim exists here in a two-fold formation, in an *active* and a *passive* form. The force which opposes the desire for looking and through which the latter is eventually abolished is *shame*.[12]

Reik, not surprisingly as a former student of Freud's, emphasizes the gendered sexual tension resulting from the visual opening of the domestic interior through the window in *Of Love and Lust*. However, moving beyond Freud, Reik specifically addresses the role of window "dressings" as the primary means for deactivating the powerful engagement of both the active/scopophilic and passive/narcissistic gaze latent in the domestic window.

Reik, apparently unconcerned with the rigorous and "skeletal" aesthetic demands of modern domestic architecture, does not concern himself with the problematic relationship between the use of curtains and the architectural representation and presentation of the interior. In the postwar era the photographic and textual representation of domestic architecture in popular magazines and professional journals increasingly emphasized the importance of transparency. Numerous articles appearing in the latter 1940s and early 1950s highlighted the benefits of "indoor outdoor living" and the domestic harmony possible with an increased visual fluidity between inside and outside.[13] In September 1949 *Architectural Forum* argued that "outdoor space, with a large glass area overlooking it, [should] be considered a minimum standard for modern homes."[14] Likewise, a 1949 feature on Richard Neutra's Tremaine House, titled "A Modern House Uses its Setting to Help Provide Luxurious Living," described the glass-walled pavilion as "not so much framed by nature as fitted into it."[15] In these publications "good living" was aesthetically and ideologically married to the architectural opening of the inside to the outside.[16] However, it was more than just an architectural "opening up" that occurred in this period, it was also the activation of the domestic interior itself as a space of visuality, distinctly organized to be seen.

In the postwar era well-known modernist housing initiatives in the United States aimed to build popular acceptance of modern domestic architecture by celebrating its compatibility with contemporary family life, flexibility of plan and program, and affordability.[17] Steel and glass construction was prominently credited with enabling such advances in the modern American lifestyle.[18] Indeed, the exposed steel frame and glass curtain wall became a key feature in the promotion of modern domestic architecture in the United States. Among the numerous editorial features on modern houses that appeared during this period, photographs of transparent window walls and sliding glass doors invisibly dividing the indoors from the outdoors were all but obligatory. While often curtains or other window treatments are visible in the photographs, they are nearly always drawn back, further emphasizing the cinematic frame of the window.

In an advertisement for the fashionable Southern Californian home furnishings store, Frank Bros., appearing in *Arts & Architecture* in 1953, the modern American lifestyle itself was put on offer (Figure 3.5). A deliriously happy young family —mother and daughter immobilize father in a welcoming embrace—foregrounds an image of an idealized modern domestic interior, singularly delineated from the white space of the page by the graphic outline of the window wall.[19] Further within the same issue, a nine-page article presenting architect Craig Ellwood's Case Study House features identical interiors, indeed the very same photograph used in the Frank Bros. advertisement, but this time, however, the image appears as

3.5
Frank Bros. advertisement, *Arts & Architecture* (June 1953)

architectural "fact" rather than advertising fiction.[20] Throughout the heavily illustrated article the photographer's camera is frequently positioned outside the house, looking through unobstructed glass doors and walls towards precisely ordered modern interiors. Enveloped in darkness with select areas of high-key lighting, the house is portrayed with a moody, dramatic quality in many of these photographs. Significantly, in both the light-hearted narrative of the Frank Bros. advertisement and the darker *mise-en-scène* of the editorial feature, the Ellwood interiors are framed for the voyeur. The reader is granted the pleasure of the scopophilic gaze, enticed to explore and measure these spaces against her own.

   The aesthetic conventions utilized by architectural journals and their advertisers would have been familiar to the mid-century popular audience. Borrowing from the visual language of classic Hollywood cinema, architectural photography in the postwar era presented readers with a known vantage point. Laura Mulvey identifies the scopic conventions of classic Hollywood cinema in her seminal essay *Visual Pleasure and Narrative Cinema*. In describing the visual environment of the cinematic experience, Mulvey calls attention to the contrasting lighting conditions which result from the audience's position surrounded by darkness and looking towards the luminous screen. It is precisely these visual conditions, according to Mulvey, that create a context in which voyeuristic separation can easily occur. Mulvey writes, "Although the film is really there to be shown, it is there to be seen, conditions of screening and narrative conventions give the spectator an illusion of looking in on a private world."[21] In both the Frank Bros. advertisement and the Ellwood editorial feature, the scopophilic gaze is focused by the widescreen window frames and the contrasting lighting conditions upon the fetishized consumer landscape of the modern domestic interior. As Mulvey suggests, "cinematic codes create a gaze, a world, and an object, thereby producing an illusion cut to the measure of desire."[22] The visual culture of the postwar domestic interior, much like the period's cinema, embodied the binary tension of the scopophilic and narcissistic gaze, of both desiring to view these private spaces and to see oneself within in them.

Control

The scopophilic gaze, with its affinity for voyeurism, is perfectly suited for the illusory world of advertising and editorial features; however, sensitivity to exposure and surveillance in relation to the domestic glass wall soon became a significant issue for individuals and families inhabiting such spaces. An article in the *New York Times* called attention to the problems arising from the use of window walls and large expanses of glass in domestic architecture, reporting that some residents of glass buildings "develop dizziness" as well as "a fear of being watched."[23] According to Dr. Jules Masserman, a psychiatrist interviewed for the article, "people have a yen for views—and they like to look at each other . . . but when they think that they, too, are being watched . . . they put up drapes, curtains, and French shades."[24] As a result, residents found themselves questioning the rationale for a view if unable to look out. Faced with this incongruity, as Masserman reported, residents of glass-walled apartments and houses soon found themselves "depressed all over again."

This relationship taken to an extreme is the focus of Michel Foucault's analysis of the panopticon. Exploring the power relations between the surveyor and the surveyed, Foucault theorizes the psychic tensions and self-regulation produced by this scopic dialectic. Foucault argues, "He who is subjected to a field of visibility, and who knows it, assumes responsibility for the constraints of power; he makes them play spontaneously upon himself; he inscribes in himself the power relation in which he simultaneously plays both roles; he becomes the principle of his own subjection."[25]

Christopher Wilson similarly considers the complexity of the relationship between the "view in" and "view out" but in direct relation to the context of the domestic realm. In particular Wilson problematizes any simple distinction separating the "view out" from the "view in," suggesting instead a more nuanced understanding of the "domestic glance." As Wilson argues, "A domestic glance, as its name implies involves the concepts of surveillance, privacy and social relations, all in relation to a domestic setting or living arrangements. Surveillance here refers both to 'looking out' and also to 'being looked at.'"[26] Finding such balance between "looking out" and "being looked at" became a critical question in the postwar period. Mechanisms for optimizing the domestic glance and minimizing the scopophobia produced by the window itself were needed in these new glass-walled dwellings.[27] How to maintain this balance without obstructing the view out or questioning the logic of modern glass architecture became an additional challenge. Within this context, electric lighting gained increasing significance, providing means for the scopic and psychic regulation of the domestic environment.

In the later 1940s and throughout the 1950s in the United States a number of articles offering advice on how to best incorporate electric lighting into the domestic interior appeared in the *New York Times, Saturday Evening Post, Vogue, House and Garden,* and *Flair*. These articles addressed the integration of new electric lighting techniques into domestic spaces as a central aspect of "home decoration," offering readers basic "how to" guidelines. One such article, "Making the Most of Lighting," appeared in the *New York Times* in October 1948.[28] Using familiar, non-technical language, the article describes three primary roles of light in the home: attraction, comfort, and personality. "Attraction" refers to the use of light for "direction of interest," necessary for emphasizing "the good and important features of the home," while "comfort" addresses utilitarian applications of light for activities such as reading, cooking, and dressing. "Personality," or lighting for a specific mood or atmosphere, is the third use of light and receives the greatest attention throughout the article. As the author proposes, "Every hostess wishes to make her home a true expression of herself. . . . [O]n entering the living room, the guest should sense the personality of his hostess. To make this possible, painstaking care should be taken in light planning." Like Reik's suggestion that the domestic interior is a spatial continuation of the woman's own body, in this article electric light is proposed as a medium with which the "hostess" (housewife) could extend a psychological image of herself for all those who enter or view this space.

The article continues describing a variety of lighting techniques that could be used to create tailored visual narratives—from social formality with a brightly illuminated ceiling, to an intimate atmosphere with lighting located below eye level. Throughout the feature lighting scenarios for entertaining, where the correct "personality" serves as an expression of social and aesthetic sophistication, are most closely detailed. Like the perfectly set dining table and neatly ordered living room in the Frank Bros. advertisements, domestic lighting is presented as a primary means of portraying one's restraint and good taste, something akin perhaps to the "modesty" signified previously by the curtain. Through such popular "how to" articles, electric lighting was positioned as a central element in the social scripting of the home, as well as a means of visually regulating the domestic scene.

In controlling the balance of light and dark areas in the domestic interior, the "hostess" was able to retain something of the domestic glance while also composing the *mise-en-scène* of the "view in." This simultaneous address of both the scopophilic gaze and scopophobic condition has significant resonance with the popular cinema of the day, and in particular, reveals connection with the contemporary codification of Hollywood cinematography. *Painting with Light*, the first book written by a Hollywood cinematographer describing the craft appeared in 1949. Importantly this "how to" book was intended for the amateur photographer and general reader rather than industry professionals.[29] John Alton, the author, was an established cinematographer well known for his work in the film noir genre. In the book, Alton describes his "Theory of Illumination" as comprised of two principal aims—lighting for "quantity" and lighting for "quality."[30] Alton identifies "quantity lighting" as concerned with the distribution and balance of light for proper exposure of film, whereas "quality lighting" addresses "orientation," "mood or feeling," "aesthetic pleasure," and "depth." In this latter category particularly, there is a clear connection with the "how to" articles then appearing in popular architecture journals and magazines.

Most striking, in his discussion of "depth," Alton notes the importance of the voyeuristic gaze in composing the cinematographic scene. He writes, "At night, when we look into an illuminated room from the dark outside, we can see inside but cannot be seen ourselves. A similar situation exists in the motion picture theatre. . . . We sit in the dark looking at a light screen; this gives a definite feeling of depth."[31] While Alton refers to this visual effect in photographic terms as "depth," what he describes is a psychological image-space constructed through the distribution of dark and light and the manipulation of the gaze, such as that found in contemporary representations of modern domestic architecture. The dark condition in which the viewer is located in juxtaposition to the glowing window (as screen) creates a situation wherein the gaze is activated and recognized simultaneously. However, in determining the scene, the "hostess," like the cinematographer, retains some control as author in orchestrating the conditions of performance, providing a tenuous balance between the gaze and the domestic glance. Indeed as Alton suggests, the limitations of the screen allow the image to be framed as "the director thinks the audience would like to see it. The success of any particular film depends a great deal upon the ability of the director to anticipate the desires of the audience."[32] In composing the domestic scene, then, the "hostess" was expected to "anticipate" the desires of the voyeur. Induced by the gaze, this expectation was pregnant in the glass apertures of the modern domestic environment.

Deception

With the manifestation of the coded visual conventions of Hollywood cinema in the postwar domestic environment, the private interior took on a quality of "to-be-looked-at-ness." The psychological implications of such visual exposure are described by Jacques Lacan, the French psychoanalyist, in his 1953–1954 *Seminars*. Here he articulates the potent and ever-present condition of the gaze from the vantage point of the individual behind a glass window. In particular, Lacan calls attention to the complexity of the construction of the gaze and the recognition of one's role as both subject and object within such an environment. The passage merits quoting at length:

> I can feel myself under the gaze of someone whose eyes I do not even see, not even discern. All that is necessary is for something to signify to me that there may be others there. The window if it gets a bit dark and if I have reason for thinking that there is someone behind it, is straightway a gaze. From the moment this gaze exists, I am already something other, in that I feel myself becoming an object for the gaze of others. But in this position, which is a reciprocal one, others also know that I am an object who knows himself to be seen.[33]

Intense interest in the American lifestyle during the postwar period—as viewed through the glass wall or picture window—established a context wherein the domestic interior itself became an object of the scopophilic gaze and a signification of desire.[34] Photographs of "indoor outdoor" domestic architecture were accompanied by texts pronouncing these environments as representations of the "good life." In such postwar narratives, the modern domestic interior was identified as a bellwether of American culture. As Joseph Barry argued in *House Beautiful* in 1953,

> The test of American civilization is not the height of its literary, musical, or artistic peaks, however important they are on the cultural landscape. It is the quality of the daily life itself. . . . The greatness we search [for] is greatness in the lives of our people. The true and the beautiful we try to combine with the good—and we call it the good life.[35]

However, the "good life" as promised in architectural journals and shelter magazines was not always received as such, most notoriously perhaps, in the case of the Farnsworth House. The iconic glass-walled house Mies van der Rohe designed in 1951 for Dr. Edith Farnsworth in Plano, Illinois, while unquestionably a sublime feat of ethereal modernism, failed to provide a domestic space that Farnsworth herself could comfortably occupy. In an interview from 1953, Farnsworth described her experience: "In this glass house with its four walls of glass I feel like a prowling animal, always on the alert. I am always restless."[36] Acutely aware of the gaze and of the exposure of every object and surface within her glass house, Farnsworth complained, "I don't keep a garbage can under my sink. Do you know why? Because you can see the whole 'kitchen' from the road on the way in here and the can would spoil the appearance of the whole house."[37] Farnsworth recognized, perhaps too acutely, that the "view in" had to be composed and maintained in relation to the aesthetic expectations of the modern domestic lifestyle. To include a garbage can within the "view" would destroy the illusion.[38] In order to preserve the integrity of the "image" of modern domesticity framed within the glass walls of her house, Farnsworth hid her garbage can in a closet. Eventually Farnsworth refused to be compliant with the demands of the gaze; she rejected the furniture Mies had specified, put up drapes and enclosed herself within the glass pavilion.

The pressure to maintain the illusion of a perfect domestic environment—modern, clean, stylish, and efficient—was intense and sustained across a variety of popular media in the postwar period. Many illustrated features and "how to" articles emphasized "the look," how things "should look," and how they "look best," affirming the pervasive visuality of the domestic environment. Like the plot of a film noir movie in which the heroine must never reveal her fear, the domestic appearance was to be maintained at all costs—a "look" staged for the viewer or voyeur rather than the convenience or comfort of the inhabitant. An article in *Life* magazine in 1949 announced the role of architectural photography in creating "glamourized houses" and how the right lighting and exposure could make modern houses "look dramatic" (Figure 3.6).[39] The caption appearing beneath Julius Shulman's iconic photograph of the Kaufmann Desert House (1946) describes how "drama" was created through double exposure—first for artificial light and second for twilight. Only through the deception of layering separate photographic exposures on a single image—one adjusted to the electric lighting inside the glass house, and another for the natural light on the landscape—was it possible to visually compose this image of a highly dramatic and seamless indoor–outdoor domestic environment.

The anxiety of maintaining appearances within the "to-be-looked-at-ness" of the domestic environment has been associated with the exponential growth of psychoanalysis and increased prescriptions of tranquilizers in the postwar era.[40] While causality in such matters may be difficult to identify, certainly the suggestion that psychological comfort could be provided by controlling the aesthetic conditions of the domestic environment, particularly with planned lighting, seems to be evidence of psychic fissures related to the performativity of these spaces. In 1957 *Vogue* ran an article, "The Light Changes," which argued that what "most American houses need" is more and better light. The article begins with a description of a domestic scene: "A party at which everyone is gay and sparkling, tactful and soothing, by turns—and always at the right moments: where everyone has a pleasant sense of well-being; and where all the guests, and the house itself, *look* their best, is one that every hostess dreams of giving."[41] In order to realize this dream of "looking her best," the author proposes that the hostess can call upon "a powerful ally: a new lighting plan," which "more than any other single factor, determines how people feel."[42] The author refers repeatedly to the relationship between the "look" of the domestic environment and how those within it "feel." Even more explicitly, the author suggests that lighting designers, as trained specialists in the composition of light are "as much authorities on human emotions, reactions, moods, as they are

3.6
Richard Neutra,
Kaufmann Desert
House, Palm Springs,
1946, *Life* magazine (April
1949) (Photograph by
Julius Shulman)

on fluorescent fields . . . as a lighting expert must also, by definition, be a practising psychologist."[43]

With this essay I have sought to identify "traces of the look" in the American postwar domestic environment, unraveling a space finely constructed through a composite of the physical, psychological, and discursive. This investigation has revealed the role of powerful, yet familiar, scopic regimes in the design, promotion, and experience of the modern domestic interior. Partially or fully wrapped in glass, the postwar domestic environment was permeated with the binary tensions latent in the glass itself—male/female, active/passive, exterior/interior, scopophilic/scopophobic. The "to-be-looked-at-ness" of this environment resulted in the development of key mechanisms for controlling the domestic *mise-en-scène*. The adoption of cinematic conventions in the popular imaging of domestic architecture and interiors reinforced the perception of these spaces as ideal, thereby increasing the anxiety of measuring up to the precise standards of the "good life." New technologies such as electric lighting were proposed as a means of "dramatizing" the interior, establishing a "mood," and crafting a psychological self-portrait to be seen and "felt" by guests or the imagined voyeur. Rather than turning away the gaze architecturally as Loos had, or, as Reik suggested, insulating oneself from view (and the temptation for voyeurism or exhibitionism) with curtains, in postwar America the glass walls of the modern house became shop windows. As one would expect with any good retail display, dramatic lighting and careful staging served as both an enticement and acknowledgment of the gaze. But the vector of desire and signification traveled in two directions. In an advertisement for Panaview sliding aluminum doors and windows that appeared in *Arts & Architecture* in 1954, the disembodied head of an attractive young woman floats on the white space of the page and is held in place by the graphic suggestion of a Panaview window-wall (Figure 3.7).

The geometric widescreen frame encloses each of the model's eyes as she looks out at the reader. The text of the advertisement tells the reader of the great promise latent in this young woman's look. It reads, "The dream in her eye comes true with Panaview."[44] The anxiety of the gaze then, was not singularly

3.7
"The Dream in Her Eye,"
Panaview advertisement,
Arts & Architecture
(December 1954)

scopcphobic, in many ways this fear was more one of failing to achieve the correct "look"—scopophilia turned obsessively narcissistic.

In postwar America's modern domestic interior, as portrayed across popular media, the "view out" became the "view in." The complexity of such a scopic and psychic construction is described by Foucault, who argues, "Power has its principle not so much in a person as in a certain concerted distribution of bodies, surfaces, lights, gazes; in an arrangement whose internal mechanisms produce the relation in which individuals are caught up."[45] The framing of the domestic interior through the picture window or window wall as a perfectly maintained consumer landscape where "everyone is gay and sparkling" and "has a pleasant sense of well-being" placed enormous expectations upon the individual responsible for this environment. This then is also a gendered condition. In the postwar era, the domestic realm unquestionably was the purview of the female head of household.[46] In the cinematic framing of the domestic environment, an exposed garbage can became a challenge to a woman's own identity and her identification with an ideal imposed by the glass wall itself.

Notes

Acknowledgments: The research informing this chapter was made possible through the generous financial support of Victoria University of Wellington. Additionally, I would like to thank David Travers for kindly allowing me to republish the classic layouts from *Arts & Architecture* magazine appearing in this essay. I am also grateful to Sarah Sherman, Reference Librarian, Special Collections and Visual Resources at the Getty Research Institute for her assistance in obtaining key images from the Julius Shulman Archive.

1. Beatriz Colomina, *Privacy and Publicity: Modern Architecture as Mass Media* (Cambridge, MA: MIT Press, 1994), 233.
2. Ibid., 255.
3. Ibid., 260.
4. On the representation of American consumer lifestyles and the home as a site of consumption in Cold War propaganda see, Susan E. Reid, "'Our Kitchen is Just as Good': Soviet Responses to the American National Exhibition, 1959," in *Cold War Modern: Design 1945–1970*, eds. David Crowley and Jane Pavitt (London: V&A Publishing, 2008), 154–160; and more generally on the Cold War domestic environment, Elaine Tyler May, *Homeward Bound: American Families in the Cold War Era* (New York: Basic Books, 1988).
5. Thermopane advertisement, *Architectural Forum*, August 1949: 4–5. On suburban postwar culture, see Lynn Spigel, *Welcome to the Dreamhouse: Popular Media and Postwar Suburbs* (Durham, NC: Duke University Press, 2001), 1–2.
6. See for example, Irene Cieraad, "Dutch Windows: Female Virtue and Female Vice," in *At Home: An Anthropology of Domestic Space*, ed. Irene Cieraad (Syracuse, NY: Syracuse University Press, 2006), 31–40.
7. Regarding the influences of psychoanalysis on the development of modern architecture, see Sylvia Lavin, "Open the Box: Richard Neutra and the Psychology of the Domestic Environment," *Assemblage*, no. 40 (December 1999): 6–25; and *Form Follows Libido: Architecture and Richard Neutra in a Psychoanalytic Culture* (Cambridge, MA: MIT Press, 2004).
8. Christopher Alexander, "From a Set of Forces to a Form," in *The Man-made Object*, ed. Gyorgy Kepes (New York: G. Braziller, 1966), 96–107, quote appearing on 96.
9. Theodor Reik, *Of Love and Lust: On the Psychoanalysis of Romantic and Sexual Emotions* (New York: Farrar, Straus and Company, 1957).
10. Ibid., 488.
11. Ibid. Reik had studied with Freud in Vienna in the early 1910s and became an important advocate for psychoanalysis in the United States after immigrating in 1938.
12. Sigmund Freud, "The Sexual Aberrations," in *The Basic Writings of Sigmund Freud*, trans. and ed. A.A. Brill (New York: Random House, 1995), 537.
13. Typically such discussions of "indoor outdoor living" were focused on a generalized understanding of the domestic environment, rather than specific room typologies. However, photographic illustrations accompanying such popular articles often featured living rooms and kitchens, but less frequently bedrooms where the notion of unobstructed transparency and fluidity was more problematic. When the bedroom was specifically addressed in this context, commonly the orientation of the bedroom towards an isolated or visually protected landscape is emphasized rather than the use of window treatments (which would foil the "indoor outdoor" flow). For example the 1943 exhibition featuring modern Californian residential architecture held at the Museum of Modern Art, New York City, praised the "judicious orientation and placing of the windows and entrances [to] insure privacy and at the same time [to] permit a sense of mobility, freedom, and openness." This statement appeared above a photograph of a bedroom with a room-length panoramic window—unfettered by any window treatments—looking out upon a private landscape. See "Five California Houses," *Bulletin of the Museum of Modern Art* 10, no. 4 (April 1943): 10–11.

14   William W. Wurster, "The Outdoors in Residential Design," *Architectural Forum*, September 1949: 68–69.
15   "A Modern House Uses its Setting to Help Provide Luxurious Living," *Architectural Forum*, September 1949: 52–58.
16   Colomina similarly argues for the pervasiveness of the postwar desire for transparency, describing the emergence of "see-through house[s]" as "mass phenomena," arguing that, "it was not just the house: it would seem that everything in the house had to be see-through, from the Pyrex cookware to Saran Wrap to windows in ovens and washing machines and so on." Beatriz Colomina, *Domesticity at War* (Barcelona: Actar, 2006), 164.
17   Arguably the best-known of these initiatives is the Case Study House program begun by John Entenza, publisher and editor of the influential journal *Arts & Architecture* (1938–1967). See Dolores Hayden, "Model Houses for the Millions: Architects' Dreams, Builders' Boasts, Residents' Dilemmas," in *Blueprints for Modern Living: History and Legacy of the Case Study Houses,* ed. Elizabeth A.T. Smith (Cambridge, MA: MIT Press, 1998), 197–211. As she suggests, "The Case Study House program confidently promised to deliver a world free from old domestic stereotypes: socially innovative, because the houses would be suited to modern lifestyles; aesthetically innovative, because they would be distinguished by modern designers; and technically innovative, because new approaches to construction techniques would be considered and new materials developed in wartime would be used" (Hayden, 207).
18   In the 1950s, all but one of the Case Study houses utilized steel framing. Hayden, 207.
19   Frank Bros. advertisement (appearing opposite editorial masthead), *Arts & Architecture*, June 1953: 4–5.
20   "The New Case Study House," *Arts & Architecture*, June 1953: 20–29.
21   Laura Mulvey, "Visual Pleasure and Narrative Cinema," in *Feminist Film Theory*, ed. Sue Thornham (New York: NYU Press, 1999), 58–69; quote on 61.
22   Ibid., 68.
23   Judy Klemesrud, "Light-Shy Tenants Taking a Dim View of Glass Walls," *New York Times*, November 28, 1967, 52.
24   Ibid.
25   Michel Foucault, *Discipline and Punish* (London: Penguin, 1977), 202.
26   Christopher Wilson, "Looking at/in/from the *Maison de Verre*" in *Negotiating Domesticity: Spatial Productions of Gender in Modern Architecture*, eds. Hilde Heynen and Gülsüm Baydar (London: Routledge, 2005), 234–252; quote on 234.
27   As illustrated in numerous articles from the period that suggested various ways to ensure "privacy" in modern glass-walled houses, see for example, "When Wide Open Spaces are Outside Looking In," *New York Times*, January 12, 1946, 12; Mary Roche, "Glass-Wall Houses Give Full Privacy: Designers on Coast Show Novel Lay-outs," *New York Times*, July 8, 1946, 19; "Outsize Windows Hard to Curtain," *New York Times*, July 18, 1949; Betty Pepis, "New Ways with Windows," *New York Times*, May 7, 1950, 200; and Betty Pepis, "Behind Glass Walls," *New York Times*, February 3, 1952.
28   Richard Kelly, "Making the Most of Lighting," *New York Times*, October 3, 1948, 21.
29   John Alton, *Painting with Light* (New York: Macmillan, 1949; Berkeley: University of California Press, 1995). Citations refer to the University of California Press edition. In the introduction, Alton suggests that his book is intended for use in developing lighting techniques for "still photography" and for "kindred souls who also delight in capturing bits of light at rest on things of beauty" (xli).
30   Alton, 33.
31   Ibid.
32   Ibid.
33   Jacques Lacan, *The Seminar of Jacques Lacan,* ed. Jacques-Alain Miller, trans. John Forrester, Book 1 of *Freud's Papers on Technique, 1953–1954* (Cambridge: Cambridge University Press, 1988), 215.

34 Similarly, in her discussion of the conventions of classic Hollywood cinema, Mulvey writes: "In their traditional exhibitionist role women are simultaneously looked at and displayed, with their appearance coded for strong visual and erotic impact so that they can be said to connote to-be-looked-at-ness . . . she holds the look, and plays to and signifies male desire." Mulvey, 62–63.

35 Joseph A. Barry, "The Next America will be the Age of Great Architecture," *House Beautiful*, April 1953: 116–125, 168–170, 194–196, quote on 116.

36 As quoted in Alice T. Friedman, *Women and the Making of the Modern House: A Social and Architectural History* (New Haven: Yale University Press, 2006), 141.

37 The complicated history of the Farnsworth House and its design, in particular the thorny relationship that developed between Farnsworth and Mies in the final years of its construction, is detailed in Friedman, 126–147.

38 Colomina has suggested that the view through the picture window or window wall "is not a private space but a public representation of conventional domesticity." Colomina, *Domesticity at War*, 168.

39 "Glamourized Houses," *Life* 26, April 11, 1949: 146–148.

40 Colomina, *Domesticity at War*, 164.

41 Alison Bisgood, "The Light Changes," *Vogue* 129, no. 1 (January 1957): 137–139.

42 Ibid., 137.

43 Ibid.

44 "The Dream in her Eye, Comes True with Panaview," Panaview advertisement appearing in *Arts & Architecture*, December 1954.

45 Foucault, 202.

46 As Esther da Costa Meyer has argued, "With the advent of industrialization, concomitant economic pressures caused severe strains in the traditional value system of American society. The transformation of the home from a place of production to one of consumption had great impact on women's personalities, and led to a drastic change from the Protestant values of thrift and self-denial to an ethic of self-indulgence and self-fashioning." Esther da Costa Meyer, "La Donna è Mobile: Agoraphobia, Women, and Urban Space," in *The Sex of Architecture*, ed. Diana Agrest, Patricia Conway, and Leslie Kanes Weisman (New York: Harry N. Abrams, 1996), 141–155.

Part 2

Ideological Objects
Design and Representation

Chapter 4

The Allegory of the Socialist Lifestyle
The Czechoslovak Pavilion at the Brussels Expo, its Gold Medal and the Politburo

Ana Miljački

One of the most famous events marking the Cold War tension's capacity to infiltrate all aspects of life revolved around a washing machine (GE: sunshine yellow). The image of Nixon and Khrushchev standing together at the American Exhibition in Moscow in 1959, observing a scene of suburban domestic life, is second only to images of Sputnik and the first lunar landing in its ability to allegorically summarize the "peaceful race"—Khrushchev's term of endearment for the Cold War—that held the world in balance for the four decades after the Yalta Conference of 1945 (Figure 4.1). On June 24, 1959, the first day of Nixon's visit to the Soviet Union, Khrushchev and Nixon also talked about missile capabilities and the freshly endorsed "Captive Nations Resolution" (which condemned Soviet involvement in Eastern European states). The capacity of washing machines and television sets to conjure up enough symbolism to push the missiles and political oppression into the background of the collective, global imaginary in this instant, dramatizes the extent to which lifestyle was one of the most captivating and symbolically powerful registers of the Cold War. Powerful—precisely because it implicated the private lives and daily decisions of the masses on both sides of the divide.[1]

Anxiety: Of Interpretation

The juxtaposition of relative luxury to relative scarcity, which was certainly the punchline of the reports on the "kitchen debate" in the American press, describes the most basic circumstances of life, and therefore of practicing architecture as well, on the opposing sides of the iron curtain. However, this juxtaposition itself has often obfuscated the importance that the concept of lifestyle had in the postwar discourse

Ana Miljački

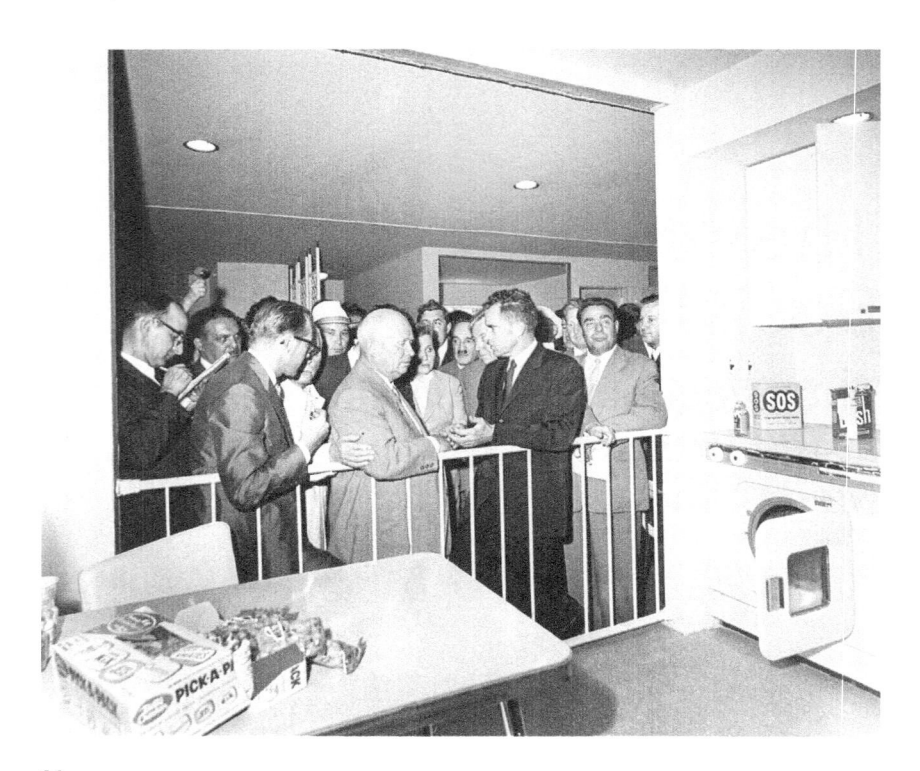

4.1
Soviet Premier Nikita Khrushchev and US Vice President Richard Nixon reviewing the American Kitchen, American Exhibition, Sokolniki Park, Moscow, 1959

of the Second World. The issue of the "correct" interpretation of Socialist Lifestyle—including everything from an appropriately socialist aesthetic, through appropriate modes of production, to ideas about "reasonable consumption"—induced much anxiety in postwar Czechoslovak expert discourse. But on top of the constant anxiety of interpretation a few themes surfaced with relative consistency: teamwork (as an idea that was conceptually grander than even the biggest structural change in the field produced in the name of socialism—the 1948 nationalization of the entire profession), synthesis (as a codeword for the thing that a team of experts does really well together), and, of course, standardization (as the chief qualifier of production that would ensure the command economy's victory over the free market). Each of these three issues would, in their own right, produce possible aesthetic effects, and since they were ideologically aligned at their basis, their combined aesthetic effect was rarely questioned as such. But this is not to say that the aesthetic interpretation of Socialist Lifestyle was not a particularly problematic issue when posited not only as a possible result of collectively vetted socialist methods, but also simultaneously as the very register of ideological correctness.

The question of the appropriate aesthetic was finally closed—or so the Czechoslovak architects thought—in 1953 at the first Conference of Czechoslovak

Architects, when socialist realism was officially adopted as their visual program (relatively late given the discussion about socialist realism started in the 1930s in the Soviet Union and among the Czech architects) accompanied by the pronouncement that Czech architects would rely on the work of the "the most progressive architecture in the world: the architecture of the Soviet Union."[2] No sooner did the Architects' Conference write the above statement into law than Khrushchev's famous speeches made it obsolete, or at least open to reinterpretation and adjustment.[3] Calling Stalin's version of socialist realist architecture "decadent" and "formalist," by which he meant expensive and misguided, in 1954, and exorcising the ghost of the dead Stalin from Soviet socialism in 1956, Khrushchev's speeches launched the Czech architectural field into a frenzy of discursive maneuvering and "self-critique."[4] The first timid (and slightly panicked) responses to Khrushchev's 1954 keynote at the All-Union Builders' Conference began to appear on the pages of the key Czech architecture journals in 1955. And while his 1956 "Secret Speech" sponsored another round of discussions on "self-criticism," by the end of 1955 it seemed that the field, led in this discussion by one of the masterminds of the nationalization of the Czechoslovak construction industry, Otakar Nový, had settled on a viable way to absorb Khrushchev's demands: socialist realist style was not to be applied mechanically in Czechoslovakia, at stake was no longer socialist realism's image but its method instead. While this official conclusion on the *correct* way to interpret Khrushchev's speeches may at first seem like a simple semantic issue, replacing "style" with "method" ensured that the discourse on socialist realism was *appropriately* adjusted, while it allowed for everything said and done until that point to remain, without being retroactively dubbed a complete error. And while this adjustment brought relief to some, it left the issue of the more difficult task of actually practicing the new and improved, and still economically minded, mass-produced and humanist architecture open to formal interpretation, anew.

Just a year before the American Exhibition in Moscow, at the Brussels Expo in 1958, the showdown between the two emergent superpowers of the Cold War (represented there with equally oversized pavilions) involved models of Sputnik and color television sets. Against the backdrop of this "friendly competition," sited literally in the shadow of the large Soviet pavilion, the Czechoslovak pavilion, the least daring of architectural statements among the Eastern Bloc countries represented at the Brussels Expo, received a gold medal (Figure 4.2).

The Brussels Expo was the first real opportunity to show the rest of the world how well things were going in socialist Czechoslovakia.[5] And thus, although it was not immediately clear what it might look like, the Czechoslovak pavilion was officially charged with producing the "total socialist synthesis" according to a new and better interpretation of the socialist realist method of work, and was retrospectively taken as the most glorious example of both (new socialist realist) image and method. It is in part because its making and evaluation left an unprecedented paper trail and because of its subsequent, legendary success in the Czech context (which remains naturalized as such even in the very recent publications on the project) that the history of the Czechoslovak pavilion aptly demonstrates— sometimes in excruciating detail—the strange Second World dance that took place

Ana Miljački

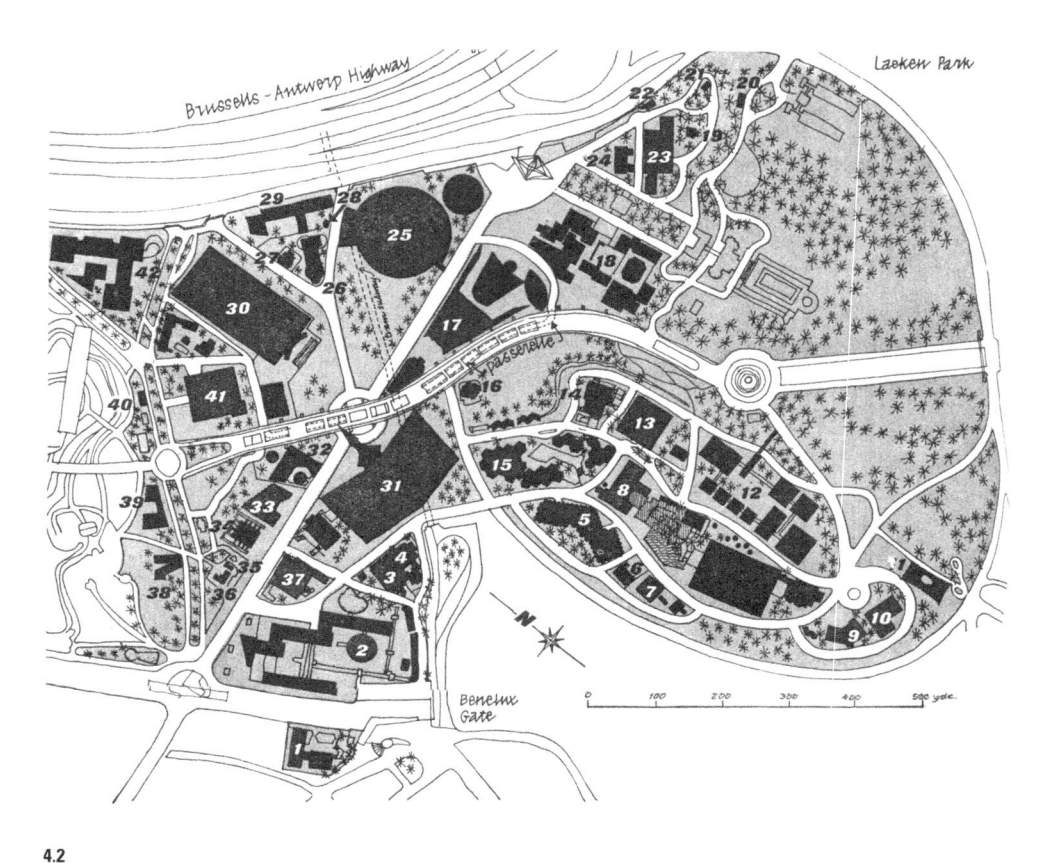

4.2
Map of the main portion of the Brussels Exhibition site, produced for *Architectural Review* (August 1958). The Soviet Pavilion is number 30, the US Pavilion is number 25, and the Czechoslovak Pavilion is number 42, to the north of the Soviet Pavilion.

regularly between state ideologues and state architects as they struggled to practice within the socialist utopia that, by the way, they had no choice but to live in.[6]

The Script: Propaganda through Perfection

The drafting of the first textual description, the libretto, for the Czechoslovak exhibit began in May of 1956, and its "ideological task" was discussed and finessed from 1956 until the actual opening of the Expo. The libretto's basic ambitions were: one, "demonstrating the upswing of the material and cultural life in Czechoslovakia as the success of the socialist organization of the society," and two, "showing our great will for friendly cooperation with all the people of the world, in all aspects of life."[7] As the exhibit was taking place in the West, "after many years of propaganda presenting Czechoslovakia as an enemy," this early libretto also proposed that the exhibit's task would be to fight misconceptions about life in Czechoslovakia most likely held by lay audiences—the first important one being that Czechoslovakia was the enemy of the West. Propaganda had always been the ultimate program of international expositions, but in the context of this exposition (held in a Western country just three years before the Berlin Wall was erected), the 1956 libretto interestingly urged specifically against sloganeering: "It is best to get at this through exhibiting sophisticated products of our industry and in the concrete results of our attention to man, definitely not through unsubstantiated statements, phrases or other cheap examples."[8] Thus, although this early version of the libretto was not for everyone's eyes (and perhaps because it was not), it could freely describe the problems with sloganeering propaganda. Given the presentation's mandate to communicate to the West, it was acceptable for the libretto to capture with some distaste the awareness of the prosaic and generally ineffective standard propaganda methods.[9] Perhaps more importantly, the fact that this type of statement appears in the libretto at all, should signal the extent to which "phrases and cheap examples" had permeated the daily life of socialist Czechoslovakia by the mid-1950s.

The second misconception that the exhibit was charged with dismantling was articulated in the libretto as Czechoslovakia's dependence on the Soviet Union. Czechoslovak officials wanted to represent Czechoslovakia as a sovereign country with unique characteristics and a capacity to contribute to world civilization—somehow different from all other people's democracies—and still willingly on the socialist path. In fact, the libretto urged that it had to be "conclusive from the exhibition that our successes stem from fulfilling our plans and they open up a perspective for future comprehensive development."[10] In order to attest to that, the material in the Czechoslovak exposition was charged with competing with the Western world in terms of the "formal perfection of objects and pavilions, their production quality and novelty of the materials used," all the while going well beyond the Western countries in terms of the ideological content of the exhibition, simply by definition (capitalism < socialism). Formal perfection was a tall order, especially since it was not accompanied by any specific criteria for its evaluation, but it is the vagueness of this term coupled with the highest—and competitive—ambitions that opened the door to experimentation, insofar as applied and theater artists and architects allowed themselves to interpret the libretto as an invitation to forget about the possible ideological repercussions of their work (should it not rank high enough in the general exposition assessments) and make something "perfect" by their own standards.

Teamwork: All for Architecture

Soon after the socialist government was installed in Czechoslovakia in 1948, and the entire field of architecture and construction was nationalized, all of the prewar, avant-garde architects found their new home in the national firm Stavoprojekt. Three leading architects from the Prague Stavoprojekt office—František Cubr, Josef Hrubý and Zdeněk Pokorný—won the closed competition for the Czechoslovak Pavilion, organized by the government soon after Khrushchev's Secret Speech, in 1956.[11] Their pre-1948 work consisted of tasteful, middle-of-the-road, modern commercial projects. Their collective roster of exhibits already included the Milan Triennale in 1947, exhibitions of the work of Stavoprojekt in 1953 and 1954, as well as the Czechoslovakia exhibit in Moscow in 1955.[12] Even though their prewar avant-garde production would have been seen as a liability until 1954, after Khrushchev's speeches it was less of an issue, and their experience abroad counted in the context where competition with the West was imagined and articulated in terms of a universally applicable register of perfection of form and novelty of materials, however vague these notions actually were. Although there is no literal evidence of this sentiment (a paper trail of it would have been damning), taking into account the ambitions of the libretto, which is to say, of the officials in charge of the Czechoslovak presentation in Brussels, and the choice of the Cubr, Hrubý, and Pokorný team of architects, it becomes clear that the unspoken agreement on the issue had to have been that only someone with real insight into Western production could possibly set the bar high enough for the Czechoslovak pavilion, its conceptual coherence and its contents. Importantly, however, among the competition entries, the proposal presented by Cubr, Hrubý and Pokorný was by far the most formally restrained. It was a very timid and controlled interpretation of how one might design following the new socialist realist method (Figure 4.3). The building was clean, as in ornament-less, which was an absolutely direct reading of a portion of Khrushchev's requests, and it was minimally expressive formally, which was in 1954 also described as a virtue by Khrushchev.

According to the chief architects' presentation in the journal *Architektura ČSR* in 1958, and before their pavilion had received its gold medal, the main intentions of the architectural aspects of the project were: "a) the urbanist integration of the object into its surroundings, b) deployment of views to the exterior and interior, c) production of an understanding of the whole, d) fulfillment of higher technical goals."[13] They were "conscious of the fact" (in their own words) that the individuality of the pavilion would be above all ensured by the individuality of the content—of the themes "coming from the specific cultural and production milieus." Each of the points listed by the architects preemptively anticipated critique. For example, the notion of "higher technical goals" squarely fit within Khrushchev's most recent pronouncements, even though it could have been seen as contradictory to his call to modesty and frugality; technical development was also the basis of all the conversations on prefabrication that underpinned Czech standardization efforts which were already underway in 1948. Furthermore, technical virtuosity was the least controversial of all possible interpretations of "formal perfection" that the officials had asked for. On the other hand, issues of integration (with the surroundings) on the urban scale or a widely accessible reading of the totality of the pavilion were both described in such a way that anything contrary to what the architects claimed they were interested in would have seemed simply absurd. No one could argue for non-integration or lack of understanding.

Given that they were navigating a terrain littered with contradictory ambitions—perfection asked for by Czechoslovak officials, modesty asked for by Khrushchev, and of course a presentation of Czechoslovak national identity structurally necessitated by the Expo (and underlined by the same officials who asked for perfection), the architects' claim that the building would derive from the content of its exhibits has to be seen as a clever rhetorical attempt on their part to transfer away some of the responsibility for the project. This political maneuver

Allegory of the Socialist Lifestyle

4.3
Above: František Cubr, Josef Hrubý, and Zdeněk Pokorný (Architects), Sketch of the winning entry, Czechoslovak Pavilion, Brussels Exhibition, 1958
Below: František Cubr, Josef Hrubý, and Zdeněk Pokorný (Architects), Model, Czechoslovak Pavilion, Brussels Exhibition, 1958

paralleled in reverse the critique leveled at the building by the head of the Czech architect's union (and one of the Expo architects' colleagues), Josef Gočár, just before the Expo opened. Protecting himself preemptively, Gočár went on record warning that the Czechoslovak pavilion was "too individualistic"—even though it was stripped of socialist realist ornament, it still seemed too indulgent, neither modest nor standardized enough.[14] The form/content split invoked by the architects positively and with the hope of eventually effecting an ever-better synthesis of the two constituted a preemptive discursive maneuver, not unlike Gočár's own. The pavilion architects' reversal of Stalin's old (now obsolete) request for works of art and architecture that would be socialist in content and national in form, that is, their proposal that the Czechoslovak pavilion for Brussels was first and foremost derived from Czechoslovak content made any critique of the pavilion automatically also a critique of the country.

The scenario for the Czechoslovak pavilion drafted by architect Jindřich Santar, proposed to present "One Day in Czechoslovakia" through work, culture and leisure. The hope was that "One Day in Czechoslovakia" would naturally mesh with the larger theme of the Expo ("for a more human world"), while presenting the excellence of life under socialism in the full superlative force of the Cold War propaganda, albeit without sloganeering.[15] In direct response to Santar's call, the Czechoslovak pavilion was programmed with a large glass exhibit, multimedia cultural programs, an industrial exhibit, images of daily life in socialist Czechoslovakia, as well as a working restaurant and sections dedicated to energy, children, and free time. Thus the content that architects hoped to rely on for effect (and inspiration) was provided by a series of familiar pre-socialist Czech and Slovak themes: glass, toys, textile crafts, industry, and food. Therefore, specifically Czechoslovak life and lifestyle were to be a testament to the greatness of socialism in Czechoslovakia (not vice versa). This strategy, "a day in life of Czechoslovakia," should remind us of the more famous (and even strikingly similarly titled) American strategy for Moscow which took place a year later, in 1959; multiple and fast-changing images of life in the United States functioning as a testament to the greatness of capitalism. In another significant parallel to the American exhibit in Moscow, the Czechoslovak multimedia program (the most highly recognized portion of the Czechoslovak exhibit—and most likely the main reason for the great number of visitors to the Czechoslovak pavilion) introduced a multi-screen technology—Polyecran—that among other things screened a film made specifically for it, *Spring in Prague*, experimenting with non-linear means of storytelling (Figure 4.4).[16]

The other important portion of the Czechoslovak multimedia presentation relied on a non-verbal hybrid between projection and theatrical action to relay its propaganda material. This new theatrical form developed by director Alfred Radok and stage designer Josef Svoboda was dubbed Laterna Magika in reference to the seventeenth-century beginnings of projection technologies.[17] The energy installation was embellished with a lightshow that the prewar avant-garde groups (like the 1920s artist collective Devětsil, or even architectural critic Karel Teige himself) would have loved, the heavy industry was literally whited out into abstraction (with a coat of paint), and theater set designer and architect Josef Svoboda's rendition of antennae

Allegory of the Socialist Lifestyle

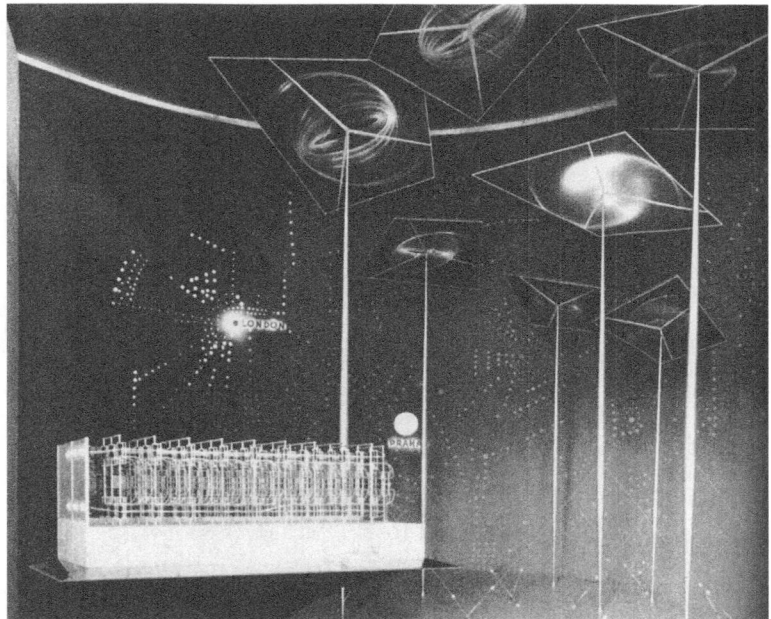

4.4
Above: Emil Radok (director and scriptwriter), Josef Svoboda (set designer and architect), and Jan Fischer (composer), Polyecran presentation of the *Prague Spring* movie, Czechoslovak Pavilion, Brussels Exhibition, 1958
Below: Josef Svoboda (set designer and architect), Antenae Installation, Czechoslovak Pavilion, Brussels Exhibition, 1958

Ana Miljački

4.5
Above: Designer Antonín Kybalov touching up a scaled model for the installation dedicated to issues of Czechoslovak fashion and taste, for the Czechoslovak Pavilion, Brussels Exhibition, 1958
Below: Multimedia installation dedicated to Czechoslovak advancements in energy production, Czechoslovak Pavilion, Brussels Exhibition, 1958 (Photograph by Alexander Paul)

as a fragile, but nonetheless techno-futuristic forest, casually nodded to Czech surrealism while serving as the evidence that television sets existed somewhere in Czechoslovakia as well (Figures 4.4 and 4.5). It is important to highlight here that all the effort to find the right tone and content on to which to hang the required perfection of objects and architectural form resulted in the equation of the content of socialist lifestyle with its historical opposite.

Synthesis: One Building for All

The main approach to the building presented a symmetrical façade of nearly classical proportions, two monolithic cubes at each end divided by a translucent glazed section bar and topped off by four shallow-pitched roofs (Figure 4.3). Three hub programs anchored the plan, each fitting into a square and "holding down" three points of a large flipped "L", while the comparatively irregular and curved shape of the restaurant animated the ground captured by the "L" of the main pavilion. While the anchored and more strictly programmed cubes were opaque and introverted, clad in tiles especially engineered for this purpose, the two arms of the "L," which for the most part have to be seen as rather grand circulation spaces, were entirely clad in glass and included areas that were double height.

When recounting the way in which they had produced their pavilion, the three architects talked about their insistence on designing the inside and the outside simultaneously. Most importantly they discussed their decision to not pursue the design of a single, total space that would provide the possibility for an uncomplicated and complete comprehension of the whole—they referred to this type of space as *monoprostor*, or mono-space.[18] They were particularly interested in differentiating views, spaces, interest, and producing more of a flow and a complex organization of spaces that would consciously juxtapose dramatically charged moments to spaces of pause and rest.

This decision to produce a complex experience in lieu of a singular object building becomes relevant when the Czechoslovak pavilion is seen against the backdrop of the Soviet one (Figure 4.6). Just as the literal urban relegation of the Czechoslovak pavilion into the background of the Soviet one directly reflects the political configuration of the Cold War relationship, the fact that unlike the Soviet pavilion the Czechoslovak one evacuated its center, can be seen not only as the acknowledgment that the center of its political system was already presented by its towering neighbor pavilion, but also that insofar as the Czechoslovak presentation at the Expo could be seen as a function of a conscious interpretation of socialism in Czechoslovakia at this point, "understanding socialism"—like living it—involved active participation by every one of its subjects.

Both the Czechoslovak and USSR pavilions greeted visitors with a long modernist stair—whose horizontality suggested and length allowed that many visitors should occupy it at once; it was a collective stair, embellished in both cases with a melodramatic, figural sculpture in an unmistakably socialist realist heroic contortion (Figure 4.7). But where the USSR pavilion opened into a single expansive space commanded by a larger than life-size figure of Lenin, the thinness of the Czechoslovak pavilion's entry foyer allowed immediate views to the restaurant structure (Figure 4.6). The second arm of the "L" was thicker, and the exhibition

Ana Miljački

4.6
Above: Central space of the Soviet Pavilion, Brussels Exhibition, 1958 (Photograph by Allan Hallstone)
Below: View through the window of the Czechoslovak Pavilion main building onto the restaurant wing, Brussels Exhibition, 1958 (Photograph by Alexander Paul)

Allegory of the Socialist Lifestyle

4.7
Above: Andrei Boretskii, Dubov, Iu. Abramov, and A. Polianskii (Architects), front entry, Soviet Pavilion, Brussels Exhibition 1958 (Photograph by Allan Hallstone)
Below: František Cubr, Josef Hrubý, and Zdeněk Pokorný (Architects), exterior plaza and front entrance, Czechoslovak Pavilion, Brussels Exhibition, 1958

displays in it were organized following the logic of the installation throughout the pavilion—objects came in and out of view, modulating the experience. The exterior of the restaurant was visually accessible from the installation on heavy industry, framing the leisurely life of the visitors, so to speak, into the most important of the exhibitions. Thus life, culture, and industry cross-referenced one another into a "total work" of socialist lifestyle.

Writing just as the Expo opened (and well before their work was endorsed by the gold medal) the architects' description of the project echoed the language used and the requirements described in the scenario and librettos that had preceded it.[19] And although their description also relatively accurately portrayed some of the pavilion's effects, suggesting self-confidently the architects had succeeded in producing exactly what everyone was hoping they would, this circular argument—"we were asked to produce a synthetic socialist whole and we produced a synthetic socialist whole"—is a clue for another layer of interpretation. Seen away from all of the ideologically motivated descriptions that surrounded it at the time, the building was in fact a rather strange combination of a classical exterior, lighter structural elements, glass, and large sculptures with an unmistakably socialist realist tone. Thus stuck halfway between the classicism of socialist realism and a new type of the architectural whole—an atmospheric meandering experience—it clumsily embodied the post-Khrushchev-speeches problem of finding the correct expression for the socialist realist method in architecture.

Endorsement: The Gold Medal and the Politburo

In the Czech context no one noticed the pavilion's developmental pains—its gold medal ensured that the tautological rhetoric of the desired product and the produced end result prevailed over any critical comparison of the Czechoslovak pavilion to the surrounding ones.

The Czechoslovak exposition, whose mandate from the outset was to represent all the great things about the peoples' democratic Czechoslovakia through concrete examples of excellence in technology and culture and by embodying the very ethos of socialist lifestyle, was the third-most-visited pavilion in 1958.[20] Six million people walked through it during its life at the Expo. The "functioning" of this nearly classical political allegory was thus paradoxically proven by the numerous awards and visitors, all supplied by the (peaceful) Western competition.

A month after the Expo closed, the Czechoslovak politburo sent its assessments of the Czechoslovak exhibit at the Expo "from the ideological point of view" to Karel Polaček, who was at that time both the Minister of Industry and the president of the government's committee for the Expo in Brussels.[21] The great success of the Czechoslovak pavilion and its installations at the Expo secured it a rather positive evaluation. The report began by stating that the Czechoslovak exhibit had completely fulfilled its political mandate. All the investments and energy that had gone into preparing the exhibit had "paid off":

> The primary concept of the scenario of our exhibit whose goal was to show the organic connection between work, life, and culture of

Czechoslovak people, which meant not isolating culture and art into separate pieces, but infusing the entire pavilion with them was proven correct. That concept gave the pavilion its wholeness, made it more attractive and through concrete examples of the work of our people it pointed to the harmony between the material and cultural standards of our people and the inseparability between culture and economy when it comes to the construction of socialism in our country.[22]

When the pavilion architects Cubr, Hrubý, and Pokorný described their strategy for focusing the attention of the visitors, they argued that the "mono-space" was useful for exhibits and buildings of a more singular character, often institutional or commercial space. Instead, they strove for a type of space that would manage to attract the attention of the weary exposition visitors, in a state of distraction:

> The kind whose attention it is necessary first to capture, focus and then keep, and eventually intensify. All that leads to a non-forceful way of guiding the visitor through gradually different and differentiated environments, inspiring him to continue exploring the additional sections of the exhibit.[23]

So this pavilion, later described as continuously undulating, well-lit, and handsomely arranged, was designed with a tired peripatetic subject (of capitalism) in mind.[24] When the allegorical mandate of the exhibit is combined with the pressures of the daily reality of the Expo, their conceptual overlap unwittingly turns the somewhat distracted exposition visitor into the perfect approximation of that happy, leisurely, and (maybe somewhat distracted, but) curious subject of socialism. The project is layered with meaning, which depending on how much credit is given to the officials and the designers in this case could be seen as part of a brilliant propaganda strategy, or as a series of ideological contradictions that ultimately bring socialism and capitalism closer together instead of differentiating them. Therefore, the Czechoslovak presentation embodies allegory on two levels: the consciously produced one of the socialist lifestyle and, on a meta level, the allegory of the Cold War itself.

The Czechoslovak Brussels pavilion was the first real opportunity for architects and artists to test their often-cited ideas about expert team work; it brought together the country's top architects, set designers, and artists—which, despite the Czech discourse on the topic, was not the norm in their respective practices. Partly due to the aspirations about a way of working already present in the Czech discourse, the Western endorsement of the Czechoslovak presentation in Brussels was not seen as a contradiction, but rather as proof that everyone was impressed and convinced, nearly ideologically "converted" in fact, by the great achievements of Czechoslovakia. The politburo's report boasted about the exhibit in exactly these terms.

Although the participation of Czechoslovak artists in the group presentation called "50 Years of Modern Art" was deemed a failure, the experiment in theater, and the experimental multi-screen narrative "Polyecran" were seen as such overwhelming successes that the politburo suggested more than once in the course of its report that these novel theater and film technologies needed to be developed further, and their development should be supported by whatever means available (Figure 4.4).[25] They were to be patented specifically for large international gatherings and, as a result, both were presented again at the Montreal Expo in 1967.[26] Also, the politburo report requested that the Laterna Magika and the Polyecran exhibits, as well as various other aspects of the Czech presentation, be adjusted for re-presentation to the domestic audiences of Czechoslovakia. Both the main pavilion and the restaurant were transported to Prague in 1960 and installed in different locations, bringing this "successful example of synthesized architecture, design and art" back into the context from which it had purportedly sprung. One hundred thousand Czechs and Slovaks visited it in Prague after its opening.[27] The pavilion, meant to represent life in Czechoslovakia in every piece of its make up and above all in its totality, was now presented to Czechoslovakia to contemplate. Although it was important for its domestic audiences to see how this work was appropriately embodying the ethos of socialism—which remained the most important topic of the expert design discourse—their reception of it was hardly academic. In Prague, the pavilion and the re-exhibition of some of its artifacts were made didactically accessible, showing citizens what it was now perhaps possible to produce, and maybe own and enjoy, or certainly at least imagine, as part of daily life in Czechoslovakia.

The final relationship of all the parts of the Czechoslovak exhibition was described shortly after the Expo closed by Czech critics as "synchronized." In the literary paper *Výtvarná Pracé*, the editor Sergej Machonin waxed poetic:

> Frankly, the most peculiar thing about that exhibit was that somehow everything there was happening at once. What tumult of thoughts, what multitude of daring technical solutions, what lavishness of forms, what endlessness of variations. A single great experiment. How you would like to get a taste of communism here for a moment—even you, who did not want to![28]

For the Czechoslovak designers and officials the "experiment" of Brussels was from the outset a self-conscious attempt to persuade its visitors that the socialist side of the "peaceful competition" of the Cold War was the more desirable side of the two—by giving them a taste of the "great" socialist culture, both in the content of the presentation and allegorically through the logic of the complex whole.

Neither the special issue of *Domus* nor the *Architectural Review* dedicated to the Brussels Expo so much as mentioned the Czechoslovak pavilion, although both were tasked with highlighting the architectural jewels of the 1958 Brussels Expo.[29] This however did not particularly affect the Czech architects' newly gained self-assuredness in the areas of formal synthesis, material experimentation, and teamwork. Opportunities to test and establish in practice a project whose logic appropriately reflected and supported socialism (beyond the usual standardized housing production) had been rare until 1958. But for the consequent effect of the Czechoslovak Brussels pavilion, even more important than this rare opportunity was the rhetoric produced around the pavilion's success. The subsequent readings of the Brussels pavilion—perhaps more than the building itself—literally helped crystallize what the project was and what architecture could do for socialism (besides standardize mass housing). The general recognition of the alignment of the rhetoric, the method, and the aesthetic product that had ultimately fashioned the success of the Brussels pavilion, at least as it was understood from within the Czechoslovak architectural and cultural context, "confirmed" that architecture had to be conceived as a complex and synthetic environment in order to properly engage and represent socialist lifestyle. After the Brussels Expo, the Czechoslovak architectural field finally had a formal and aesthetic model to follow.

Notes

Acknowledgments: An early draft version of this paper was presented in the *Architectural Histories of Organization* seminar held at the Radcliffe Institute for Advanced Study in January 2010. I want to thank Timothy Hyde for organizing that engaging exchange, and the participants in the seminar for a lively and constructive discussion, and generous suggestions on how to sharpen the focus of the paper.

1   There have been some efforts to consider Socialism's interest in the topic of lifestyle in the last decade, or if not exactly its interest in lifestyle then at least the practical effects that living under socialism had on the private lives of its denizens. The first important book on the topic was David Crowley and Susan Reid, eds., *Style and Socialism: Modernity and Material Culture in Post-War Eastern Europe* (Oxford: Berg, 2000). But it is only in the last few years that something approaching a critical mass of interesting and critical work has begun to accumulate, importantly embracing the Cold War logic in a more even-handed way across the iron curtain than was previously the case in historiography of this era. To name only two that have already had, or I believe will have, a great impact on future work in this area: David Crowley and Jane Pavitt, eds., *Cold War Modern: Design 1945–1970* (London: V&A Publishing, 2008) and Greg Castillo, *Cold War on the Home Front: The Soft Power of Midcentury Design* (Minneapolis: University of Minnesota Press, 2010).

2   The resolution of the 1953 conference described the tasks of Czechoslovak architects in thirty-four logistical points, including the launching of a theoretical institute (which would not—unlike other institutes for the research of housing, or standardization—be dedicated to experimenting with the production of ideological foundations for the work of architects), cooperation with Soviet architects, involvement in the architecture school curriculum, and cooperation with scientific institutes. Crucially, it also underlined the importance of relying on the work of the "the most progressive architecture in the world: the architecture of the Soviet Union," and using the methods of socialist realism. In fact the first point of the resolution addresses the need to establish methods of educating architects in the ways of "Marxism-Leninism and socialist aesthetics." "První konference delegatů českých a slovenských architektů ve dnech 2–5 července 1953 v Praze—rezoluce," *Architektura ČSR* 12 (1953): 105–106. Unless otherwise noted, translations are the author's own.

3   I am referring here to Khrushchev's speech delivered on December 7, 1954 at the "All-Union Conference of Builders, Architects and Workers in the Building Materials Industry, in Construction Machinery and Road Machinery Industries and in Design and Research Organizations" in Moscow, and his February 1956 "Secret Speech," widely held as the de facto beginning of de-Stalinization in the Soviet Union, or in some cases as the beginning of the end

of Socialism in the Second World. See Nikita Khrushchev, "On Wide-Scale Introduction of Industrial Methods, Improving the Quality and Reducing the Cost of Construction," and "On the Personality Cult of Joseph V. Stalin," both in Thomas P. Whitney, ed., *Khrushchev Speaks: Selected Speeches, Articles, and Press Conferences, 1949–1961* (Ann Arbor: University of Michigan Press, 1963). Nearly every academic text that deals with postwar architecture in the Second World relies on these speeches as real epistemic breaks in the field, which in my opinion reproduces their mysterious status without adding much explanatory value. For evidence of this type of treatment see, for example, David Crowley and Susan Reid, eds., *Style and Socialism*.

4   There are numerous projects across the Soviet Union and the Eastern Bloc that could serve as the perfect paradigmatic representatives of Stalin's socialist realism, from the famous Seven Sisters (Stalin's highrises) in Moscow (including the buildings of the Moscow State University or the Hotel Ukrain), built in the later 1940s and early 1950s, to the 1950s' monumental Stalin Allee project in Berlin. I am purposefully differentiating this, by no means simple, version of aesthetic socialist realism from the "socialist realist method" that the Czech architects settled on after Khrushchev's speeches. Khrushchev identified the formalism of the avant-garde, often attacked by the theorists of socialist realism, with socialist realism's own formalism and the most common interpretation of his speech goes against the monumentality, and often classicism, of Stalin's aesthetic motto "socialist in content, national in style."

5   Even if that meant falsifying the reality, as Rostislav Švácha suggests in his unpublished article manuscript "Architektura 1958–60," presented to the author in 2004.

6   The really well-produced and comprehensive 2008 book on the Czechoslovak participation in the Brussels Expo, which accompanied an exhibition in Prague on the same theme, certainly exudes the excitement about the Czech 1958 "success" in Brussels. Although some of the authors included in this compilation do take a more critical stance towards the actual products and the ideologically precarious position of the artists and architects that produced them (notably Martin Strakoš's articles on the Czechoslovak architectural production of the period), much of the book plays up the "success" in almost the same terms it was described in, in 1958. For the most part this stance does not diminish the rest of the critical work produced by the authors, but it does testify to the extent to which this 1958 "success" has been naturalized among Czech historians. See Daniela Kramerová and Vanda Skálková, eds., *Bruselský Sen: Československa učast na světové výstavé Expo 58 v Bruselua životní styl 1. poloviny 60. let* (Prague: Arbor Vitae, 2008).

7   Libretto by a professor at the Applied Arts School (VŠUP) in Prague, Adolf Hoffmeister, and a documentary film director, Milan Tichý, dated May 25, 1956; see Adolf Hoffmeister and Milan Tichý, "Navrh rámcového libreta československé expozice na světové výstavě v Bruselu v. r. 1958," 1, Ministerstvo školstvý, box 1570-22 II Brussel, National Archive, Prague.

8   Adolf Hoffmeister and Milan Tichý, "Navrh rámcového libreta československé expozice na světové výstavě v Bruselu v. r. 1958," 2.

9   The standard propaganda pronouncements, spelled out in words and posted on walls, were not erased in their entirety, they were instead replaced for this occasion by the poetry of Vítězslav Nezval, a modern Czech poet.

10 Adolf Hoffmeister and Milan Tichý, "Navrh rámcového libreta československé expozice na světové výstavě v Bruselu v. r. 1958," 8.

11 The entire field of architecture was nationalized in 1948 and "Stavoprojekt" was the name given to the new, single national network of architectural offices.

12 The team Cubr, Hrubý and Pokorný designed the exhibit celebrating ten years of the People's Democratic Czechoslovakia in Moscow. See "Výstava 'Deset let lidově demokratického československa,' Moskva 1955," *Architektura ČSR* 15, no. 1–2 (1956): 24–26. The same issue of *Architektura ČSR* published another of Pokorný's exhibits in Brno.

13 František Cubr, Josef Hrubý, and Zdeněk Pokorný, "Československy pavilion a exposice," *Architektura ČSR* 17 (1958): 664.

Allegory of the Socialist Lifestyle

14   Per information he got from Karolina Šimůnková from the National Archive, Czech architectural historian Martin Strakoš reports on Gočar's opinion about the pavilion presented at a meeting of the Union of Architects; see in particular his note 36, page 100. Martin Strakoš, "Architektura Expo 58 v Bruselu a Československý pavilion," in *Bruselský Sen*, 100.

15   See, Jindřich Santar, "Československá expozice na Světové výstavě," *Architektura ČSR* 17, no. 9–10 (1958): 684.

16   A comparison between Josef Svoboda's Polyecran (and even Laterna Magika) to the Eameses' multi-screen design and presentation for the US Exhibit in Moscow 1959 is more than appropriate at this point. Not only are the strategies related enough that the Czech presentation should enter the genealogy of multimedia and intermedia design, thus perhaps upsetting the all-too-simple history of these techniques that have placed the Eameses' single-handedly at the front of the intermedia and multi-screen design, but the fact that both sides across the iron curtain used lifestyle and non-linear narrative structures to convey (and convert to) their side of the story complicates the narratives of both of these Cold War histories. Perhaps recognizing the similarity in the Czechoslovak Brussels 1958 and US Moscow 1959 strategies, the Soviet officials invited the Czechs to bring their Brussels presentation to Moscow right after (and most likely in response to) the US presentation. For a specifically Eames-centric description of the multimedia developments of the late 1950s see Beatriz Colomina, "Enclosed by Images: The Eameses' Multimedia Architecture," *Grey Room* 2 (Winter 2001): 6–29, as well as Beatriz Colomina, *Domesticity at War* (Cambridge, MA: MIT Press, 2007). Also Greg Castillo's presentation of the famous kitchen debate is a refreshingly balanced view of what Khrushchev might have wanted to get out of the US presentation in Moscow. Castillo paints a plausible picture of a smart Soviet leader, in opposition to the usual duped and stunned framing of him with regard to this event. See specifically Castillo, "The Trojan House goes East," *Cold War on the Home Front*, 139–172. When it comes to the histories of intermedia and filmic practices, Gene Youngblood dedicated a chapter to Czech Polyecran presentation at Expo 1967 in Montreal in his famous *Expanded Cinema*; see Gene Youngblood, *Expanded Cinema* (New York: E.P. Dutton and Co., 1970).

17   After its debut in Brussels, the Laterna Magika form was made part of the national Czechoslovak theater and given its own dedicated building, where multiple shows a day still attract numerous tourists.

18   František Cubr, Josef Hrubý, and Zdeněk Pokorný, "Československy pavilion a expozice," 664.

19   Several versions of the libretto track the development of ideas and their eventual ideological embodiment in the architectural and exhibition proposals. In the end the librettos were superseded by Jindřich Santar's scenario. Jindřich Santar with V. Jasanský, J. Novotný, and A. Pludok, "Základní scénař exposice ČSR na Světové výstavě v Bruselu 1958," Ministerstvo školstvý, box 1570–22 II Brussel, National Archive, Prague.

20   According to a Czech historian Alena Andlerová. See, Alena Andlerová, "My v Bruselu 1958," *Umění a řemesla* 4 (1987): 37–42.

21   Vaclav Slavík and Zdeněk Urban (odělení ÚV KSČ), "Zhodnocení čs. Exposice na Světové výstavě v Bruselu z hlediska ideologického," Ministerstvo školstvý, box 1570-22 II Brussel, National Archive, Prague.

22   Vaclav Slavík and Zdeněk Urban (odělení ÚV KSČ), "Zhodnocení čs. Exposice na Světové výstavě v Bruselu z hlediska ideologického," 2.

23   František Cubr, Josef Hrubý, and Zdeněk Pokorný, "Československy pavilion a exposice," 659.

24   Rostislav Švácha describes it thus in "Česká architektura 1956–1963," in *Ohniska znovuzrození. České Umění 1956–1963*, ed. Marie Judlová (Prague: Galerie Hlavního Města Prahy, 1994).

25   For a period description of Polyecran and Laterna Magika see Jan Grossman, "Výtvarné Hledisko Laterny magiky a Polyekranu" *Výtvarne Umění* 5 (1961). And for a historization of Laterna Magika and Polyecran's place among other artistic and cinematic developments both of the period and generally, see René Rohan, Camille Morineau, and Vít Havránek, eds., *Laterna Magika: New Technologies in Czech Art of the 20th Century* (Prague: Kant, 2002).

26 In 1967 the intermedia practices that Polyecran and Laterna Magika represented perfectly fit the spirit of the Montreal Expo, saturated with similar presentations. For a description of intermedia practices including the use of the Polyecran technology at the Expo 1967 in Montreal, see Gene Youngblood, *Expanded Cinema*.
27 See Alena Andlerová, "My v Bruselu 1958," *Umění a řemesla* 4 (1987): 37–42.
28 Sergej Machonín, "Z Experimentu rodí se nové umění," *Výtvarná Práce* 11 (1958): 2.
29 The *Architectural Review* even had a section singling out six outstanding pavilions: German, Dutch, Yugoslavian, Spanish, Swiss, and Japanese. No mention was made of the Czechoslovak pavilion or medal. See *Architectural Review* 124, no. 739 (August 1958): entire issue. See also "Expo 58," *Domus*, no. 345 (August 1958): 1–30.

Chapter 5

Assimilating Unease
Moholy-Nagy and the Wartime/Postwar Bauhaus in Chicago

Robin Schuldenfrei

László Moholy-Nagy's debut as leader of the New Bauhaus in Chicago was auspicious (Figure 5.1). A high-profile *New York Times* article in September of 1937, "America Imports Genius," hailed his arrival along with that of three other men of "genius": Albert Einstein, Thomas Mann, and Walter Gropius. The article cautioned, "The hospitality that America extends to these men should not be merely physical, but spiritual. We should not be in too great haste to 'Americanize' them—in the sense of attempting to indoctrinate them with all the beliefs we already hold. To make the most of their presence here we must think not only of what we have to tell them but of what they have to tell us."[1] Despite this plea, Moholy-Nagy was quick to claim America as his own. Especially as Europe plunged into war, Moholy-Nagy's unambiguous public statements reflected his desire to ingratiate himself with the country that he hoped would move the world beyond the war: "The present world crisis will bring unforeseen problems to all of us. We shall have to make decisions of great consequences, both to ourselves and to the nation. Whether or not Hitler wins, whether or not we get into the war, we shall undergo great strains because an equilibrium has been disturbed. Europe has lost the leading position which it had in culture and technics. America is now the country to which the world looks."[2] This last observation is an early iteration of a position which would be taken up by a number of critics of art and architecture in the postwar period, but a tension can nonetheless be detected in Moholy-Nagy's language—an uneasiness with which émigrés, understandably, conducted themselves, underscored here by Moholy-Nagy's references to "us," "we," and "the nation." The émigrés' anxiety about their status in the United States was often palpable; their anxiety about the war Europe brought to the world propelled their efforts to continue their work in spite of that uncertain status.

5.1
The New Bauhaus, 1937, Chicago, IL (Photograph by Herbert Matter, 1938)

When the New Bauhaus opened in October of 1937 as the self-proclaimed successor of the famed German institution, which had itself gone through several iterations, lastly in Berlin, before closing in 1933, the United States was still emerging from its Great Depression, while—from the perspective of the emigrant former members of the German Bauhaus—the situation in Europe was becoming more dire.[3] When the Second World War broke out, the European Bauhäusler, who had experienced the darkening situation first-hand, were more politicized and also ready to contribute to the war effort in more practical ways, perhaps, than their American counterparts; although individual architects and artists took varied positions on the swiftly changing situation, the American public generally remained wary of entering another major war after the experience of the First World War. Many of the Bauhäusler now plunged adeptly into their new American cultural milieu, winning over government bureaucrats, private businessmen, and other officials, later capitalizing on these relationships during the postwar boom. As America welcomed fleeing members of the Bauhaus, as well as other modern artists and architects from across Europe, there was an assimilation of European modern forms and ideas to American conditions.[4] This assimilation occurred over a relatively short period of time, as Moholy-Nagy reflected in 1946: "When I came to this country ten years ago, I had to relearn completely my ideas about design. I had thought that European measures could be applied to America immediately with the same results as over there. . . . I never would have believed that a grown-up person could learn as much as I had to learn in this country."[5] In the case of Moholy-Nagy at the New Bauhaus and its successor, the School of Design in Chicago, it is striking how the exigencies of the circumstances in which he found himself in America, and the very anxiety that this new situation generated, carried him almost overnight from a left-leaning artistic milieu to American government collaborations and very pragmatic assistance to his new country.[6] Gropius was later able to assert, "When Moholy-Nagy built up the Institute here in Chicago, he had the vision to lay its foundations in such a way that indigenous American design could be stimulated and developed."[7] It was during the war years that the protagonists of the New Bauhaus—by this time, the School of Design—it will be argued, laid the groundwork for their acceptance in postwar America, both in terms of design research and connections established with American individuals and institutions. The school began to prepare for possible entry into war very early on, before Pearl Harbor, and, while the country was still in the midst of the war, looked to a planned segue from its wartime work to preparations for the postwar period, declaring as early as 1942 that it was adapting its program for "the present emergency as well as to the problems of postwar production."[8] Indeed, the school's ability to contribute novel, practical solutions to the war effort aptly positioned its mode of modern design for participation in postwar technological progress and the boom-time affluence that accompanied it.

In the process, under Moholy-Nagy, the attempt to revive and continue the Bauhaus experiment in America necessarily transformed the project the German institution had pursued. Perhaps surprisingly, this transformation was marked by an intensified turn towards the usefulness of design. This essay situates that development, and Moholy-Nagy's school's contribution to postwar modernism in

America, in the context of its involvement in the nation's war effort and the opportunities for anxious assimilation of émigrés like Moholy-Nagy that it afforded. While demonstrating the continuity between wartime efforts and the postwar boom, this chapter examines the ways in which these activities contributed to the increased acceptance of modernism in America, and the Chicago school's role therein—as well as the ways in which this connection to the war was formative for American postwar design.[9] The project Moholy-Nagy pursued through iterations of the design school he directed in wartime Chicago was indeed one of designing, and teaching, in war for a time and circumstances beyond war.

Anxiety, Assimilation, Integration

Although they had been given plumb positions of power in institutions of higher learning, an act that in and of itself indicates a large amount of faith in them, former members of the Bauhaus had reason to be anxious about their tenuous status.[10] For the most part, the newcomers arrived with just the material possessions and artworks that they could bring with them, often with larger art collections left behind in trust with the hope of eventual exportation, with very little money (savings, if there were any, generally had to be left in Germany) and varying levels of proficiency in English, and they faced very different educational structures, cultures, and expectations in their new positions.[11] Hal Foster has asserted that Moholy-Nagy's prior critique of capitalism became muted after his arrival in the United States, and that the American version of the Bauhaus ideal revealed a belief on the part of Moholy-Nagy that the "modernist evolution in abstract styles was commercial design."[12] This is undoubtedly largely so. Yet for Moholy-Nagy this assimilation to American capitalism and the realm of the businessman-supported, non-profit institution (rather than government support which had been the—tenuous—mainstay of the German Bauhaus) was likely brought on more by pragmatism than core belief.[13] Dismayed by the commercial world's reaction to the work of his fellow artists, he worried privately, "the provocative statement of modern art is constantly annulled by checkbook and cocktail party. Am I on the same way?"[14] The tangible design contributions that he and his colleagues were able to make in their new country thanks to a certain partial but rapid assimilation were one palliative for the anxiety created by their uneasy status.

Former Bauhaus members were also quick to serve the US government in concrete ways. They were asked to join committees for which they gave generously of their expertise and time. For example, Gropius was a key member of the Harvard Group of the American Defense Committee, work for which he was warmly thanked by the group's leader in a letter of 1941: "I want to tell you how grateful we are for your contribution to the work of the Group and above all for your personal interest and sympathy."[15] Likewise, Moholy-Nagy served on the City of Chicago's Civil Defense Commission, was a key member of the Chicago Metropolitan Area camouflage section, and worked closely on various initiatives with the Office of Civilian Defense in Washington. They did so even as, during the war years, and thereafter, the relationship between the émigrés and their new government was not one based on open trust. The FBI kept extensive files on Gropius, Mies, and others.[16] Moholy-Nagy's citizenship process was held up by several years by the FBI's investigation of him, which prevented the Naturalization Service from granting him citizenship until the FBI case closed.[17] Gropius was obliged to report his travel itinerary to the authorities every time he left Cambridge.[18] Yet he worked closely with American government officials to further their postwar aims. As Karen Koehler has brought to light, by 1944, in collaboration with the United States War Information Bureau, Gropius allowed a propagandistic radio play to be written about him for a series called *America, the Haven*.[19] A work of fiction, it was intended to reach retreating German working-class soldiers and was meant to be aired in areas of Germany liberated by the Allies.[20] It celebrated his life's work, touting a "cultural trust" placed in him and the achievements that he was to continue in America. The text from the radio play, written under the auspices of the United States War Information Bureau, frames Gropius's position in this manner: "I am an exile and yet I shall live. I will continue my work. . . . For there is a trust placed in me. A cultural trust."[21] It was perhaps this idea of "cultural trust" that formed the lens through which American officials saw the usefulness of the European émigrés and, in turn, what émigrés saw as their offering to America: the exportation of their ideas, forms, and educational working methods to the United States. But they also quickly offered pragmatic new design-objects and inventive solutions to wartime problems.

Of the émigrés' many responses to the instability of their position in America, a crucial one was to anchor and stabilize themselves not only through their design contributions and their teaching positions, but through their formal and informal social networks. They used a web of connections to each other to share information and opportunities in a foreign land and culture. And they helped each other to anchor themselves to interested, prominent Americans in the cultural sphere, such as Philip Johnson at the Museum of Modern Art, as well as the business realm, through figures such as Walter Paepcke, head of the Container Corporation of America (CCA), who backed the New Bauhaus financially and fostered further support for the institution through his network of contacts. Through Moholy-Nagy and the school, Gropius and Herbert Bayer came to know Paepcke closely, who, for his part, awarded them design commissions under the auspices of his company. These prominent Americans could help stabilize the positions of the newcomers, through key introductions, via direct financial support for their projects, by providing help in obtaining financial backing via a third party, or by lending expertise in navigating governmental and other systems which could help to establish them.

It is also significant that designers who moved from Germany, such as Gropius, Mies, Moholy-Nagy, Marcel Breuer, Ludwig Hilberseimer, and Erich Mendelsohn, showed little desire to return after the war despite the fact that the rebuilding of Germany would have afforded them many opportunities to build. Instead they were particularly committed to forging a career in their new country and pursuing the opportunities they saw for their work in America. This was in contrast to other groups of émigrés in the realm of art and culture, such as George Grosz, Bertolt Brecht, Theodor Adorno, and Max Horkheimer, who all returned to Germany. Moholy-Nagy, in New York in 1945 for a meeting of the American CIAM organization (Congrès Internationaux d'Architecture Moderne), which was promoting postwar planning, was astounded to find "most French refugees dead-set on going back to France and England at the first possible moment."[22] He felt of these compatriots who intended to return to Europe that it was "a great pity that we cannot bind them (with love and money) to this country."[23] Of especial importance to Moholy-Nagy was this "binding" to his new country through as rapid an assimilation as possible.

In tandem with his efforts at assimilation, Moholy-Nagy frequently used the idea of "integration" to describe his vision of the design process, and this vision might be seen to correspond to the situation faced by these designers in America, too. Registering the anxiety surrounding technology in this period, Moholy-Nagy wrote often of a sought-for integration of the human and the technical world: "We feel that after the war, conditions will have a task of greatest importance for us: the integration of the neglected values of art and humanities with a hypertrophic technology."[24] Such an integration was also foundational to his teaching aims: "By now technology has become as much a part of life as metabolism. The task therefore is to educate the contemporary man as an *integrator*, the new *designer* able to re-evaluate human needs warped by machine civilization."[25] In war, the use of new materials and technologies clearly had devastating consequences. In Moholy-Nagy's view this reality increased the need to use new knowledge and new design to positive wartime ends that could mitigate these consequences, from designing camouflaged shelter for citizens during attacks, to new safety equipment for those on the battlefields, to using the design process for restorative occupational therapy for those returning from war, all to be discussed here. The anxiety about the devastation caused by technological prowess that followed the First World War, which had been largely replaced by excitement in 1920s Weimar Germany, including at the original iteration of the Bauhaus, once again resurfaced for many during the Second World War.[26]

The *Chicago Sun* newspaper aptly summed up the school in wartime in this manner: "The work carried forward by this group can no longer be described as revolutionary, but rather as a unified and imaginative approach to both fine arts and design technology. Some changes in emphasis have come about in response to American ways of living."[27] For Moholy-Nagy, adapting to America while integrating technology to serve the needs of man would also have to attempt to counteract the horrors of war. An era which had held so much promise seemed to have reached an impasse. Moholy-Nagy characterized the situation in this manner:

> To state the case is almost too simple:
>
> The industrial revolution opened up a new dimension—the dimension of a new science and a new technology which could be used for the realization of all-embracing relationships. Contemporary man threw himself into the experience of these new relationships. But saturated with old ideologies, he approached the new dimension with obsolete practices and failed to translate his newly gained experience into emotional language and cultural reality. The result has been and still is misery and conflict, brutality and anguish, unemployment and war.[28]

In response, Moholy-Nagy called for a well-balanced social organization to come out of a form of education in which everyone was utilized to his highest capacity. Although many designers, companies, and industries articulated their eager preparedness for the promised postwar boom ahead, in terms of retooling for peacetime production and consumption, Moholy-Nagy saw the need, even during war, to design *beyond* war—not just in terms of material goods, that is, but to envision for a future with a place for design and design education in a *society* beyond war.

This was the basis for the American version of the Bauhaus in Chicago—a stated repositioning toward the cultural realm and toward a concern for humanity. While the nexus of technology and culture had always been part of the German Bauhaus's aims, in its series of prewar iterations it did not broadly succeed in designing for a different society, despite its efforts to engage new industrial technology. What ultimately distinguishes the American institution in the war years from the original Bauhaus is the extent of its concern for pragmatic design solutions and the humane use of technology in aiding civilization—areas, namely, in which the war epitomized all that had gone wrong—concerns which also provided the New Bauhaus/School of Design's orientation toward the eventual postwar period.

During Moholy-Nagy's time at the German Bauhaus (he left in 1928, following Gropius's resignation) its legacy was assured through the highly successful *visual* iteration of ideas about modernism that the institution embodied. Indeed, the symbolically resonant objects produced at the Bauhaus under Gropius are much more likely to be found in museums today than any products of the New Bauhaus/School of Design—but these iconic modernist designs—chess sets, ashtrays, silver and ebony tea services—represented luxury objects in ideology, form, and type. Though ostensibly intended for mass production, they were expensive, difficult to fabricate, and remained out of reach of the many, failing to accommodate the altered economic realities necessary for the sale of modern objects on a mass scale.[29] This difficulty can be traced partly to the fact that the German Bauhaus was still profoundly shaped by the nineteenth-century heritage of *Kunstgewerbe*, or arts and crafts, and its post–World War I revival, which explicitly attempted to recover that heritage via the high-quality art object of the craftsman.

The New Bauhaus, on the other hand, partly by virtue of lacking a strong anchoring tradition, but also due to the exigencies of the coming war, would serve to cement and intensify a tendency away from craftsmanship toward a new emphasis on engaged, practical experimentation and pedagogical innovation. This trend was reflected in the school's first curriculum, which added "scientific subjects" (which included the fields of geometry, physics, chemistry, mathematics, and economics including statistics and marketing) as one-third of the preliminary course program, giving them a weight on a par with the two other categories of "basic design workshop" and "analytic and constructive drawing." As Moholy-Nagy wrote in the institution's first catalogue, the school's ambitious task was "to contrive a new system of education which, along with a specialized training in science and technique leads to a thorough awareness of fundamental human needs and a universal outlook."[30] The German Bauhaus had had lofty goals for its design with regard to the masses, but even these declared aims were outstripped by the new focus formulated by Moholy-Nagy in Chicago, which signalled the extent to which a new social mode of design would require radically changed foundations. Moholy-Nagy's Chicago school went much further to put a new production paradigm for design into institutional and pedagogical practice.

Other émigrés were also important facilitators of the Bauhaus legacy in America, and the housing and urban solutions proposed by these architects and their students for the postwar period were arguably as grounded in offering real solutions as those of Moholy-Nagy's school's were for design. Still, in the American phase of their careers the other key protagonists were notably focused on either art-related issues at art schools (Anni and Josef Albers at Black Mountain College, followed by Yale) or architectural concerns at schools of architecture (Gropius and Breuer at Harvard, Mies at IIT). Moholy-Nagy, in comparison, had a special, if especially precarious, platform—as the leader of a newly founded, independent school of *design* (and not as a division of a larger, less flexible, institution), from which to attempt to bring about an—of course vastly altered—version of what he and his colleagues in Dessau had sometimes envisioned.[31] Moreover, Moholy-Nagy's singular commitment to, and practice of, the labor-intensive Bauhaus educational working methods permitted him to conceive of changed design practices, in the pragmatically charged social and political context of the realities of the wartime situation, while, in the pedagogical setting of the school, actively undertaking the kind of transformations he thought this new practice would require. War and precarity provided the impetus to achieve a form of practical, problem-driven design that the original, still elite-oriented Bauhaus had never managed to fully put into practice. The uniqueness of the New Bauhaus/School of Design lay in its particularly remarkable unification of this effort in a school (like the former Bauhaus) and its community-oriented pedagogical practices, and in the singular way in which it integrated contingent war-related demands into these modes of learning. In doing so, the school's activities were always looking to a time and condition beyond the war. Not least for this reason, the research engaged in on behalf of the war effort, and its products, also had implications for changes in design processes in the postwar period.

War Efforts

As the nation's circumstances changed—initially on the brink of war, then at war, and then facing the transition to postwar, peacetime production—the new Bauhaus reacted (while going through its own institutional reorganizations, into the School of Design). The school re-tooled its existing courses and introduced many new ones in order to focus on the evolving practical problems facing the country. Keeping the idea of working with industry at the forefront of the school's mission, Moholy-Nagy used the phrase "war industry" to refer to the war-related work in this period.[32] By this he meant efforts to design with and for industry in such a way as to directly aid the war effort: students worked on portable runways for temporary airfields and air-raid shelters, shock-proof helmet construction and a shock-absorbing wire-cloth pillow for helmets, an infra-red oven that cooked food at four times the usual rate, and parachute clothes.[33] An airplane door was designed in plywood, and the school experimented with a new system of friction welding of clear acrylic plastics intended

Assimilating Unease

for the swifter repair, in the combat zone, of the easily shattered plexiglass and Lucite domes of airplanes.[34] Another useful product developed at the school was a new kind of barbed wire, sent to Washington for testing, intended for repairing holes in the plastic gunners' hoods on bombers.[35] Also devised during this period by student Elic Nekimken were rubberized-cloth flotation units that could be connected with notebook rings to form a lifebelt or raft (Figure 5.2). George Marcek contributed a ventilated helmet for a patient with a skin disease, which also potentially could protect healthy men from the sun's rays. A mobile machine gun unit by student Nolan Rhoades was intended to be constructed out of a few structurally simple parts

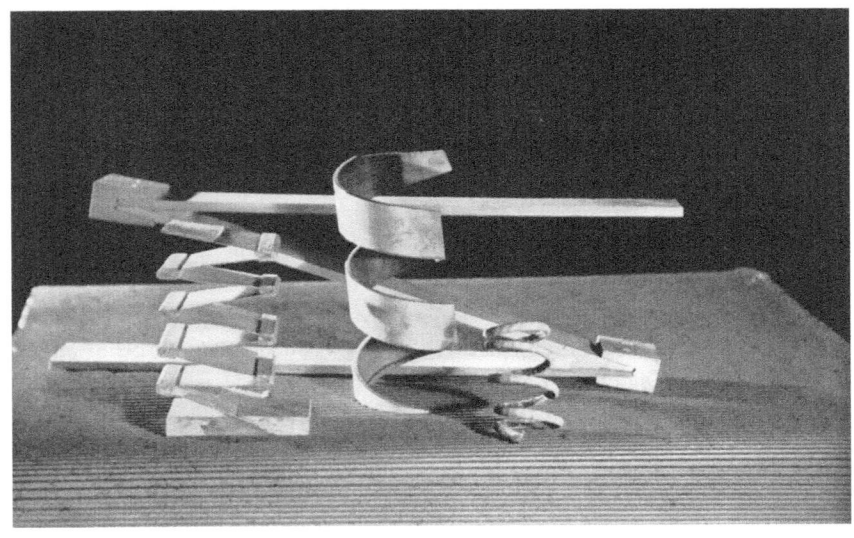

5.2
Above: Elic Nekimken, Life Belt Units, Student work, School of Design, 1942
Below: Four types of wooden springs ("V" or Victory Spring shown front left), Student work, School of Design, –early 1940s

welded together in an assembly line using standard automobile power, allowing for mass production at low cost; it was also designed to be light enough for two men to handle and to break down into stackable units for shipment. Rhoades's designs of a "guerrilla supply bomb" and "plastic balloon skin" made out of "weather proof cellophane and cheesecloth bound by alternate rectangular patterns of glue" illustrate the school's investigations in materials studies. These objects reached varying levels of actualization—some objects remained innovative ideas and never progressed further than the design phase—but they represent the school reacting systematically and creatively to perceived needs. Other ideas progressed to the prototype stage, exhibited as mock-ups both at the school and beyond. Finally, some ideas advanced to the degree that they could be manufactured and tested at the school, and then sent on to contacts in industry or defense authorities.

Wooden springs were perhaps one of the school's biggest innovations (Figure 5.2). Beginning in June 1941, students, working with faculty, designed at least twenty-four different spring prototypes in plywood or laminated wood.[36] The threat of a metal shortage stimulated this project, and it was successfully carried out before the ban on metal went into effect.[37] With it, wood ceased to be viewed as a mere substitute for steel and came to be appreciated as a structural material in its own right, especially because it withstood specific pressures and, unlike metal, could recover from fatigue when rested.[38] One of the school's prototypes, the "V" spring (for victory), was found to hold the same amount of compression weight and to withstand ten years' wear, proving as durable as metal springs.[39] Importantly, the V-spring was comprised not of large sheets of plywood, which was also beginning to be rationed for war use, but rather of small strips of veneer sealed with resins which conserved its moisture content and protected it from variations in humidity.[40] These strips were hinged at alternate ends and folded over wedges, zigzag fashion, at the joint of each "V," so that the size and shape of the wedges determined the amount of elasticity in the spring.[41]

The wood spring represented the school's first successful attempt at direct cooperation with industry; after it developed a prototype, a manufacturer conducted large-scale tests which led to its perfection and use.[42] A model wood-spring mattress was displayed by the Seng Company, a large furniture firm, at the 1942 Chicago furniture fair.[43] Moholy-Nagy reported that the school received its first check for $2,500 in November of 1942, as an advance royalty payment on the wood springs.[44] The experiments with wooden springs also directly led to the development of an experimental stool in plywood, using the same application of technology as the springs. (One might note here, perhaps in tribute to his drive to find wood replacements for metal, that in these years the students apparently affectionately referred to Moholy-Nagy as "Holy Mahogany."[45]) Throughout these efforts, Moholy-Nagy was driven by a concomitant desire to articulate wartime designs toward postwar hopes, as is evidenced by his report to Nikolaus Pevsner in March 1943: "Through our success with the wood spring experiments … a large furniture manufacturer is interested in our bent wood solutions. This type of furniture can be seen as a forerunner of simplified and healthier design, having the potentialities of replacing the over-stuffed upholstered furniture."[46]

Elsewhere, individual designers such as, most notably, Charles and Ray Eames conducted wartime experiments in the novel use of plywood, veneers, and glues for leg splints and airplane nose cones and stabilizers that would likewise directly contribute to the war effort and then later find wide application in the Eameses' iconic furniture designs. Comparable schools of art and design, such as Cranbrook, however, neither assisted so assiduously in wartime design efforts, nor did they tend to attempt such direct cooperation with industry.[47] War-related activities at Black Mountain College were limited mainly to participation in the Enlisted Reserve Corps program, which was intended to provide officers with "leadership qualities" for the military by allowing enlisted students to defer service in order to complete their education first; the school was also approved by the US Relocation Authority to accept American-born Japanese transfer students from the Pacific coast.[48] Likewise, schools of architecture, which did offer some war-related courses (for example, camouflage courses were taught at the architecture school of the University of Pennsylvania, and troops were offered camouflage instruction under the auspices of the Landscape Architecture Department at Harvard), did not dramatically reorient themselves to the war in the same manner as the School of Design, nor did they pursue wartime collaborations with industry in the same way.

For the duration of the war, the Chicago school's war-related design activities were consistently undertaken with an eye toward design transformations to come once the war was over. The school sought to engage in industrial research and development for war-fettered companies that could not spare their own designers or engineers for new product studies—an effort that effectively positioned the school and its students for the postwar period, giving it the opportunity to offer well-trained potential employees and expertise, as well as possible prototypes.[49] Already having established itself and its work, the school was called upon for design solutions by outside manufacturers. Beyond the wooden springs, the school sought to design other consumer goods with possible lasting application around the wartime shortages, as steel and other metals were withdrawn from civilian use. For example, a large mail-order company asked the school to experiment with a metal-less design for a chair for infants that had formerly been made of a canvas back and seat and metal frame.[50] Tackling the problem, students devised wood substitutes—a painted, easy-to-assemble, inexpensive version for lower-income homes, and a streamlined, bent-and-polished plywood example. They also experimented with substitutions for wooden dowels, alternatively testing the combination of resin with paper and cotton. Other materials which had been essential to the functioning of the workshops—such as rubber, paper, and plastics—were also rationed, necessitating further innovations.[51]

As a result of these investigations and new designs, Walter Paepcke, the Chicago businessman and key benefactor of the school, wrote on the school's behalf to the War Production Board:

> Dr. Moholy-Nagy has recently had a conversation with Capt. Benjamin Gelb of the Consumer Product Branch of the WPB [War Production Board]. The School is most anxious to be recommended for a research

Robin Schuldenfrei

5.3
Above: Fiberboard chairs, Student work, School of Design, early 1940s
Below: Fiberboard chair, Student work, School of Design, 1940–1945

> contract on new types of household goods and domestic appliances. . . . It [the school] trains and educates young men and women to become practical industrial designers of all war and postwar products. . . . I am convinced that the School could do an excellent job on research assignments for the Consumer Product Branch. I am recommending it most highly for favorable consideration in this connection.[52]

Here was an attempt to position the school not only for more formal wartime commissions but also for postwar production.

Other furniture designs, similarly born out of wartime shortages, show the ways in which the school was already thinking about the transition to postwar furniture needs. Prototypes developed in the early 1940s illustrate the degree to which students were already engaged in work which featured low cost materials, mass production, and the ability to be packed flat (which saved shipping costs initially, but also allowed the user to easily store items of furniture). These prototypes include an inventive series of fiberboard chairs; some designs were entirely made of fiberboard whereas others used a tubular steel support structure (Figure 5.3). Further examples include the plywood "knock-down chair" by Robert Zinns of 1942, in which flat pieces of plywood were slotted into each other in lieu of fixed joints. Other experiments with plywood joints indicated that they could be strengthened by enlarging the gluing surface of the plywood edges.[53] Jack Waldheim's "Z-Chair" used thin laminated wood instead of solid wood or thick plywood and featured a single, continuous, Z-shaped wooden support to form the base, legs, and armrests. In the immediate postwar period, wartime problematics and aesthetics continued to influence furniture designs such as Robert Beard's 1947 "Collapsible Chair," which could fold up completely flat, and Allan Johnson's design for a cot which compressed, accordion-like, to a small size. Like many other designers and companies in this period, the school looked to the factory re-tooling that would follow the war, and many prototypes coming from the school in the postwar period were specifically designed to be manufactured on the same machines that had been producing ammunition parts.[54] Military production and use of plywood, Moholy-Nagy envisioned, would lead to veneer or plywood furniture manufactured using the same type of blanking dies used in airplane factories for wings and in fuselage construction.[55] Therefore the school devoted much design focus to lightweight, easily manufactured, laminated veneer and plywood furniture prototypes to be shaped on automatic molds that would only require several minutes per piece.

Amid these innovations, Moholy-Nagy was quick to assert that this ingenuity struck a long-established, particularly American note, as he told a newspaper interviewer:

> [T]he old American spirit of patent furniture has been reawakened in the students. Between 1830 and 1880 thousands of new ideas for furniture were submitted to the [United States] patent office. It was an ingenious American development. . . .

> Now we have taken it up again. And by being trained in the understanding of motion, joints, the transition of forces by lever, and the role of pivots and folds, and by combining this knowledge with new materials and new machines such as the infra-red oven for plastics and the electrical bending machine for plywood, the students have made a number of astonishing designs.[56]

This mannered assertion of a link to a particular aspect of American heritage, one that the United States had always used to distinguish itself from the traditions of Europe—that of American ingenuity—could be seen as one more important way to keep the school situated in its context, despite its foreign director and the many émigré members of its staff. The conditions under which they were working, the continuing precariousness of their personal situations, were likely never far from their minds.

The "War Courses" at the School of Design in Chicago

Beyond designing around wartime shortages and addressing war-related needs (and with an eye towards the period to follow), the school also offered an assortment of other new "war courses" during these years. The majority of these were designed to take up immediate wartime training needs—although even the survey art lecture course was retained and transformed to cover the Social Usefulness of Twentieth Century Art and its Relation to a Nation at War.[57] As the school's summer session brochure of 1942 intoned, "In a country at war education and vocational training are faced with the problem of achieving maximum results in minimum time without sacrificing the objectives of general education. The School of Design in Chicago—because of its past educational policy—has readily adapted its program to the requirements of the present emergency."[58] At a time when America's entry into the war expediently drained schools across the country, the School of Design's war courses significantly boosted the school's enrollment; as Moholy-Nagy reported, "the year 1942 was more positive for the School than we had the right to expect. Through the preparation of war courses—camouflage, war designs and experimentation with substitutes—we had our highest enrollment counting the day and night students together—over 230 students in the last semester."[59]

In accordance with the recommendations of the Wartime Commission for Higher Education, students could use summer session credit towards regular semester work, speeding up the timetable to graduation.[60] (In a nod to wartime privations students attending the summer session held in the countryside outside Chicago were instructed that it was "absolutely essential" to "bring all their ration cards, marked towels and one woolen blanket."[61]) The school's intensified program sought to keep "constant pace with war-time . . . requirements" while also making provisions for those "engaged in the war effort [by day] to pursue their education" through evening classes.[62] It also came to terms with the fact that it was losing students to military recruitment, but did not forego the opportunity to publicize the fact that it was supplying the military with well-trained recruits who were especially suited to meeting new situations with resourcefulness and inventiveness.[63]

Later on, war veterans were directly served too, as the school, working closely with the Veterans' Administration, designed a special course of study specifically for those attending under the terms of the GI Bill, allowing veterans to condense two-year courses into one year of study.[64] At times, veterans outnumbered regular students by a ratio of 4:1.

War-related classes offered by the school were much more practical and results-orientated than the earlier curriculum and included: Model Airplane Building, which taught the principles of aeronautics, including experiments in plane design; Design in Plastics Research, which investigated the potentialities of thermo-setting and thermo-plastics; and a course called Mechanical and Architectural Drafting Training for the War Industries.[65] Other wartime courses included a general course on Mechanical Drawing and Architectural Drafting, Blue Print Reading, and Photography for War Services.[66] In Production Illustration students now learned techniques potentially useful for the war effort, including explosion, x-ray, and cut-away illustration, axonometric projection, photomontage, super-imposition, and single and stroboscopic motion projections. The school quickly re-organized, and in some cases, re-staffed, in order to provide these valuable wartime technical skills.

Notably, it also sought to use its particular expertise in visual design to aid in the war effort. A Visual Propaganda in Wartime course, also called the War

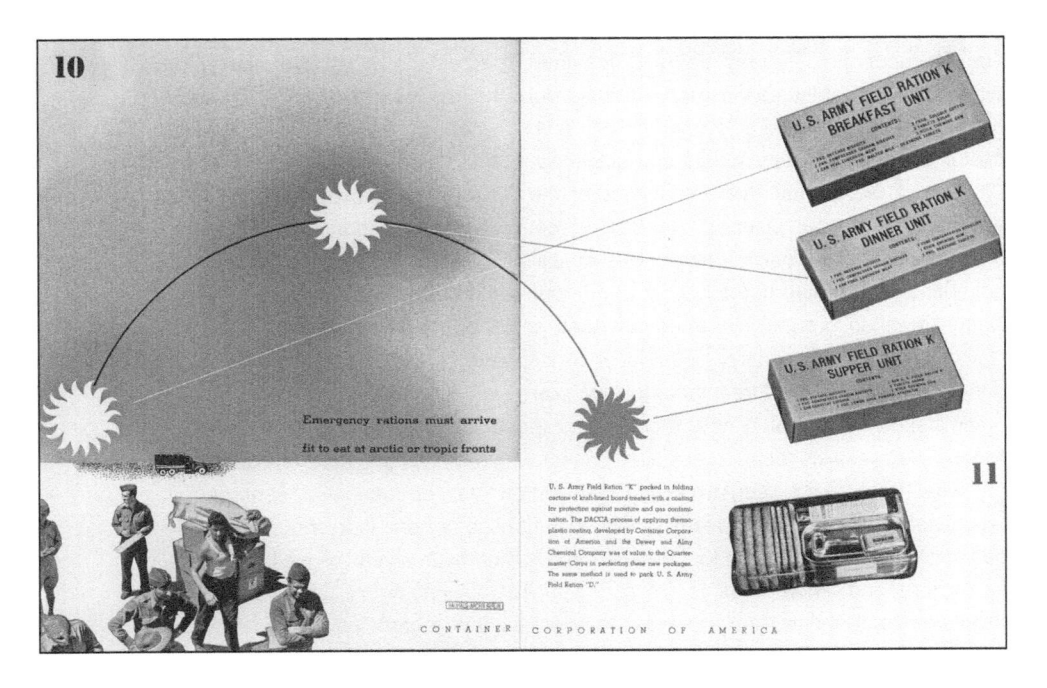

5.4
Gyorgy Kepes, *Paperboard Goes to War*, Booklet for the Container Corporation of America
(Chicago: Brookes & Sons Company, 1942)

Displays course, working in cooperation with the Army, focused on silkscreen poster design, display, and mobile exhibition design, with the goal of educating civilians on topics such as air-raid precautions, accident prevention, and first-aid. The posters produced in this course had unsubtle slogans, common for the period, such as The People are on the March, Wipe Out the Enemy, War Loan for the Future, and Smash Anti-Semitism.[67] Posters designed by student Richard Filipowski, *Care Saves Wear* and *Deliver Us from Evil* (both from 1943), won prizes in Chicago and New York, respectively. For his graphic design contributions towards the war effort, Gyorgy Kepes, an instructor at the school, was awarded a War Committee citation for "extraordinary service rendered our Government."[68] Faculty, such as Kepes, and former Bauhaus members in the close-knit circle of émigrés surrounding the school, such as Herbert Bayer, as well as students, also created designs for the Container Corporation of America in support of the war effort. Sponsored by the company's president and benefactor of the school, Walter Paepcke, they—and other European modern artists—designed informational booklets, such as Kepes's *Paperboard Goes to War* (Figure 5.4) and advertisements—for example, one by Herbert Bayer that informed citizens: "Paperboard that goes to war is paper that wasn't burned. Save waste paper! Sell or give to local collections." By providing crucial wartime information to citizens in a graphically compelling—and thus memorable—manner, these designers were able to aid the war effort on a wide scale.

Constructive Interventions: Rehabilitation and Therapy

The Occupational Therapy course, designed to create a new framework for rehabilitating disabled servicemen returning from the war, was another cornerstone of the school's wartime effort and gave it a chance to give its ideas about holistic design education a very public and social application. Sponsored by the Deputy Director of the Mental Hygiene Service of the Illinois State Department of Public Welfare, the school planned the training course in conjunction with veterans' hospitals, working closely with various officials. Envisaging that the war and the postwar period would demand a large number of personnel for this task, Moholy-Nagy identified groups in immediate need of rehabilitation, such as Army and Navy aviators suffering from operational stress, soldiers experiencing breakdowns during training, and injured industrial workers, and sought to train a corps of rehabilitation personnel in new modes of responding to their needs.[69] Ultimately, Moholy-Nagy envisioned a larger-scaled project with new types of hospitals designed for what he termed "constructive rehabilitation" (as opposed to "sentimental rehabilitation"). These institutions would have housed general workshops, in which patients would have worked for periods from six months to a year, as well as special workshops and laboratories for more advanced recovery work that would take from one to three years.[70] He was prescient in this regard: psychiatric-hospital admissions doubled between 1940 and 1956.[71] The school's effort to respond to this projected need highlights the degree to which Moholy-Nagy consistently thought not just in a pragmatic vein, but also about how the design school might address postwar social needs and societal changes.

By further developing its foundational teaching strategies to serve the projected onslaught of postwar recuperative needs, in what it viewed as a "constructive problem of education," the school broke with traditional modes of therapy and instead applied contemporary ideas and practices in education, psychological research, psychoanalysis, and even scientific motion studies to its program of rehabilitation.[72]

Two new courses were implemented for training rehabilitation personnel: Rehabilitation I, which focused on sensory experiences, especially visual expression, and workshop exercises, and Rehabilitation II, which tackled issues more unusual for a design school—occupational, physio- and psychotherapy, psychiatric integration, mental hygiene, scientific motion studies, family counseling, and problems of industrial workers, namely fatigue and monotony.[73] Proposed rehabilitative activities for patients were similar to those already taking place at the school—photography, basket weaving, leather work, plastics, and other crafts, as well as writing, poetry, and drama. Students in the course produced sample pieces to simulate the work of bed-ridden patients.[74] Both the head of the Illinois Neuropsychiatric Institute and Franz Alexander, a notable psychoanalyst and physician at the Chicago Institute for Psychoanalysis (a fellow Hungarian, whom Moholy-Nagy had known at the University of Budapest, and who had worked previously in Berlin), supported the program, sending students, nurses, and social workers to attend classes as well as arranging for Moholy-Nagy's appearance before several medical conventions.[75] The school also offered a related evening lecture series on the topic of rehabilitation, which featured twenty-seven experts in the fields of psychoanalysis, occupational and recreational therapy, "psycho-drama," and other areas focused on the issue of addressing the potential needs of returning disabled men.[76]

The courses sought to serve a wider population using key Bauhaus ideas and classroom exercises. Through them, the school was able to reach a different variety of pupil—not self-pronounced artists but rehabilitation facilitators and, indirectly, the injured. These courses thus offered a new opportunity to use Bauhaus methods in support of a long-standing Bauhaus belief, held particularly strongly by Moholy-Nagy himself, in the creative potential of every individual. To that end, therapists, aides, nurses, and laymen were all trained to view rehabilitation as a practice of restoring confidence in the disabled servicemens' own creative abilities.[77] As Moholy-Nagy explained, "Rehabilitation has different facets, but its main direction is at present to restore the patient physically and psychologically to the previous level of his normal status, by reestablishing his self-confidence and giving him opportunity to participate in purposeful production."[78]

Concerned with both cultivation of psychological well-being and a productive end result, the rehabilitation courses, termed "constructive occupational therapy" by Moholy-Nagy, represented another effort to apply Bauhaus ideas to American circumstances. Occupational therapy may seem an odd choice for a design school, but its inclusion was much in keeping with Moholy-Nagy's own pedagogical methodologies and with teaching practices developed at the German Bauhaus. What Moholy-Nagy termed "the Bauhaus approach" in occupational therapy was intended to "awaken hidden capacities, increase self-confidence, leading to inventiveness and resourcefulness" through exercises aimed at self-discovery and "the awakening of consciousness about personal creative abilities."[79] Particularly evident in these rehabilitation courses would have been the sensory-based, process-oriented pedagogic practice that Jeffrey Saletnik has described, in reference to the original Bauhaus, as "design-as-process."[80] This approach, which viewed art objects as permanent exponents of the process of their conceptualization and making, was continued by Moholy-Nagy at the School of Design, as well as by other former Bauhäusler at other institutions in America. Moholy-Nagy sought, innovatively, to use methods of art-making developed at the Bauhaus, methods that remained at the core of his school in Chicago, to aid in the recovery of war-related disabilities, in another pragmatic mobilization of art in response to a perceived need and towards constructive ends. These courses also embodied a new application of the school's focus: methods of design pedagogy, combined with the application of science and technology, were developed and implemented not in pursuit of a well-designed, useful *object*, but rather toward the aim of cultivating *individuals* as productive participants in the ongoing design of postwar American society.

The Art of Camouflage

The second National Defense Course devised by the School of Design during the war years was the Principles of Camouflage course, offered alternately as the Industrial Camouflage course (Figure 5.5).[81] Given under the auspices of the Office of Civilian Defense in Washington, it presented another opportunity to test out the School's ideas about the integration of practices and knowledges across varied fields in a new mode of "design." Moholy-Nagy had been in discussion with various military and government representatives about introducing camouflage training into the school's workshops as early as the spring of 1941; following the December attack on Pearl Harbor and his subsequent appointment to the Chicago Metropolitan Area camouflage section, he devised the course for the 1942 spring semester and then reached out to government officials to obtain official sponsorship for it. The development of the course so early in the war brought inquiries to the school on behalf of other institutions interested in offering camouflage courses, and Moholy-Nagy sought to organize a camouflage instructors' conference in Chicago to bring together teachers of camouflage courses from around the country with the goal of creating a common policy. This proposal was superseded by the Office of Civilian Defense's decision to organize camouflage instruction nationally, and an invitation to send a member of the School of Design to Fort Belvoir, Virginia for training followed.[82] Gyorgy Kepes, after leading the school's initial Principles of Camouflage course in the spring of 1942 and then receiving certification at the Army Engineer School at Fort Belvoir, was made head of the newly created Camouflage Department.[83] The students in these courses included current pupils at the school, members of the pre-inducting class, which was also open to high school seniors, and professionals, such as architects and engineers.[84] The Office of Civilian Defense especially encouraged architects and engineers to participate in the training as "the ones to whom protective concealment problems will best be referred when such decisions are made by the War Production Board"; with completion of the course,

Assimilating Unease

5.5
Camouflage Course, Student work, School of Design, 1942–1943

they would be qualified to "prepare plans, in accordance with principles established by the OCD [Office of Civilian Defense]"[85] The class was a War Services Project, and the work produced by the students was considered official government documentation. Several of the school's students went on to work for the Army's Camouflage Research Department or to active camouflage battalions in Europe.[86]

The course went beyond teaching the expected basic skills of military and industrial camouflaging of tanks, trucks, airplanes, and factories. Kepes led the students in designing a wide range of camouflage options that would conceal potential targets from ground observation, including by snipers, tanks, and submarine periscopes, as well as by low-altitude observation balloons, and from aerial attack methods, such as area bombing, timed precision bombing, dive bombing, and low-flying hedgehopping.[87] To aid the design process, students were trained in the fundamentals of aerial bombardment and the problems, including current modes of camouflage, that were typically faced by bombers.[88] From expert lecturers, they were instructed in infrared and night photography, the physiology of the eye and optics, atmospheric conditions, and certain landscape problems. In seeking new modes of camouflage, the students studied nature and animal camouflage, visual illusions, geometrical optics, techniques of basic photography, photo-topography, and stereoscopic photography, as well as practical skills such as estimation of costs for military bids.[89] Two films made at the school, *Exhibition Work of Camouflage Class* (1943) and *Design Workshops* (1944), show the students actively at work on camouflage problems—for example, utilizing aerial photographs to identify potential targets, or using principles of abstraction to conceal regular forms and patterns (Figure 5.6). This kind of application of various types of technical skills to a wide range of problems—both very concrete and also more conceptual—was different from the crafts-based Bauhaus training of an earlier, perhaps more innocent era, but it did continue the technological legacy of the school, adding to its American iteration a greater urgency and new forms of integration of art and science.

The school was in the unique position to combine science, technology, and art to aid the war effort, and the potential contribution of the visual artist toward this effort was continually stressed in the school's wartime program. As Kepes pointed out in his introductory lecture for the 1942 camouflage course,

> The present emergency demands a reorientation into new fields of activity.... Camouflage requires the combined knowledge of people with a great variety of training—architects, engineers, painters, sculptors, graphic artists. They are finding a synchronization of their divergent knowledge in the fulfillment of this urgent task. This synchronization may be achieved only through ... a mutual exchange of knowledge in each particular field. Thus the aim of this course is to acquaint the participants with all the factors involved in camouflage, enabling them to utilize their expert knowledge efficiently.[90]

According to the course outline, the school consciously tried to avoid what it saw as "economic waste ... caused by the inertia of professional isolation" whereby

Assimilating Unease

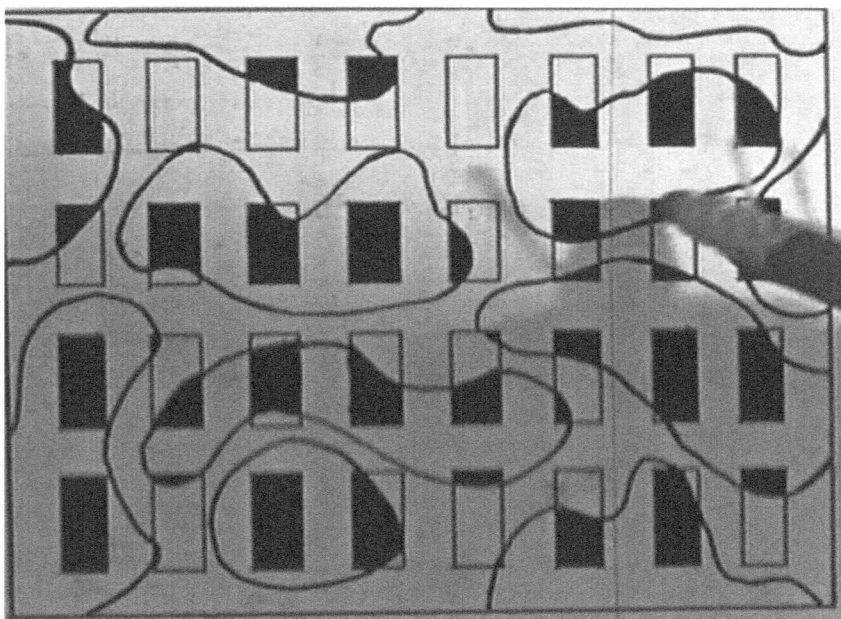

5.6
Camouflage Course, Student work, School of Design, 1942–1943 (Film stills, *Design Workshops*, 1944, 16mm, color, silent)

"the painter saw only painting problems, the architect only architecture, [and] the engineer only engineering." This was true of the school's entire, broader design effort, which, like the course, took as its goal to engender "the necessary flexibility which emerges from a mutual grasp of each other's problems."[91] The philosophy behind the camouflage course supported its practical undertaking to combine the skills of several different professions and improve upon past methods of camouflage by merging specialties and disciplines. The Bauhaus had always striven to realize such a praxis across different fields of art and design; the war effort provided the School of Design with a clear impetus to achieve this melding by orienting it toward pressing, practical, and productive ends.

Beyond the collaboration with the Office of Civilian Defense for the camouflage course, the school also proposed itself as the site of an entire camouflage "research laboratory," which would have prepared volunteers for civilian and military camouflage tasks and also trained teachers who could in turn train others. While the school was never fully expanded into this laboratory, it did conduct further research and development work, much of it highly situational. For example, specialists and students worked on potential methods of changing the appearance of the city of Chicago in order to camouflage it enough to confuse the enemy. The city presented unique difficulties due to its large lake and rivers; since it was supposed that general bombing could not be avoided, the idea was for precision bombing to be rendered inaccurate via large-scale camouflage.[92] Moving beyond standard blackout techniques, which interrupted travel and were ineffective for bodies of water, the group proposed a "moving-light" plan using "halation units," large systems of lamps placed in patterns that would cast strong, confusing glows over or near target areas, rendering potential targets, such as workers' homes, factory sites and airfields, invisible under a luminous haze; by extending this lighting out over the lake, the contour and location of Chicago's lakefront, its most obvious marker, would have been distorted.[93] Students studied color combinations, geometrical optics, lights and shadows, fog and smoke, and other undisclosed means of pockmarking the city so that a bomber would have difficulties finding a target.[94] Faculty were hard at work as well; Kepes took on the problem of the nightly flares at the steel mills, which were easy beacons for bombers, by conducting laboratory experiments, the results of which proposed turning green flood lights on the steel mills to render their red flames nearly invisible.[95]

A large role was played by Moholy-Nagy personally too: he was appointed a member of the Mayor's personal staff under the auspices of the City of Chicago's Civil Defense Commission, a group in charge of camouflaging Chicago against air attack, especially the Lake Michigan waterfront. After completing a survey of the area in small planes and patrol boats, Moholy-Nagy worked on a number of potential methods of disguising distinctive elements of the city—the camouflaging of the oil storage tanks along the city's south shoreline, for instance.[96] "The whole city could be camouflaged, if that were necessary," Moholy-Nagy told the *Chicago Daily News* in 1942. "It depends on how much money could be spent on such a project. . . . Dummy buildings could be built on barges in the lake to change the contour of the city. In this way the Loop could be projected a mile or two into the water. The drives could be covered over with painted burlap. Or scaffoldings could be built to resemble street intersections, or landscaped, to break up the length of the drives."[97] He also proposed obliterating the steel mills from the air through the use of smoke and suggested a signal in response to which janitors in every city building would throw a chemical in the boiler resulting in an instant blanket of blackness, blotting out the entire area. The role of artificial light and light manipulation in obscuring targets drew on one of Moholy-Nagy's own longstanding, primary artistic interests, giving him an opportunity to capitalize on his previous experiments.

A June 1942 article in the journal *Civilian Defense* labeled Moholy-Nagy and Kepes "among the best informed men in America on camouflage techniques," both in terms of theory and practical application.[98] It noted also, centrally, that camouflage should not be undertaken by individual organizations, industrial plants, or agencies, but must be operated on a community scale. Camouflage thus entailed in an uncanny way an almost seamless merging of important, originary Bauhaus ideals—the joining of the arts in work on a common goal, one that had aspects of both artistry and technology, and which could be undertaken only through working *as* a community and *within* a larger community.[99]

War Art: An Exhibition

Important samples of the school's research and new inventions were presented to the public in a wartime exhibition entitled *War Art*.[100] This exhibition represented, at once, another of the school's efforts to disseminate its activities into the surrounding society, its foundational interest in improving means of visual communication generally, and the acute need it felt to substantiate the school's accomplishments in a situation characterized by competing, urgent priorities and constraints on funding and other resources. Organized by Moholy-Nagy and featuring work by students from the School of Design and the Illinois WPA Arts and Crafts Project, the exhibition ran just months after the American entry into the war, from April to May of 1942, at the Renaissance Society of the University of Chicago. (A related exhibition, under the auspices of Gyorgy Kepes's camouflage workshop, featuring much of the same work, was mounted at the school in 1943.[101] This exhibition was captured in a twenty-one-minute color film made at the school, *Exhibition Work of Camouflage Class*.) The *War Art* exhibition at the Renaissance Society was conceived to demonstrate not just the work that was being done at the school or under the auspices of the WPA but, more generally, "new developments in art in their application to war activities."[102] As Moholy-Nagy explained: "We are aware that many individual artists have contributed to the war objectives by their work, ideas and suggestions. These contributions, however, have not been generally publicized."[103] Even before Pearl Harbor, he noted, his own school had already begun to reorganize its work to meet anticipated needs; following that event, a much greater emphasis was being placed on actual war requirements, particularly domestic defense. The exhibition was accordingly intended to illustrate the "contribution of the creative artist and the craftsman as he adapts himself to the urgent needs of today."[104]

A relatively simple one-room exhibition, most of the designs on display were mounted posters on walls or small-scale models. In addition to elucidating

5.7
Above: Gyorgy Kepes or Ralph Graham, *War Art*, Catalogue cover for exhibition at the Renaissance Society, Chicago, 1942
Below: Exhibition of the Camouflage Workshop, School of Design, 1943 (Film still, *Exhibition Work of Camouflage Class*, 1943, 16mm, color, silent)

typical camouflage problems, it included a camouflage demonstration using two light boxes to show how light and shadow could conceal the character of forms. Also on display were designs of new materials, such as the cellophane and cheesecloth plastic "skin," and designs featuring existing materials utilized in novel ways, such as the rubberized cloth flotation units. By the exhibition's opening, some of the designs were already in active use at army, navy, and air training bases.[105] A number of designs were not allowed to be exhibited, however, as they were subject to censorship in the name of national security.[106] Curatorial files note that some of the restricted work included scale models of operations for landing and loading ordnance, and diagrammatic charts of airplane motors, ammunition components, and safety and production methods.[107]

In the catalogue accompanying the show, Moholy-Nagy described the circumstances of his wartime educational program: "In a country at war, education and vocational training are faced with the problem of achieving maximum results in minimum time." He then connected them with the school's unique pedagogic vision and practices. The school, he pointed out,

> because of its educational policy—has readily adapted its program to the present emergency. Its class room and workshop training, the coordination of hand and brain, helps to make the individual resourceful and inventive. He knows from direct experience how to handle the tools of the craftsman, the basic machines of industry, and the problems of contemporary science and art. With such an integrated training of art, science and technology the students of the school were able to attack civilian and military tasks with courage, achieving surprising results, many of which have good possibilities.[108]

Moholy-Nagy also noted how, within the wartime context, he was directing his school to a broader conception of the kinds of needs to which design, both through its products and its practices, could respond. He saw the economic and technical needs that the war had brought to the fore and which would persist in altered form once the war was over, not in isolation, but rather in the context of the larger "human" side of need, of which the war and its effects formed powerful evidence. It was in the context of this perception and its implications for design praxis that the school's contributions to the war effort could be understood: "The creative and inventive mind of the artist has always been alert to human needs. So today, the arts, the applied or practical arts in particular, are serving to meet the urgent needs of the present, and new techniques and development are utilized to aid in the national effort."[109]

This exhibition, then, demonstrated the tangible results, in the context of war, of the school's successful merging of technology and science, emphasized, singularly, by its evolving educational program for the creative problem-solving abilities of the trained artist and designer. Calling into new service the basic artistic skills that had always been taught at the school, including exercises in understanding and manipulating light, research into color and surface effects, the scientific testing of differing materials, and the visualization of form in three-dimensional space or other views, such as aerial perspectives, the school could demonstrate that it had the capabilities to carry out the practical and productive designs that it espoused.[110] It thus continued to aim for what the original catalogue for the school had proclaimed in 1937: simply, the development of "a new type of designer, able to face all kinds of requirements, not because he is a prodigy but because he has the right method of approach."[111] In showing its contributions to the war effort at this exhibition, the school was able to very visibly legitimate itself on several levels; it demonstrated that its unconventional teaching practices—which were being introduced in various institutions scattered across the country by former Bauhäusler now working in them but put into practice systematically at the New Bauhaus and the School of Design, under difficult and uncertain circumstances—could produce distinctively useful, practical results. This institution, led almost exclusively by foreigners who had moved to the United States from Germany, was ready to make serious contributions to a new homeland's war effort.

In doing so it was working to address more general problems at stake for design that were brought forward by the war-exhibition format—such as the relationship between the visual and practical qualities of design products and the relationship between individual designers and a broader community. In presenting new ideas via new objects to a nation at war, the school and its protagonists were able to show that they at the school, and its mode of modern design more generally, were in the process of pragmatically facing the nation's challenges—both in the present time of crisis, in which the attack on Pearl Harbor had led many Americans to question their country's defensibility and readiness for war, and for the envisioned peacetime to follow. It was not enough to simply design for war and for peace in a pedagogical vacuum, and so the school strove to successfully communicate its design practice, largely through the objects it generated, to a broader public. Indeed, this communicative element was integral to the expanded conception of design that the Chicago iteration of the Bauhaus was struggling to put into practice. The *War Art* exhibition, as well as other exhibitions didactically demonstrating the products of the school's workshops, were concrete examples of the school's members mitigating their uneasy status, and that of the school, to a wartime and postwar audience, as part of its broader attempt to forge a new relationship between design and its audiences.

Creative Violence: Conciliatory Postwar Visions

This essay has sought to underscore the novel pragmatism of Moholy-Nagy's version of the Bauhaus—the degree to which the school in its American incarnation in Chicago was able to quickly adapt to the changed circumstances of a nation at war and to instigate an array of concrete solutions to wartime problems, introducing its new mode of design and design education in the midst of the war effort and positioning it, through this effort, for the changed peacetime to follow. Under Moholy-Nagy the New Bauhaus/School of Design addressed the war by offering specific programs and courses, forging key alliances with offices of the military, and using the school as a laboratory for solutions for the war effort. This pragmatism manifested itself in the extent to which, under the leadership of Moholy-Nagy, the school managed to offer real design solutions to a nation at war—from useful objects made of non-rationed materials to visual design to innovative teaching practices. But it also reflected a significant and radical attempt to pursue, to a new degree, in changed forms, and under different circumstances, a holistic, integrated reconception of design as a social and pedagogical practice with links to diverse forms of knowledge and artistic and industrial production.

This project, which had begun at the German Bauhaus, received a charged, bold new formulation under Moholy-Nagy's direction and the pressure of events and acute circumstances in wartime Chicago. The combination of the broad anxiety produced by the war and the narrower anxiety felt by immigrants such as Moholy-Nagy—positioned precariously in the society that had received them and seeking to contribute skills and pedagogical practices that they had brought with them to fight against the state they had fled—seemingly provided the impetus for the émigrés to effectively redirect their efforts toward the kind of social transformation that the German Bauhaus Moholy-Nagy had been a part of had previously proclaimed but largely failed to usher into being. The result was a successful melding of art and technology with science to devise technically advanced objects and educational models for the war effort—a melding that arguably represented a realization to a new degree of the Bauhaus's originary ideals. While in Germany Bauhaus members often wondered why industry did not embrace their designs, in the United States Moholy-Nagy quickly and successfully cooperated with complex American bureaucracies, such as the Office of Civilian Defense, and private investors alike. Although the war found many Bauhäusler working in the United States in new capacities, furthering various aspects of the original school's methods and ideals, Moholy-Nagy particularly saw his work in America as a continuation of the German Bauhaus's organization and pedagogical methodologies, ones that he also viewed as potentially very useful to the war effort. A letter he wrote to the Wartime Commission of the US Education Department a few months after America's entry into the war captures what he saw as his school's contribution:

> Our educational method, the coordination of hand and brain, the integration of workshop and intellectual training, may offer a good approach to your present problems, especially if the training in dexterity includes the basic machines of industry. . . . Continuing the educational work of the Bauhaus, the integration of art, science and technology, we have found that the youth of this country is very receptive to this type of training. It helps to make the individual resourceful and inventive, quick in decisions, courageous in approaching civilian and military tasks.[112]

The war indeed formed an urgently compelling new challenge for the reconception of design and design training that the "Bauhaus method" had embarked upon. The pragmatic approach that Moholy-Nagy frequently trumpeted to those he had to win over was joined by a philosophical one, itself bearing some congenial affinities with American philosophical Pragmatism, one in which Moholy-

Nagy and his fellow instructors and students used their particular areas of expertise to address problems of war, simultaneously cultivating a postwar role for modern design in America as a form of process-oriented, social problem-solving to be cultivated through new practices of pedagogy.[113] As the United States had watched the events unfolding in Europe with mounting alarm, Moholy-Nagy had not ceased to proclaim the potential social benefits of this design philosophy, as here in 1940, with an eye towards the role of design in war and beyond: "Training in design is training in [the] appreciation of [the] essence of things. It is penetrating, comprehensive. It includes development of various skills in using materials, but goes much beyond that. It involves development of attitudes of flexibility and adaptability to meet all sorts of problems as they arise."[114] In the face of war, Moholy-Nagy and his school had stood self-consciously at the ready, practically and ideologically. Moholy-Nagy was keenly aware of the circumstances when he made this statement—as a foreigner in a nation on the eve of war leading a school without particularly stable financial or social backing—and he did not shy away from using wartime contributions to both mitigate his own uneasy status and, at the same time, assimilate the school and its design practices.

Even before the war broke out, perhaps channeling what he had seen in Europe as he fled, Moholy-Nagy cautioned, according to the *New York Times*, that no artist may "dodge his epoch. He may be crushed by it, or he can become bitterly aggressive, or can make use of it in various creative ways. The Bauhaus would make use of it in a creative way."[115] The wartime experience to follow further influenced this insistence that crises were to be met creatively and that design had a crucial role to play in this response. Moholy-Nagy framed his position sharply, emphasizing the parallels between the war effort and the design effort, acknowledging the violence they both entailed: "We have to use creative violence to redesign our life, just as we are using a scientific-technological violence to win the war."[116] But as Moholy-Nagy explained in 1944, he saw art as a tool also, or ultimately, for harnessing aggression, suggesting that war could not but be detrimental to creativity, that the object of design in war—even when it was working directly on the war effort—was to design beyond war: "Art as [an] expression of the individual can be a remedy by sublimation of aggressive impulses. Art educates the receptive faculties as well as revitalizes the creative abilities. In this way art is rehabilitation therapy through which confidence in one's creative power can be restored."[117] In the midst of such a devastating war, a wariness about human potential abounded, and Moholy-Nagy saw in education, including design education, a possible guard against future violence: "We have to have a staff ready whose members have had time and concentration to watch closely the symptoms of war in our youth and to map a course for the future."[118] Moholy-Nagy's version of the Bauhaus in America during the war years took up the mantle of social responsibility with great vigor. Whereas the earlier Bauhaus had also conceived of art as standing at the center of a social project, it was during the war years that art found a guiding productive purpose in the activities of the new incarnation of the institution—whether employed to help veterans recover, to aid civilian instruction, or to design equipment or camouflage for use in the war. The "creative violence" Moholy-Nagy spoke of was to be applied also to the practices of design itself, as an antidote to aggression and violence, in the name of cultivating a new generation that would not lead the world back into war as its predecessors had. This reformatory conception of design training was tidily summed up by Moholy-Nagy in 1943, describing his school as one that educates "by going back to the fundamentals and building up from there a new knowledge of the social and technological implications of design. The new generation of designers, who have such a training, will be invulnerable against the temptations of fads, the easy way out of economic and social responsibilities."[119] Moholy-Nagy's iteration of the Bauhaus in Chicago gave this conception a new urgency, making its case for the future value of the results of its instruction for the country: its role was to produce designers who would assume social, technological, and economic responsibility in the postwar period—following in the footsteps of those who had designed during the war, both for it and for the time beyond it.

Moholy-Nagy looked to the restorative power of art in the postwar period, putting a fragmented civilization back together again. In 1940 he had expressed his broad conception of design still in terms of peacetime life: "A designer trained to think with both penetration and scope will find solutions, not alone for problems arising in daily routine, or for development of better ways of production, but also for all problems of *living and working together*. There is design in family life, in labor relations, in city planning, in living together as *civilized human beings*."[120] Once at war, the school continued to look ahead to future peacetime design needs—framed not to consumer ends, but rather in terms of production as benefiting of society: "After the war a great conversion from war to peace production will take place. Such inventiveness and resourcefulness are the qualities of the educational method of the School of Design in Chicago, these qualities will help the individual to find his right place in peacetime production. This should be to the mutual benefit of himself and the community."[121]

In his graduation speech to the small class of 1942, Moholy-Nagy contended that in a time of war, it was a great privilege to be allowed the exercise of one's skill in design—a privilege granted by society, made for its future benefit, bringing with it an obligation to use one's creative skills for the "productive and harmonious existence of a new generation."[122] It was this obligation that the New Bauhaus had sought to assume through its wide-ranging participation in the war effort—in the service, ultimately, of a more peaceful future in the postwar period, in which design would continue to play a socially beneficial role. This participation necessarily entailed collaboration and compromises, through which Bauhaus émigrés such as Moholy-Nagy, who had arrived under tenuous circumstances, managed to contribute much in several short, but crucial years. In Moholy-Nagy's characterization of these contributions, and of the school's functioning during the war years, as "a great privilege," one continues to hear, perhaps, the conciliatory outlook that underscores the school's anxious beginnings. The task of the present generation, he declared in 1944, to which the New Bauhaus/School of Design had sought to contribute the resource of an invigorated design process and pedagogy, was the "preservation and refinement" of the "*individual* within a harmonious *social* existence, the value of which will be measured in terms of cooperation and social usefulness."[123] When Moholy-Nagy died in November 1946, he was denied the further privilege, as he presumably would have seen it, of seeking to address design to the new and different social challenges of the boom period following the war, in which modern design was poised for far greater popular acceptance, though not without costs for the social design vision that the wartime Chicago design school under Moholy-Nagy had sought to put into practice. Moholy-Nagy had looked forward to the possibility of a vibrant postwar future, one in which the possibilities in a new country must have seemed expansive—but he presumably did so with an acute awareness of the persisting challenges of living together as human beings.

Notes

Acknowledgments: This essay has benefited from thoughtful suggestions by Kathleen James-Chakraborty, Karin Koehler, Marton Orosz, and John Ackerman, all of whom I would like to thank. For invaluable assistance at the research stage and for responding to numerous inquiries thereafter, I thank Catherine Bruck at the University Archives, Illinois Institute of Technology; Valerie Harris at the Special Collections, University of Illinois at Chicago; Sabine Hartmann and Wencke Clausnitzer-Paschold at the Bauhaus-Archiv Berlin; Hattula Moholy-Nagy at the Moholy-Nagy Foundation; Karen Reimer at the Renaissance Society at the University of Chicago; and Margaret Zoller at the Smithsonian Archives of American Art. I would also like to thank the Humboldt University, Berlin for funding travel, research, and the reproduction of illustrations. Earlier versions of this paper were presented at the *Global Bauhaus* conference in 2009 at the Martin-Gropius-Bau Berlin (held in conjunction with the exhibition *Modell Bauhaus / Bauhaus: A Conceptual Model*) and at the Dessau Institute of Architecture in 2011 as part of *Dessauer Gespräche / Dessau Talks*. I would like to thank the organizers and audience members at both of those events for the opportunity to present this work and for their thoughtful discussion.

1. "America Imports Genius," *New York Times*, September 12, 1937, sec. 4.
2. László Moholy-Nagy, "Relating the Parts to the Whole," *Millar's Chicago Letter* 2, no. 23 (August 5, 1940): 6.
3. On the recommendation of Walter Gropius, who had initially been offered the position, the organizing representatives of the Association of Arts and Industries invited Moholy-Nagy to be the school's director. He arrived in Chicago in July of 1937 to meet with the association's board, agreeing to lead the newly established institution, which opened in October. The school changed names and iterations frequently in its initial years of operation: it began as The New Bauhaus: The American School of Design in 1937 but was closed in 1938 by the Association of Arts and Industries. In 1939 it became independent from its original benefactors and was reopened and renamed the School of Design in Chicago. In the spring of 1944 it became the Institute of Design; it persisted in this form, despite Moholy-Nagy's death in 1946, until 1949, when it retained its name but became a school within the Illinois Institute of Technology, as it remains today.
4. For a detailed analysis of the reception of European Modern Architecture in the United States, including a nuanced discussion of the tenuous position of Bauhaus émigrés, of attempts at assimilation vis-à-vis the contemporary culture of the United States, and of the many myths surrounding their success, see Kathleen James-Chakraborty, "From Isolationism to Internationalism: American Acceptance of the Bauhaus," in *Bauhaus Culture: From Weimar to the Cold War*, ed. Kathleen James-Chakraborty (Minneapolis: University of Minnesota Press, 2006), 153–170. See also James-Chakraborty, "Changing the Agenda: From German Bauhaus Modernism to U.S. Internationalism," 235–252, and Franz Schulze, "The Bauhaus Architects and the Rise of Modernism in the United States," 224–234, in Stephanie Barron, *Exiles and Emigrés: The Flight of European Artists from Hitler* (New York: Harry N. Abrams, 1997). In

Domesticity at War (Cambridge, MA: MIT Press, 2007), Beatriz Colomina examines the architectural context in the immediate postwar years, viewing the engagement with the Second World War as the event that finally created the conditions for the development of modern architecture in the United States (12). She argues that there was a shift from war to domesticity to product design which resulted in a milieu that she terms an "obsessive, embattled domesticity" (19).

5   László Moholy-Nagy, Transcript of "Conference on Industrial Design, A New Profession" held at the Museum of Modern Art for the Society of Industrial Designers (11–14 November 1946), 54, 60, Institute of Design Records, University Archives, Paul V. Gavin Library, Illinois Institute of Technology, Chicago (hereafter cited as Institute of Design Records, IIT). Moholy-Nagy's expertise on design education was held in high regard by 1946. He was introduced at the conference by Joseph Hudnut, dean of the architecture school at Harvard, as "the most able and vigorous and successful pioneer in educational discipline based upon objective analysis of the modern scene. We imitate him at Harvard, and he is imitated all over the world, chiefly because he has been able to see a role for the architect and the designer in the kind of training which he is developing which, I think, is going to be a keystone in the education of this new profession" (59–60).

6   Helping to smooth this transition would have been the post-Depression circumstances during Moholy-Nagy's initial years in the United States, in which many government officials had participated in the administering of New Deal and WPA (Works Progress Administration) projects and thus would have been sympathetic to leftist ideals. The decision to let certain émigrés into the United States was sometimes predicated on how the government viewed their potential contribution to the country.

7   Walter Gropius, in "Three Addresses at the Blackstone Hotel on the Occasion of the Celebration of the Addition of the Institute of Design to Illinois Institute of Technology" 17 April 1950, 11, offprint, Institute of Design Records, IIT.

8   School of Design, *1942–43 Course Catalogue* (Chicago: School of Design, 1943), Institute of Design Collection, Special Collections, Daley Library, University of Illinois at Chicago, Chicago (hereafter cited as Institute of Design Collection, UIC).

9   For sources that examine connections in design from wartime to postwar boom time, see especially Donald Albrecht, ed., *World War II and the American Dream: How Wartime Building Changed a Nation* (Cambridge, MA: MIT Press, 1995); Andrew M. Shanken, *194X: Architecture, Planning, and Consumer Culture on the American Home Front* (Minneapolis: University of Minnesota Press, 2009); and Jean-Louis Cohen, *Architecture in Uniform: Designing and Building for the Second World War* (New Haven: Yale University Press, 2011). Although the focus here will be primarily on Moholy-Nagy, many other émigrés with key skills in art, architecture, and design, some who had been affiliated with the Bauhaus and some who had not, also contributed to the war effort in many ways, large and small. For example, former Bauhäusler Herbert Bayer, working closely with Edward Steichen as curator, designed the 1942 *Road to Victory* exhibition at the Museum of Modern Art, which drew on powerful visual narrative, intended to have maximum impact on the audience, to celebrate America and its resolute strength in entering the war; Bayer also designed the installation for MoMA's 1943 *Airways to Peace: An Exhibition of Geography for the Future* and devised a series of flexible display units for posters and war propaganda that was used for traveling exhibitions put on by the US government. Following the war, he continued to aid US government efforts—for example, contributing the design for the 1957 United States Information Agency exhibition *Volk aus Vielen Völkern* (*Nation of Nations*) in Berlin. See Arthur A. Cohen, *Herbert Bayer: The Complete Work* (Cambridge, MA: MIT Press, 1984), 300–308. Modern German architects Erich Mendelsohn and Konrad Wachsmann advised the US government about traditional German building techniques and materials (and their relative combustibility), aiding the 1943 construction of a full-scale "German village" on the Dugway Proving Grounds in Utah. Fellow German émigrés Paul Zucker, Hans

Knoll, and George Hartmueller oversaw the construction of authentic interior furnishings, and Antonin Raymond, a Czech émigré, advised on a companion "Japanese village." The two villages were repeatedly bombarded and rebuilt, in order to ascertain the most effective means of their destruction. Mendelsohn also advised on typical German factory construction, especially their roofs' susceptibility to incendiary bombs. See Jean-Louis Cohen, 231–239.

10 For a contextualized discussion of the extent to which the exile experience of Walter Gropius was characterized by his efforts to avoid political controversy and separate art from politics, as manifested in his avoidance of historical specificity in the design and contents of the 1938 Museum of Modern Art exhibition and accompanying catalogue, *The Bauhaus, 1919–1928*, see Karen Koehler, "The Bauhaus, 1919–1928: Gropius in Exile and the Museum of Modern Art, N.Y., 1938," in *Art, Culture, and Media Under the Third Reich*, ed. Richard A. Etlin (Chicago: University of Chicago Press, 2002): 287–315. Koehler notes the fear of—and hostility towards—new immigrants in 1938, the year that the exhibition opened. Anti-German and anti-Bolshevist propaganda was commonplace (Bauhaus artists had the potential to be identified pejoratively as either Germans or Bolsheviks), and in a period of continued unemployment in the United States, the new émigrés were also regarded as potential labor competition (296–300). See also Koehler, "Angels of History Carrying Bricks: Gropius in Exile" in *The Dispossessed: An Anatomy of Exile*, ed. Peter I. Rose (Amherst: University of Massachusetts Press, 2005), 257–280. For a wide-ranging study on exiled artists and architects of this period, see Barron, *Exiles and Emigrés: The Flight of European Artists from Hitler*.

11 Herbert Bayer is said to have arrived in New York with less than twenty dollars in his pocket. Sibyl Moholy-Nagy claimed that Moholy-Nagy, by insisting on speaking German, "lost most of his English vocabulary" en route from Chicago to Mills College in Oakland, where he had been invited to conduct a summer school in 1940. Sibyl Moholy-Nagy, *Moholy-Nagy: Experiment in Totality* (New York: Harper Brothers, 1950), 180. William H. Jordy has noted that Mies relied on others to translate for him during his initial four years in the United States before making an effort to speak English. Jordy, "The Aftermath of the Bauhaus in America: Gropius, Mies, and Breuer," in *The Intellectual Migration: Europe and America, 1930–1960*, ed. Donald Fleming and Bernard Bailyn (Cambridge, MA: Belknap Press of Harvard University Press, 1969), 516. Once America entered World War II, uncertainty and isolation ensued, as Sibyl Moholy-Nagy's diary entry of December 11, 1941, starkly captures: "War with Germany—that means severing the last connections with my family. No more letters." Sibyl Moholy-Nagy, "Domestic Diary of America's Participation in the Second World War," 11 December 1941, 5, Sibyl and László Moholy-Nagy Papers, Archives of American Art, Smithsonian Institution, Washington, DC (hereafter cited as Moholy-Nagy Papers, Smithsonian). Beyond physical and economic hardship, there was also the continuing emotional hardship of emigration, to which an entry in Sibyl's diary from the end of the war gives insight: "Laci [Moholy] came home. There is an unwritten code among emigrants—even when you are married. Every reference to Europe or to the past is guarded, casual, uttered only after the emotion behind it has been secured safely with an enforced dose of self-control. There is an emigrant etiquette, and Laci has adhered to it the same as I." She then goes on to report their reactions to the end of the Second World War: "So the European victory, the defeat and death of the greatest objective enemy we have known in our life-time, the end of twelve incredibly strenuous years, was mentioned between us only in passing." Sibyl Moholy-Nagy, Diary, 13 May 1945, Moholy-Nagy Papers, Smithsonian.

Part of the wartime and postwar endeavors of Bauhäusler such as Ludwig Mies van der Rohe, Gropius, and Moholy-Nagy were activities related to, understandably, simply trying to help family, friends, and colleagues who remained in Germany. The difficult realities of wartime and especially postwar Europe highlights another reason why Moholy-Nagy and others were to stay in the United States. Letters between Lilly Reich and Mies show that he supplied his extended family, Reich and her family, and former clients such as Carl Crous with CARE (Cooperative for American Remittances to Europe) packages—pre-packaged staples that could be purchased for delivery to Europe. Reich repeatedly wrote Mies, asking for goods such as coffee, tea, rice, and eggs, and thanking him for the packages as they arrived safely. Once installed at Harvard, Walter and Ise Gropius began a tireless campaign assisting friends and colleagues trying to leave Germany, and they, like Mies, also sent provisions. They began a "Bauhaus Fund" which mailed parcels to former Bauhaus members remaining in Germany. The Moholy-Nagys, with little disposable personal income, and positions that were continuously unstable, sent a tremendous amount back to Europe. Sibyl's sister, in a letter thanking Sibyl for the latest food package, writes of the relief it gave, and reports of a darkening situation, in which the hitherto lack of food and clothing was made worse by the newer shortages in electricity, gas, and at times, water. Eva Pietzsch to Sibyl Moholy-Nagy, 3 January 1947, Moholy-Nagy Papers, Smithsonian. Subsequent letters detail their "fight to feed themselves" ("*Kampf ums fressen*"). The Moholy-Nagys also sent CARE packages, funds, and other assistance to friends, including the contemporary dancer Gret Palucca and artists Paul Citroen, Raoul Hausmann, and Kurt Schwitters. Lloyd C. Engelbrecht, *Moholy-Nagy: Mentor to Modernism*, 2 vols. (Cincinnati: Flying Trapeze Press, 2009), 1:272, 2:673–677.

12 Hal Foster, "The Bauhaus Idea in America," in *Albers and Moholy-Nagy: From the Bauhaus to the New World*, ed. Achim Borchardt-Hume (London: Tate Publishing, 2006), 97.

13 The original Bauhaus, especially under Gropius, as well as its predecessor led by Henry van de Velde, had always sought to minimize reliance on government support through commercial work and had the stated goal of forging an alliance with industry, yet it was unable to substantially achieve this; in America Moholy-Nagy did not have the option of receiving comparable, direct financial support from the government, although he actively sought it as a sponsor of the school's wartime activities. He also spent a great deal of energy courting companies, large and small, for funding, materials, and technical equipment. Without a stable source of income, his school was perpetually in crisis. After its original board of directors dissolved the school within its first year, Moholy-Nagy re-opened without a board that would fund the school, but rather with a "sponsors committee" of prominent cultural figures. Later, benefactor Walter Paepcke formed a board to support the school, a body to which Moholy-Nagy was not always deferential, having a strong personal vision for his school. Paepcke also tried to interest local institutions of higher learning in annexing the school and called in Gropius, Bayer, and Breuer to assess whether Moholy-Nagy could be advised in the direction the school should take to become more stable (see Alain Findeli's description of the "Moholy Affair" in "Design Education and Industry: The Laborious Beginnings of the Institute of Design in Chicago in 1944," *Journal of Design History* 4, no. 2 [1991]: 97–113). Gropius, ensconced in the stability of Harvard, and Mies at IIT weren't forced to face general financial difficulties nor were they responsible for contending with drops in student enrollment, both greatly exacerbated by the war. (The GSD dropped to twenty-six students and began admitting women to take up the places of absent male students. See Jill Pearlman, *American Modernism: Joseph Hudnut, Walter Gropius, and the Bauhaus Legacy at Harvard* [Charlottesville: University of Virginia Press, 2007], 200–201. At the School of Design, which had always admitted women, it was only during the war that it had more female than male students.)

14 Letter, Moholy-Nagy to Sibyl Moholy-Nagy, 26 April 1944, reprinted in Sibyl Moholy-Nagy, *Moholy-Nagy: Experiment in Totality* (New York: Harper Brothers, 1950), 216.

15 Harold J. Coolidge, American Defense, Harvard Group, to Gropius, 10 January 1941, Walter Gropius Papers, Harvard.

16 For discussion and reproduction of key FBI documents, see Margret Kentgens-Craig, *The Bauhaus and America: First Contacts, 1919–1936* (Cambridge, MA: MIT Press, 1999), 238–240 and Appendix.

17 A letter of explanation was sent to Moholy-Nagy from Joseph Edelman, an attorney retained by Moholy-Nagy to expedite his case. The letter also pointed out that other Hungarians had been naturalized within a period of six months to a year and a half, whereas at this point in the

process Moholy-Nagy had already been in the United States for eight years. Part of the FBI investigation seems to have been due to Moholy-Nagy's involvement, while in America, with the Hungarian Democratic Council, which sought to foster democracy in Hungary. See Edelman to Moholy-Nagy, 23 March 1945, and Moholy-Nagy to Andrew Jordan, District Director, US Department of Justice, 12 November 1945, Moholy-Nagy Papers, Smithsonian. Moholy-Nagy, after much effort and outreach in many directions, finally obtained his naturalization papers on April 10, 1946 (seven months before his death).

18 Karen Koehler, "The Bauhaus Manifesto Postwar to Postwar: From the Street to the Wall to the Radio to the Memoir," in *Bauhaus Construct: Fashioning Identity, Discourse and Modernism*, ed. Jeffrey Saletnik and Robin Schuldenfrei (London: Routledge, 2009), 28. See also a copy of the 1942 US Department of Justice "Regulations Controlling Travel and Other Conduct of Aliens of Enemy Nationalities" in the Walter Gropius Papers, Harvard.

19 For an extended discussion of this fictional radio play and its significance see Koehler, "The Bauhaus Manifesto Postwar to Postwar," 24–28.

20 Ibid., 26.

21 Ibid., 25.

22 As reported by Sibyl Moholy-Nagy in a letter to Robert Tague, 9 June 1945, Bauhaus Archive, Berlin.

23 Moholy-Nagy, letter to Robert Tague, 14 July 1945, Bauhaus Archive, Berlin. Moholy-Nagy seemed determined to stay from the very beginning, writing from Chicago, not long after his arrival, to Sibyl, who was still in London, "You ask whether I want to remain here? Yes, Darling, I want to remain in America. There's something incomplete about this city and its people that fascinates me; it seems to urge one on to completion. Everything seems still possible. The paralyzing finality of the European disaster is far away. I love the air of newness, of expectation around me. Yes, I want to stay." Moholy-Nagy letter to Sibyl Moholy-Nagy, 8 August 1937, reprinted in Sibyl Moholy-Nagy, *Moholy-Nagy: Experiment in Totality*, 145.

24 Moholy-Nagy to Dr. P.P. Keppel, Carnegie Corporation of New York, 7 January 1943, Institute of Design Collection, UIC.

25 Emphasis in original. László Moholy-Nagy, *Vision in Motion* (Chicago: Paul Theobald, 1947), 64.

26 This technological anxiety was compounded by the development of far more devastating, atomic weapons (a key local role was played by Enrico Fermi's laboratory at the University of Chicago) and their deployment at Hiroshima and Nagasaki; Moholy-Nagy reacted by painting *Nuclear I* and *Nuclear II* in early 1946. See Timothy J. Garvey, "László Moholy-Nagy and Atomic Ambivalence in Postwar Chicago," *American Art* 14, no. 3 (Autumn 2000): 22–39.

27 A.B.D. "School of Design on Threshold of Fourth Year," *The Chicago Sun*, January 3, 1942.

28 László Moholy-Nagy, *Vision in Motion*, 10. *Vision in Motion* was predominantly written in 1944, as the war still raged on, although it was not published until 1947, after the war's conclusion and also posthumously.

29 See Robin Schuldenfrei, "The Irreproducibility of the Bauhaus Object," in *Bauhaus Construct*, 37–60. Exceptions are mainly objects produced in the years that Hannes Meyer led the school, after the departure of Moholy-Nagy: several textiles from the weaving workshop were mass produced, and the Bauhaus wallpapers, not the iconic objects usually associated with the original Bauhaus today.

30 Moholy-Nagy, *The New Bauhaus* Catalogue (Chicago: School of Design, 1937), 4, Institute of Design Collection, UIC.

31 Among the varied continuations of the Bauhaus project in America, the New Bauhaus (and its later iterations) under Moholy-Nagy remained the institution most closely linked to the original Bauhaus's structure, program, and desired end results. Copious correspondence demonstrates that Gropius remained closely affiliated and invested in the school's future throughout its stormy history, beginning by nominating Moholy-Nagy as its first leader, then, over the years, advising Moholy-Nagy on how to structure the institution, lending his name to its initiatives, and stepping in periodically to reassure the school's administration and benefactors.

32 Moholy's "naive" use of this term (largely) preceded the advent of today's vast, for-profit military-industrial complex. See, for example, Moholy-Nagy, letter to George Kepes, 19 November 1942, Bauhaus Archive, Berlin. Kepes's name will be cited throughout this essay in accordance with how it appears in the original source quoted. The Hungarian Kepes was born with the first name "György," but (presumably as an act of assimilation) he used the German form of his name, "Georg," for the period of his Berlin years, then "George" during his initial years in America, later reverting back to "Gyorgy" but without the umlaut.

33 For images and short descriptions of these projects, see Box 23, Volume 7, Institute of Design Records, IIT.

34 Letter, Moholy-Nagy to Walter B. Kirner, National Defense Research Committee, 7 January 1944, Bauhaus Archive, Berlin.

35 "Design for Wartime Living and When Peace Comes," 1943, newspaper clipping of unidentified source, Institute of Design Collection, UIC.

36 László Moholy-Nagy, "Modern Designs from Chicago," *Modern Plastics*, December 1942; reprinted in: *Timber of Canada*, February 1943, 19.

37 "New Slant on New Product Planning: How Outside Help, from Private Research Groups and Schools, Can Ease War Plant Job of Finding Products for Tomorrow, Give Designers a New 'Lift,'" *Modern Industry*, June 15, 1943, 46–47. War Production Board (WPB) Limitations Order L-49 set severe restrictions on the total amount of iron and steel available for the manufacture of furniture springs. See *Official Weekly Bulletin of the Office of War Information, Washington D.C.* 3, no. 41 (October 13, 1942). The next *Bulletin* reported that used metal beds and bedsprings were being sold at inflated prices and ordered a review of all cases in which jobbers, manufacturers, and distributors might be violating the provisions of the general maximum price regulations for such items. *Bulletin* 3, no. 42 (October 20, 1942). On November 1, the production of metal springs for civilian use was banned altogether, and by December policies had been put in place to encourage the use of wooden springs, with the provision that furniture with wooden springs could not be approved for sale without demonstrable laboratory test reports showing that the new springs met standards prepared by the Office of Price Administration in cooperation with the National Bureau of Standards. *Bulletin* 3, no. 49 (December 8, 1942). The school's experiments with wooden springs began well in advance of these directives, putting the school at a distinct advantage.

Similarly, the Museum of Modern Art in New York adapted its popular *Useful Objects* annual exhibition series to contend with wartime restrictions, opening *Useful Objects in Wartime* in 1942. On display were household objects featuring non-priority materials; the Conservation and Substitution Branch of the War Production Board made recommendations to the museum about possible inclusions and omissions. No metal objects were selected for the display, which relied heavily on glass and ceramic objects, and presented some unusual materials, such as a cornhusk doormat. The museum's bulletin featured images of common household objects such as steel ladles and Bakelite dishes with a large "X" struck through them, noting for which sector of war production the material was being requisitioned—for example, Lucite and Plexiglas for airplane construction and nylon for parachutes. Also included in the exhibition were articles designed in response to requests by men and women in the army and navy and supplies necessary for civilian defense. See "Useful Objects in Wartime," *Bulletin of the Museum of Modern Art* 10, no. 2 (December 1942–January 1943): 1–21. See also Mary Anne Staniszewski, *The Power of Display: A History of Exhibition Installations at the Museum of Modern Art* (Cambridge, MA: MIT Press, 2001), especially 209–235.

38 "New Slant on New Product Planning," 46–47.

39 "'Sleep Like a Log' on New Wood Springs," *Bruce Magazine*, May–June 1943, Institute of Design Records, IIT.

40 László Moholy-Nagy, "Modern Designs from Chicago," reprinted in: *Timber of Canada*, February 1943, 20.

41 "Wooden Springs," *Business Week*, October 31, 1942.
42 "New Slant on New Product Planning," 46–47.
43 "Wooden Springs," *Business Week*.
44 Moholy-Nagy to Kepes, 19 November 1942, Bauhaus Archive, Berlin.
45 "The New Springs," 34–35, undated, unidentified article, Institute of Design Records, IIT.
46 Moholy-Nagy to Nikolaus Pevsner, 18 March 1943, Bauhaus Archive, Berlin. The by now long-standing idea of promoting modern materials for furniture to replace stuffed upholstered furniture—an idea that modern architects had promoted vigorously in 1920s Europe—got renewed currency in Moholy-Nagy's Chicago context, where the modern plywood, Lucite, and metal chairs being designed at the school were introduced to a midwestern audience that would not necessarily have been familiar with the earlier European developments.
47 Moholy-Nagy's ideas may have directly influenced Charles Eames; according to R. Craig Miller, during the time that Eames was teaching design at Cranbrook (September 1939–June 1941) and simultaneously working in the Saarinen office, he often went to Chicago on weekends to consult with Moholy-Nagy. See Miller, "Interior Design and Furniture," in *Design in America: The Cranbrook Vision, 1925–1950* (New York: Abrams, in association with the Detroit Institute of Arts and the Metropolitan Museum of Art, 1983), 109. In comparison to the School of Design, Cranbrook did not offer comprehensive work in industrial design and in the late 1930s and early war years had considerable difficulty in maintaining a design department; for a period during the war, the department was closed (1943–1944). Likewise the metalcraft department was suspended for most of the duration of the war, due to shortages.
48 Black Mountain College Newsletter, "The College in a World at War," November 1942: 4–5.
49 "New Slant on New Product Planning," 46–47.
50 "Design for Wartime Living and When Peace Comes."
51 Alain Findeli, "Design Education and Industry," 100.
52 Walter Paepcke to Donald M. Nelson, War Production Board, 3 February 1944, Institute of Design Collection, UIC.
53 Moholy-Nagy, "Modern Designs from Chicago," 20.
54 See, for example, "Industrial Design: New Forms for Postwar Hardware," 51–53, unidentified journal, Institute of Design Records, IIT. The article, which featured prototypes being developed at the school, noted, "War production already hums twenty-four hours a day in many plants, and we are scheduled to reach total conversion next June. This means that re-tooling will follow when the war ends, bringing with it sweeping changes in the accustomed forms of all our manufactured products" (51).
55 Al Bernsohn, "The New Wood that Bends," April 1941, 23, unidentified journal, Institute of Design Records, IIT.
56 Emery Hutchison, "Stories of the Day," *Daily News*, June 28, 1944.
57 School of Design, *National Defense Courses* Brochure (Chicago: School of Design, 1942), Institute of Design Collection, UIC.
58 School of Design, *Summer Session 1942* Brochure (Chicago: School of Design, 1942), Institute of Design Collection, UIC.
59 Moholy-Nagy to P.P. Keppel, Carnegie Corporation of New York, 7 January 1943, Institute of Design Collection, UIC. In the fall of 1942 Moholy-Nagy could report that the school had 206 students of whom 134 were in the camouflage course. Moholy-Nagy to Robert J. Wolff, 6 October 1942, Bauhaus Archive, Berlin.
60 School of Design, *Summer Session 1942* Brochure (Chicago: School of Design, 1942), Institute of Design Collection, UIC.
61 School of Design, *Summer Session 1943* Brochure (Chicago: School of Design, 1943), Institute of Design Collection, UIC.
62 School of Design, *Day and Evening Classes 1943–1944* Brochure (Chicago: School of Design, 1943), Institute of Design Collection, UIC.

63 For example, see Moholy-Nagy to P.P. Keppel, Carnegie Corporation of New York, 7 January 1943, Institute of Design Collection, UIC.
64 'School of Design, *Report on Public Relations Activities* (Chicago: School of Design, February 6, 1945), 1–2, Institute of Design Collection, UIC.
65 School of Design, *Academic Year 1942–1943* Brochure (Chicago: School of Design, 1942), Institute of Design Collection, UIC.
66 School of Design, *Summer Session 1943* and *Photo Classes 1943* Brochures (Chicago: School of Design, 1943), Institute of Design Collection, UIC.
67 For these posters and others, see Box 25, Volume 9, Tab D, Institute of Design Records, IIT.
68 This was awarded by the Society of Typographic Arts. Raymond Heer, Secretary, The Society of Typographic Arts to George Kepes, 22 December 1942, Gyorgy Kepes Papers, Archives of American Art, Smithsonian Institution, Washington, DC (hereafter cited as Kepes Papers, Smithsonian).
69 Paper given by Moholy-Nagy at the 1943 Annual Meeting of the American Psychiatric Association. Moholy-Nagy, "New Approach to Occupational Therapy," 1943, 1–9, Institute of Design Collection, UIC. Organizations across the United States, including other art-related cultural institutions, also began to address this need—specifically, the potential for artists, the arts generally, and museums to aid in the recovery process. For example, an exhibition at the Museum of Modern Art in New York, *The Arts in Therapy* (1943), looked to the potential role of the crafts in occupational therapy and the psychiatric use of media such as painting, sculpture, and drawing in therapy. The museum sponsored a contest for objects and projects of therapeutic and recreational value; second prize was awarded to School of Design members Juliet Kepes (wife of Gyorgy Kepes) and Marli Ehrman (head of the textile workshop) for a multi-textured, multi-sensory cloth children's book. See "The Arts in Therapy," *Bulletin of the Museum of Modern Art* 10, no. 3, (February 1943): 1–24.
70 Moholy-Nagy, "New Approach to Occupational Therapy," 3.
71 See William Leuchtenberg, *A Troubled Feast* (Boston, MA: Little, Brown, 1973), 104; cited by Jean-Louis Cohen.
72 Moholy-Nagy, "Orientation Course in Occupational Therapy," 1, Institute of Design Collection, UIC.
73 Ibid., 3–4.
74 John Craig, "Stories of the Day," *Chicago Daily News*, February 26, 1943.
75 Sibyl Moholy-Nagy, *Moholy-Nagy: Experiment in Totality*, 185.
76 Letter from Moholy-Nagy to Friends of the School of Design, 27 September 1943, Walter Gropius Papers, Harvard.
77 School of Design, *Summer Session 1943* Brochure.
78 Moholy-Nagy, "New Approach to Occupational Therapy," 1.
79 Ibid., 4.
80 See especially Chapters 1 and 2 of Jeffrey Saletnik, "Pedagogy, Modernism, and Medium Specificity: The Bauhaus and John Cage" (Ph.D. diss., University of Chicago, 2009), 18–121.
81 School of Design, *National Defense Courses 1942* Brochure (Chicago: School of Design, 1942), Institute of Design Collection, UIC. Another example of the school's work with local officials and government bodies was an informational booklet on camouflage that was produced by the course as a WPA (Work Projects Administration) activity, sponsored by the Chicago Metropolitan Area Office of Civilian Defense. See "Selected List of References on Camouflage," November 1942, Institute of Design Records, IIT. The School of Design was not the only school to offer such a course; during the war years, institutions of higher education from Paris to Burma, as well as across the United States, offered courses of instruction on camouflage. See Chapter 6 "Camouflage, or the Temptation of the Invisible," of Jean-Louis Cohen, *Architecture in Uniform*, 187–219, especially therein "Didactics of Camouflage, from Chicago to Brooklyn," 195–201.

82 Moholy-Nagy, letter to Walter Paepcke, 18 March 1942, Institute of Design Collection, UIC, and Moholy-Nagy to George Kepes, 19 November 1942, Bauhaus Archive, Berlin. During this period, Moholy-Nagy notes, he was also being apprised by officials of the structure of similar courses being organized at Pratt Institute in New York.
83 Kepes underwent 85 hours of specialized training from June 22–July 4, 1942. See Certificate, The Engineer School, Fort Belvoir, Virginia, Kepes Papers, Smithsonian.
84 School of Design, *Summer Session 1943* and *Principles of Camouflage* Course Brochure (Chicago: School of Design, 1943), Institute of Design Collection, UIC. Over 100 students graduated from the course.
85 School of Design, *Principles of Camouflage* Course Brochure.
86 Including Myron Kozman, Robert Preusser, and Jesse Reichek. John L. Scott, with László Moholy-Nagy and Gyorgy Kepes, "A Bird's-Eye View of Camouflage," *Civilian Defense*, July–August 1942: 10.
87 George Kepes, "Introductory Lecture for the Camouflage Course" (lecture summary, School of Design in Chicago, September 16, 1942), 1–4, Institute of Design Collection, UIC.
88 Means of obscurement that had come into use which were studied included artificial light patterns, blink lights, mercury vapor, false fires, mirror devices, and other forms of light projection. "Outline of the Camouflage Course at the School of Design in Chicago, 1941–1942," 3–4, Institute of Design Collection, UIC.
89 Ibid.
90 Kepes, "Introductory Lecture for the Camouflage Course," 1.
91 "Outline of the Camouflage Course at the School of Design in Chicago, 1941–1942," 1.
92 M. Seklemian, "A Study of the Principles of Camouflage Conducted at the School of Design Chicago," September 1942–January 1943, Institute of Design Records, IIT.
93 Ibid.
94 "Kelly and Army Plan Hiding of City from Foe," *Chicago Daily News*, May 8, 1942.
95 Ibid.
96 Donald S. Vogel, letter to George J. Mavigliano, 2 September 1983, in Mavigliano, "The Chicago Design Workshop: 1939–1943," *Journal of Decorative and Propaganda Arts* 6 (Autumn 1987): 42.
97 "Kelly and Army Plan Hiding of City from Foe." Moholy-Nagy also noted: "Germany is reputed to have spent $1,000,000 in camouflaging the Fokker aircraft factory at Amsterdam alone. Chicago, of course, has some special problems of camouflage. There is the lake, which like a sore thumb sticks out and points to the city and to its largest industrial arm, the steel mills. Then there is the river, like a road sign. And the many beautiful parks, all good landmarks for fliers."
98 John L. Scott, with László Moholy-Nagy and Gyorgy Kepes, "Civilian Camouflage Goes Into Action," *Civilian Defense* 1, no. 2 (June 1942): 8.
99 Prompted by precisely this wartime difficulty of camouflaging cities, fear of aerial bombardment, and later the atom bomb, the decentralization of the city became an important aspect in postwar planning, impacting the location and shape of communities, industrial dispersion, and centers of knowledge and science. See, for example, Peter Galison, "War against the Center," *Grey Room* 4 (Summer 2001): 5–33; David Monteyne, *Fallout Shelter: Designing for Civil Defense in the Cold War* (Minneapolis: University of Minnesota Press, 2011); Jennifer S. Light, *From Warfare to Welfare: Defense Intellectuals and Urban Problems in Cold War America* (Baltimore: Johns Hopkins University Press, 2003); Matthew Farish, "Disaster and Decentralization: American Cities and the Cold War," *Cultural Geographies* 10, no. 3 (2003): 125–148; Margaret Pugh O'Mara, *Cities of Knowledge: Cold War Science and the Search for the Next Silicon Valley* (Princeton, NJ: Princeton University Press, 2004).

100   Other war-focused exhibitions and art-related activities were mounted across wartime America; for example, the Museum of Modern Art in New York presented an extensive series of exhibitions including *Britain at War* (1941), *Art in War* (1942), *Road to Victory* (1942), and *Camouflage for Civilian Defense* (1942), for which a second version was also prepared for touring in 1942–1943. The museum sponsored competitions, placing a selection of the entries on display, including the photography contest *Image of Freedom* (1941) and three poster competitions (former Bauhaus member Xanti Schawinsky's poster was among the winners): *National Defense Posters* (1941), *United Hemisphere Posters* (1942), and *National War Posters* (1942). A roster of circulating wartime exhibitions that traveled to ninety-three cities across America was also developed in this period. See "The Museum and the War," *Bulletin of the Museum of Modern Art* 10, no. 1 (October–November 1942): 3–19.

101   Sibyl Moholy-Nagy, *Moholy-Nagy: Experiment in Totality*, 184.

102   *War Art* Press Release, The Renaissance Society at the University of Chicago Records, The Archives of American Art, Smithsonian Institution, Washington, DC (hereafter cited as Renaissance Society Records, Smithsonian).

103   *War Art* (Chicago: Renaissance Society, 1942). An example of this small exhibition catalogue is available in the Renaissance Society Records, Smithsonian, in the Institute of Design Collection, UIC, and Institute of Design Records, IIT.

104   *War Art* Press Release, Renaissance Society Records, Smithsonian.

105   For example, according to the *War Art* press release, the "visual education charts" for teaching camouflage and mechanical skills.

106   *War Art* Press Release, Renaissance Society Records, Smithsonian.

107   Also restricted were designs of: camouflage for ordnance operations; three-dimensional illuminated panels that showed radio and weather charts; and specially designed furniture for officers' lounges and a servicemen's recreation center. See curatorial files, The Renaissance Society.

108   *War Art* (Chicago: Renaissance Society, 1942).

109   Ibid.

110   For a complete list of the skills taught as well as general aims, see the original 1937 school catalogue, Moholy-Nagy, *The New Bauhaus* Catalogue (Chicago: School of Design, 1937), Institute of Design Collection, UIC.

111   Ibid., 4.

112   Moholy-Nagy to F.J. Kelly, Executive Director, Wartime Commission, US Office of Education, 13 March 1942, Institute of Design Collection, UIC.

113   Armed with a letter of introduction from mutual educator and colleague Charles Morris, Moholy-Nagy met with John Dewey in November 1938 in New York; at that meeting Dewey gave him his recently published book *Experience and Education*. Dewey was among the academics and intellectuals, such as Gropius and Alfred H. Barr, that Moholy-Nagy had enlisted to support his school. Dewey's 1934 *Art as Experience*, particularly Dewey's belief in the *process* of the development of a work of art as an *experience*, rather than simply the resulting work of art itself as the main object, likely would have influenced, and dovetailed with, Moholy-Nagy's own educational philosophies, especially those behind the first-year Basic Course. *Art as Experience* was a required text of the Product Design workshop, and Moholy-Nagy refers to Dewey's practices directly in *Vision in Motion* (71). See also Alain Findeli, "Moholy-Nagy's Design Pedagogy in Chicago (1937–46)," *Design Issues* 7, no. 1 (Autumn 1990): 4–19, especially 13–15.

114   Moholy-Nagy, "Relating the Parts to the Whole," 6.

115   Ruth Green Harris, "The New Bauhaus: A Program for Art Education," *New York Times*, May 29, 1938.

116   Moholy-Nagy quoted by Reed Hynds, "Blueprint for the Post-War World," *St. Louis Star-Times*, January 22, 1942.

117 László Moholy-Nagy, "The Task of this Generation: Reintegration of Art into Daily Life," *Department of Art Education N.E.A. Bulletin*, 1944, n.p. (2), offprint, Institute of Design Records, IIT.
118 Moholy-Nagy to P.P. Keppel, Carnegie Corporation of New York, 7 January 1943, Institute of Design Collection, UIC. Moholy-Nagy would continue to be disturbed by man's injurious power. For a discussion of Moholy-Nagy's concerns about the destructive power of nuclear energy following the dropping of the atom bomb on Hiroshima and his own 1945–1946 radiation treatments for leukemia, including a thorough discussion of his 1946 paintings *Nuclear I* and *Nuclear II*, see Garvey, "László Moholy-Nagy and Atomic Ambivalence in Postwar Chicago," 22–39.
119 László Moholy-Nagy, "Design Potentialities," (1943) in *New Architecture and City Planning*, ed. Paul Zucker (New York: Philosophical Library, 1944), 686–687.
120 Moholy-Nagy, "Relating the Parts to the Whole," 6. For a discussion of Moholy-Nagy's pedagogical aims at the new Bauhaus—including the conviction that the school should offer an education combining humanistic and technical spheres and emphasizing the integration of the designer into society—as well as Moholy-Nagy's belief that the designer could bring an integrated, humanistic element (including a biologically necessary "organic design") into a technologically mediated new form of vision, see also Reinhold Martin, *The Organizational Complex: Architecture, Media, and Corporate Space* (Cambridge, MA: MIT Press, 2003), 53–58.
121 School of Design, *Day and Evening Classes 1943* Brochure (Chicago: School of Design, 1943), Institute of Design Collection, UIC.
122 Sibyl Moholy-Nagy, *Moholy-Nagy: Experiment in Totality*, 188.
123 Moholy-Nagy, "The Task of this Generation," n.p. (1). Emphasis in original.

Chapter 6

The Anxieties of Autonomy
Peter Eisenman from Cambridge to House VI
Sean Keller

Since the middle of the nineteenth century, existentialist thought has centered around the anxious relationship of freedom and determination. In the primal scene of modernism—repeated by Kierkegaard, Nietzsche, Heidegger, Sartre, and Camus—the human subject, numbed by social conventions, is seized by a vertiginous realization of his existential freedom from such determinations. Modernist aesthetics has played out a mirrored theme through the concept of autonomy: the artwork that strives to be free from external determination must confront the dilemma of self-determination. In what follows I want to suggest that exactly these issues—at the level of the dwelling subject and of the architectural object—propelled the seminal first decade of Peter Eisenman's writing and practice.

Anxiety for Autonomy
Eisenman opens his 1963 dissertation for the University of Cambridge with a rejection of tendencies that he believes are misleading postwar architecture, specifically the attempt to ground design in the "actual"—a term he uses to refer to the supposed demands both of function and of the *Zeitgeist*.[1] To Eisenman this exaggerated emphasis on the "actual" results in either a naive empiricism that wrongly imagines architecture as an applied social science—surveying, analyzing, and solving quantifiable design problems—or a contrary escapism that takes "refuge in mannerism and the cult of self expression."[2]

More specifically, Eisenman has claimed that his dissertation was a direct response to another—that of former Cambridge undergraduate Christopher Alexander—the text which would become the popular design methods book, *Notes on the Synthesis of Form*.[3] Eisenman was not wrong to identify the growing influence of data-driven functionalism in the early 1960s. Under the banner of "design methods" such approaches were beginning a decade-long run at the center of architectural research and debate. The University of Cambridge itself would play an important role in the design methods movement through the Centre for Land Use and Built Form Study (today the Martin Centre) founded by Alexander's classmate Lionel March in 1966.[4] Though rooted in pre-existing rhetorics of functionalism—and at Cambridge explicitly understood as a revival of the most hard-nosed strand of Soviet Constructivism—the sudden appeal of quantitative design methods in the 1960s was a direct result of the Second World War. Chief among the war's effects was the introduction of electronic computing, which combined with operations research and a centralization of Britain's building industry to create an environment in which architecture (among many other fields) turned to quantitative methods as an indication of rigor, seriousness, objectivity, and intellectual weight (not to mention fundability). Anxious at the emergence of this tendency, Eisenman's reaction was, as he has termed it, "dialectical."[5] Perhaps more than intended, the term is apt, since his rebuttal of the design methods approach was itself largely shaped by the postwar interest in logic, methodology, rigor, and—conceptually at least—computation.

In contrast to postwar functionalism, Eisenman's first concern in his dissertation is with architecture as a communicative act, the success of which, he argues, depends upon the clarity of its medium:

> The essence of any creative act is the communication of an original idea from its author, through a means of expression, to a receiver. The means of expression must be such as to transmit the original intention as clearly and fully as possible to the receiving mind. This need for clarity and comprehensibility, so much stressed by the Gestalt psychologists, is critical to the development of any means of communication.[6]

Emphasizing the deeply disorienting condition of the postwar world, Eisenman argues that effective communication will require the establishment of a hierarchy among the "elements" of the "architectural equation." Within this hierarchy, "temporal ends"—"intent, function, structure and technics"—must be subservient to "absolute ends":

> ... our social, economic and technological environment has become so overwhelmingly distended that no significant order can be perceived by the individual. . . . [The] need for individual expression is a legitimate one, but if it is to be satisfied without prejudice to the comprehensibility of the environment as a whole, a general priority system must be proposed; and it will be argued here that such a system must necessarily give preference to absolute over temporal ends.[7]

Influenced by Colin Rowe's application of Rudolf Wittkower's methods to modernism, and by his own "revelation" before Giuseppe Terragni's work in Como, Eisenman proposes that it is form, as an absolute end, that must be raised to "a position of primacy" in a hierarchy of architectural concerns. Yet, in order to serve as a secure and ideal basis of clear architectural communication, form itself must be subdivided and a distinction made between generic and specific form: "The term generic form is here understood to mean form thought of in a Platonic sense, as a definable entity with its own inherent laws."[8] Generic form has a "transcendent or universal nature" with properties that "stand above any aesthetic preferences." There are also, in this argument, only two types of generic form: linear and centroidal (Figure 6.1) each possessing "certain inherent dynamics, and these must be understood and respected if any grammatical usage or interpretation of a given solid is to be attempted." Going further—and anticipating his later discovery of Noam Chomsky's linguistic theories—Eisenman next makes an important distinction between architecture and the "pictorial" examples of the Gestalt theorists:

> ... we must introduce the notion of movement, and postulate that an experience of architecture is the sum of a large number of experiences—each one of them apprehended visually, it is true as well as through other senses; but accumulated over a much longer time span than is required for the initial appreciation of a pictorial work; and building up into a conceptual, not a perceptual, whole. And since this whole is conceptual it must have a clarity of concept; its argument must be intellectually as well as visually comprehensible.... The need for formal clarity and unmistakable reference to some well-understood archetypal solid thereby becomes still more urgent, since the person experiencing any organisation must be able to hold in his visual and somatic memory at the end of the process everything which has impinged upon it since the beginning.[9]

Thus, Eisenman's career began with an argument that architecture should be understood as a logic of form: a set of conceptual operations rigorously based on the universal properties of a small number of primary geometric elements. Nor was this intensely argued position short-lived. Merged with ideas from Chomsky and conceptual art, it continued to provide the ground of Eisenman's practice at least through the 1972 publication of *Five Architects*, where the argument made in his dissertation provides the intellectual framework for his first houses:

> There is often an attempt made to rationalize architecture in terms of its program.... [In 1957] Sir John Summerson represented this position quite explicitly when he attempted to make a case for a theory of architecture with such a programmatic basis. In essence, Summerson said the source of unity in modern architecture is in the social sphere, in other words, in the architect's program. But ... if the program is to sustain such an emphasis, it should be able to specify and distinguish what the facts of a particular situation are, and except for certain physical laws, facts in a programmatic sense are in reality a series of value judgements. Much of the oeuvre of modern architectural theory is involved in a basic dilemma precisely because it has refused to distinguish between problems of fact and problems of value, and, more

Sean Keller

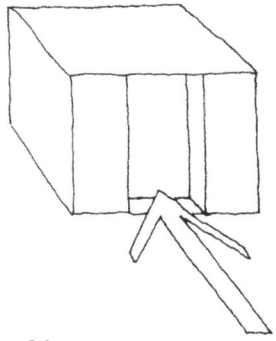

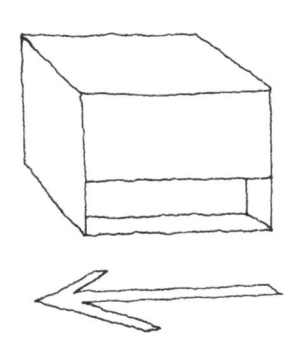

26.
DISTORTION OF GENERIC STATE DIFFERENT FOR AXES PERPENDICULAR OR PARALLEL

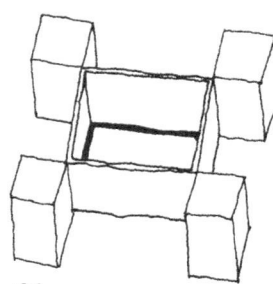

27.
CENTROIDAL SYNTAX:
ACKNOWLEDGEMENT OF CENTER
RECOGNITION OF ABSOLUTE HORIZONTAL
ARTICULATION IN SOME WAY OF CORNERS

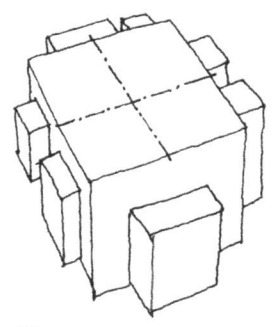

28.
LINEAR SYNTAX:
LINEAR NATURE OF FORM
EXPRESSION OF DOMINANT AXIS
AND DOMINANT PLANE OF REFERENCE
ARTICULATION OF ENDS.

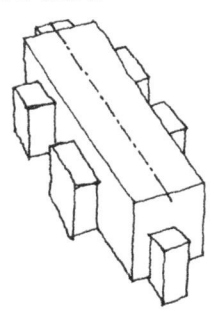

29.
INTERNAL CONFLICT PRODUCES DISTORTIONS:
CENTROIDAL THEATRE IN GENERIC STATE MAY
BE DISTORTED BY SPECIFIC CONDITIONS TO PRODUCE
A LINEAR FORM

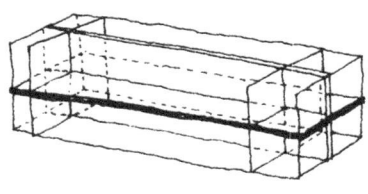

6.1
Peter Eisenman, centroidal and linear syntaxes, "The Formal Basis of Modern Architecture," 1963

specifically, because it has refused to recognize problems of form as predicated by anything except ideas of social and technological change or as matters for stylistic and aesthetic speculation. . . .

The making of form can, for instance, be considered as a problem of logical consistency, as a consequence of the logical structure inherent in any formal relationship. The making of form in this sense is more than the satisfaction of functional requirements and more than the creation of aesthetically pleasing objects, but rather the exposition of a set of formal relationships. [10]

This logic of form was meant to provide architecture with autonomy from the field of ever-shifting postwar demands, thereby offering Eisenman an escape from his anxiety of the "actual." Anxiety is the correct term here because Eisenman was concerned with what he understood to be the very existence of architecture itself—its autonomy—which design methods threatened to subjugate to the rule of other, ostensibly more scientific, fields. Eisenman's concern was an existential anxiety *for* architecture, for its existence in the wake of the Second World War (Reyner Banham's epochal conclusion to *Theory and Design in the First Machine Age* had raised the same question, while offering an opposing answer).[11] Yet, while in this early period he presented autonomy as a universal antidote to the anxieties of the postwar condition, Eisenman would soon discover both that autonomy contained its own internal anxieties and that it offered, not relief, but a provocation to further anxiety.

Anxieties of Autonomy

After completing his dissertation at Cambridge, Eisenman returned to the United States, began teaching at Princeton University, founded and ran both the Institute for Architecture and Urban Studies in New York and the influential journal *Oppositions*, and began his architectural practice. The first results of the practice were designs for a series of houses, some built, some not: House I (1967–1968, in fact, an addition to an existing house), House II (1969–1970), House III (1969–1971), and so on through the punningly named House El even Odd (1980). The numbering of these projects, in place of the traditional use of clients' names, reflected both Eisenman's ongoing interest in a quasi-logical exploration of architectural design and his new engagement with the New York art scene of the 1960s, especially conceptual art and minimalism.

The house series began as an extension of the logic of form described in Eisenman's dissertation, but now deployed as a syntax for the generation of architecture. Directly recalling the analytic drawings of the dissertation, the houses were presented through increasingly extensive sets of axonometric diagrams (Figure 6.2) that suggested an autonomous, semiautomatic, process of formal generation: step-by-step a simple initial volume seems to be multiply subdivided, shifted, sheared, rotated, and intersected to arrive at a densely complex, though apparently arbitrary, end state. Eisenman was explicit about the presumption of logic behind the first houses:

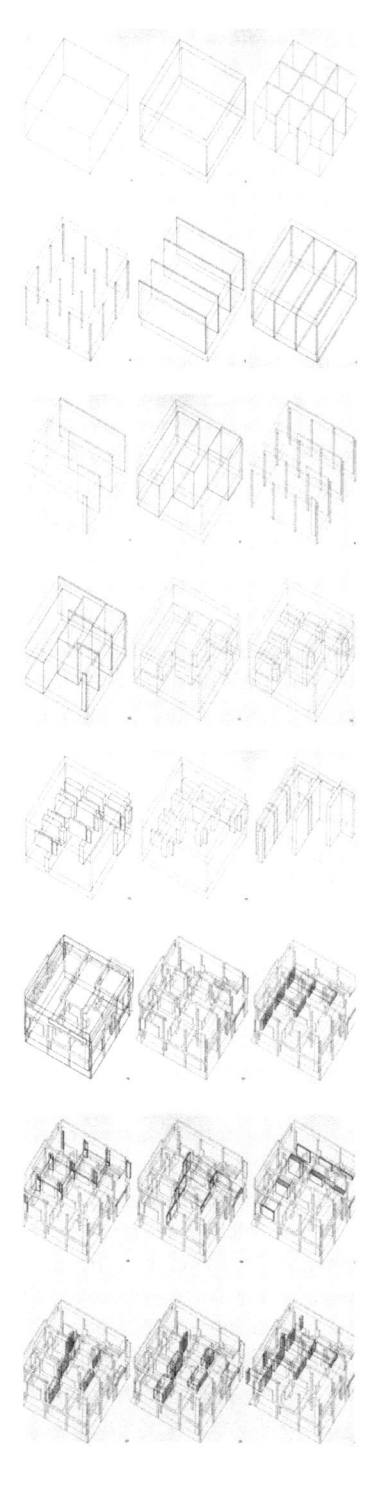

6.2
Peter Eisenman, diagrams of House II, 1972

House I was an attempt to conceive of and understand the physical environment in a logically consistent manner, potentially independent of its function and its meaning....

House I posits one alternative to existing conceptions of spatial organization. Here there was an attempt, first, to find ways in which form and space could be structured so that they would produce a set of formal relationships which is the result of the inherent logic in the forms themselves, and, second, to control precisely the logical relationships of forms....

[Interpreting this underlying logic] does not depend entirely on the observer's particular cultural background, his subjective perceptions, or his particular mood at a given time, all of which condition his usual experience of an actual environment, but rather it depends on his innate capacity to understand formal structures.[12]

Echoing the architect, critics understood the early projects in these terms: in House III "the basic volume of the cubes was progressively elaborated and refined through a rigorous and systematic series of 'movements' . . ."[13]

Yet simultaneously Eisenman was deploying techniques that challenged the idea of logical consistency and began to open up possibilities for indeterminacy, even anxiety, within the autonomous design methods he was advocating. Primary among these was the multiplication of "formal structures" underlying each project. For example, in House I "the formal structure was in a sense over-stressed or over-articulated so that it would become a dominant aspect of the building. One means to over-stress such a structure was to suggest two simultaneous structures which overlay and interact."[14] Each of the overlaid structures is intended to indicate a "deep structure" of diagonally shifted volumes, which is not directly perceivable. Thus—despite initial appearances, common critical readings, and Eisenman's own suggestions—the set of diagrams for any one of the houses does not chart a single continuous sequence of development, and it surely does not follow a linear "logic" in the sense that each stage is necessarily determined by the preceding.[15] Instead each set of diagrams is best read as a record of multiple simultaneous determinations of the project, which are superimposed in the final state. The aim, about which Eisenman became increasingly articulate, was a building that would stimulate a process of continual, irresolvable interpretation, as any element could be read as the trace of multiple, overlaid formal processes.

The nonlinear design process of the houses was neatly revealed by a short film, *Castelli di Carte: Transformations Series B*, that Eisenman made for the 1973 Milan Triennale. The film of over one thousand frames was composed of diagrams of House IV that flip by, rapidly building up from simple initial forms—a cube of lines, a cube of planes, a solid cube—to a complex palimpsest resembling the built house and then decomposing again into the initial cubes. While there are short passages of the film that convey a sense of organic development, the overall effect is dominated by jarring cuts between alternative "interpretations" of the house. Even Eisenman was surprised by the film's disjunctive quality and its demonstration that "What seemed to be a logical set of moves . . . was shown to be flawed."[16]

With House II (Figure 6.3), Eisenman extended the conceptual ambiguity to the elements of the composition. For example, the distinction between column and plane, which House I sought to maintain, was collapsed, so that a thin vertical element could be understood equally well as a positively determined "column" and as the residue of an imaginary intersection of a planar solid and a prismatic void. Eisenman described this as a shift toward a general use of conceptual "bi-valency."[17] This possibility of a simultaneity of interpretations—which had been taken up from Rowe and Robert Slutzky's concept of "phenomenal transparency," and which in the dissertation had existed uncomfortably along with the drive for universal clarity—became the central technique of what Eisenman began to call "conceptual architecture." The creation of such an architecture—though initiated by an ideal of logical consistency—paradoxically seemed to require ever greater levels of ambiguity in the material building. Where the dissertation had suggested that form would sit atop a hierarchy of elements that included structure and materiality, the houses were designed not just to subordinate, but to negate such physical concerns:

> All of the apparent structural apparatus—the exposed beams, the freestanding columns—are in fact non-structural. . . . Once one has understood that they are not structural one must ask what are they? Why are they where they are? Take them away, or change their shape, and what have you got?[18]

Similarly, the only possible materialization of a "conceptual architecture" came to be an anti-material "Cardboard Architecture," which blurred traditional distinctions of representation and scale:

> Cardboard is used to question the nature of our perception of reality and thus the meanings ascribed to reality . . . the term raises the question of the form in relation to the process of design: is this a building or is it a model?[19]

Last in this catalogue of bi-valencies was the dominance of axonometric conception, prominently displayed by the layers of diagrams in which each house was encrusted. Evoking the prewar avant-gardes, especially De Stijl and Constructivism, this mode of representation, as Kenneth Frampton has pointed out, "always allowed one to distance oneself from the immediate presence of the space."[20]

The complexity and ambiguity of Eisenman's "conceptual architecture" become particularly apparent when contrasted with the work of Sol LeWitt, to which Eisenman made reference, and which the houses, or at least their diagrams, superficially resemble.[21] As Rosalind Krauss has argued, the work of LeWitt and other Minimalists—Donald Judd, Robert Smithson, Robert Morris—was not a celebration of Cartesian thought, but an undermining of such "false and pious rationality"

6.3
Peter Eisenman, House II, Hardwick, Vermont, 1969–1970

through an "absurdist Nominalism" (Judd's famous "just one thing after another").[22] Krauss points out that in works like *122 Variations of Incomplete Open Cubes* (1974; Figure 6.4) "[t]he babble of a LeWitt serial expansion has nothing of the economy of the mathematicians language."[23] In contrast, Eisenman, during this same period, framed his practice through Chomsky's revival of "Cartesian Linguistics" and remained committed to the "deep structure" of a presumed architectural logic. This opposition in attitude explains the opposition in results: it is only because of his belief in a transcendental logic of conception that Eisenman felt compelled to create houses that were so complex in their material realization, while LeWitt could use "the idea of error" to spit out arrays of mindless forms.[24] Similarly, the relationship to historical context also diverges: where LeWitt produced deadpan parodies of postwar computation, Eisenman battles the logic of functionalism with an equally earnest logic of form.

The cumulative result of the techniques Eisenman developed in the first houses was a frequently repeated anxiety over the work's status as architecture, an anxiety most fully reflected in the book, *Peter Eisenman's House VI: The Client's Response*, particularly in Paul Goldberger's article, "The House as Sculptural Object,"

Sean Keller

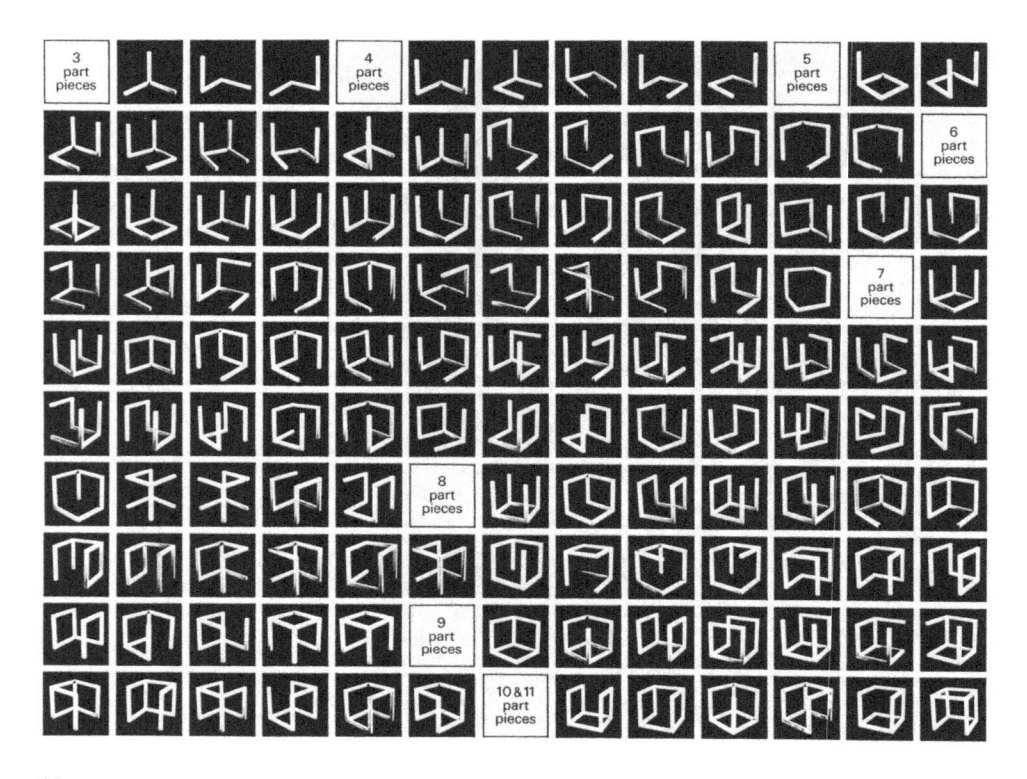

6.4
Sol LeWitt, *Variations of Incomplete Open Cubes*, 1974

reprinted there.²⁵ In fact Eisenman was encountering precisely the problems that other logicians of medium-specificity had faced: having claimed that the essence of architecture rested in formal concepts, Eisenman's efforts to construct buildings driven purely by such concepts seemed to result in something that might not be architecture at all.

    While his "conceptual architecture" of the 1970s was still intended as a response to the anxiety for autonomy described in his dissertation, Eisenman incompletely, but importantly, began to shift from formal logic to formal ambiguity as the means of achieving this autonomy. Through the course of the house series the dissertation-like claims for a transcendent, ahistorical architectural logic were increasingly replaced by anxiety-making ambiguity within the formal processes—a trend eventually shaped by Eisenman's involvement with the anti-foundationalism of Jacques Derrida during the 1980s. Yet, the desire for an autonomous architectural logic has never entirely disappeared: it recurs for example in Eisenman's recent descriptions of his career as an exploration of architecture's "interiority."²⁶ In fact, we might best read the house series—and Eisenman's entire oeuvre—as an anxious use of formal logic: one which simultaneously suggests and frustrates the notion that his architecture is generated by some autonomous, rigorous, self-determining process (see the parallel discussion of Eisenman's "humanism" below). This character of his work was established by the early 1970s, when Eisenman determined that his anxiety *for* the autonomy of postwar architecture could only be addressed through the anxieties *of* the autonomous architectural object.

Autonomy for Anxiety

While Eisenman initially intended his formal logic as a response to the anxieties of the postwar condition, he eventually came to understand that his formalism—especially when deployed to create domestic space—produced anxiety of its own. In regard to the house series, Eisenman has written that the extreme formalism of the projects, their stripping away of semantic references, and their multiplication of competing conceptual readings all work to produce a Brechtian estrangement—denying any comforting associations of "house" and forcing the occupants to consciously grapple with the architecture.[27] Thus, while an interest in formal autonomy runs consistently from his dissertation forward, the purpose of this autonomy shifts from the assuagement of anxiety to its provocation.

This shift, signs of which first appear in the late 1960s, grows out of the unavoidable difficulties of materializing his highly abstract, supposedly pure, formal logic as actual buildings—at the seam between the conceptual deep structure and the physical structure of the house itself. Here examples of "conceptual" work in other media, especially sculpture, proved instructive to Eisenman, as he refined his understanding of such an approach in architecture:

> . . . the idea of an architecture as distinguished from a painting will always contain in the idea, ideas of functional and semantically weighted objects such as walls, bathrooms, closets, doors, ceilings. There is no conceptual aspect in architecture which can be thought of without the concept of pragmatic and functional objects, otherwise it is not an architectural conception. . . . To make something conceptual in architecture would require taking the pragmatic and functional aspects and plac[ing] them in a conceptual matrix, where their primary existence is no longer interpreted from the physical fact of being a bathroom or closet, but rather the functional aspect bathroom or closet becomes secondary to some primary reading as a notation in a conceptual context.[28]

Paradoxically, then, in an essay devoted to "conceptual architecture," Eisenman found himself needing to claim that—in contrast to work like LeWitt's sculptures—architecture was differentiated by pragmatics and function, precisely those concerns of the "actual" that his dissertation had rejected. The position advanced here—which represents the key to the House series and perhaps to all of Eisenman's most convincing work—is that architecture is, in fact, defined by the contradictions and tensions between the pragmatic and the conceptual, between the actual and the autonomous.

Though described in "Conceptual Architecture," the full potential of this tension was not immediately applied, so that through the publication of *Five Architects* Eisenman largely continued to maintain the detached, neo-Platonic tone of his dissertation:

> At present most buildings are burdened by their very description as "museums" or "country houses" with a weight of cultural meaning which is here meant to be neutralized by the opposition of an equally loaded term [cardboard]. . . .
>
> In House II there is a concern for space as the subject of logical discourse. Such a logical structure of space aims not to comment on the country house as a cultural symbol but to be neutral with respect to its existing social meanings.[29]

This attitude shifted with the publication of House III (Figure 6.5), when Eisenman—in an article titled "To Adolph Loos and Bertold Brecht"—recognized that the "questioning" provoked by the logical structure was a primary and deep attribute of the project, though he strained to insist that such provocation arose "quite unintentionally" (a claim which the dedication to Loos and Brecht greatly undercuts):

> It has become clear to me that any attempt to express this concern for the [logical] structure of the form in the actual form itself tends to isolate the individual from the environment of that form. . . .
>
> . . . Since a structure per se has no meaning, any understanding of it is dependent on some sense of itself—its logical consistency, its appearance of certainty or completeness. . . . This expression of the formal system produces an architecture divested of traditional meaning, that admits no adjustment and alteration; it excludes the design of those things which, through design, reinforce traditional meaning, such as interior finishes, the location and style of furniture, or the installation of lighting. Consequently while the architectural system—the formal structure—may be complete, the environment "house" is almost void. And quite unintentionally . . . the owner has been alienated from his environment.
>
> In this sense, when the owner first enters "his house" he is an intruder; he must begin to regain possession—to occupy a foreign container. . . . The interior "void" resulting from a complete architectural structure seems to act as both a background and a foil, almost as a conscious stimulant for the activity of the owner. . . . In such a situation, choosing interior finishes, adding walls, placing furniture, and installing lighting, is no longer concerned with the purpose of fitting some preconceived idea of good taste or completing some "set piece" scheme of either the owner or the architect.[30]

Here, it is helpful to draw a brief comparison with Viktor Shklovsky's classic description of such "defamiliarization"—a description that Krauss also raises

6.5
Peter Eisenman, House III, Lakeville, Connecticut, 1969–1971

in her essay on Eisenman.[31] Importantly, for Shklovsky, it is precisely the amnesia-inducing "automatism"—even "algebrization"—of everyday perception that art should work against (his well-known illustration is Tolstoy's inability to say whether he had, or had not, dusted a divan). By impeding communication art "deautomatizes" perception. In these terms, Eisenman's work presents an interesting case in which one automatism, that of domestic mindlessness, is interrupted and deautomatized by the presence of another, the automatism of a formal logic, which in itself is equally mindless. Alone either automatism would be mindless—a point suggested by the ironical epigraph from Shklovsky in Krauss's essay on LeWitt—it is only their confrontation that is simulating. Shklovsky gives several methods by which poetry impedes language, and Eisenman's approach is closest to the "roughening" of language through repetition which makes pronunciation difficult. Yet, Shklovsky says, in art this repetition cannot become the regular rhythm of prose or folk song, but must itself be disrupted. This too applies nicely to Eisenman's difficult repetitions.

Oddly, while the text accompanying House III marks Eisenman's full grasp of the potentially estranging effects of his logical structures, it is also the most traditionally functional of all of the houses in the series—a point emphasized by one pleasantly surprised reviewer:

> Even though the drawings indicated places such as "kitchen," bedroom," "bath," etc., it was difficult for me to interpret how the volumes so indicated represented . . . spaces that people could actually live in with even a modicum of comfort and privacy. . . .

> Not until I was actually inside the house did I gradually come to realize that not only does it function as a house, but it performs well as one, perhaps even better than many that avow a great concern for function. . . .
>
> The arrangement of spaces could hardly be more practical or functional. . . . You begin to appreciate . . . that the form and the function of this house are one, that they are inextricably bound to each other, and that neither could exist as it does without the other.[32]

Eisenman must have recoiled from such apparent praise. The next, and last, of the houses to be built, House VI (Figure 6.6), proved to be an emphatic rejection of this all-too-easy reconciliation of conceptual rigor and quotidian existence, and the culmination of his exploration of autonomy and domestic anxiety. Taking the Brechtian rhetoric seriously, House VI was a direct, not incidental, attack, via "logical

6.6
Peter Eisenman, House VI, Cornwall, Connecticut, 1972–1975

structure," on residential norms, as evidenced by a catalogue of instantly notorious—and lovingly photographed—affronts: the column that displaced guests at the dining table; the column on hinges that compensated for a too-narrow doorway; the sink in an upstairs closet; the inverted red "stair" suggesting that the entire house might be flipped over; and—most primally—the slot in the bedroom floor dividing the beds of man and wife (Figure 6.7).

Yet the disruptions of the project ran deeper than such practical provocations. House VI not only disrupted the general concept "house," it was also an inversion of specific tropes of De Stijl houses, by which Eisenman hoped to achieve a "reduction of metaphor."[33] This entailed emptying the meaning of the horizontal datum; the contradiction of the horizontal and vertical emphases; the inversion of his own earlier houses in order to place the "façades" at the center; and the opposition of oblique conception and frontal experience. Through this radical questioning of architectural metaphors—which, of course, required an acknowledgment of them—House VI moved out of the Platonic world of form and into the history of architecture itself. Doing so allowed Eisenman to challenge fundamental assumptions that the previous houses had left intact:

> What was a facade? Why should it be on the outside? Was it a cultural or formal referent? Would it be possible to invert the conception and reality of the facades of the first four houses and place them at the center . . . ? That is, one would walk through the space to come to the "entry" (or beginning) of conception.[34]

Lastly, at its deepest level (to use Eisenman's own metaphor), House VI attempted to destabilize the very conceptual structure on which it was based:

> House VI, then, represents a change. In House II and IV the architectural notations existed to produce a mental landscape, to suggest an alternative reality and an alternative experience and meaning of architecture. But in House VI, the experience of the physical environment does not lead to any mental structure. . . . In other words a particular juxtaposition of solids and voids produces a situation that is only resolved by the mind's finding the need to change the position of the elements. . . . This produces within the mind a sense of tension or compression in a particular space that is not created through the juxtaposition of real walls, but is instead in our conception of their *potential* location. . . .[35]

Collectively, the new strategies of House VI seemed to mark an important shift for Eisenman away from his early Platonism and into another, less idealist, position. Eisenman himself has made this observation, as well as Krauss, who has drawn a somewhat strained parallel to her own transition from "formalism" to "structuralism."[36] Yet, whatever transition occurred with House VI, it was far more subtle and incomplete than a simple change of ideological uniforms. Take, for example, this scene:

6.7
Above: Peter Eisenman, House VI, dining area with red and green stairs, Cornwall, Connecticut, 1972–1975
Below: Peter Eisenman, House VI, bedroom, Cornwall, Connecticut, 1972–1975

> *House VI, Eisenman and Robert A.M. Stern seated at opposite ends of a couch.*
>
> *Stern*: You've rather turned five thousand years of culture upside down, it seems to me.
>
> *Eisenman*: Well, I think that architects have traditionally been very slow to understand that culture has been turned upside down all by itself. When we have science fiction movies, the people from Mars come down, and they speak in mathematical terms—in mathematical terms because it's a universal language. This house, in a sense, speaks in mathematical terms the Martians could understand.
>
> What that is saying is that you don't have to be from the elite of society, you don't have to know architectural history, cultural history, social history. You just have to come and experience the house. This is a house that any man can understand and be sensitive to because it speaks in universal terms. . . .
>
> . . . It doesn't speak in the classical conventions that only the learned and the elite understand. It's a house for everyman. That's exactly what I'm saying, and it speaks to the America of today, not to the patrician America of two centuries ago.
>
> *Stern*: (*In a voice-over.*) Whether for Every-Man or Every-Martian, House VI is most compelling as a dream monologue of the subconscious.[37]

Here, in the mid-1980s, is Eisenman still talking about the importance of his architecture being universally comprehensible, even reassuringly so—precisely the issue that motivated his dissertation two decades earlier. Yet, what is comically emphasized is that it is the very striving for universal comprehension, outside cultural (or even planetary) specifics, that turns the house into an alien outpost. This brief exchange exposes a long-running conundrum: even after House VI, is Eisenman's conception of the subject—"Every-Man or Every-Martian"—posthumanist? In one somewhat exaggerated sense, yes: he forcefully rejects all "patrician" cultural references in favor of an abstract mathematical language. But, in another sense, no: Eisenman obviously continues to believe that this formal language reaches a "deeper" universal subject that lies beneath the cultural "surface." (Here the impact of Chomsky's "Cartesian" linguistics continues. Eisenman's reference to Martians is also similar to Shklovsky's reference to Tolstoy's use of a horse as a narrator— each relies on a "deeper" sensibility to defamiliarize human conventions.)

In a provocative essay on this issue, Sarah Whiting has described a "stark contrast" between Rowe's humanism and Eisenman's posthumanism, which she sees beginning with Eisenman's dissertation. This overlooks the continuity, argued for here, of Eisenman's early position with that of Rowe (and "early" sometimes stretches surprisingly late, as in the interview with Stern).[38] Such a clear distinction, which Eisenman himself has tried to retroactively construct, is only possible if one exaggerates both Rowe's humanism and Eisenman's shift into some form of posthumanism. In fact, in his 1973 addendum to "The Mathematics of the Ideal Villa," Rowe is at pains to point out the "limitations" of his method—including its inability to deal with content and its possible tedium.[39] There is nothing in his tone that suggests a humanist revival, and Rowe's only positive claim for his formalism closely echoes Eisenman: it may be widely accessible because it relies on few external references. On the other side, while Eisenman did begin developing a formalism of "exteriority," which split from the object-oriented approach of the Rowe/Wittkower lineage, this began only with the Cannaregio project of 1978.

Further complicating any theoretical parsing is Eisenman's return, even in the late 1980s, to an explicitly existentialist vocabulary and to the consequences of the Second World War:

> With the scientifically orchestrated horror of Hiroshima and the consciousness of the human brutality of the Holocaust it became impossible for man to sustain a relationship with any of the dominant cosmologies of his past; he could no longer derive his identity from a belief in a heroic purpose and future. Survival became his only "heroic" possibility. . . . For the first time in history, man was faced with no way of assuaging his unmediated confrontation with an existential anxiety.
>
> Man now lives in this *in extremis* condition. . . . This uncertainty calls into question the symbolism of all such markers of identity, not just those ultimate ones, but the daily institutions of church, school, house. The estranging vector moving out from the center is not subject to man's volition, and no post-modern retreat into simulated symbols of a benign past can mask it. The anxiety that the architecture of this book addresses, and to which it resolutely responds, exists.[40]

Thus, despite attempted rewritings, it is crucial to recognize the distinction between Eisenman's existential—and therefore modernist—anxiety and a (post)structuralist condition, in which, strictly speaking, there would be no subject for which anxiety could exist. Eisenman's anxious entanglement with autonomy, with its particular focus on domesticity, developed only because he began with, and carried forward, this earlier existential anxiety. Or, to revise Whiting's description, it is not that there was a rupture *between* Rowe and Eisenman, but a rupture *within* each of their intellectual frames. This is essentially the description Eisenman himself gave in his 1976 essay "Post-Functionalism":

> This new theoretical base changes the humanist balance of form/function to a dialectical relationship within the evolution of form itself. The dialectic can best be described as the potential co-existence within any form of two . . . tendencies. One tendency is to presume architectural form to be a recognizable transformation from some pre-existent geometric or Platonic solid. . . . This tendency is certainly a relic of humanist theory. However, to this is added a second tendency that sees architectural form in an atemporal, decompositional mode. . . . Here form is understood as

a series of fragments—signs without meaning dependent upon, and without reference to, a more basic condition.[41]

By defining his practice around an anxious logic of formal generation, Eisenman devised an approach that he could claim was inherent to architecture (its "interiority") but which also both reflected and provoked the anxieties of the postwar condition.

Notes

1. Peter Eisenman, "The Formal Basis of Modern Architecture" (Ph.D. diss., University of Cambridge, 1963); facsimile published by Lars Müller (Baden, 2006). A summary of the theoretical portion appeared as "Towards an Understanding of Form in Architecture," *Architectural Design* 33 (October 1963): 457–458.
2. Eisenman, "The Formal Basis of Modern Architecture," 29.
3. "Discord Over Harmony in Architecture: The Eisenman/Alexander Debate," *Harvard Graduate School of Design News* 2 (1983): 12; Christopher Alexander, "The Synthesis of Form: Some Notes on a Theory" (Ph.D. diss., Harvard University, 1962); revised as *Notes on the Synthesis of Form* (Cambridge, MA: Harvard University Press, 1964).
4. For more on the context of postwar Cambridge see my "Fenland Tech: Architectural Science in Postwar Cambridge," *Grey Room* 23 (Spring 2006): 40–65.
5. "Discord Over Harmony in Architecture: The Eisenman/Alexander Debate," 12.
6. Eisenman, "The Formal Basis of Modern Architecture," 25.
7. Ibid., 29.
8. Ibid., 33.
9. Ibid., 72–73.
10. Peter Eisenman, "Cardboard Architecture: House I," in *Five Architects: Eisenman, Graves, Gwathmey, Hejduk, Meier* (New York: Wittenborn & Company, 1972; New York: Oxford University Press, 1975), 15. Citations refer to the Oxford edition.
11. Eisenman returned to this theme most explicitly in "Post-Functionalism," *Oppositions* 6 (1976): i–iv.
12. Eisenman, "Cardboard Architecture: House I," 15–17.
13. David Morton, "One man's fit . . .," part of "House III: Miller Residence, Lakeville, Conn.," *Progressive Architecture*, May 1974: 92.
14. Eisenman, "Cardboard Architecture: House I," 16.
15. My focus here is limited to Eisenman's contemporaneous descriptions of his early writings and houses. An assessment of his many complicated, and likely contradictory, *retrospective* descriptions of these projects is beyond the scope of this essay. The most complete of these histories appears in Peter Eisenman, *Diagram Diaries* (New York: Universe Publishing, 1999).
16. Peter Eisenman, "Diagrams of Interiority," in Eisenman, *Diagram Diaries*, 75. My description is based on a videotape of the film shown in the exhibition *Eisenman/Krier: Two Ideologies* at the Yale School of Architecture, Fall 2002. Louis Martin curated the Eisenman portion of the show.
17. Peter Eisenman, "Cardboard Architecture: House II," in *Five Architects*, 26.
18. Eisenman, "Cardboard Architecture: House I," 16.
19. Ibid., 15.
20. Kenneth Frampton, preface to *Peter Eisenman's House VI: The Client's Response*, by Suzanne Frank (New York: Whitney Library of Design, 1994), 13.
21. See Peter Eisenman, "Notes on Conceptual Architecture: Towards a Definition" *Casabella* 359/360 (November/December 1971): 49–57. This essay was published, in some sense, about a year earlier in *Design Quarterly* 78/79 (1970), "a special double issue on 'conceptual

architecture.'" However, in keeping with the spirit of the issue, the main body of the text did not appear, leaving only the footnote numbers scattered over four pages, and the footnotes themselves. Accompanying biographical information indicated that a copy of the article (presumably with the full text visible) could be requested from Eisenman. Reference here will therefore be to the *Casabella* publication.

22 Rosalind Krauss, "LeWitt in Progress," *October* 6 (Fall 1978): 46–60.
23 Ibid., 55.
24 Krauss herself calls attention to this idealism—what she calls Eisenman's "hermeneutic phantom"—in an essay written just before the one on LeWitt. See Rosalind Krauss, "Death of a Hermeneutic Phantom: Materialization of the Sign in the Work of Peter Eisenman," dated June 1977, in *Houses of Cards*, by Peter Eisenman (New York: Oxford University Press, 1987), 166–184. Krauss's argument is greatly complicated by her simultaneous alignment of, and distinction between, her early Shklovskian formalism and Eisenman's Wittkowerian "conceptualism."
25 Frank, *Peter Eisenman's House VI*; Paul Goldberger, "The House as Sculptural Object," *New York Times Magazine*, March 20, 1977. All of the "responses" to the project—from the owners Dick and Suzanne Frank, the critics, and Eisenman himself—similarly describe the house as a difficult but ultimately domesticated creature. There emerges a quasi-ritualistic pattern in which commentary on the formal abstraction and functional anomalies of the house is always immediately balanced by remarks about the phenomenological pleasures of inhabiting it: openings and obstructions appear in all the wrong places, but the play of light is beautiful; the owner bangs his head, but learns to bend down and appreciate the architectural lessons he is learning. If the existence of the book is evidence of the anxiety the house provoked—not many dwellings demand a written response—its content demonstrates the overwhelming strength of the domestic norms Eisenman was supposedly flaunting.
26 Peter Eisenman, introduction to *Eisenman Inside Out: Selected Writings, 1963–1988* (New Haven: Yale University Press, 2004), vii; and Peter Eisenman, "Diagrams of Interiority," in Eisenman, *Diagram Diaries*, 44–93.
27 Peter Eisenman, "House III: To Adolf Loos and Berthold Brecht," part of "House III: Miller Residence, Lakeville, Conn.," *Progressive Architecture*, May 1974: 92.
28 Eisenman, "Notes on Conceptual Architecture," 51.
29 Eisenman, "Cardboard Architecture: House II," 27.
30 Eisenman, "House III: To Adolf Loos and Berthold Brecht," 92.
31 Viktor Shklovsky, "Art as Technique" (1917), in *Russian Formalist Criticism: Four Essays*, trans. Lee T. Lemon and Marion J. Reis (Lincoln, NE: University of Nebraska Press, 1965), 3–24; Krauss, "Death of a Hermeneutic Phantom," 168.
32 Morton, "One man's fit . . . ," 92–94.
33 Peter Eisenman, "House VI," *Progressive Architecture* (June 1977): 59.
34 Ibid.
35 Ibid.
36 Krauss, "Death of a Hermeneutic Phantom."
37 Robert A.M. Stern, "Dream Houses," *Pride of Place: Building the American Dream*, episode 3, directed by Murray Grigor (Films for the Humanities: 1986), VHS.
38 Sarah Whiting, "Euphoric Ratio," in *Tracing Eisenman: Peter Eisenman: Complete Works*, ed. Cynthia Davidson (London: Thames & Hudson, 2006), 91–111.
39 Colin Rowe, "The Mathematics of the Ideal Villa," in *The Mathematics of the Ideal Villa and Other Essays* (Cambridge, MA: MIT Press, 1976), 1–27.
40 Peter Eisenman, "Misreading Peter Eisenman," in *Houses of Cards*, 170/2.
41 Eisenman, "Post-Functionalism," iv.

Part 3

Societies of Consumers

Materialist Ideologies and Postwar Goods

Chapter 7

"But a home is not a laboratory"
The Anxieties of Designing for the Socialist Home in the German Democratic Republic 1950–1965

Katharina Pfützner

In the first fifteen years of the German Democratic Republic's (GDR) existence cultural politicians attempted to define a suitable approach to the design of objects for the domestic realm. This approach, rooted in an anxiety to shape an alternative, distinctly socialist idea of the modern home, drew on the doctrine of socialist realism and rejected modernism. During the same period, the industrial design community of the GDR continued to support a modernist approach to design, which manifested itself in the large-scale emergence of professionally designed mass-produced objects for domestic use that followed a modernist idiom. This divergence between official rhetoric and design practice points to a significant conflict which will be the focus of this essay.

Although it gave rise to much tension and anxiety, this conflict has not yet been examined and explained satisfactorily. Instead there has been a tendency to downplay the dispute. Scholars have generally acknowledged some early socialist realist polemic against "formalist" (i.e. modernist) design and against the Bauhaus.[1] But the existence of modern designed objects dating from the second half of the 1950s has led some accounts to conclude that, after a brief flurry of condemnations in the early 1950s, the official denunciation of modernism was somehow reversed and industrial design was exempt from larger efforts to establish a socialist realist culture.[2]

Furthermore, the two rival perspectives have so far remained rather obscure. While several writers on GDR design have cited some of the early anti-modernist polemic, there has been little serious engagement with the underlying position it was informed by.[3] As a result the rejection of modernist design and of the

Bauhaus heritage has tended to be portrayed exclusively as a response to international Cold War politics, while disregarding the impact of domestic cultural-political concerns.[4] Meanwhile the modernist approach adopted by GDR designers has been similarly misconstrued. Scholars often assume that the official denunciation of the Bauhaus effectively prevented GDR designers from appropriating its ideas and attribute the modern quality of GDR design to their seeking *stylistic* inspiration from concurrent West German or Scandinavian design, rather than considering a more direct, but unauthorized, domestic appropriation of the Bauhaus heritage.[5] In fact, both parties to the dispute appear to have been motivated by a persistently articulated anxiety to fulfill the cultural needs of the citizens of the GDR, although they evidently diverged on the exact nature of such needs.

This essay argues that postwar design in the GDR was fraught with considerably more anxiety than has been suggested so far. To this effect it will focus on the previously neglected domestic concerns which, it contends, primarily fueled the discord in question. It will also argue that the conflict was serious and sustained, lasting until at least the mid-1960s, and that therefore the apparent divergence between design practice and rhetoric must be explained in terms of GDR designers having a substantial degree of independent agency. This indicates the importance of questioning prevailing assumptions arising from orthodox explanatory models, such as the totalitarian paradigm in the case of GDR historiography, while interpreting evidence from a wide variety of sources.[6]

The Socialist Realist Home

In the immediate postwar period the GDR officially adopted the Soviet doctrine of socialist realism to guide efforts to promote the establishment of a new socialist culture. The core idea of this doctrine, as outlined in a number of high-profile newspaper articles at the time, was that the arts were instrumental in raising the social consciousness of the people. Therefore it was considered necessary that cultural output impart important themes and values in a comprehensible and inspiring manner.[7] This provided the argument for a sweeping rejection of "formalism," understood as a prioritization of form over content or meaning, which advocates of socialist realism identified in modern art, particularly in abstract art, but also—far less plausibly—in modernist architecture and design.[8] Instead, artists were urged to critically appropriate Germany's classical cultural heritage, which was viewed as offering guidance on "how to speak to the people in an artistic language that is intelligible to the people."[9] A further significant aspect of the socialist realist position was its national orientation. In the GDR the appropriation of the German cultural heritage and the rejection of international tendencies, such as modernism, were claimed to be vital to counteract the perceived erosion of the German national consciousness resulting from the significant cultural influence exerted by the "imperialist" United States over the Federal Republic of Germany at this time.[10] In a resolution passed at the third party congress of the ruling *Sozialistische Einheitspartei Deutschlands* (SED) in July 1950 "formalism" was thus described as rooted in "cosmopolitanism" and infamously declared a "weapon of imperialism."[11]

These general and abstract principles, summed up by the slogan "*national in form, socialist in content*," clearly did not constitute straightforward guidelines for practitioners. In fact, many cultural spheres in the GDR struggled with the doctrine's interpretation, giving rise to widespread discussions in the early 1950s—the so-called Formalism Debate. Designers had particular difficulties with the idea of "socialist content," as the applied arts, unlike the fine arts, had no tradition of prioritizing the communication of complex themes or narratives. Further complications arose when it became clear that "kitsch" and historicist imitation were also to be avoided.[12] Industrial design, still in its infancy and therefore lacking the support of dedicated theorists and without any Soviet precedent to refer to, largely relied on architects to translate socialist realist principles into the realm of design.[13]

Among architects it was Kurt Liebknecht, president of the GDR's authoritative German Academy of Architecture, who most vocally sought to advance an interpretation of the doctrine for his field.[14] He proclaimed in published texts and speeches that socialist realist buildings and interiors should express the new social order in existence in the GDR—the "reign of workers and peasants."[15] This meant, he argued, that domestic interiors for the working population of the GDR should be embellished with decorative elements derived from architectural styles which had characterized the dwellings of the ruling classes of bygone eras—he particularly recommended Neo-Classicism, but also advocated Renaissance, Baroque, Chippendale, and Biedermeier.[16] Modernist architecture, on the other hand, with its explicit rejection of ornament, was deemed to lack meaning; it was considered too intent upon a radical rupture with cultural tradition, on the one hand, and with notions of national difference, on the other, to provide suitable inspiration for socialist realist interiors.[17] This perspective culminated in the highly problematic equation in the sphere of design of modernism with "formalism" and its consequent rejection. The modular furniture manufactured by the renowned *Deutsche Werkstätten Hellerau*, for example, especially Bruno Paul's popular system *Wachsende Wohnung*, was repeatedly denounced as "formalist" (Figure 7.1).[18]

Liebknecht's argument that the appropriation of certain historical styles would lead to domestic interiors which best reflected the ideal of "socialist content" seemed further strengthened by the claim that the resulting output coincided with the aesthetic preferences of ordinary people within the socialist society.[19] Consequently the "taste" of the people was repeatedly invoked by supporters of this approach, as for example, very potently, by the General Secretary of the SED's Central Committee Walter Ulbricht, a trained cabinet maker, who asserted in an address delivered at a 1952 interior architecture seminar that:

> The furniture which has been manufactured in the Bauhaus Style does not conform to the aesthetic preferences of the modern people of the new Germany. To this day some of our people's enterprises thoughtlessly imitate such primitive furniture design and do not recognize the high expectations that the working population now have on the formal beauty and comfort of our furniture.[20]

7.1
Above: Architect Ernst, Furniture range for living room and study, manufactured by VEB Ostthüringer Möbelwerke Zeulenroda, polished walnut. Example of an "exemplary" socialist realist interior, *Besser leben—schöner wohnen!* exhibition, Berlin, 1953.
Below: Bruno Paul, Furniture range *Wachsende Wohnung* (model 558), 1935, manufactured by VEB Deutsche Werkstätten Hellerau. Example of an "inadequate" modernist interior, *Besser leben—schöner wohnen!* exhibition, Berlin, 1953.

Evidently, just as socialist realist art was considered art which was intelligible to ordinary people, socialist realist design ultimately came to be seen as design which appealed to their aesthetic preferences.

The applicability of these ideas was subsequently broadened to include other household objects, when Walter Heisig, director of the Institute for Applied Art, addressed a gathering of designers in 1953 to outline the official socialist realist position on industrial design.[21] This stance included demands that designers should adhere to the wishes of the working population, who were presented as desiring "multi-colored, vibrant [furnishing] fabric patterns, which are bright and seem optimistic," rather than drab or abstract—clearly echoing the references to the population's aesthetic preferences found in architectural discourse.[22] It also entailed the adoption of the socialist realist architects' belief in the need for applied decoration. As a result Heisig bemoaned a prevailing tendency in the glass and ceramic industry to simplify forms and eliminate decoration and held up as exemplary two eighteenth-century laundry presses with elaborately carved handles, one "formed like a human figure, the other like a horse with a fishtail." This remained the officially promoted position on "socialist design" for the domestic realm for more than a decade and, while references to it disappear from published discourse in the mid-1960s, it was never actually officially overturned.

The Functionalist Socialist Home

The industrial design community of the GDR, on the other hand, supported a modernist approach to the design of domestic objects, or more specifically, an approach primarily informed by what Paul Greenhalgh has termed *Pioneer Modernism*—the socially engaged, anti-historicist, and technologically progressive output of a group of design movements, which had emerged in Europe in the 1910s and 1920s.[23] According to articles in specialist literature, designed artifacts, and oral history interviews, GDR designers particularly sympathized with the social utopian conception of design as a means to provide practical and affordable products for all layers of society, which had been formulated in modernist circles, and perhaps most forcefully at the Bauhaus, before the war. It had led to a functionalist approach to design, which prioritized an object's practical usability and its suitability for mass production, while negating the need for ostentation and social differentiation and consequently rejecting historicism and decoration.[24]

While Bauhaus publications were extremely rare in the GDR after the war, a number of former Bauhaus students had begun to work in industry or taken up posts in the GDR's main art schools or associated design institutes. In addition, the Dutch architect Mart Stam, who had taught some courses as a visiting teacher at the Bauhaus in the late 1920s, had settled in the GDR after the war and taken up leading posts in art schools in Dresden and later in Berlin. The presence of these people ensured that all industrial design students in the GDR were exposed to modernist ideas, which were passed down as former students became teachers, although officially industrial design education was claimed to follow socialist realist principles.[25]

At that time many designers in the GDR expressed the view that the socialist society represented a unique opportunity to adopt a genuinely functionalist approach to design.[26] After all, class distinctions had been eradicated, theoretically removing the need for objects to act as status symbols, and manufacture was no longer motivated by profit, thus eliminating the need to subject products to cyclical style changes or to infuse them with an inflated sense of value through the application of decorative detailing. This accounts for the designers' rejection of additive decoration for domestic objects, particularly if historically inspired, as articulated here by a prominent critic:

> The elimination of functionally superfluous formal detailing on our appliances is . . . not just technologically, but also ideologically justified. The sumptuous carvings applied to Renaissance and Baroque furniture were of politico-functional (psychological) significance for the ruling class. . . . As member and creator of a classless society, the worker has no need to rule anybody with pomp, or to set himself apart from his fellow class members through his furniture. . . . What the worker does need is a simple, beautiful environment in which he can be comfortable after work.[27]

Instead GDR designers insisted, in line with Bauhaus ideas and in disagreement with socialist realists, that the most important consideration for a designer was the "function, the intended use or the purpose of a product."[28] Accordingly the home was seen as a place, "in which the human being takes center stage and is assisted by the things around him."[29]

Finally, industrial designers in the GDR also shared the modernist idea that designed objects should be capable of being mass produced in order to reduce costs and reach the largest possible number of users. Right from the outset, when advocates of socialist realism demanded an orientation on traditional craft skills and techniques, Mart Stam had called for "cheap, good, sound, and highly tasteful furniture for 95 percent of the population. . . . Such furniture cannot be hand crafted. For this purpose we need to be able to think industrially."[30] Some time later designers also supported the concomitant process of standardization, claiming that "modern socialist industrial design can only be realized on the basis of standardized production, in which that product becomes standard which corresponds to the real needs of society and of the individual."[31]

This approach to the design of objects for domestic use indisputably contravened official guidelines derived from the doctrine of socialist realism. Yet, close scrutiny of contemporary discourse suggests that rather than considering it an expression of dissent against the notion of a specifically "socialist design" for the home, it should be seen as an attempt by GDR designers to frame an alternative idea, which to them seemed more compelling than the official doctrine.

The Campaign against "Formalism" (1950–1955)

The substantial divergence between these two outlined positions inevitably led to considerable anxiety. The situation was particularly serious during the first half of the 1950s, the period of the Formalism Debate, which saw a fierce and concerted campaign by party ideologues to establish a socialist realist design approach and eliminate "formalism" with the help of newspaper articles, public exhibitions, speeches at party and professional conferences, and interventions in educational institutions.

Several exhibitions were organized to inform the general public about how they should endeavor to live. For example, the 1952–1953 exhibition *Industriewaren von heute* (Today's Mass-Produced Goods) displayed "exemplary" home-ware items, including ceramics, glass, and furnishing textiles, alongside what a press review described as "beautiful exemplars of our centuries-old national heritage, which can still provide inspiration today."[32] A more confrontational approach was adopted with the furniture exhibition *Besser leben—schöner wohnen!* (Better Living—More Beautiful Dwelling!) in 1953. It contained "exemplary" furnishings next to antique furniture from which to seek inspiration, as well as "negative examples" of "formalist" furniture from current production.[33]

Noncompliant designers or organizations were also often publicly named and criticized in speeches and articles. During a conference organized in conjunction with the *Besser Leben* exhibition Kurt Liebknecht denounced the *Deutsche Werkstätten Hellerau*, who "to this day refuse to accept that function cannot be the sole determinant in furniture design" and thus "continue to build simple, clean, box-like furniture and modular furniture" and "furniture, which lacks top and base moldings and is barely contoured, which is thus still formalist."[34] He also condemned furniture designed by Mart Stam as being "derived from hospital furnishings and dictated solely by function and hygiene. What is such furniture doing in the home, where aesthetic design considerations predominate? The root of this phenomenon is the formalist notion of the machine for living in" (Figure 7.2).[35] Stam had been named and confronted persistently since the beginning of the campaign.[36] After losing his posts as director of the School for Applied Art in Berlin-Weißensee and of the associated Institute for Industrial Design in 1952, he left the GDR in January 1953.[37]

Despite a significant degree of political pressure, however, the campaign to establish a socialist realist design approach seems to have had an almost negligible impact on the GDR's domestic material culture. This is indicated by contemporary criticism, as well as by a general lack of surviving evidence of designed and mass-produced objects that conform to the doctrine.[38] This suggests that GDR designers, who were reported to respond to the demands of the doctrine only with serious reluctance, managed to avoid cultural-political intervention relatively successfully.[39]

The campaign came to an end in the mid-1950s, following a reorientation in the architectural sphere after Stalin's death. In December 1954 Nikita Khrushchev addressed the All-Union Builders' Conference in Moscow to call for the adoption of industrial building methods and the elimination of additive decoration in favor of

7.2
Mart Stam, Study interior (probably from the Weißenhof Siedlung), 1927. Example of a "formalist" interior in catalogue of *Besser leben—schöner wohnen!* exhibition, Berlin, 1953

greater cost-effectiveness and speed of construction.[40] Although articulated in the context of architecture, the argument against the prevailing interpretation of the doctrine on grounds of cost effectiveness was equally valid for industrial design. It seems to have undermined the official position on design in the GDR sufficiently to end the campaign, but did not lead to its official renunciation, thus resulting in a subsequent period of ambiguity and unease.

Thaw, Negotiation, Challenges (1956–1962)

The years between 1956 and 1962 were noticeably more peaceful than the early 1950s, as "anti-formalist" rhetoric became less intransigent and habitual. For instance, design exhibitions were now organized to promote design in general, rather than specifically socialist realist design, and these were reviewed in the press without reference to the national heritage, socialist realism or "formalism."[41]

Design discourse published in specialist literature in this somewhat liberalized environment was dominated by practitioners and theorists, whose texts explored and tested the boundaries of the guidelines established during the recent Formalism Debate. Initial contributions were very cautious, frequently articulated between the lines or following extensive citations of progressive critics from the USSR, where the rehabilitation of the Soviet modernist heritage was gathering momentum in the wake of the Twentieth Party Congress in 1956.[42] The designer Horst Michel, for example, chose to eschew explicit references to the modernist heritage, while calling for bright, flexible, and functional living spaces, as well as

7.3
Franz Ehrlich, Cabinet and table from furniture range *Serie 602*, 1956, manufactured by VEB Deutsche Werkstätten Hellerau, ash wood (Photograph by Friedrich Weimer)

forms he described as sensible, enduring, and appropriate, and condemning "historicist representation."[43] Of course, conformist demands to support the doctrine also continued to be published.[44]

Later contributions were less timid; in March 1958 one critic explicitly declared that "the developments of the last hundred years have clearly demonstrated that the adaptation of historical models for industrial mass production does not result in design but in kitsch," before acclaiming the latest furniture produced by the *Deutsche Werkstätten Hellerau*, including the modular system *Serie 602* by Bauhaus graduate Franz Ehrlich (Figure 7.3).[45]

This process of challenging official restrictions did not remain confined to the realm of theoretical arguments. The GDR designers' affinity for a functionalist approach was also reflected in the objects they designed. These began to emerge on a significant scale in the GDR during the second half of the 1950s. Ranging from straightforward plastic household articles, including buckets, brushes, and tableware, to more complex technical goods, such as cameras, radios, and television sets, these products were all functional and mass produced, and exhibited forms that were restrained and lacked historically inspired additive decoration, as well as any fashionable or emotive detailing.

However, to attribute this spate of functionalist objects solely, or even largely, to a supposed cultural-political course change and consequent, fully authorized change in design practice, would be to ignore a concurrent, immensely transformative development for which ample evidence does exist—the consolidation of the industrial design profession and its exploding impact on the manufacturing industry. In 1958 the first cohort of industrial design students graduated from the School for Applied Art in Berlin-Weißensee, among them the future state secretary Martin Kelm, and immediately began to design for industry. Enduring industry connections were also established by the Weißensee school from the mid-1950s on, by the Institute for Applied Art in Berlin, where Heisig reported a noticeable increase in industry collaborations from 1957, and by the Institute for Design and Development, which had been set up in 1959 in affiliation with a former craft school in Halle.[46] In June 1958 this school had been restructured to become the second academic institution in the GDR to educate industrial designers—the School for Industrial Design Halle-Burg Giebichenstein. Furthermore the specialist journal for industrial design, *Form und Zweck*, began to be published in 1956–1957 and the Fourth German Art Expo, the first to include work by industrial designers, was held in Dresden in 1958.[47] Therefore the emergence of functionalist objects during the second half of the 1950s can be seen as the result of designers taking advantage of an increased influence over industry to express their challenges to the official position on design in material form.

The Fifth German Art Expo and Renewed Escalation (1962–1965)

The argument that the appearance of functionalist objects in the GDR in the late 1950s should not be attributed to a cultural policy reversal is further supported by a renewed intensification of the conflict in the early 1960s. By then objects designed for domestic use had reached such a high degree of aesthetic reduction that they were commonly characterized in insider circles as "grey, angular, stackable."[48] This blatant collision with official expectations led to widespread disapproval voiced in cultural-political circles.[49] The re-escalation erupted publicly on the occasion of the opening of the Fifth German Art Expo in Dresden in 1962, where the recent work by industrial designers was showcased. It was triggered by a highly critical review of the industrial design exhibition, which singled out particular exhibits and their designers.[50] The review's publication in the national daily newspaper *Neues Deutschland* in October 1962 caused further extensive discussions in professional circles and among the general public.[51] The article's author, cultural editor Karl-Heinz Hagen, resurrected much of the familiar rhetoric which had previously dominated discourse during the Formalism Debate. He complained about a prevailing "tendency towards cold aestheticism, dull monotony and impoverished artistic forms, culminating in naked functionalism," which indicated to him that the exhibiting designers "essentially persist in their formalist viewpoints." Echoes of the Formalism Debate could also be found in his objections to an insufficient use of decoration. A set of plain white cylindrical vases designed by Hubert Petras, for example, were described as unartistic and expressionless (Figure 7.4). Similarly, Hagen's disapproval of formal simplicity, affecting glassware, furniture, and even technical equipment, had a familiar ring. Jürgen Peters' geometric radio set *Stereo 72* was claimed to evoke medical equipment and led Hagen to proclaim that "a home is not a laboratory" (Figure 7.5).

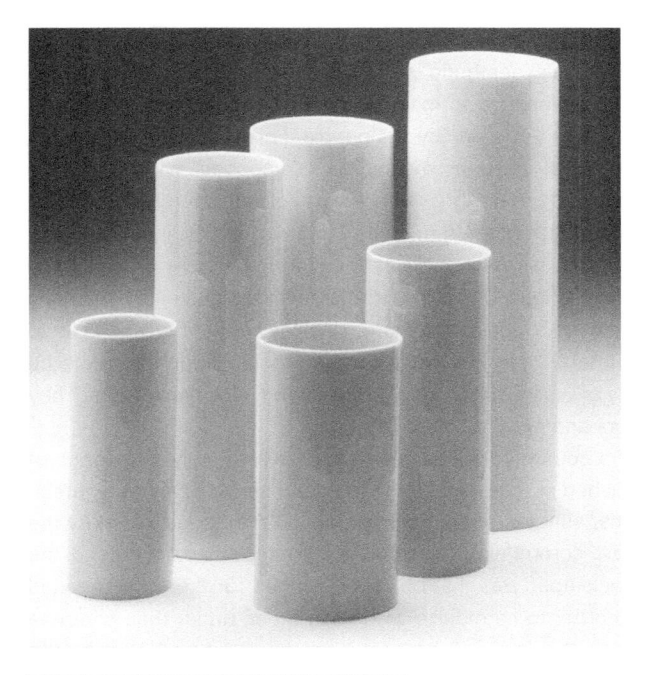

7.4
Above: Hubert Petras, Cylindrical vases, 1961, manufactured by VEB Porzellanwerk Lichte-Wallendorf (Photograph by Klaus E. Göltz)
Below: Sigrid Kölbel, Jacquard furnishing fabric, *V. Deutsche Kunstausstellung* exhibition, Dresden, 1962

Finally, Hagen's critique also reveals a familiar anxiety about the adequate satisfaction of the population's aesthetic preferences. His choice of language suggests concerns that the simplified forms, the subdued colors, and the lack of figurative decoration would not be *valued* by the people. For instance, he trivialized Petras's undecorated cylindrical vases as meaningless "chopped, white porcelain tubes" and lamented mockingly that Sigrid Kölbel's grey shaded furnishing fabrics featured abstract geometric patterns, rather than figurative motifs, indicative of a trend that would "eventually allow every bungler to cover up his lack of imagination with a few lines and dashes" (Figure 7.4). This collision with the perceived aesthetic preferences of the people also again dominated Walter Ulbricht's response to questions raised on this matter during a party conference in December 1962; he claimed that "the majority of workers will not want to inhabit such drab rooms. They want bright, friendly colors and tasteful vases."[52]

GDR designers countered these charges quite resolutely in a series of articles, which were published in specialist literature over a period of about eighteen months and took positions, either explicitly or implicitly, on the issues raised by the critique. One of the most commonly articulated arguments used to defend the aesthetic restraint of their output was that objects designed for the home needed to be relatively neutral in order to harmonize with each other, rather than compete for attention.[53] This aspect, they argued, had not been taken into account by the critics of the exhibition, as spatial limitations had, for the most part, not allowed the recreation of lifelike domestic scenarios.[54]

The designers also challenged the ideologues' authority on the alleged aesthetic preferences of the population. To this effect a November 1962 memo from the Institute for Applied Art in defense of the exhibition included transcriptions of the guestbooks, which confirmed the visitors' almost unequivocal approval.[55] This strategy highlights a curious situation: as has been shown, claims to have authority on the wishes of the people had been made by both sides since the Formalism Debate in the early 1950s, yet because the GDR lacked conventional market mechanisms and an established market research system, it was almost impossible to know what the country's consumers really wanted to buy. While claims made in line with the official cultural policy of the SED were not usually supported with any evidence, designers of the Institute for Applied Art had often referred to guestbooks from design exhibitions in order to authenticate their own expertise on the population's aesthetic preferences.[56] These indeed confirmed that the overwhelming majority of visitors approved of the exhibits, merely expressing their dismay at the difficulties in procuring these products in retail outlets. Yet, although such exhibitions were usually very well attended, it is doubtful that the preferences of the majority of the population were accurately reflected in the sample that frequented design exhibitions, let alone signed guestbooks.

The designers' defiance was also reflected in their practice, as they continued to design functionalist products for domestic use. For instance, the development and production of rectilinear modular radio systems persisted despite the vilification of Jürgen Peters's *Stereo 72* and led to such products as the *RK1*, the *RK2*, and the *Heliradio* system, jointly designed by freelance designers Clauss Dietel

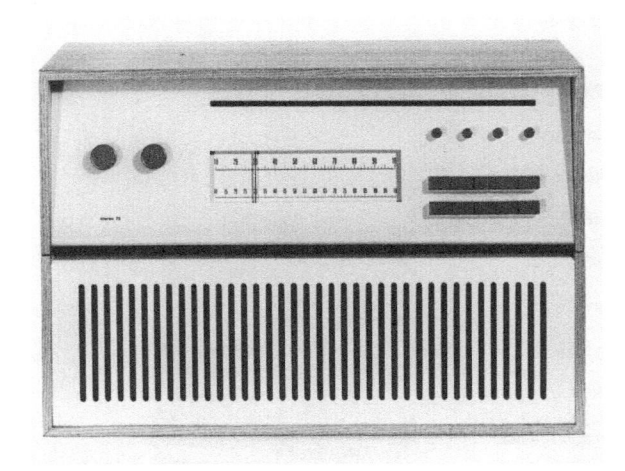

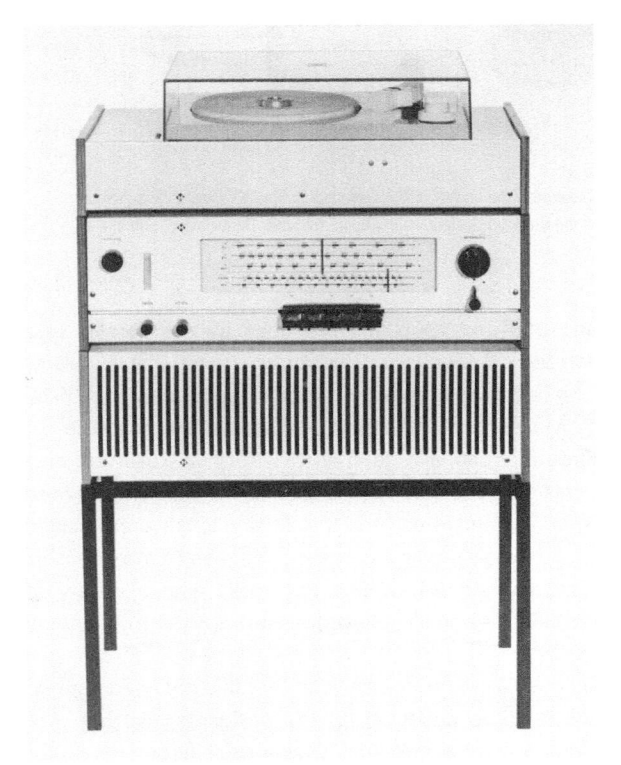

7.5
Above: Jürgen Peters, Radio system *Stereo 72*, 1962, designed for VVB Rundfunk und Fernsehen (not manufactured) (Photograph by Georg Eckelt), Stiftung Haus der Geschichte der Bundesrepublik Deutschland, Sammlung Industrielle Gestaltung, Berlin
Below: Clauss Dietel and Lutz Rudolph, Stereo system *Heliradio*: RK3 (tuner) + P1 (record player) + L20 (speaker), 1965, manufactured by Gerätebau Hempel KG, Limbach Oberfrohna (Photograph by Georg Eckelt), Stiftung Haus der Geschichte der Bundesrepublik Deutschland, Sammlung Industrielle Gestaltung, Berlin

7.6
Margarete Jahny and Erich Müller, Tableware range *Europa*, 1965, manufactured by VEB Glasfabrik Schwepnitz (Photograph by Christel Lehmann), Stiftung Haus der Geschichte der Bundesrepublik Deutschland, Sammlung Industrielle Gestaltung, Berlin

and Lutz Rudolph between 1960 and 1965 and produced by the semi-private manufacturer *Gerätebau Hempel KG, Limbach Oberfrohna* (Figure 7.5). Similarly, stackable pressed glassware in subdued forms and colors was designed in 1965 by Margarete Jahny and Erich Müller, both employees of the Central Institute for Design, despite Hagen's criticism of dark and geometrically formed glassware only three years earlier; *Europa* was subsequently popularized as the official tableware for the national hotel chain *Interhotel* and remained in production for several decades (Figure 7.6).[57] And finally, Hubert Petras's cylindrical vases and many similar vessels remained in production in plain white, as well as decorated with a variety of ornamental motifs. Evidently GDR designers enjoyed almost complete autonomy from cultural-political directives.

It would be erroneous, however, to conclude that this renewed flare-up in the early 1960s was entirely inconsequential for the designers involved. The condemned radio system *Stereo 72*, which had been designed by Jürgen Peters for the state-run Industry Association for Radio and Television Equipment in 1962, did not go into production. Neither did the more elaborate home entertainment system *Rundfunk-Stereo-Phono-Fernsehen*, which the designer subsequently developed for the same client in 1964, although it had been publicized in a mainstream interior design magazine and shown at trade shows (Figure 7.7).[58] Yet, while this certainly seems to have caused Peters considerable frustration, he was clearly not intimidated enough by public criticism to refrain from designing further home entertainment

7.7
Jürgen Peters, Home entertainment system *Rundfunk-Stereo-Phono-Fernsehen*, 1964, designed for VVB Rundfunk und Fernsehen (not manufactured), shown with furniture range *Leipzig 4* on title page of interior design magazine *Kultur im Heim* (Photograph by Georg Eckelt)

systems, which were no less functionalist than the first.[59] The controversy also had implications for the designer of the decried cylindrical vases, Hubert Petras. In April 1963 he wrote to the director of the Institute for Applied Art to complain of harassment by local SED functionaries in response to Hagen's review.[60] He was sufficiently traumatized by these events to eventually give up his practice and did not resume work again until 1966, when he took up a teaching position at the Burg Giebichenstein design school.

Evidently advocates of socialist realist design were not in a position to intervene directly in manufacturing decisions. This suggests that, despite the authoritative nature of public rhetoric, GDR politicians were *not* united behind the official idea of design for the socialist home. The socialist realist position appears to have been upheld mainly in cultural-political circles, while the designers' modernist approach with its compelling social and economic arguments seems to have found tacit approval from at least some elements within the leadership of the GDR, particularly among those involved in economic and industrial administration.

Nevertheless, cultural ideologues were able, at times, to exert influence through media campaigns with unpredictable and potentially devastating consequences. Hence the dispute remained a persistent source of anxiety throughout its duration.

In the mid-1960s socialist realist design rhetoric faded noticeably. This period saw significant structural changes, which progressively allied the discipline of industrial design, represented by the Institute for Applied Art, to the manufacturing industry and reduced its exposure to the influence of cultural politics. In September 1962 the director of the Institute for Applied Art, Walter Heisig, was replaced by the industrial designer Martin Kelm, who zealously pursued the establishment of closer industry connections. Consequently the institute was renamed Central Institute for Industrial Design and in January 1965 it was moved from the Ministry for Culture to the German Office for Metrology and Product Testing, a central body which reported directly to the Council of Ministers and was responsible for quality control and assurance for domestically manufactured goods.[61] From this time on, references to the idea of socialist realist industrial design seem to have disappeared from discourse completely and the enduring conflict, although never officially resolved, could be considered put to rest.

Conclusion

Postwar design for the domestic realm was steeped in anxiety in the GDR, as designers and party ideologues disagreed on the idea of the modern socialist home. As this essay has shown, the resulting conflict was both grave and sustained, lasting from the early 1950s until the mid-1960s. This is suggested not only by the significant rhetorical continuities between the polemic of the early 1950s and the early 1960s, but also by the designers' sustained engagement with aspects of the official position in the intervening period, whether attempting to accommodate, amend, or subvert it.

This essay has also demonstrated that the dispute in question can be explained without reliance on significant external influences, as a domestic disagreement between competing visions of a "socialist design" for the domestic sphere, which diverged on the supposed needs and desires of the socialist consumer. SED ideologues made no reference to Soviet industrial design and although the Soviet rehabilitation of its own modernist heritage coincided with a comparative lull in the GDR design dispute, the subsequent renewed intensification of the conflict in the GDR in the early 1960s clearly defied the revised Soviet course. This cautions against an over-attribution of change or continuity in the socialist realm to Soviet intervention or imposition of authority.

Finally, the existence of functionalist objects for domestic use from this period and the relative absence of designed objects that conform to official expectations confirm the presence within GDR culture of spaces not only for negotiation, but also for a substantial degree of noncompliance. This finding clearly collides with conventional notions about life in the GDR. It demonstrates that the rhetoric recorded in published or archived documents can sometimes have very limited authority and draws attention to the value of interrogating material culture, both for the objects it contained and those it did not.

Notes

Acknowledgments: I am very grateful to all who have contributed, but special thanks for support beyond the call of duty are due to Günter Höhne, for his generosity in sharing his address book of GDR designers with me, to Gisela Haker of the Bundesarchiv, who eased the difficulties of long-distance research, and to Fiona Loughnane and Joe Morrissey, who read and constructively commented on various earlier drafts. I also want to thank Robin Schuldenfrei for being such a diligent editor and, of course, my supervisor Mick Wilson.

1. See, for example, Paul Betts, "The Bauhaus in the German Democratic Republic: Between Formalism and Pragmatism," in *Bauhaus*, ed. Jeannine Fiedler and Peter Feierabend (Cologne: Könemann, 2000), 42–49 and Eli Rubin, *Synthetic Socialism: Plastics and Dictatorship in the German Democratic Republic* (Chapel Hill: University of North Carolina Press, 2008), 43–50.
2. See, for example, Paul Betts, "The Politics of Post-Fascist Aesthetics: 1950s West and East German Industrial Design," in *Life after Death: Approaches to a Cultural and Social History of Europe during the 1940s and 1950s*, ed. Richard Bessel and Dirk Schumann (Cambridge: Cambridge University Press, 2003), 291–321 and Eli Rubin, "The Form of Socialism without Ornament: Consumption, Ideology, and the Fall and Rise of Modernist Design in the German Democratic Republic," *Journal of Design History* 19, no. 2 (2006): 158–159.
3. For an exception see Katharina Pfützner, "'Cold, Clean, Meaningless': Industrial Design and Cultural Politics in the GDR 1950–1965," in *Contested Legacies: Constructions of Cultural Heritage in the GDR*, ed. Matthew Philpotts and Sabine Rolle (Rochester, NY: Camden House, 2009), 107–110. Greg Castillo has also recently examined the socialist realist position on interior architecture and furniture design in Greg Castillo, *Cold War on the Home Front: The Soft Power of Midcentury Design* (Minneapolis: University of Minnesota Press, 2010), 49–57.
4. In particular in Betts, "Bauhaus," 42–49 and Paul Betts, *The Authority of Everyday Objects: A Cultural History of West German Industrial Design* (Berkeley: University of California Press, 2004), 89–92.
5. See Paul Betts, "Building Socialism at Home: The Case of East German Interiors," in *Socialist Modern: East German Everyday Culture and Politics*, ed. Katherine Pence and Paul Betts (Ann Arbor: University of Michigan Press, 2008), 110, and, specifically in relation to furniture, Castillo, *Cold War*, 173–201.
6. This popular theoretical framework tends to conceptualize a "totalitarian" state and its institutions as a monolithic entity that controls all aspects of life effectively and with a unified, coherent aim derived from a single ideology. For a brief discussion of the various "totalitarian" models, as they might pertain to GDR historiography, see Corey Ross, *The East German Dictatorship: Problems and Perspectives in the Interpretation of the GDR* (London: Arnold Publishers, 2002), 20–25.
7. For more details see N. Orlow, "Wege und Irrwege der modernen Kunst," *Tägliche Rundschau*, January 20, 1951: 4.
8. See Orlow, "Wege" and Wilhelm Girnus, "Wo stehen die Feinde der deutschen Kunst? Bemerkungen zur Frage des Formalismus und des Kosmopolitanismus (1)," *Neues Deutschland*, February 13, 1951: 3.
9. Orlow, "Wege." Unless otherwise noted, translations are the author's own.
10. See, for example, Orlow, "Wege" and Wilhelm Girnus, "Wo stehen die Feinde der deutschen Kunst? Bemerkungen zur Frage des Formalismus und des Kosmopolitanismus (2)," *Neues Deutschland*, February 18, 1951: 3. This influence was not limited to popular culture; the US military administration also played an active role in the revival of modernist culture in the postwar years, as outlined by Betts, *Authority*, 139–145 and Castillo, *Cold War*, 31–46.
11. These specific sections of the resolution were cited by Kurt Liebknecht, "Im Kampf um eine neue deutsche Architektur," *Neues Deutschland*, February 13, 1951: 3.

12   For an example of the explicit rejection of historicist imitation see the exhibition catalogue *Besser leben—schöner wohnen! Raum und Möbel* (Berlin: Deutsche Bauakademie und Ministerium für Leichtindustrie, 1954), 88, and on the official rejection of "kitsch" see the SED resolution printed in Hans Lauter, *Der Kampf gegen den Formalismus in Kunst und Literatur, für eine fortschrittliche deutsche Kultur* (Berlin: Dietz Verlag, 1951), 156–157.

13   Industrial design had not been recognized as a specialized discipline by Soviet art discourse under Stalin, according to Susan E. Reid, "De-Stalinization and Taste, 1953–63," *Journal of Design History* 10, no. 2 (1997): 178.

14   For an overview of architectural discourse in the GDR at this time see Andreas Schätzke, *Zwischen Bauhaus und Stalinallee: Architekturdiskussion im östlichen Deutschland 1945–1955* (Braunschweig and Wiesbaden: Vieweg, 1991), and for a very thought-provoking article on Soviet socialist realist architecture see Catherine Cooke, "Beauty as a Route to 'the Radiant Future': Responses of Soviet Architecture," *Journal of Design History* 10, no. 2 (1997): 137–160.

15   From a paper presented at the Interior Architecture Conference on 17 November 1953, printed in *Besser leben*, 17.

16   Ibid., 21–33.

17   Ibid., 13–17.

18   Ibid., 46, for example.

19   See, for instance, Lauter, *Kampf*, 96, and "Die neuen Aufgaben der Innenarchitektur und der Möbelindustrie," *Thüringer Tageblatt*, January 29, 1954, page number unavailable, press clipping in archive *Sammlung industrielle Gestaltung*.

20   From an excerpt of the address cited in "Wir wollen besser wohnen," *Sonntag* 4, April 20, 1952, page number unavailable, press clipping in archive *Sammlung industrielle Gestaltung*.

21   This institution, responsible for industrial design in the GDR from its foundation in 1951 to its dissolution in 1990, underwent several changes in name and affiliation over the years, which has led to some confusion in recent scholarship. Originally set up as the Institute for Industrial Design (*Institut für industrielle Gestaltung*) attached to the School for Applied Art in Berlin-Weißensee, it was renamed Institute for Applied Art (*Institut für angewandte Kunst*) in July 1952, when it was also disconnected from the school and incorporated instead into the Ministry for Culture. In October 1963 it was renamed Central Institute for Design (*Zentralinstitut für Formgestaltung*) and in January 1965 moved from the Ministry for Culture to the German Office for Metrology and Product Testing (*Deutsches Amt für Meßwesen und Warenprüfung*) (DAMW). Further structural and name changes are omitted here, as they fall outside the temporal scope of this essay.

22   Heisig's speech was subsequently printed in *Zu den aktuellen Fragen der angewandten Kunst in Industrie und Handwerk* (Berlin: Institut für angewandte Kunst, 1953). This and the following citations: ibid., 7–8.

23   Paul Greenhalgh, ed., *Modernism in Design* (London: Reaktion Books, 1990), 1–24.

24   See, for example, Annelise Fleischmann (1924), "Economic Living," in Frank Whitford, *Bauhaus* (London: Thames & Hudson, 1984), 209–210 or Walter Gropius (1926), "Bauhaus Dessau—Principles of Bauhaus Production" in *Form and Function: A Source Book for the History of Architecture and Design 1890–1939*, ed. Tim and Charlotte Benton (London: Crosby Lockwood Staples, 1975), 148–149.

25   See minutes of a meeting on 25 January 1953 in the School for Applied Art in Berlin-Weißensee provided in *Drei Kapitel Weißensee: Dokumente zur Geschichte der Kunsthochschule Berlin-Weißensee 1946 bis 1957*, ed. Hiltrud Ebert (Berlin: Kunsthochschule Berlin-Weißensee, 1996), 279–281.

26   See, for example, Mart Stam (1950), "Entwurf 'Institut für industrielle Gestaltung'," in *Drei Kapitel Weißensee*, ed. Ebert, 79–81; Hermann Exner, "Zu den neuen Möbeln von Franz Ehrlich und Selman Selmanagić," *Bildende Kunst* 3 (1958): 191–194; or Ekkehard Bartsch, "Standardisierung—Vielfalt—Formgestaltung," *Form und Zweck* 2 (1965): 7–12. These beliefs

were also retrospectively confirmed by many GDR designers in interviews with this author, particularly by Ekkehard Bartsch (2006), Erich John (2008), and Martin Kelm (2008).
27 Exner, "Zu den neuen Möbeln," 194. For another explicit rejection of ornament see Erich John, "Die Schönheit unserer Technik," *Bildende Kunst* 1 (1963): 3–13.
28 Martin Kelm, "Künstlerisch-ästhetische Fragen der Industrieformgestaltung," *Bildende Kunst* 1 (1964): 4.
29 Jürgen Peters, "Die Entwicklung der Rundfunk- und Fernsehindustrie aus der Sicht des Formgebers" *Form und Zweck* (1961): 29–38.
30 See Mart Stam, "Arbeitstagung des Instituts für Innenarchitektur, Referat Stam, 14.3.52" in *Drei Kapitel Weißensee*, ed. Ebert, 163.
31 Bartsch, "Standardisierung," 12.
32 Hans W. Aust, "Industriewaren, die das Volk verlangt," *Tägliche Rundschau*, January 17, 1953, page number unavailable.
33 *Besser leben*, 75–76.
34 Ibid., 45–46.
35 Ibid., 15–16.
36 See, for example, Lauter, *Kampf*, 89 and Ebert, *Drei Kapitel Weißensee*, 107.
37 For more information on the Institute for Industrial Design see note 21.
38 For examples of contemporary criticism see Heisig's assessment in *Zu den aktuellen Fragen*, 6, or Peter Bergner, "Über das Moderne," *Form und Zweck* (1956–1957): 119–122.
39 The designers' lack of enthusiasm for the doctrine was an openly discussed irritation at the time; see Bergner, "Moderne," 119.
40 For relevant excerpts of Khrushchev's speech, as translated and published in the GDR in 1955, see Schätzke, *Zwischen Bauhaus*, 158–160.
41 See for instance the 1956 industrial design exhibition review by Werner Miersch, "Eine Ausstellung schöner und zweckmäßiger Industriewaren," *Das Blatt* 8 (1956), page number unavailable, press clipping in archive *Sammlung industrielle Gestaltung*.
42 On the Soviet rehabilitation of aspects of modernism see Victor Buchli, "Khrushchev, Modernism, and the Fight against *Petit-bourgeois* Consciousness in the Soviet Home," *Journal of Design History* 10, no. 2 (1997): 161–176; Reid, "De-Stalinization;" or Iurii Gerchuk, "The Aesthetics of Everyday Life in the Khrushchev Thaw in the USSR (1954–64)," in *Style and Socialism: Modernity and Material Culture in Post-War Eastern Europe*, ed. Susan E. Reid and David Crowley (Oxford: Berg, 2000), 81–100. For an example of a challenge which was supported by references to Soviet discourse, see Hermann Exner, "Die neue Wohnung—Spiegelbild ihrer Bewohner," *Sonntag*, September 2, 1956, page number unavailable, press clipping in archive *Sammlung industrielle Gestaltung*.
43 This position can be found at the core of most of Michel's texts; the specific expressions cited here stem from Horst Michel, "Das Angemessene," *Bildende Kunst* 11/12 (1956): 652.
44 For examples see Bergner, "Moderne," 120 and Walter Heisig, "Fortschritte der industriellen Formgestaltung," *Form und Zweck*, 1956/57: 34.
45 Exner, "Zu den neuen Möbeln," 194
46 For more on the establishment of industry connections by the Weißensee art school, see Ebert, *Drei Kapitel Weißensee*, 228. Evidence of an increased collaboration with the manufacturing industry by the Institute for Applied Art can be found in its plans and reports from 1951 to 1958 in Bundesarchiv Berlin-Lichterfelde (BArch BL) DR1/7986. For more on the foundation and work of the Institute for Design and Development, see Jörg Petruschat, "'Take me plastics'," in *75 Jahre Burg Giebichenstein: 1915–1990; Beiträge zur Geschichte*, ed. Renate Luckner-Bien (Halle: Burg Giebichenstein, 1990), 234.
47 The title of the publication was changed to *form+zweck* in 1967.
48 The original expression, "*grau, eckig, stapelbar*," was relayed to the author in interviews with several GDR designers, including Christa Petroff-Bohne (2008), Alfred Hückler (2008), and

Katharina Pfützner

Günter Reißmann (2008). A further reference to it can be found in a published interview with GDR designer Dietmar Palloks in Jens Semrau, ed., *Was ist dann Kunst? Die Kunsthochschule Weißensee 1946–1989 in Zeitzeugengesprächen* (Berlin: Lukas Verlag, 2004), 278. Its precise origins have thus far remained elusive.

49 See, for example, the Ministry for Culture report on the work of the Institute for Applied Art from February or March 1962 (BArch BL DR1/8000) and the internal report on the Fifth German Art Expo by the central executive of the Union of Visual Artists (*Verband Bildender Künstler*) from 3 October 1962 "Thesen zur Einschätzung der V. Deutschen Kunstausstellung," 8 (BArch BL DR1/8067).

50 Karl-Heinz Hagen, "Hinter dem Leben zurück: Bemerkungen zur 'Industriellen Formgestaltung' auf der V. Deutschen Kunstausstellung," *Neues Deutschland*, October 4, 1962: 4.

51 See BArch BL DR1/7961 for a letter from 23 October 1962 by Friedrich Engemann, head of the recently established Industrial Design Council (*Rat für Industrieform*), to the Ministry for Culture, listing the large range of groupings and institutions who had asked him to take a position on the published article. For an indication of the response by the public see replies from readers published in *Neues Deutschland* in January 1963 alongside a follow-up article by Willi Köhler, "Wonach streben die Meister der angewandten Kunst? Noch einmal zur Ausstellung Industrielle Formgestaltung in Dresden," *Neues Deutschland*, January 4, 1963: 3.

52 Walter Ulbricht, "Antwort auf Fragen der Delegierten: Auszug aus der Diskussionsrede auf der Bezirksdelegiertenkonferenz in Leipzig am 9.12.1962," *Leipziger Volkszeitung*, December 15, 1962: 5.

53 For example in John, "Schönheit," 12.

54 See, for example, an unpublished and undated analysis of the exhibition produced in the Institute for Applied Art entitled "Einschätzung der V. Deutschen Kunstausstellung: Industrieform," stored under *Jahresdokumentation 1962* in the archive *Sammung industrielle Gestaltung*, or a memo entitled "Bemerkungen zur Ausstellung der angewandten Künste auf der V. Deutschen Kunstausstellung mit besonderer Berücksichtigung der Industrieformgestaltung," which had originated in the same institution on 26 November 1962 (BArch BL DR1/8067).

55 See memo entitled "Bemerkungen zur Ausstellung der angewandten Künste auf der V. Deutschen Kunstausstellung mit besonderer Berücksichtigung der Industrieformgestaltung" from 26 November 1962 (BArch BL DR1/8067).

56 See, for example, Heisig, "Fortschritte," 34.

57 For more information on the Central Institute for Design see note 21.

58 See Jürgen Peters and Helmut Wawoczny, "Bausteinserie Rundfunk-Stereo-Phono-Fernsehen," *Kultur im Heim* 4 (1964): 6–9. In a 2008 interview with this author, Jürgen Peters confirmed that in his opinion the manufacture of these systems was prevented by the director of the Industry Association for Radio and Television Equipment as a direct result of the Hagen article in 1962.

59 For an indication of Peters' exasperation see Jürgen Peters, "Combi—Vision 70—Rafena," *Kultur im Heim* 2 (1965): 6.

60 Hein Köster, former custodian of the *Sammlung industrielle Gestaltung*, refers to documents to this effect in the collection's archive in Hein Köster, "Schmerzliche Ankunft in der Moderne: Industriedesign auf der V. Deutschen Kunstausstellung" in *Wunderwirtschaft: DDR-Konsumkultur in den 60er Jahren*, ed. Neue Gesellschaft für Bildende Kunst (Cologne: Böhlau Verlag, 1996), 101. These documents could not be recovered during a visit in 2008, but in a 2007 interview with this author Hubert Petras recalled that he was prohibited from exhibiting in his home town.

61 See *Gesetzblatt der Deutschen Demokratischen Republik* 2.92, September 24, 1965: 667–669.

Chapter 8

Architect-Designed Interiors for a Culturally Progressive Upper-Middle Class
The Implicit Political Presence of Knoll International in Belgium

Fredie Floré

In the first decade following the Second World War, Knoll International, a renowned American-based producer of "international style" furniture, entered the Western European market. It did so by selling production licenses to local furniture companies. One of these was Kunstwerkstede De Coene (De Coene Art Workshop), a Flemish family business specializing in the design and production of wooden furniture, interiors, and building elements and internationally known for its impeccable craftsmanship. In 1954 De Coene obtained the Knoll production licenses for "the Benelux countries"—that is, Belgium, the Netherlands, and Luxembourg—and the Belgian Congo.[1] In the Benelux, as in other parts of Western Europe, Knoll furniture provided a welcome solution for the booming administrative sector, which was in need of suitable, modern office furnishings. However, it was not long before Knoll also entered the domestic sphere. As design historian George H. Marcus explains, the "renewed functionalist style," as represented by, for example, Knoll, "was brought into domestic interiors as highly paid architects began to build and furnish houses for their corporate clients."[2] In Belgium in the 1950s and 1960s, as in several other European countries, Knoll easily found its way into the homes of a culturally progressive upper-middle class. In 1965, the Flemish design and architecture critic K.-N. Elno described the situation clearly when he wrote: "It [Knoll International] equips managers' offices . . . in large banks and commercial enterprises and it further finds its way into the living rooms of the upper economic stratum of Western affluent society."[3]

Fredie Floré

This chapter discusses the "import" of Knoll International to Belgium. In doing so, it investigates the impact of the American-based company on the cultural and political identity of De Coene. Taking into account the history of the Flemish furniture firm and its postwar conviction for economic collaboration with the German occupying forces, it argues that the purchase of the Knoll production licenses was part of a political reorientation. However, this strategy remained implicit and has never been openly discussed. Knoll's powerful marketing strategies and narratives, strengthened by the almost unanimously positive reviews in the Belgian architectural and design press, took center stage and rapidly converted Knoll designs into acknowledged international symbols of modernity.[4] Only a few critics in Belgium went so far as to add some reservations to their generally positive appreciation of Knoll products. For example, in 1962 architecture critic Geert Bekaert wondered if "this meticulous watching over perfection, this scrupulous attention to even the last detail" which characterized Knoll production perhaps also attached a sense of "inaccessibility" to it.[5] A few years later, Elno remarked on the expensive nature of the products. He believed that because of their high cost, Knoll products tended to represent within society "a certain 'aristocracy' based on material power."[6] This aspect would bother him, he explained, "if it was not so excellently integrated in a system of *values* which we, in this case 'despite' certain social aspirations, *have to* defend, encourage and bring to life."[7] These values included "a subtle flair for form and for spatial poetry."[8] Apart from guarded remarks like those of Bekaert or Elno, most critics in Belgium agreed that in general Knoll set a good example, in particular for national furniture production and home culture.[9] However it is remarkable that none of them paid much attention to the way in which Knoll collaborated with the local furniture industry or to the political nature of this collaboration.

Modernizing De Coene

The firm De Coene, based in Kortrijk in West Flanders, has a long and valued history dating back to the late nineteenth century.[10] For decades the company was known mainly for its luxurious art-deco interiors. In the 1920s and 1930s, De Coene produced furniture, carpets, stained-glass windows, lamps, and textiles for a new class of wealthy citizens. The firm furnished upper-class villas, apartments, restaurants, bars, and office spaces. Even the Belgian royal family showed an interest in the flourishing company. In 1935, for example, De Coene produced a rosewood desk for King Leopold III, following a design by architect Henry van de Velde.

During the interwar years De Coene exported a considerable volume of goods to France, Great Britain, and the Netherlands. In both the 1925 Exposition Internationale des Arts Décoratifs (International Exposition of Applied Arts) in Paris and in the 1935 World Exhibition in Brussels, the firm's participation was awarded a Grand Prix for its excellent craftsmanship and for its close affinity with the fine arts. Following the tradition of the Arts and Crafts Movement, Jozef De Coene, artist and founder of the firm, regularly invited renowned artists to take part in the design or production process. Painter Albert Saverys, for example, designed carpets and sculptor Geo Verbanck drew bronze fittings for cupboards and doors. The company was also known for its advanced technology. In 1921, De Coene had its own plywood production unit comprised of American machines. Shortly thereafter, the firm successfully developed its own type of adhesive, based on urea resin.

In the first decade after the Second World War, De Coene went through a difficult phase. The firm was convicted of being an economic war collaborator, mainly due to the fact that during the war it had produced barracks, emergency housing, and furniture for the German military and civilian services, as well as a number of fake wooden airplanes meant to mislead the allied air force.[11] As a result, De Coene was sequestered by the government and it was not until 1952 that the original owners of the firm were back in charge. Financial settlements between the firm and the government remained pending until 1958. In this situation, the company's prospects for obtaining loans for further development were not good and, more importantly, from 1953 onwards, it risked having its profits confiscated. Faced with enormous financial losses, the new De Coene management overtly changed course. From 1953 onwards, Pol Provost, the new general director of the company, decided to invest heavily in new branches of the wood and furniture industries.[12]

In this period, the furniture, interior design, and construction departments were brought up to date and modernized. This process was marked by the 1954 acquisition of the production and sale licenses of Knoll furniture for the Benelux. In a published interview of 1998, Adolf De Coene, former general director of the firm, remembers how the purchase of the licenses signified an "enormous change" in the development of the De Coene firm: "Before the arrival of Knoll, De Coene already made so-called modern furniture, but this was not comparable with the designs by Knoll."[13] Already by the mid-1950s, Knoll was well known for its collection of modern domestic and office furniture with product lines by famous artists and designers such as Eero Saarinen, Harry Bertoia, and Ludwig Mies van der Rohe. The production of some of the Knoll designs required the introduction of new techniques in the De Coene factory. For example, Jérôme Dervichian, chief of the production of Knoll products at De Coene, recalled the arrival of a spot-welding machine and the necessary moulds to make the Diamond Chair and other furniture pieces by Harry Bertoia (Figure 8.1).[14] He noted that this technique was new to De Coene and that the Knoll company had sent the young American designer Richard Schultz to Kortrijk to instruct the De Coene staff. Schultz had been working for Knoll as Bertoia's assistant and at the time was assigned to oversee licensed production of the Bertoia series and other Knoll products in several countries outside the United States.[15] Dervichian remembers that De Coene's experienced craftsmen "were rather skeptical and suspicious" of the new technology of spot welding.[16] But Schultz, whom Dervichian describes as a "skilful intellectual," knew how to deal with this situation and deliberately chose young, unskilled workers to train in the new techniques.[17] In the 1950s, the firm also installed a new and up-to-date technical laboratory and bought an advanced press for the production of bakelized plywood (plywood plates finished with a sheet of impregnated veneer with phenol based resins). A whole range of new building products was launched: self-supporting panels, new types of plywood, doors, trailers, prefabricated houses, and glulams (glued laminated timber support beams) with a rectangular section (Figure 8.2).

Fredie Floré

8.1
Advertisement for Knoll International Brussels in the Belgian journal *Architecture*, showing images of the Diamond Chair by Harry Bertoia, 1955

8.2
Architects Fabrizio Carola and Fernand De Rijck, Glulam structure of the Brussels Expo 58 footbridge produced by De Coene, c. 1958, Kortrijk

Inspired by the Knoll collection, De Coene also developed its own contemporary furniture lines. However, this change did not imply the abandonment of its interwar activities. De Coene continued to produce furniture in the style of earlier historic periods. Moreover, irrespective of the new lines of mass-produced wares, the postwar modern and period furniture of De Coene still played an important role in the representation of upper- and upper-middle-class clients, as had been the case since the 1920s.

Knoll and the New (Political) Identity of De Coene

Buying the Knoll production licenses was in many ways a decisive ingredient in the postwar modernization process of De Coene. It not only introduced a new, modern line of furniture elements and new production techniques but also opened up new markets, in particular that of the booming office sector. Above all, it implicitly helped De Coene in shifting its political identity. After all, the association with the American-based Knoll company somewhat overwrote the memory of the company's commissions for the German occupier and the negative connotations of the firm's recent trial, which, as it was one of the first trials in Belgium on economic collaboration, had attracted a lot of public attention.[18] More specifically, it was the "international" identity of Knoll that helped to distract attention from the "local" political history of De Coene.

By the mid-1950s Knoll had built itself an international identity on several levels. First of all, although it was an American-based firm, it had strong European and even German roots. Hans Knoll, who founded the Hans Knoll Furniture Company in New York in 1938, was the son of the German furniture maker Walter Knoll, one of the first producers of Bauhaus designs.[19] A large part of the furniture Hans Knoll produced in the early 1940s was designed by the Danish designer Jens Risom. In 1946, Hans went into partnership with his wife Florence Schust-Knoll—who had studied with Eliel Saarinen at the Cranbrook School of Art and Mies van der Rohe at the Illinois Institute of Technology—and the company's name was changed to Knoll Associates. In the 1950s the Knolls further developed their connections with European émigrés and American designers who provided the company with furniture designs known today as "modern classics."[20]

Knoll's international identity was also reinforced by the sale of production licenses and the establishment of branch stores outside America. The first foreign production branches were established in 1951 in France and Germany.[21] At that time the company was called H. G. Knoll International.[22] In the following years several other countries followed suit and in 1955 Knoll International Ltd. was established with branch stores and licensees in Belgium, Canada, Cuba, Switzerland, and Sweden, together with those in France and Germany. Knoll's international network continued to grow. By the early 1970s the company was represented in no less than thirty-one countries outside America and many large cities featured Knoll showrooms, often designed or executed in collaboration with a local modern architect.[23] For example, the first showroom in the Benelux was established in 1954 on the Rue Royale in Brussels and was the result of collaboration between Florence Knoll and her interior design office, the Knoll Planning Unit (established in 1943), the

8.3
Knoll showroom, Rue Royale, Brussels, 1954

Belgian architect Constantin Brodzki, and De Coene (Figure 8.3).[24] The typical features of the Knoll "look," as described by Bobbye Tigerman, were present: iconic furniture elements in familiar arrangements, a recognizable color scheme and articulated rectangular surfaces.[25] Later on, additional showrooms were built in Liège, Amsterdam, and Antwerp.[26] In several countries, Knoll showrooms were used from time-to-time as venues for cultural events, often presenting the work of native artists. For example, in the Paris showroom director Yves Vidal and artistic director Roger Legrand organized several book launches and exhibitions of the work of fine artists such as the French painter Guy de Rougement.[27]

Finally, the international identity of Knoll was reinforced by the kind of architectural projects for which its furniture was designed and used. Knoll, and especially the Knoll Planning Unit, specialized in the arrangement of large office buildings of the so-called "international style," a term first introduced in 1932 by Henry-Russell Hitchcock and Philip Johnson with their book and exhibition on modern architecture at the New York Museum of Modern Art. Although this "style" has subsequently proved to be problematic in its definition, after the Second World War it was strongly associated with several of America's large new building programs, including the modern office building with its steel construction and largely glazed façade. A well-known example of this kind of building was the head office of the Connecticut General Life Insurance Company in Hartford (completed in 1957), designed by the architectural office Skidmore, Owings and Merrill (SOM), with an interior by the Knoll Planning Unit. SOM was known to be at the forefront of the design of American office buildings with large curtain-glass façades. However not all of their office designs fit within this type. For example, SOM's first commercial building in Europe—for the Banque Lambert in Brussels in the late 1950s—featured a façade of a geometric structure of precast concrete, a material which, according to one of the partners in the design office, Gordon Bunshaft, better suited the historical context of Belgium's capital city.[28] On the other hand, as far as the furnishings were concerned, the new Banque Lambert strongly resembled the modern corporate buildings of postwar America. The interiors of the bank were designed by De Coene and Simonis, a Brussels-based company which in the mid-1950s also chose to modernize its furniture collection and became one of the first suppliers of Herman Miller products to Belgium. As in many contemporary American office buildings, the lobby of the Banque Lambert was furnished with Mies's Barcelona Chairs and a Florence Knoll couch.[29]

Some observations can now be made on how Knoll, with its international identity, contributed to the political reorientation of De Coene. In collaborating with this American-based company, De Coene took the side of one of the former allied forces. But it also implicitly took a position in a new conflict: that of the Cold War. After all, Knoll, and thus also De Coene, clearly added to the growing visual representation of the American superpower in Western Europe, a phenomenon much criticized by many in the Eastern Bloc. As former Knoll associate Brian Lutz explains in his monograph on the company, from the early 1940s Knoll had been "established with the Washington elite, thanks to work the Planning Unit had done for clients such as Henry Stimson, the secretary of war, and Nelson Rockefeller, who was active in the foreign affairs of the Franklin Roosevelt administration."[30] Therefore, according to Lutz, "it was a logical progression for Knoll to become actively involved with the Office of Federal Building Operation—the FBO—a division of the State Department that oversaw construction, planning, and maintenance of buildings and real estate in other countries."[31] In their 1981 monograph on the company, Eric Larrabee and Massimo Vignelli point out that, after the Second World War, Knoll was able to profit from the so-called "counterpart funds" of the United States in Europe created by the Marshall Plan.[32] For example, the US State Department placed a large order with Knoll for furnishings to be used in the diplomatic facilities expansion program. This commission, paid with by counterpart funds, Larrabee and Vignelli explain, provided the starting capital for the company's overseas expansion. The 1954 license contract between Knoll and De Coene itself confirms the strong ties between the American firm and the American authorities. It stipulated that Knoll Associates and Knoll International reserved the right to sell directly "to the American government and to all public or semi-governmental American agencies or bodies on the territories assigned to the licensee and without having to grant compensation for this to the latter."[33] As architectural historian Greg Castillo points out, "Knoll was the perfect Marshall Plan partner: a charismatic entrepreneur, familiar to officials in Washington through its firm's design commissions for federal office buildings, and endowed with business contacts across Europe."[34]

Knoll products were also displayed in several pro-American exhibitions in Europe. As both Paul Betts and Castillo have shown, in the 1950s they were part of several "soft power" presentations of the United States in Western Germany.[35] They were likewise part of several editions of the *American Design for Home and Decorative Use* exhibition, first held in 1953 in the Taidehalli (Art Hall) in Helsinki as part of the larger *American Home 1953* exhibition organized by the Finnish-American Society.[36] *American Design for Home and Decorative Use* was a traveling exhibition sponsored by the newly formed United States Information Agency (USIA). It displayed over 300 American domestic commodities selected by curators of the Museum of Modern Art in New York. According to art historian Gay McDonald it "played an early and until now overlooked role in this larger story of how American domestic commodities were sent abroad specifically to inform other nations of the high standards of living enjoyed in the United States."[37] In the following year, the exhibition traveled to many other European venues, including two Belgian ones—successively the Casino in Ostend and the Ghent Museum of Decorative Arts—although it must be noted that the response in Belgium was not as evident as in Finland.[38] In short, Knoll's seductive "international style" products in Europe, in some contexts more obviously than in others, engendered specific political connotations. They became part of the overseas construction of images of a progressive American lifestyle, much condemned by many in the Eastern Bloc who believed that the Marshall Plan was part of a capitalist endeavor to erode local economies and national sovereignty.[39]

In producing, presenting, and selling Knoll products, De Coene was in effect supporting the political representation of America in the Benelux. Some of the company's assignments even directly underlined or promoted the presence of the United States in Europe. For example in 1955 De Coene signed an important contract for the construction of 1,800 trailers for the US Air Force (Figure 8.4).[40] The trailers were designed to house employees and their families in the numerous American air bases built in Europe after the war. However, it was mainly with Knoll that the De Coene firm contributed to the introduction of the postwar image of the "American way of life" in the Benelux. This took place in a quite subtle way. In overseas areas Knoll strategically labeled itself not as much as an "American," but as an "international" firm, and strongly promoted collaboration with local architects, artists and companies. Meanwhile local agents were gently instructed to develop a pro-American network. For example, Jan Saverys, the first manager of the Brussels Knoll showroom, remembers how he was advised by the Knoll company to collect the names and addresses of the architects in the Benelux who subscribed to the American journals *Progressive Architecture* or *Architectural Forum*.[41] These contacts were meant to serve as a basis for the new showroom's network. So, in its association with Knoll, De Coene contributed to a cleverly developed and locally embedded promotion of an "American way of life."

Knoll and Postwar Modern Architecture in Belgium

In Belgium, Knoll International's locally embedded promotional strategy quickly produced results. From 1954 onwards Knoll products were increasingly visible, especially in the cultural and architectural realms. This was the year in which full-page advertisements began to appear in many Belgian architectural and art journals. In the following years these journals, as well as foreign journals such as *Architectural*

8.4
De Coene, trailers for the US Air Force, c. 1955

Forum or the French *L'Architecture d'Aujourd'hui*, published advertisements for modern building, furnishing products, or technical appliances based on images that presented these products in combination with Knoll furniture. Some journals, such as the Flemish *Bouwen en Wonen*, even devoted a series of articles to the Knoll company and published pictures of diverse interiors in Belgium furnished with Knoll products: the Brussels Knoll showroom, the Brussels bar Cap d'Argent, designed by Chistophe Gevers (who from around 1956 assisted Saverys in the showroom of Knoll International in Brussels), a Brussels hotel by architect René Stapels, the reading room of the seminary in Bruges by architect Arthur Degeyter, and several domestic interiors by, for example, architects Henri Montois and Robert Courtois, or by Casimir Grochowsky and Roger Delfosse.[42]

Furthermore, Knoll furniture appeared in many exhibitions in Belgium in the 1950s. In some cases the furniture elements were part of the objects on display. For example, this was the case in the model house for the 1953 *Salon de l'Enfance et de la Famille* in the Palais des Beaux Arts in Brussels, designed and equipped by the Société Belge des Urbanistes et Architectes Modernistes (SBUAM).[43] (Constantin Brodzki, the architect who in the same period was involved in the construction of the Brussels Knoll showroom, was a member of SBUAM.) Knoll furniture was also on display in *Vormen van Heden* (Forms of Today) in Knokke in

Fredie Floré

8.5
Exhibition *Vormen van Heden* (Forms of Today), Knokke, Belgium, 1957

1957, an exhibition whose curators were K.-N. Elno and the Flemish painter Luc Peire and which was designed to show the close relationships between the fine and the applied arts (Figure 8.5). Here, several groups of Knoll furniture were shown in combination with abstract works of art.

However, in many other exhibitions the furniture elements themselves were not the protagonists of the show. *Hout, vriend van de mens* (Wood, Friend of Mankind) in Antwerp in 1955, for example, was an exhibition promoting the use of wood. One of the participating companies was De Coene and several chairs designed by Eero Saarinen stood in the exhibition space. It is unclear whether the chairs were officially part of the objects on display, but photographs show that they obtained a prominent place on the exhibition floor, not just as seating, but as part of the visual and spatial layout. Another clear example of the integrated presence of Knoll furniture in an exhibition context is the 1958 Brussels World's Fair. In this case, De Coene was able to fully demonstrate its capacities as both a supplier of wooden building components and furniture maker and at the same time to profit from its extensive network of contacts.[44] It not only constructed glulam structural frames for twenty-three pavilions, it also built two completely prefabricated buildings, delivered wood-based sheets for dozens of interiors and exteriors, was involved with an experimental wooden folded plate construction, and showcased its products in three pavilions. Moreover it produced Knoll furniture for over twenty-seven Belgian and foreign pavilions or exhibitions: Knoll furniture was present in the model house built by De Coene next to the Buildings and Dwellings pavilion, in the American pavilion, in the international fine art show *Fifty Years of Modern Art* (whose layout was designed by Peter Callebout, an architect known for his contemporary projects exploring the possibilities of wood construction), and in numerous other ways.[45]

In Belgium, as in many other countries, Knoll products soon became objects representing an elite cultural status, finding their way not only into the lobbies and executive offices of modern office buildings but also into the houses of those members of the upper-middle class who chose to live in a "modern" way. The March 1957 issue of the American journal *Architectural Forum* characterized "the Knoll interior" in this way: "as much a symbol of modern architecture as Tiffany glass was a symbol of the architecture of the Art Nouveau."[46] This symbolic value was quite successfully exported to Belgium. In the 1950s and 1960s a significant number of architects consciously integrated Knoll furniture into the visual representation of their designs, as if to underline the modernity of their work. As a symbol of modern architecture, Knoll products turned out to be quite flexible. For example, these Belgian architects did not necessarily share the same appreciation for architecture made in America and their own work often was quite different in nature.

As an example, one might focus in on one of the most important architectural assignments of the twentieth century in Belgium, that of the single family house, for example, those designed by the Walloon architectural office Groupe EGAU (Études en Groupe d'Architecture et d'Urbanisme) and by the architect Paul Felix. The Mozin House (1957–1958) by Groupe EGAU, for instance, is a steel construction which overlooks the city of Liège. Pictures of the house published in 1960 show interiors mainly filled with Knoll furniture (Figure 8.6).[47] Jules Mozin (1914–1995), the owner of the house, was one of the partners of Groupe EGAU. According to various accounts, he was fascinated by steel structures and had great enthusiasm for the Case Study Houses of Craig Ellwood and Pierre Koenig.[48] The use of "American" Knoll furnishings perhaps refers to Mozin's admiration for the Californian architecture of those years, and underlines the open spatial structure and other modernist features of his own house. Other houses designed by Groupe EGAU in this period were also furnished with Knoll furniture, such as a "house for an engineer" in Liège, on which a feature article was published in the Belgian architectural journal *La Maison* in 1960.[49]

The contemporary Flemish architect Paul Felix (1913–1981) showed appreciation for the work of a different set of American architects.[50] In 1954 in an

Fredie Floré

8.6
Above: Architects Groupe EGAU, Mozin House, Liège, Belgium, 1957–1958
Below: Architects Groupe EGAU, Interior of the Mozin House, Liège, Belgium, 1957–1958

8.7
Architect Paul Felix, Interior of the Bonduel House, Bruges, Belgium, 1959 (Photograph by R. Vanroelen)

article on the architecture of "the new world" he began by clarifying that his sympathy for modern design was not synonymous with a blind admiration for everything "made in U.S.A."[51] He praised the work of Frank Lloyd Wright, but also criticized the American taste for "the chromed glamour of luxury cars."[52] He praised the refinement of Mies van der Rohe's work, but also tentatively questioned the extent of its human qualities. The architecture for which Felix showed the most appreciation in his article was that of the country houses of Marcel Breuer. In Breuer's well-balanced play of simple geometric volumes and the frequent use of brickwork and concrete, Felix possibly saw some affinities with his own architecture. Felix's work in this period had an unpretentious modern appearance that was characterized by a clear functional and structural organization. In the published interior photographs of several of his 1950s single-family houses, Knoll furniture takes a prominent position. "The Knoll furniture elements are typical," Felix's biographers Geert Bekaert and Ronny De Meyer point out in their description of the interior of the 1954 house for Dr. Gyselen in Pellenberg.[53] Another example is that of the House Bonduel (1959) in Bruges, designed by Felix for the artist Roger Bonduel, known for his expressive metal sculptures. In both cases, the Knoll furniture first and foremost seems to underline the somewhat subdued progressive nature of Felix's architecture. In the case of House Bonduel, the rather expensive Knoll furniture elements such as the Bertoia Diamond chair were accompanied by several coffee or side tables, which the artist had designed and made himself but which were clearly inspired by the Knoll collection (Figure 8.7).[54] Bonduel recalls that it was Felix who encouraged him to buy the Knoll designs.[55] Although he was aware of the modern furniture production of several Belgian designers at that time, he chose to follow the architect's leads for the interior arrangement of his house.[56]

In conclusion, by buying the Knoll production licenses for the Benelux, De Coene took a significant step in reorienting its problematic political identity. At the same time, within the Belgian context, it introduced an additional tool for architects to express the specific modern character of their work. In some cases, as for example in the work of Groupe EGAU or Paul Felix, the architects had some sympathy with a specific niche of American architectural output. The presence of Knoll as part of their own architectural designs can be interpreted as an indicator of these sympathies, but first of all as an intensifier of the "modern" qualities of their work. This was one of the most remarkable strengths of the Knoll furniture brand. Its appealing modern design, supported by strong marketing strategies, convincingly presented itself as "international" and as a perfect tool with which to highlight the modern character of the "local" architecture, art or other (cultural) production. Houses such as that of Mozin or Bonduel only reinforced this mechanism. Interior photographs of these houses were published in the architectural and cultural press in Belgium and confirmed the seemingly perfect marriage of "international" and "local" modernity, while the political meaning of this process was left undiscussed.

Notes

Acknowledgments: The author wishes to thank Roger Bonduel, Philippe De Craene, Jérôme Dervichian, Jan Saverys, and the Stichting De Coene for their feedback and support; Rika Devos for collaborating on the research on the postwar history of De Coene; and Wendy Scheerlinck, Kaat Standaert, and Niké Vanderpoorten who wrote master's theses on themes relating to the subject of this chapter.

1   On December 24, 1953 the license contract between Knoll Associates/Knoll International Limited and the Ateliers d'Art de Courtrai/Knoll International Brussels (the corporation which De Coene had to establish within three months of signing the contract) was signed. The first license period started on January 1, 1954. See "Convention" (unpublished document, undated copy), Rijksarchief Kortrijk (Public Record Office Kortrijk), Archive of the Kantoor Controle Vennootschappen 2 in Kortrijk, pack 257, file tax assessment year 1955; and "Agreement" (unpublished document, 1 March 1961), Rijksarchief Kortrijk (Public Record Office Kortrijk), Archive of the Kantoor Controle Vennootschappen 2 in Kortrijk, pack 263, file tax assessment year 1965. The 1961 contract also mentions the date of the first contract.
2   George H. Marcus, *Functionalist Design: An Ongoing History* (Munich: Prestel, 1995), 145.
3   K.-N. Elno, "Ludwig Mies van der Rohe: genie en drama," *Tijdschrift voor Architectuur en Beeldende Kunst* 4 (1965): 77. Unless otherwise noted, translations are the author's own. For a discussion of the design criticism of K.-N. Elno, see Fredie Floré, "Design Criticism and Social Responsibility: The Flemish Design Critic K.-N. Elno (1920–1993)," in *Writing Design: Words and Objects*, ed. Grace Lees-Maffei (Oxford: Berg Publishers, 2011).
4   For examples of positive reviews of Knoll products in architectural and design journals in Belgium, see Léon-Louis Sosset, "Het meubel draagt bij tot het uitbouwen van de hedendaagse stijl. De firma Knoll," *Kunstambachten en Kunstnijverheden* 80 (1956): n.p.; Jul De Roover, "Meubelen Knoll International Brussels," *Bouwen en Wonen* 1 (1959): 3.
5   Geert Bekaert, "Tien jaar Knoll International," *De Linie* 695 (1962): 9.
6   Elno, "Ludwig Mies van der Rohe: genie en drama," 77.
7   Ibid., 78.
8   Ibid.

Knoll International in Belgium

9   See Jul De Roover, "Meubelen Knoll International Brussels," *Bouwen en Wonen* 1 (1959): 3.

10   For an overview of the history of the firm, see *Kortrijkse Kunstwerkstede Gebroeders De Coene: 80 jaar ambacht en industrie. Meubelen—interieurs—architectuur* (Kortrijk: Uitgeverij Groeninghe Kortrijk, 2006). The first historical overview of the post–Second World War activities of De Coene was published in 2002, see Fredie Floré, "De Coene na WOII: meubelproducent en bouwfirma," in *van Moderne Makelij 1952-1977. De Kortrijkse Kunstwerkstede De Coene in Antwerpen*, ed. Mil De Kooning, Ronny De Meyer, and Fredie Floré (Antwerp: Erfgoedcel Stad Antwerpen, 2002), 9–40.

11   See Ruben Majeur et al., "Ambachten en industrie onder één dak. Groei en ontwikkeling van de Kortrijkse Kunstwerkstede," in *Kortrijkse Kunstwerkstede Gebroeders De Coene*, 41–69.

12   For a discussion on the postwar investments of De Coene in new branches of the wood and furniture industries, see Rika Devos and Fredie Floré, "Modern Wood: De Coene at Expo 58," *Construction History* (2009): 103–120.

13   Hilde Bouchez, "Adolf De Coene, de trots van de oude blinde meubelmaker. U moet daar eens aan voelen. Ziet u wat ik bedoel?" *De Standaard Magazine* 42 (1998): 12–4.

14   Jérôme Dervichian, "De Harry Bertoia-stoel," in *Art De Coene. Jaarboek 1* (Kortrijk: Stichting De Coene vzw, 2000), 19–21. Another De Coene collaborator, Achilles Daelman, talks about the production of the Bertoia chairs in Belgium on the following DVD: "Achilles Daelman: Diamond Chair (1952) by H. Bertoia, Knoll," *Kortrijkse Kunstwerkstede, Ateliers d'Art de Courtrai De Coene gebr,* Terenja van Dijk and Frank Herman (Kortrijk: Erfgoedcel Kortrijk, 2009).

15   See Brian Lutz, *Knoll: A Modernist Universe* (New York: Rizzoli, 2010), 62. See also Richard Schultz, "The Outdoorsman," interview by Paul Makovsky, *Metropolis Magazine* 29, no. 10 (May 2010): 108–113.

16   Dervichian, "De Harry Bertoia-stoel," 19–21.

17   Ibid.

18   See Majeur et al., "Ambachten en industrie onder één dak," 41–69. See also Fred Germonprez, *Jozef De Coene en de Kortrijkse Kunstwerkstede* (Tielt: Lannoo, 1983), 163–219. For a spoken account of the position of De Coene within the economic field in Belgium during the Second World War, see also the DVD "De Coene and the Second World War: A Historical Analysis. Prof. Dr. Dirk Luyten SOMA/CEGES, UGent—BE," *Kortrijkse Kunstwerkstede*, Terenja van Dijk and Frank Herman.

19   See, for example, John F. Pile, "Knoll International," vol. 1 of *Encyclopedia of Interior Design*, ed. Joanna Banham (Oxford : Fitzroy Dearborn, 1995), 687–689.

20   See Lutz, *Knoll*, 40.

21   On the introduction of Knoll International in France, see for example Dominique Forest, ed., *Mobi Boom: L'Explosion du design en France 1945-1975* (Paris: Les Arts Décoratifs, 2010).

22   Jonathan M. Woodham, *Oxford Dictionary of Modern Design* (Oxford: Oxford University Press, 2006), 244.

23   See Pile, "Knoll International," 687–689.

24   For more information on Constantin Brodzki, see Pierre Loze et al., *Constantin Brodzki : Architecte* (Sprimont: Pierre Mardaga éditeur, 2004).

25   Bobbye Tigerman, "'I Am Not a Decorator': Florence Knoll, the Knoll Planning Unit and the Making of the Modern Office," *Journal of Design History* 1 (2007): 61–74.

26   The showroom of Knoll International in Amsterdam was located in a large house on the Keizersgracht, number 699. In 1971 this showroom moved to the Weesperstraat. See Dervichian, "De Harry Bertoia-stoel," 19–21.

27   See Constance Rubini, "Éditer, diffuser," in Forest, ed., *Mobi Boom,* 229.

28   See Peter Blake, "SOM Puts the Bones Outside the Skin," *Architectural Forum* (May 1959): 147–148.

29   See "Banque Lambert à Bruxelles," *L'Architecture d'Aujourd'hui,* September 1965: 100.

30 Lutz, *Knoll*, 61. According to Florence Schust the design of the office of Henry Stimson was her first job for Hans Knoll. See Lutz, 26.
31 Ibid., 61.
32 Eric Larrabee and Massimo Vignelli, *Knoll Design* (New York: Abrams, 1981), 176.
33 "Convention" (unpublished document), Rijksarchief Kortrijk (Public Record Office Kortrijk), Archive of the Kantoor Controle Vennootschappen 2 in Kortrijk, pack 263, file tax assessment year 1965, 3.
34 Greg Castillo, *Cold War on the Home Front: The Soft Power of Midcentury Design* (Minneapolis: University of Minnesota Press, 2010).
35 See Paul Betts, *The Authority of Everyday Objects: A Cultural History of West German Industrial Design* (Berkeley: University of California Press, 2004), 88 or Castillo, *Cold War on the Home Front*.
36 Gay McDonald, "The Modern American Home as Soft Power: Finland, MoMA and the 'American Home 1953' Exhibition," *Journal of Design History* 4 (2010): 387–408.
37 Ibid., 387–408.
38 At the time of writing, the author found only one substantial review on the Belgian editions of *American Design for Home and Decorative Use*. See Léon-Louis Sosset, "In de kursaal van Oostende. In het Museum voor Sierkunsten te Gent. Tentoonstelling van door het Museum voor Moderne Kunst van New York uitgelezen voorwerpen," *Kunstambachten en Kunstnijverheden* 57 (1954) 1–3. On the success of the *American Home 1953* exhibition in Helsinki, see McDonald, "The Modern American Home as Soft Power," 387–408.
39 See Castillo, *Cold War on the Home Front*.
40 See Ruben Majeur et al., "Houtindustrie De Coene: Opkomst en ondergang van een industriële groep," in *Kortrijkse Kunstwerkstede Gebroeders De Coene*, 141–169. Several articles in *Coen ende Vri*, the staff magazine of De Coene, refer to the construction of the trailers. See *Coen ende Vri* 1 and 2 (1955). In the mid-1950s the staff magazine also published a few articles on America in general, which were clearly meant to encourage a positive appreciation of the "new world" amongst employees. See L. D., "Over mensen en dingen in Amerika," *Coen ende Vri* 5 (1956): 11–2; W.D.B., "U.S.A. in vogelvlucht," *Coen ende Vri* 6 (1956): 4–5.
41 Jan Saverys, unpublished notes on Knoll International and De Coene (private archive of Jan Saverys, s.d., accessed by the author in 2000). Régine Chemay and Christophe Gevers assisted Saverys in the Knoll showroom in Brussels.
42 *Bouwen en Wonen* 12 (1958).
43 See Fredie Floré, *Lessons in Modern Living: Source Book on Housing Exhibitions in Belgium 1945–1958* (Ghent: WZW Editions and Productions, 2004).
44 See Devos and Floré, "De Coene at Expo 58," 103–120.
45 Peter Callebout designed the exhibition in collaboration with the artist Marc Mendelsohn. See Rika Devos, "Een groot fiasco? Het Expo 58-avontuur van de Belgische architecten," in *Moderne architectuur op Expo 58. "Voor een humaner wereld,"* ed. Rika Devos and Mil De Kooning (Brussels: Dexia/Mercatorfonds, 2006), 66.
46 "The Knoll Interior," *Architectural Forum* 3 (1957): 137.
47 Pierre-Louis Flouquet, "Habitation Familiale, à Liège. Architecte: J. Mozin (Groupe EGAU)," *La Maison* 4 (1960): 112–115.
48 See Mil De Kooning, "Groupe EGAU," in *Horta and After: 25 Masters of Modern Architecture in Belgium*, ed. Mil De Kooning (Ghent: Ghent University, 1999), 176–191.
49 "Habitation pour un ingénieur. Arch.: Groupe EGAU (Ch. Carlier—H. Lhoest—J. Mozin)," *La Maison* 10 (1960): 334–335.
50 See Geert Bekaert and Ronny De Meyer, *Paul Felix, 1913–1981: Architectuur* (Tielt: Lannoo, 1981).
51 Paul Felix, "De Nieuwe Wereld," *West-Vlaanderen* 6 (1954): 282–284.

52 Ibid.
53 Bekaert and De Meyer, *Paul Felix*, 50.
54 Unpublished interview with Roger Bonduel conducted by the author, Bruges, 22 January 2011.
55 Ibid.
56 In the 1950s Bonduel's work was shown several times in the same context or in the same venues as the work of young furniture designers in Belgium, for example in the Ghent Museum of Decorative Art (1956) or in the applied arts section of the 1958 World's Fair in Brussels. See Floré, *Lessons in Modern Living*.

Chapter 9

Domestic Environments
Italian Neo-Avant-Garde Design and the Politics of Post-Materialism

Mary Louise Lobsinger

While the contribution of Italian neo-avant-garde design to architectural discourse is often closely connected with the political upheaval of the late 1960s, many of the practices achieved parallel successes within the culture of high design. This dual aspect is rarely addressed in writing about the neo-avant-garde, although it is acknowledged in more commercial forums. Take for example the *Quaderna* tables designed by the collaborative Superstudio and since 1970 manufactured as part of the *Misera* series by Zanotta. An editorial featuring the tables in the Italian design magazine *Abitare* plays upon the coincidence between May 1998, the issue's publication date, and the social unrest of May 1968 (Figure 9.1). The accompanying text describes the *Quaderna* as evidence of the revolutionary spirit that once kindled "an electrifying moment when the negation of everything became the new everything."[1] The year "1968" as a placeholder signifying political revolt and as a marketing ploy enhancing the cultural value of design puts into paradoxical play a set of oppositions. Italian neo-avant-garde design practices aimed much of their creative efforts at critiquing or at least having fun with the presumed conformity underlying the social mores of a consumer-driven society. When referenced in various publications appearing decades later these same products still carry with them the aura of rebellion and anti-conformity through a strategy of persuasion aimed at a post-materialist consumer market. The mere mention of "1968" adds an immaterial quality to the physical item. This is hardly an abuse, for ambiguous readings and even an ambivalent relation to consumer culture were at work in design practices from this period. In other words, the inversion of intentions was internal to the critical project of neo-avant-gardism.

Domestic Environments

Progetto/*design:*	Superstudio (Adolfo Natalini, Cristiano Toraldo di Francia, Roberto Magris, Piero Frassinelli, Alessandro Magris), 1970
Tipologia/*typology:*	Tavolo/*table*
Produttore/*maker:*	Zanotta spa, 20054 Nova Milanese (Milano), via Vittorio Veneto 57, tel. 0362/368330, fax 0362/451038
Materiali/*materials:*	struttura di legno tamburato placcato di laminato Print, colore bianco, stampato in serigrafia a quadretti neri di 3 cm *Wooden frame electro-veneered in white Print laminate screenprinted with 3 cm black squares*
Dimensioni/*dimensions:*	cm 126x126x72 h/*126x126 cm, height 72 cm*
Prezzo al pubblico/*price:*	lire 4.060.000 IVA compresa/*L 4,060,000 including VAT*

9.1
Aldo Ballo, Photograph accompanying editorial, published in *Abitare* 373 (May 1998): 154

Ambivalence of the Grid

Superstudio's *Quaderna* tables are white plastic laminate rectangular tables, benches, and desks whose grid-scored surfaces give the visual impression of modularity and flexibility in assemblage. Superstudio labeled their first experiments with grid-based objects and environments "Istogrammi di architettura" or histograms of architecture (Figure 9.2). These investigations with the grid and cube soon evolved beyond the composition of furniture-like architectural objects to eventually collage and filmic explorations of the grid as a conceptual device deployed over vast geographies. The *Quaderna* evidenced the practicality of the grid as a compositional tool and can be interpreted as a tongue-in-cheek commentary upon the modernist trope of modularity and the repeatability of form as a rational means for mass producing objects for domestic use. As the group's politicized cultural intentions grew more ambitious, they re-conceptualized the function of the grid and, ironically taking credit as its inventor, re-named it the "supersurface." As a supersurface the grid encouraged contradictory interpretations as a device that enabled the effortless design at all possible scales—from furniture, to buildings, to environments, and most famously depicted as the *Continuous Monument* of 1970 (Figure 9.3). Through the supersurface, the collaborative also leveled a socio-political critique at the relation between design and the environment.[2]

The supersurface performed in various projects as a resilient and multi-tasking epistemological metaphor in that, as noted by philosopher Umberto Eco, "the structure of its form reflected the way in which contemporary culture viewed reality."[3] The well-publicized drawings and collages of Superstudio's work from this period are always accompanied by texts that give varied and at times conflicting interpretations of the grid's materiality and function. The supersurface has been

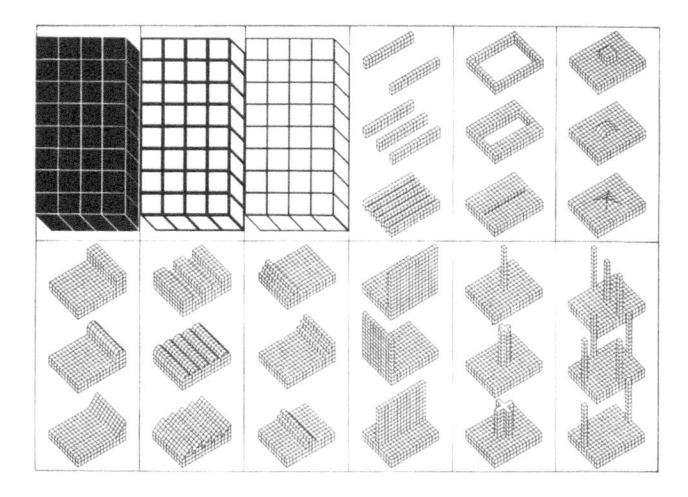

9.2
Superstudio, *Istogrammi d'Architettura*, 1969, published in *Domus* 497 (April 1971): 46

9.3
Superstudio, *The Continuous Monument: On the Rocky Coast*, photocollage cut-and-pasted printed paper, colored pencil, and oil stick on board, 1969, 18⅜ × 18⅛ inches (46.7 × 46 cm), The Museum of Modern Art, New York

described by the group as a simple reflective mirroring surface and, more luxuriously, as executed in materials such as alabaster. In realizations such as the *Continuous Monument* the supersurface serves as the enclosure for a gigantic single structure. Again function is contradictorily construed as on one hand an ecological container and on the other, more sinisterly, as a depiction of global urbanization that evidences "the horrors realized through architecture's pursuit of scientific methods."[4] Drawing upon aspirations that parallel those of conceptual art practices—such as those of Sol LeWitt—the grid surface is said to represent a "model of a mental attitude" or a field of energy enabling spontaneous communication.[5] With this latter assignment, depicted vividly in colorful collages, the grid performs as an immaterial support for human emancipation from the repressive strictures of everyday life.[6] While the depictions could be interpreted as representing technological support encouraging new subject positions through, for example, the unfettered freedom to roam— physically and psychically—the globe, they equally invoke an opposing condition.

Depicting humans mindlessly wandering through geographically disparate landscapes the grid becomes a representation of a closed socio-economic system of an accelerated capitalism where all desires are pre-scripted in advance of need or experience. From this perspective the grid as supersurface represents the rationalization of experience or what in the early 1960s the philosopher and social theorist Herbert Marcuse characterized as the effect of the "technological apparatus of an administered society."[7] At once symbolic of the democratic distribution of space, the grid in this latter instance becomes an invisible instrument of repression. These interpretations reflect well-rehearsed critiques of the role played by modernist architects and planners in the over-determination of the physical environment.

Superstudio's ambivalent use of the grid as supersurface cannot be dismissed. It compares with critical cultural thinking within creative practices that subscribed to aesthetic withdrawal or to institutional critique as well as to those questioning claims to authorship within media-dominated social conditions. The grid, whether white scored plastic surface or representing an invisible electronic net, can be interpreted as positing a retreat from the visual within the field of consumption. Likewise the supersurface's imagined generative potential, the iterability of form and repetition that comprises an infinitely extendable grid would appear to negate the designer's creative expenditure. However naive these challenges to the modus operandi of the designer, the design authorship can be decoupled from the designed object or project, the belief underlying such work assumes design can perform as a vehicle for critical thought. Taking this stance the designer, despite in reality being inextricably a construct and at the service of the market, can freely disavow complicity with consumer desires, especially those produced by authored aesthetic affect.

Whether representing the withdrawal from aesthetic presence, the global mapping of rationalizing technologies, or an enhanced cybernetic dimension, the supersurface remains intransigently paradoxical. As a conceptual apparatus it throws into relief the impossibility of distinguishing between familiar dualisms, such as the artificial and the natural, or the spectacle of reality and reality. In light of the political fallout of the 1960s, the overall effect is to perplex or make difficult the Marxian equation illustrating the relation between production and consumption within capitalism. Perhaps what the conceptual dexterity of the grid-scored surface most significantly puts into play are not questions of representation but of capacity to perform by drawing attention to the framing of reality. The grid demands the viewer-user consider or, more strongly, confront questions about how reality is structured.[8] The grid as the infinite extension of man-made sign systems orders reality as abstract. In this capacity, that of ordering reality beyond the immediately visual, the querying of the grid shifts from the interpretation of form and content to its performance. The movement of thought between the image (as contents of reality) and its support (the grid as a frame) casts doubt upon the experience of reality as either objective or subjective. Reality is framed as second nature, that is, as an ideological construct dependent upon so many socio-cultural and political conditions. In various realizations the supersurface provokes reflection upon the conditions that mediate human experience, whether physical, virtual, technological, political, environmental, or behavioral.[9] Given this, the conceptual dexterity of the supersurface seems to be secondary to what it does: it calls attention to our experience of objects, social relationships, and environments as structured. And yet, for all the conceptual play and critical potential elicited from the supersurface, it became—as the editorial published in *Abitare* suggests—evidence of the successful exportation of Italian design. In the 1960s there were, however, design practices that, if less commercially successful than Superstudio, were engaged in a similar critical cultural endeavor.

Modification of Use

In the late 1960s and early 1970s the focus of Italian experimental design practices varied from speculation upon electronically enabled environments and collaborative performances to the pedagogically motivated adaptation of poor materials to innovative structural concepts. The shared aim of these various practices might be identified as the radical modification of use. To meddle with a received function of an object, a material, or environment was theorized as a tactic that could bring about a reterritorialization of subjects and objects in space. In other words, confounding use could both change user experience and call attention to negative effects of an ever-adapting capitalist mode of production. It was theorized that the challenge to habitual uses and customary functions of an object or environment would create vacuoles of "non" communication, encouraging alternative routes of communication, or perform as a circuit breaker within that much-abused term, "the system."[10] As a means for challenging use, Superstudio's supersurface, proffered as a neutral field, disavows any presumed use in advance of users. It speaks to a withdrawal of aesthetic intention as use-value as well as the more literal structuring of experience. While the design and production of furniture destined for the marketplace or drawings for galleries present rather suspect ground for aesthetic withdrawal there were less well-publicized practices that engaged more tangible considerations of use.

During the 1970s architect Riccardo Dalisi worked with children from the Traiano Quartiere, an impoverished housing development in Naples, where he experimented with "*tecnica povera.*"[11] This work offers what might be considered a more modest approach to the idea of modification of use, framed as a politically motivated practice and creative strategy with a specific social objective. In one project the children exercised creative energies and engaged their immediate environment by using paper and found materials to make simple non-load-bearing structures that demarcated new spatial relations within the housing estate (Figure 9.4). Dalisi introduced the children to basic structural principles such as those employed by Frei Otto and Buckminster Fuller. This re-use of materials was not to be confused with the aestheticizing of waste or found objects popular in art schools. Andrea Branzi of the architecture studio Archizoom Associati, ever willing to capitalize on a moment of anti-design or participatory practice as an example of radical design, praised Dalisi's experiments as evidence of "liberated collective creativity,"[12] the outcome of which, he claimed, resisted any formulation to general principles or methodology. In an issue of *Casabella*—the voice piece of the Italian *architettura radicale* during this period—Branzi labeled Dalisi's practice "guerrilla warfare." It was a practice that focused on specific acts over future results thereby privileging user

9.4
Riccardo Dalisi. *Untitled Photograph*, 1974, published in *Architettura d'animazione* (Editore Beniamino Carucci, 1974), 72

participation over the making of artifacts for use. It was imagined that activities that spawned modifications in use might incite unpredictable lines of flight in thought and action among the children and inhabitants of the ghetto. Equally the participatory hands-on approach was considered a challenge to the normative conditions of practice and the disciplinary designation of space in advance of use. This position was predicated on notions of user participation and the employ of simple techniques to ends other than expected. Such socially committed approaches eschewed the pursuit of utopia as a future perfect place or the hype surrounding new technological means for mass communication.

Addressed to a parallel but rather different audience and ends, the projects by the Milan-based artist-architect Ugo La Pietra varied in use of materials and surrounding environment. La Pietra is quoted as polemically condemning the design profession as "the formalizers" and for making decisions based upon, as he described it, rigid and distinct categories of individual, environment, and object.[13] His work might be characterized as multimedia, installation-based environments that, operating at various scales, were intended to produce direct experiences of reality. In an experiment appropriately titled *Immersions* (*Immersione*) from 1971, a translucent acrylic globe was placed over the head and upper body of a participant who was then bombarded with new stimuli including electronic music and Styrofoam balls. Other projects such as *The Crossings* (*I percorsi*) or *Model of Comprehension* (*Modello di comprensione*) had more public and collective engagement with reality (Figure 9.5). For example, La Pietra would place PVC covered triangular structures in a street or piazza with the intent of re-framing significant tourist views, such as the Duomo in Milan. The devices employed in these projects were rather simple and yet they acted upon the viewer's experience. Some of his experiments appear in retrospect as rather comical explorations aimed at producing alternative realities. La Pietra explained the goals of these experiments in ideological terms, as intended to remove the "filters of reality" or "to liberate form."[14] Writing about La Pietra's work, the critics Gillo Dorfles and Tommaso Trini—champions of *arte povera*—rather grandly characterized his *ad hoc* pieces as "experimentations in chance that challenged environmental planning."[15] La Pietra described the experiments in phenomenological terms as explorations that tested the "degrees of liberty available within the structures of organization."[16] He wrote rather poetically that the cultural operator "with a critical sense of physics and an ability to use the image should try to upset the balance."[17] The various contraptions implemented by La Pietra were designed as instruments that could disturb the structural imposition and reinforcement of social behaviors through habitual use. La Pietra was not alone in believing that the slightest "alteration of the *system* could reveal a repressed desire for invention" or that practices that put pressure on the aural and visual could jump-start individual creativity and undo habits of social conditioning.[18]

The Florence-based design collaborative UFO produced happenings they titled *Urboeffimeri*, which loosely translates to mean "ephemeral urban happenings". The claims supporting the various projects ranged from disrupting what they described as the myths of "sociourbanism" through an array of disparate political issues popular among the left including racism, the war in Vietnam, and sexual repression.[19] The group's activities included temporary installations, performances, texts, and costume design. After 1968 UFO's positions took an ideological turn and their projects were dedicated to exposing, in their words, how "objects and ideas are the accessories of capitalism."[20] By the early 1970s their thinking, following a tendency among the Italian neo-avant-garde, added a poetic or what might loosely be called a phenomenological dimension when they began calling for the "destruction of the object."[21] In this vein, the rail against the "hypertrophy of the imaginary" or arguments for "magical territories of the imagination" parallels the intentions of groups such as Superstudio. Still UFO's rather ephemeral engagement with the modification of use did not operate upon an external urban structure nor did it directly address a traditional notion of the functionalist paradigm. Rather, as characterized by Adolfo Natalini of Superstudio in another context, this kind of work sought "a new reality within reality."[22] Similar to Superstudio's *lo spazio vissuto* ("the space of experience") experiments at the University of Florence dating from the late 1960s,

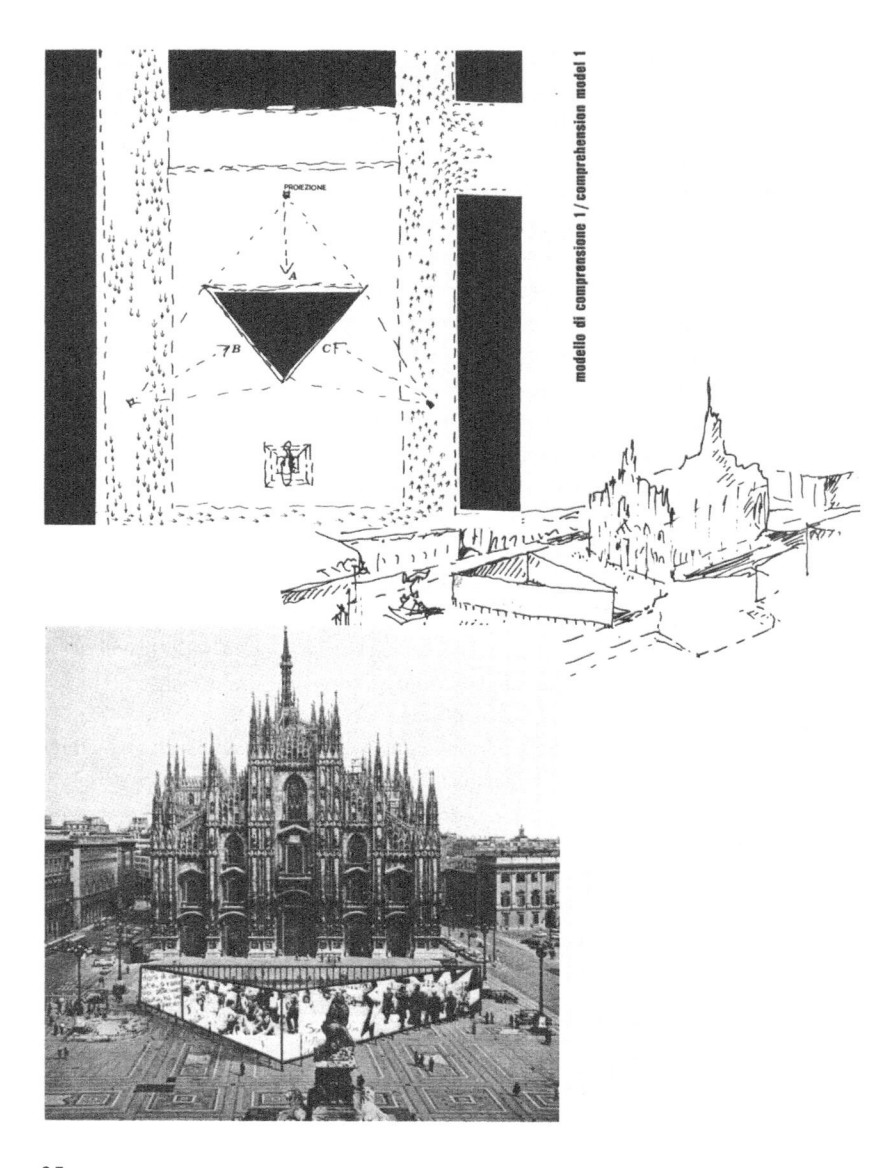

9.5
Ugo La Pietra, *Modello di comprensione,* published in *Casabella* 366 (June 1972): 47

UFO intended to "furnish architecture with destructive models of behavior," to widen its formal repertoire and predispose "the operator"—the equating of designer with user—"to new types of total action."[23] In 1969 Branzi directed the discussion of "user" and "use" away from urban or environmental structures to describe the "user" as a consumer of things, of culture and space. Presciently Branzi argued that the Marxian production-consumption equation no longer held true, for consumption now trumped production as the dominant mode of existence. However, like production, consumption enforced a social compliance. Differently from alienated conformity under capitalism, compliance within the advanced consumer society of "neo-capitalism" took the form of satiated, passive acceptance. Branzi wrote that radical practices should invent objects and environments able to resist exhausting the *raison d'être* for design within use. But equally, he exhorted designers to propose objects and projects that would enter the channels of consumption bereft of the usual, as he characterized it, vague extra, the cultural cache or aura so readily consumed. Design should confront, according to Branzi, "the spoiled consumer's bad conscience and fright on discovering objects which cannot be consumed" in any form.[24] The assumption underpinning the practices described above is based on a notion that designed objects and environments could and should awaken user-subjects to the conditions of living in a capitalist society. Practices were motivated by the belief that individual and group creativity might sponsor the formation of new social relations. This kind of thinking is an integral part of what we have come to expect from the nostalgic interpretation of 1960s as evidenced in the advertisements and blockbuster exhibitions of Italy, the land of good design.

Superstudio's project titled *A Place to Eat* (*Un posto per mangiare*) offers an apt example of a supposedly domestic object that solicits alternative uses while it simultaneously confronts any assumed idea of what a dining table should look like (Figure 9.6). Here the supersurface as deployable object divulges little of its possible functions; at best it presents itself as an inverted and rather ungainly four-legged table. The scale and organization of vertical elements as well as location in what appears to be an outdoor setting estrange the object from the discipline of sitting and eating at the table. While the structural and functional roles traditionally attributed to design are denied, the surface signals the artifice of design. Playing upon contradictory readings the object simultaneously ideologizes as it poetizes: it throws into doubt the function of design and of the thing called a table, while it poetizes the activity that momentarily defines it.[25] As a realization of *Istogrammi di architettura* it stands opposed to meaning in advance of use and is without residue to meaning after the activity has ceased. The placement, askew in a semi-natural setting, seems entirely arbitrary and may be illustrative of a tactical approach: the designers produce an object that offers an opportunity for an encounter between user, use, and environment. *A Place to Eat* presents an assault on the status of the object and its role in structuring the environment through functional, social, or cultural meaning. It offers a remedy for passive compliance to the dictates of social conformity as engagement turns users upon their own devices in structuring the environment.

9.6
Superstudio, *Istogrammi di architettura. Un posto per mangiare,* published in *Domus* 497 (April 1971): 46

Spatio-Political Turn

In the 1960s, cultural practices turned from objects to, as evidenced above, politically motivated projects that sought to frame or structure environmental situations. These kinds of practices are well documented and have been a recurring topic within art discourse.[26] Italian neo-avant-garde design practices, however influenced by experimental forms abroad, had an internal discourse that was, in political tenor, rather distinct. In 1969 the Italian art historian Giulio Carlo Argan convened a group of artists, architects, theorists, and historians to discuss the advent of new practices with socio-political aims at a seminar titled "Environmental Structures" (*Strutture ambientali*). In his introductory remarks Argan drew connections between recent architectural or spatial experiments and the political motivation to transform the social imagination. When he declares the impossibility of militating "against the system" and calls for artists to invent new modes of non-oppositional resistance, the influence of the post-1968 reformulating of Marxian practice is evident.[27] The old standard of direct oppositional revolt, the kind engaged by the historic avant-garde, was, he declared, no longer tenable. The call to the social imagination as a means of stepping beyond oppositional tactics is positioned against the old standard which pitted "technical integrationists," as advocates of total immersion in the cultural apparatus of capitalism, against "apocalyptic critics" or philosophical positions that might loosely be associated with, for example, the Frankfurt School.[28] Using the politicized anti-traditional artist term "cultural operators" Argan recommended the construction of temporal-spatial situations, similar to practices discussed above. In Argan's formulation these environments should challenge the users' or participants' habits of seeing and being; following Umberto Eco, cultural provocateurs should intervene somewhere between the externalized world of objects and the subject's internalization of environmental affects.[29] Perhaps more interesting for the architects and designers present at the event was Argan's call for a new avant-garde mandated to reformulate art as critical thought.

Participants at the seminar included some of the most prestigious critics and designers to emerge out of this period, including Gilles Dorfles, Tomas Maldonado, Giancarlo De Carlo, and Umberto Eco among others. Despite wide-ranging dissension among participants they could all concede one issue: the object as such had become a more complicated entity. Of the many possible theoretical inquiries into the relation of environment and politico-aesthetic experience from this period, Eco's—although often overlooked—is easily argued as most pertinent to the Italian practices. The turn to a semiotic reading of the environment is in part related to Eco's thesis on the pedagogic function of aesthetic production and reception. In important essays published during the 1960s, Eco evolved a semiotic subject of experience that situated at the center of every act of perception a continuously altering subjectivity, that is, an observer actively acquiring knowledge. Rather than a beholder or audience distanced from given works, Eco argued for a dynamic construal of aesthetic reception as a field of relations. The subject as well as the environment was figured as equally unstable or mutable. The purpose of art, as argued by Eco, was not to produce aura or to reconcile individuals to alienated life, or to the pressures of technological society and chaos of information-dense environments. Rather, "open works," as Eco characterized his preferred type, should enable individuals to seek "new ways of being free from within alienated conditions."[30] The politics of aesthetic experience as an open work differs radically from that of traditional art or the modality of attack and opposition engaged by the historical avant-garde.

Herbert Marcuse was an equally important influence upon experimental architecture practices of the 1960s. Like Eco, his theorizing of the condition of subjectivity offered a rationale for devising works that addressed the politics of imagination and, for some, a lighter perhaps less constricting version of Marxian thought than was emerging within the Italian Left at that time. It is worth noting that Marcuse's writings, although soon out of favor, were very popular, in particular his *One Dimensional Man*. In Italy the book became a best seller with sales reaching 170,000 copies in 1967. Marcuse analyzed social repression under what he theorized as an administered capitalism to argue that the techniques enabling the conquest of capitalist economic form—from the science of industrial production to blatant domination by means of management techniques aimed at rationalizing human behavior, such as behaviorism in the social sciences—had turned into a nefarious form, an overarching social administration. Marcuse coined the phrase "technological apparatus" to capture the extent to which the rationalizing means of control penetrated all aspects of life. Within administered society all subjective and objective experiences merged and all differences were leveled to the same, effecting an affirmative experience. In other words, the subject did not experience alienation in the traditional Marxist sense but rather was persuaded by new needs and desires that an otherwise excavated subjectivity was indeed full of life. If this was the experience of life within advanced capitalism, and it would seem that many of the Italian neo-avant-garde practices are aligned with such a diagnosis, then for Marcuse authentic freedom could only come about by devising new relationships between the techniques of social control and individual unconsciousness. In a sense, works that would alert one to the reality of empty life. Apparently contrary statements made by Marcuse for example "processes such as mechanization and standardization might actually release individual energy into unchartered realms of freedom beyond necessity" readily invoke the contradictory aspects of Superstudio's supersurface or La Pietra's environmental interventions.[31] And as we shall see, Marcuse's seemingly counterintuitive recommendation for stricter conditions of repression parallels Archizoom's proposal for an urban machine that heightens alienated experience to bring about the destruction of obsolete forms of existence. And later in Marcuse's *Essay on Liberation*, penned in response to the events of 1968, he advocates for artists to reproduce conditions that might enable the emergence of an aesthetic dimension from within technological society. By then Marcuse was championing the destruction of culture and calling for what he termed the "Great Refusal" which meant, refusing to participate in the "system."

It should be noted that not all participants in Argan's *Strutture ambientali* seminar agreed with the privileging of the imagination as a place or space of some authentic human condition. Emerging from the margins of the conference proceedings are voices of dissent, contesting the idea of the open work and dismissing all the talk about imagination as merely a form of escapism that forfeited the political. One of the more strident attacks came from Andrea Branzi of Archizoom.

Capitalist Machine

While much of the theoretical support for various radical design practices can be accounted for or interpreted through the writings by popular philosophers such as Marcuse and Eco, there were other political influences within Italian design culture. Archizoom resumed its critique of the relation between design and politics at a seminar held at the Politecnico di Torino in 1969 titled *utopia e/o rivoluzione* ("utopia and/or revolution"). Archizoom and members from the Torino-based radical groups Gruppo Strum and Anonima were the sole representatives of Italian practices at an event that included members from various British, American, and French collaboratives. In a text accompanying a project titled "The Theater of Power" (*Il teatro del potere*) Archizoom launched a polemical argument describing the conditions of social relations within capitalism. The text is heavily indebted to the Italian New Left, especially to Mario Tronti's seminal "The Factory and Society" (*La fabbrica e la società*) as published in *Quaderni rossi* in the early 1960s.[32] Archizoom paraphrases Tronti's analysis when they claim that the disappearance of distinctions between consumption and production had produced an economic model identical to the relations between factory and supermarket. This model now circulated within society organizing life, work, and the urban sphere across the plan of capital. Following Tronti, the organization of the factory had passed, Archizoom argued, from containment within the spatial sector of the factory to society where internalization had transformed the social into an urbanized global work force.[33] What on the surface appeared as technological progress was evidence of a mode of capitalism that had pervasively adapted technological rationality as ubiquitous organizational technique. The plan of capital presupposed a closed system; the more rational it becomes the more abstract it was, from factory organization to cognitive behavioral techniques. Archizoom argued—following Tronti and Raniero Panzieri before him—that capitalism was far from rational, and it irrationally and voraciously pursued new levels of integration and at every step produced false states, abstract states, of equilibrium.[34] Adapting this interpretation of capitalism led Archizoom to conclude that it was no longer useful to invent new forms of design or to propose imaginary better future worlds. Such efforts merely avoided reality and distracted from the problem at hand. They responded to this endgame capitalism by offering formless structures and monoforms that they argued would best service the motor of capitalism. An urbanism comprised of empty structures to be occupied would allow "quantity" in the Marxian sense, to circulate, accumulating freely, and in keeping with the imperative to offer nothing to consume, the proposal failed to provide any pretense to quality or value-added by means of design.[35] This rather literal interpretation of Tronti's theory of the new form of capitalism was transposed to perform as the intellectual support for Archizoom's seminal project, No-Stop City (Figures 9.7 and 9.8). It would be repeated with little refinement or elaboration in venues such as *Casabella*, *In. Argomenti e immagini di design*, *Domus*, and *Architectural Design* until about 1973.[36]

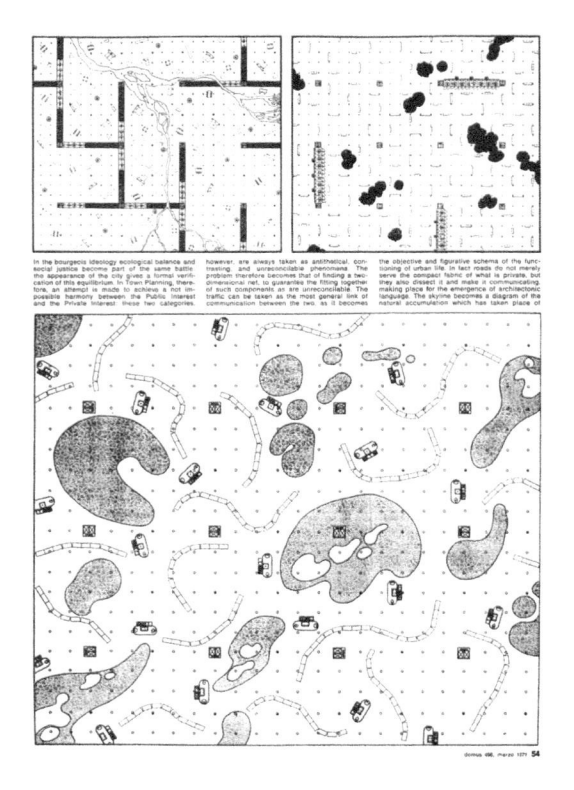

9.7
Archizoom, *No-Stop City. Residential Parkings. Climatic Universal Sistem*,
published in *Domus* 496 (March 1971): 54

      The didacticism of No-Stop City pushes the notion of the modification of use to an extreme limit. The idea of "use" that the project calls into question belongs to the old Marxist equation implicating use value and exchange value. No-Stop City is based on an analogy between factory and supermarket as the most efficient vehicles for integrating production and consumption on all levels of existence. It depicts the urban environment or city as a machine for producing use value absolutely bereft of exchange value. The city rendered as a single manufacture, as a coherent socio-economic form, is the place where the unity of capital realizes itself. The project proposes an ideal where ease of circulation harks back to more benign utopian propositions of the early twentieth century. But the difference lies with the condition of closure that allows for the ceaselessly efficient circulation of quantity—people and goods—bereft of quality. No-Stop City is not purely negative. It does propose a future realization, an end point to which the effortless circulation is geared: the irrationality of the system will, they predict, bring about the demise of capitalism. According to Archizoom's formulation the system, capitalism, when freed of internal resistances will be thrown into an accelerated state that eventually handicaps its

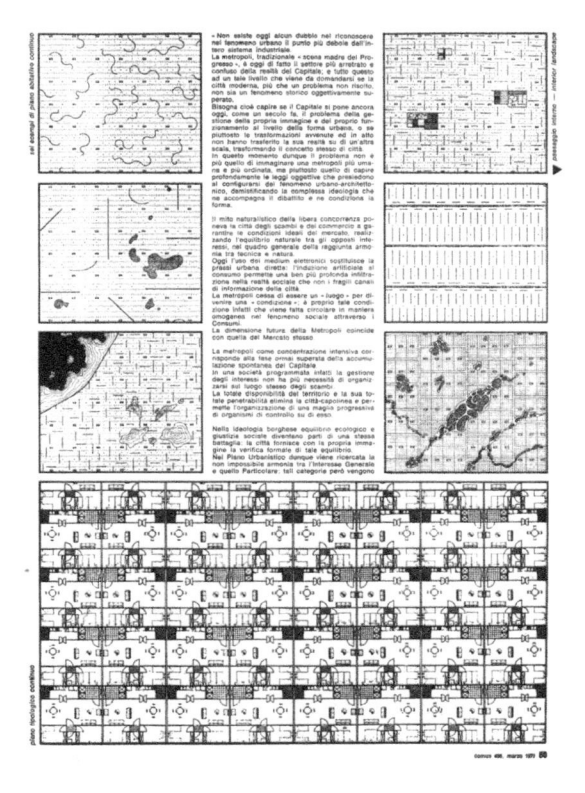

9.8
Archizoom, *No-Stop City. Residential Parkings. Climatic Universal sistem,*
published in *Domus* 496 (March 1971): 50

ability to manufacture new desires to consume and thus it will be left without new markets to conquer. To be driven into a state of total equilibrium or stasis, would mean death for a system dependent on continuous growth. For lacking motivation for and by consumers, the whole system comes to a standstill. In this way, Archizoom speculated by means of a polemical, manifesto-like urban proposition that capitalism could bring about its own destruction. If designers relinquished the aura that stoked consumption, then the seeds of failure would be found from within the very mechanisms of capitalism's success. The narrative was a close crib of Tronti's analysis.[37]

The containment implied by the factory and supermarket analogy also critiqued what the designers perceived as the manufacture of false separations within everyday life under capitalism—as if leisure and work, production and consumption were discrete and not the product of social relations. The repeatability of living cells and parking stalls demystified the abstract construction of, for example, Nature and Culture. While Tronti is clearly the source of this critique No-Stop City also recalls Marcuse's prescriptive approach to urban planning: to imagine the city as a machine and mechanize it accordingly through the stricter zoning of functions and the use of repetitive forms. Marcuse predicted that implementation of such techniques would exacerbate alienation and bring about revolt. As Branzi described it, No-Stop City was not an image of a better world. It was neither a utopia nor an alternative to present reality. Nor was No-Stop a proposition for the future rather it was intended to bring about a new critical awareness in the present.[38]

In conclusion, in Marcuse's formulation, ideology inhibited action and veiled human experience of reality. He argued that the veil of ideology could be pulled aside through either creative experience or contrarily, the enforcement of more stringently repressive conditions. Such notions were considered intolerably naive by the theorists of the Italian New Left, and yet Italian designers reading across various political analyses and theories, borrowed freely to support their practices. Most were not so optimistic as to believe in a future technological utopia or that creativity might liberate a repressed subjectivity, but offered alibis and the means—in whatever form—for making reality present, to prod the staid imagination.[39] The use of the grid, the factory, the supermarket, electronic gadgetry, as well as paper geodesic domes spoke eloquently of the desire to overcome the distance between image and reality, the abstract and the natural, architecture and the mechanisms of capitalism. Perhaps most importantly the designers well understood the role played by design as the elixir of capitalist consumption. Returning to the merchandized radicality of Superstudio's supersurface as an enduring exemplar of the Italian neo-avant-garde: now more than forty years later it would seem symptomatic of all it was meant to counter; the obsession with the new, the status of the object, the designer's signature as marketable commodity in a world where nothing seems to be new. Archizoom's ironic declaration of the elimination of quality from the equation of consumption or the belief that designers merely contributed an aesthetic filter that made repression palatable are the obverse side of aesthetic withdrawal. In the end, the paradox rests with the fact that practices which once advocated for a world freed from the pollution of design became internationally renowned designers of that very successful export: "Italian Design."

Notes

Acknowledgments: I would like to thank Robin Schuldenfrei for organizing the session at the annual meeting of the Association of Art Historians at Glasgow in April 2010 for which this paper was prepared and for her extraordinary effort in bringing this anthology to publication. For permission to republish images I would like to thank Archizoom Associati (A. Branzi, G. Corretti, P. Deganello, M. Morozzi, D. Bartolini, and L. Bartolini), Marirosa Toscani Ballo for Aldo Ballo, Riccardo Dalisi, Ugo La Pietra, Superstudio (A. Natalini, C. Toraldo di Francia, R. Magris, G.P. Frassinelli, A. Magris, A. Poli (1970–1972), *Casabella* and *Domus* (copyright Editoriale Domus S.p.A., Rozzano Milan, Italy), and the Museum of Modern Art, New York. The research is currently funded by a Social Sciences and Humanities Research Council Grant.

1   *Abitare* 373 (March 1998): 154. Unless otherwise noted, translations are the author's own.
2   Mildred S. Friedman, Introduction to Sottsass, "Superstudio on Mindscapes," *Design Quarterly* 89 (1973): 5. Also see the description in *In-arch*, Istituto nazionali di architettura, (Florence: Centro Di, 1978).
3   Umberto Eco, "The Open Work in the Visual Arts," in *The Open Work,* trans. Anna Cancogni (Cambridge, MA: Harvard University Press, 1989), 87–93.

4   Superstudio, Cristiano Toraldo di Francia, Alessandro Magris, Roberto Magris, Piero Frassinelli, Adolfo Natalini, "Superstudio on Mindscapes," *Design Quarterly* 89 (1973): 17.
5   Ibid., 19: "If the instruments of design have become as sharp as lancets and as sensitive as sounding lines, we can use them for a delicate lobotomy. Thus, beyond the convulsions of overproduction, a state of calm can be born, in which a world without products and refuse takes shape, a zone in which the mind is energy and raw materials, and also a final product, the only intangible objects of consumption."
6   See Superstudio's contribution to the exhibition and catalogue curated and edited by Emilio Ambasz, *Italy: The New Domestic Landscape* (New York: MoMA, 1972).
7   Herbert Marcuse, *One Dimensional Man: Studies in the Ideology of Advanced Industrial Society* (Boston, MA: Beacon Press, 1964), 23.
8   Rosalind Krauss, "Grids," in *The Originality of the Avant-Garde and other Modernist Myths* (Cambridge, MA: MIT Press, 1987), 21.
9   Tomás Maldonado, *Design, Nature, and Revolution: Toward a Critical Ecology* (New York: Harper & Row Publishers 1970, 1972 1st US edition), 3.
10 Gilles Deleuze, "Control and Becoming," *Negotiations 1972–1990* (New York: Columbia University Press, 1990), 175.
11 See Riccardo Dalisi, *Architettura d'Animazione: Cultura del proletariato e lavoro di quartiere a Napoli*. (Assisi-Rome: Editore Beniamino Carucci, 1974). See "Architettura nelle lotte di Quartiere," *In. Argomenti e immagini di design* 13 (Autumn, 1974).
12 Andrea Branzi, *Casabella* 364 (1972): 58–59.
13 Ugo La Pietra, "Counterdesign as Postulation," in *Italy: The New Domestic Landscape*, 227.
14 Ugo La Pietra, "Il sistema disequilibrante," in *Il sistema disequilibrante 1* (Milan: Edizione Galleria Toselli, 1970), 6.
15 Gillo Dorfles, "Testo introduttivo," and Tommaso Trini, "Dalla Chiarificazione Globale di Ugo La Pietra," in *Il sistema disequilibrante 1*, 4–5; 9–14.
16 La Pietra, *Il sistema disequilibrante*, 6.
17 Ibid., 6.
18 La Pietra, "The Reappropriation: The Alteration of Urban-Institutional Space as Means of Individual Experience," in *Contemporanea 1973–1974*, exhibition catalogue compiled by Palma Bucarelli (Florence: Centro Di, 1973), 298. Italics author's.
19 "Gli UFO," *Marcatrè* 41–42 (1968): 73.
20 Lapo Binazzi, "From the Object to Survival," *Contemporanea*, 301.
21 "Gli UFO," 73.
22 Adolfo Natalini, "Arte visive e spazio coinvolgimento," in *Ipotesi di Spazio*, presented by L. Ricci (Florence: G+G, 1972), 24–25.
23 Ibid., 24.
24 Andrea Branzi, "Architettonicamente," *Casabella* 334 (1969): 36.
25 See Benjamin Buchloh's citation of Roland Barthes when discussing Sol LeWitt's proto-Conceptual work of the early 1960s and the paradigm of oppositional artistic practice inherited from the historic avant-garde in "Conceptual Art, 1962–1969" *October* 55 (Winter 1990): 111. For the original context see Roland Barthes, "Myth Today," in *Mythologies* (1972), trans. Annette Lavers (New York: Hill and Wang, 1993, 27th edition), 158–159.
26 Buchloh, "Conceptual Art" 104–143. There are many recent publications that could be cited in this context, such as Tom McDonough, *"The Beautiful Language of My Century," Reinventing the Language of Contestation in Postwar France, 1945–1968* (Cambridge, MA: MIT Press, 2007); Larry Busbea, *Topologies: The Urban Utopia in France, 1960–1970* (Cambridge, MA: MIT Press, 2007); Felicity D. Scott, *Architecture or Utopia: Politics After Modernism* (Cambridge, MA: MIT Press, 2007); Dominique Rouillard, *Superarchitecture: Le Futur de l'Architecture 1950–1970* (Paris: Éditions de la Villette, 2004); or Alexander Alberro, *Conceptual Art and the Politics of Publicity* (Cambridge, MA: MIT Press, 2003).

27 Giulio Carlo Argan, *Strutture ambientali* (Bologna: Cappelli Editore, 1968), 39.
28 Argan is referring to Umberto Eco's characterization of affirmative practices in *Apocalittici e integrati* (Milan: Bompiani, 1964).
29 Argan, *Strutture ambientali*, 38–39.
30 Eco, *The Open Work*, 136.
31 Marcuse, *One Dimensional Man*, 247.
32 Mario Tronti, "La fabbrica e la società," *Quaderni rossi* 2 (1962): 1–30.
33 Archizoom, "Relazione del Gruppo Archizoom," *Marcatrè* 50–55 (1960): 96.
34 Raniero Panzieri, "Sull'uso del capitalismo della macchina," *Quaderni rossi* 1 (1960): 47.
35 *Marcatrè* 50–55, 100.
36 *Casabella* 350 (July–August 1970): 43–52.
37 Mario Tronti, "The Strategy of Refusal," republished in Paolo Virno and Michael Hardt, *Radical Thought in Italy: A Potential Politics* (Minneapolis: University of Minnesota Press, 1996), 29–30.
38 Archizoom, *Marcatrè,* 95.
39 Herbert Marcuse, *Essay on Liberation* (Boston: Beacon Press, 1969), 26.

Part 4

Class Concerns and Conflict: Dwelling and Politics

Chapter 10

Dirt and Disorder
Taste and Anxiety in the Homes of the British Working Class

Christine Atha

In this chapter the various approaches taken to the aesthetic education of the working classes through a didactic literature of design reform are examined in the context of moral hygiene, social reform, and postwar politics. Whether perceived or real, the intransigence of the working-class consumer in pre- and postwar Britain necessitated the production of considerable amounts of aesthetic and political propaganda around design and its consumption. Straddling the period from 1937 to 1954, the texts under discussion here concentrated on the sanitization of the working-class home and its occupants and represent the attempts made by political agencies during these years to correct and civilize working-class taste and produce a "discriminating" working-class public. This specific period is particularly fertile with texts encompassing as it does the aftermath of two world wars and the social reconstruction these precipitated.

A range of discourses surrounding hygiene and cleanliness are inscribed in both the literature of design reform and that of health and mental improvement. Dirt and disorder were natural companions present in aspects of furnishing, furniture, ornamentation, and interior decoration in the working-class home. Those design texts under scrutiny here were emphatic about the correlation between cleanliness and hygiene in the home and the effects of this on its occupants and their taste. Constant representation of the working classes and lower-middle classes as lacking good taste betrayed not only an anxiety about these social upstarts and their parvenu aspirations, but also revealed worries about their suitability for new homes and the new way of life brought about in Britain in the period between the wars and after 1945.[1] If the literature of design reform stressed the trained and discerning eye, the white space, and the clean line it was because it had a distinctly mysophobic view of the working class. This was present in descriptions of the corpus of the working classes as "crippled" by bad taste.[2] They had "crude" vision and were therefore insensitive to their surroundings.[3] These descriptions of working-class taste paralleled those views of their environment discussed by health and social reformers.

Christine Atha

The Management of Domesticity and the Clean Home

If the general well-being of the consuming public demanded that they become discriminating in all aspects of their lives, then the model citizen was to demonstrate the good taste and clean living that accompanied it. In the period from 1937 to 1954 the literature of design reform and mediation reveals to the working-class consumer a sense of dissatisfaction, and an uneasy relationship with their decisions about taste, and a general disillusionment with the quality and design of the material goods in their homes.

It was through this literature that the British government's message of environmental refurbishment and material renewal was delivered, but this was set alongside another narrative that proclaimed the need for social renewal and a re-engineered class structure. The focus of this discussion was once again, as it had been in the nineteenth century, centered about the management of the home, its décor and its furnishing. The home, as the new front line of engagement with the consuming public, was the most promising realm through which to make contact with the sensibility of the working classes, and to subsequently exert influence. It was in the home that changes could be brought about to the tastes and views of the working class essential to their social reformation.

Ordinarily we might not regard class considerations to be useful as an indicator of a particular viewpoint. However, in this reappraisal of the pre- and postwar position and in re-reading these pamphlets and booklets, books and guides, government directives and marketing literature, the presentation of the class motif is deeply felt, and the reformation of the working class is read into and through the materials under consideration. Chief amongst the authors of these texts were Anthony Bertram and Nikolaus Pevsner, both keen proponents of modernist principles and, up to a point, socialist values, and who best communicated the anxiety around the poorly furnished, ill-decorated, and over-ornamented home, and their language betrays this (Figure 10.1).

We are more familiar perhaps with them at this time for their work on individual artists and their general art criticism, but here they turn their attention to design and daily life. Bertram and Pevsner used BBC broadcasts and their publications to set out an aesthetic education manifesto for a consumer perceived by them, rightly or wrongly, to be intent on resisting its benefits.

Without always acknowledging it overtly, the working class is implicated in these texts as "the vast majority of our countrymen" and ultimately as "the indiscriminating public."[4] We get some indication of their tone through the terms used within descriptions by Anthony Bertram, Nikolaus Pevsner, and others of the designs favored by the working classes: dishonest, vulgar, common, crude, coarse, cheap, uncivilized, ugly, violent, jazzed up, disgusting, crippled, mongrel, bogus, sham, and inappropriate.

The anxiety attached to the selection of domestic goods, with particular instructions for avoiding the selection of the *wrong* type of goods, was manifest within these texts as a clear direction to choose modern, clean, and functional exemplars. The open disparagement of articles of furniture and objects consistently

Dirt and Disorder

10.1
Above: Cover, Anthony Bertram, *Design in Everyday Things*, 1937
Below: Cover, Nikolaus Pevsner, *Visual Pleasures from Everyday Things*, 1946

portrayed as "dishonest," "disfigured," and essentially lumpen, in both words and images, pointed towards the decent and respectable instead, and to what was most appropriate socially, emphatically clean, and with no potential hiding place for dirt. Some might view this as benign paternalism but we can also see this as an expression of distrust and deep anxiety in the face of working-class sensibilities and habits perceived as being both unclean and uncontrolled.

From its inception, the aesthetic education project engendered an atmosphere of anxiety and discontent amongst its various proponents but also amongst those who were to be its recipients. Speculating about the most effective mechanisms for communicating with the consuming public, while at the same time building bridges with the consumer goods and construction industries, those responsible for implementing change trod an uneasy path between the economic needs of the nation and their own misgivings about the aesthetic capacities of its citizenry. This same anxiety was felt by a doubtful public led to be distrustful of their own capabilities in these matters by a literature that seemed to stress the primary problems with decoration, novelty, display, and cheap goods as those unique to their class and inherent in their physical disposition.

On yet another side there were protestations from the retail trades and manufacturers about the predisposition to bad taste amongst the majority of the British public, in both pre- and postwar periods. In these endeavors to inculcate taste into an often less-than-compliant public we see the respective governments of the day at times anxious and confused, occasionally benign and paternalistic, generally resigned, but nevertheless determined to transform the reluctant working-class subject into a creature of good taste and one of clean habits.

Clean Homes

Slum clearance had been an ongoing project during the interwar years. The plight of these slum dwellers was documented in some detail in *The Road to Wigan Pier* by George Orwell published in 1937 by the Left Book Club. Working-class homes were, Orwell admitted, indescribably dirty with dark, overcrowded interiors, albeit through poverty, not by choice:

> Bishops, politicians, philanthropists and what not enjoy talking piously about "slum clearance" because they can thus divert attention from more serious evils and pretend that if you abolish the slums you abolish poverty.[5]

There is little doubt that the housing that many working-class families occupied in the interwar years was often dirty, infested, and unhygienic and that these slum conditions were widely recognized as inhuman and the source of many often fatal diseases. Indeed there was another extensive literature around these health education issues, and with their focus also clearly on cleanliness in the home, it was not difficult to see how the discourse surrounding modern design found a firm place alongside it.

(below) *The shapes have gone to seed a bit and the pressed decoration bears little relation to them. Decoration is not necessarily wrong, but what is the point of the bits applied to these pieces?*

(above) *"Modernistic" or "jazzy" shapes, which may have a novelty appeal when first seen but would not prove good living companions. There are many details in this photograph worth critical scrutiny.*

10.2
Gordon Russell, *How to Buy Furniture*, Council of Industrial Design, 1947

In the literature of design reform we see the working class depicted as "disabled" by poor taste and "enabled" by the clean forms of modernism. References to the beneficial effects of the clean and uncluttered interior are juxtaposed with prejudicial descriptions of overornamented furniture.

In Figure 10.2, the captions read:

> (above) "Modernistic" or "jazzy" shapes, which may have a novelty appeal when first seen but would not prove good living companions. There are many details in this photograph worthy of critical scrutiny. (below) The shapes have gone to seed a bit and the pressed decoration bears little relation to them. Decoration is not necessarily wrong, but what is the point of the bits applied to these pieces?[6]

The principles of the *existenz-minimum*, the minimum requirements for the best possible quality of life, were to be adapted for the British estate dweller and the sanitization of the working-class home achieved through the introduction of "no-nonsense" and unadorned fitted modern furniture, an organized kitchen, and the introduction of laundry facilities.[7] This was to be viewed as a statement of personal and moral hygiene synonymous with the desired transformation of the citizen and their taste. Reformation of the postwar economy would depend on a distinct change in the consumer and in their habits. Any anxieties about the moral health of the masses were to be transferred to their tastes in furniture and furnishings, as the one might be perceived as being very clearly displayed in the other. This would be a difficult transformation.

Resistance to changes in their taste and its expression in the domestic sphere was an essential component of the careful grip the working classes maintained over their cultural preference and its manifestation. The pleasure and satisfaction supplied by over-embellished surroundings to occupants of the working-class home would persist and with it the intense unease felt towards what was often described as its almost degenerate condition by the design reformers.

Prewar Design and the *Everyday Thing*

As Anthony Bertram indicated in *Design in Everyday Things*, the task of educating the masses was not for the faint hearted: "The anger of the untrained must be braved. It is simply not true that everyone is born with the capacity to judge design."[8] Bertram's BBC broadcast series from 1937, *Design in Everyday Things*, was an early attempt at what we might recognize today as a community consultation exercise combined with local discussion groups. At the request of the BBC Bertram had visited forty towns to discuss design in detail with citizens of all types and professions. Discussion groups were also formed for each of the broadcast talks and group leaders were directed to ask the questions contained in the *Design in Everyday Things* booklet that accompanied the broadcasts (Figure 10.1). In his introduction Bertram made it clear that his talks were addressed to the working classes who were socially and economically "the vast majority of our countrymen."[9]

The series had a mixed reception but Bertram sounds disingenuous in his response later to reactions to its perceived didactic nature: "A few correspondents and one radio critic in a popular paper indignantly suggested that under my apparently mild exterior I had sinister *educational* [Bertram's italics] motives."[10]

The purpose of the broadcasts had been stated clearly enough in the text of the accompanying booklet and education was stressed as the main purpose of the BBC Talks department output. Perhaps Bertram bridled at the *type* of education that had been implied. In Bertram's own descriptions of the problem his broadcasts set out to remedy, he identifies disorganized and dysfunctional families as occupants of homes furnished by those "crippled" by their bad taste and in need of rescue by aesthetic education, stating: "A man who has been long crippled must learn to walk again: it is no use for him to protest that he could walk once years ago without advice or support. Education, then, and only education, can heal this social crippledom."[11]

After the first talk *What does the Public Want?*, broadcast on October 4, 1937 at 8pm, of the two questions that were suggested for group discussion the second had a distinctly leading tone: "2. Why do you think people buy imitation goods—electric fires that flicker, things made in a plastic material treated to look like wood? Isn't such design dishonest? And is veneer an example of this?"[12]

In the sixth talk in the series on November 8, 1937, the topic for discussion was *Housing the Workers*. The preamble to the discussion is laden with statistics and some very useful figures:

> Nearly 1,500,000 houses, built since the war, have been subsidized by the State. It has cost well over £175,000,000. On slum clearance alone since 1930 £1,200,000 has been paid by the Exchequer; but about 25,000 people are leaving the slums every month. Are these vast sums being well used?[13]

Attaining a deeper understanding and appreciation of the benefits of well-designed goods and housing might have been the intention of *Design in Everyday Things* but concerns about the way design affected the lowest paid in the country might have been directed better.

The issue of new housing and home furnishing featured prominently in the booklet and the broadcasts had been intended to address the changing face of Britain at that time. The physical descriptions that are found within the text must have fascinated, and at times puzzled the reader, with their portrayal of the malformed and disabled body, crude vision, and poor palate. As illuminated by the text, "the very crude eye" of the working class when cast over cheap furniture is incapable of discerning good ornament from bad, but more importantly does not distinguish details in the quality of manufacture or craftsmanship.[14] In this respect we might also say that the *crude eye* seeks imitation rather than the original, as it has no capacity to judge pure design. It is difficult to understand why Bertram was so biased. Bertram's description of what he refers to as "good ornament" and the form of the beautiful object suggests again the problematic nature of the coarse and uncultivated working class used only to bad stamped ornament, unable to afford anything better, and given to other types of equally abhorrent physical decoration, "Good ornament is only possible today in relatively expensive goods—the sort of things we use in our best clothes. . . . Form . . . can be quite sufficiently beautiful without trappings and trinkets, make-up and tattooing."[15]

Remaking the working class in the image of the dignified and honest form would not be a simple case of their visual re-awakening but a form of spiritual healing and bodily wholeness achieved through the nature of the honest thing. The call from Bertram to heal the "social crippledom" of a lack of taste, was also vitally connected to learning how to live again once they moved to their new modern homes.[16]

The Popular Taste: Carpets and Corruption

Prior to the Second World War the situation of industrially manufactured and mass-consumed goods had been assessed by Nikolaus Pevsner in his book *An Inquiry into Industrial Art in England* published in 1937 (Figure 10.3).

In it he acknowledged that the plight of the working classes was understood to be inherited from the social strictures of the nineteenth century:

> In fact these horrors would scarcely have arisen, had not the industrial development of the nineteenth century deprived the poorer classes of so much joy in life. A splendor which reality does not concede is brought into our humble surroundings by meretricious industrial products, which achieve in permanence some of the elating effect that for a few hours is bestowed upon us by the Hollywood heroes' fantastic mode of life in the pictures.[17]

This description of the working class as overpowered and overwhelmed by the opiate affects of those popular but "meretricious" goods through inherited traits suggests subjugation by poor design, while at the same time proposing class insensibility to better goods. This crusade against shoddy design and its degrading effects echoed the same concerns Ruskin had expressed about the advent of mass-produced goods.[18] There is no reference to any of the innocent pleasures that these same "meretricious" goods might have brought into, by implication, joyless lives. The working class were therefore in essence first subjected to the adverse affects of their lack of taste and then condemned to their moral degradation through the shoddy goods that they couldn't help but choose. Pevsner continues,

> Looked at from this point of view, the question of design is a social question, it is an integral part of *the* social question of our time. To fight against the shoddy design of those goods by which most of our fellow men are surrounded becomes a moral duty.[19]

For Pevsner, there could be no better example of "shoddy design" than that seemingly offered by carpets. Dirt and disorder are read in the pattern of imitation Oriental carpets while the standard patterned carpet attracts an equally

10.3
Cover, Nikolaus Pevsner, *An Enquiry into Industrial Art in England*, 1937

disturbing critique from Pevsner as an emblem of the chaotic character. On the body or on the floor, patterns were synonymous with a lack of good taste and poor hygiene. However, rather confusingly for his argument, patterned carpets in dark shades were the most universally popular and ubiquitous flooring types in both middle-class *and* working-class homes of the period. Not only that, they were without doubt almost entirely of poor design. Pevsner had found this in his surveys of manufacturers and retailers. "My main problem here was this: Why are modern carpets in England so appallingly bad in design? To find an answer to these alarming questions it was important to have especially detailed evidence from carpet manufacturers."[20]

We might at first wonder about the aesthetic capabilities of such an erudite scholar being brought to bear on carpets but in fact there was much to say about them that corresponded rather well with the problematic elements within painting at the time. He continues, "The dominant patterns for the last eight or nine years have been derived from a deplorably misunderstood Continental cubism, the prevailing colors being in brown, a blatant orange and, in more recent years, a grass-green no less blatant."[21]

Pevsner's extensive, and somewhat exhaustive, discussions with manufacturers and retailers of such carpets revealed in them a rather surprising and ill-concealed contempt for their own products and by implication, the consumers who bought them. Bemused by the popularity of these bad designs, and at a loss to imagine who it was that might be purchasing their goods, manufacturers and retailers exclaimed surprise at their continued success in selling them. Curiously, and with an obvious fascination, Pevsner quotes them at considerable length:

> One man spoke of the modern "bastard stuff" which he has to turn out: . . . and a third said in a forlorn way: "I wish you could tell me who the people are who buy my stuff. I have never been in a house with carpets like that." There was also a fourth director whose expressions in front of his products varied between "hideous," "horrible," "beastly" and "nasty," and a fifth who seemed to get a perverse joy and self-tormenting pride out of displaying his worst bestsellers. I still remember the sound of his: "Now look at this, isn't it a brute?"[22]

Were these displays of horror at the goods they were selling for the benefit of the enquirer or did they reveal a more profound distaste? Was class in fact at the heart of these observations of "having never been in a house with carpets like that" and furthermore was it actually thoroughly embedded in the culture of exclusivity that surrounded retail environments? The salesperson and their retail domain were also subject to established British social mores. Class-consciousness in Britain was obvious to Pevsner and he saw the exclusivity in styling as symptomatic of its existence, but he also uses it as an argument for more acceptance of the modern movement: "Therefore a style of our age must be an unexclusive style, and its merits must be collective merits not distinguishing one individual or one class."[23]

Design, Dirt and "Carpets of Dark Hair"

Design, a book by Anthony Bertram published by Penguin in 1938, was based upon the *Design in Everyday Things* broadcasts and was arranged in nearly the same manner as the radio programs. If there was concern over rehousing the poorer elements of British society, in Bertram's attempt to put our minds at rest by refuting claims about their domestic practices and defending the uncivilized working-class family and their right to a new home, he sounds unconvinced:

> Bathrooms are always supplied, of course, and I hope nobody still thinks coals are kept in them. That is one of the silliest lies. I have never seen a case of misuse, and what is more, I have heard of none from all the experts I have talked to. It is a wicked legend that must have grown up from one or two cases.[24]

This is the essential problem in both Bertram's and Pevsner's portrayals of the working-class domestic domain. The home, as the domestic sphere and realm of habitation of the working class, is presented as a demoralized and dejected place in this literature. In spite of a fascination with the working class for their artisan origins, their leisure activities and entertainments, their social traditions and conventions, Bertram promotes the idea of disorder in their behavior, the over-decorated, and in all the sentimental paraphernalia and memorabilia on display. Removal of all extraneous and superfluous everyday things is strongly recommended as disorder rules in the form of miscellaneous objects and decoration, and moreover dirt is suspected, if not actually seen, in workaday furnishings. The destructive and intrusive tendencies of the "slumming" philanthropists of the Victorian period is reinvented and reinvigorated in Bertram's close examination of the working-class interior portrayed as one that is overly ornate, inevitably dirty, and furnished with their hallmark dark hair carpets—a concern he shared with Pevsner: "When we step out with bare feet onto the white rug, we feel beautifully safe; which we never do with black hair or all over patterns in dark shades. It is not that we suspect houses of being dirty but we like to *see* that they are clean."[25] Furthermore suggestions that patterns were perhaps pleasant or functional in some way are met with suspicion and in this case directly refuted: "When I was broadcasting I had a letter from a man who said that he liked patterned Indian carpets "because they are easy to keep clean." What he meant, of course, was that they do not *show* the dirt; which is rather an unhygienic confusion of thought."[26] This expression "an unhygienic confusion of thought" sums up the attitude to the ordinary person and their individual taste. The crude eye was at work again here, unable to distinguish pattern from dirt, with confused thinking allowing for no clarity of vision.

The thorough cleansing of all "useless" ornament and frippery instilled a moral agenda as well as one that promoted cleanliness. It effectively removed any undesirable manifestations of taste. The hope for modernism in the home was in its creation of a regimen of labor and time, and with the kitchen as its focal point, it would recreate the notoriously cluttered working-class domestic context in its own image unencumbered by useless possessions. The removal of family activity from the kitchen and the suggested imposition of clean, clutter-free enclosed cabinets displaces objects, "whatnots and bric-a-brac" from dirty shelves to the confines of sanitary storage.[27] The gradual elimination in the postwar period of the structure of two downstairs rooms in council housing, and with it the culture of the "front parlor" so familiar from the back-to-back or slum house, also re-ordered working-class behavior.

The Literature of Design Reform Postwar and the New Working Class

The literature of design reform in the interwar years had attached itself to a set of political agendas intent on social and industrial reform where the modernist principles it espoused might be placed for greater effect. If the modernist project had failed to capture the imagination of the working class before the Second World War then afterwards the chance represented itself with new opportunities to educate a generation deprived of goods and ready to make a new nation. Government would seek to create change in civic cultures and reconstruct the demos in the British postwar situation through the development of new housing and new consumer products that would "civilize."

The New Towns Bill introduced by Lewis Silkin, the Minister for Town and Country Planning, in May of 1946 emphasized the way in which design would also democratize:

> Our aim must be to combine in the new town this friendly spirit of the former slum, with the vastly improved health conditions of the new estate but it must be a broadened spirit embracing all classes of society. The former slum dweller, or dweller in the poorer part of a town, has a good deal to learn from those better off, and vice versa.[28]

This view of the transforming and reforming aspects of new towns was founded in a widely shared belief that the residents of these new environments would replace the perceived social disorder of the slums with a newly ignited civic pride, family order, and initiative. It may have been the intention that over the course of time improved home conditions would have an effect and that the slum mentality would dwindle as a result of increased exposure to new environments and modern fitted interiors. The "dirty" conditions associated with slum life would be eradicated once and for all and the postwar working-class interior would be thoroughly cleansed through a deeper understanding of and training in the principles of good taste.

The aesthetic project, its protagonists hoped, would succeed by inscribing the desired taste not only within their habitat but also within working-class social structures themselves. If the attempts made by various political agencies to correct and civilize working-class taste and produce a "discriminating" working-class public were to be successful then instruction in the principles of taste was to be critical to raise standards. Anxiety about their taste raised doubts about the integrity of the working class and finally confirmed deep anxiety about the quality of the working class home and domestic realm. The emphasis on hygiene slowly shifted to the moral composition of the family, its leisure pursuits, and subsequently its taste.

Posters produced by the Central Office of Information for the promotion of new towns and life in postwar Britain, distributed at home and abroad, alluded to the green and pleasant land, which was being created for the working class, and to the burgeoning economy. This was idealized and represented in utopian images such as *Life in Britain Today—A Typical British Recreation Centre* by C. W. Bacon from 1947 that promoted the British way of life on the way to postwar prosperity (Figure 10.4).

Part of the text reads:

> Workers in such industries must live near their factories or workshops, and consequently townships tend to spring up round the groups of factories. Everything possible is done, however, to avoid any kind of unhealthy congestion in these communities and, in addition, the surrounding countryside

Dirt and Disorder

10.4
C. W. Bacon (artist), *Life in Britain Today—A Typical British Recreation Centre*, Central Office of Information Poster, 1947

is protected to provide a "green belt" where workers can spend their leisure time at various games and pastimes. In this, as in other things, the British liberal way of life leads to a continual improvement in the social conditions and the health of the workers, for the efficiency and well-being of the nation are based on their good health.[29]

In *Visual Pleasures from Everyday Things* by Nikolaus Pevsner published by the Council for Visual Education in 1946, the text analyzed various objects in order to "establish criteria by which the aesthetic qualities of design can be judged."[30] In the analysis of the perfect new entities of radiograms, pots, and dishes, investing their forms with beauty and sensitivity, tastefulness and moderation pointed out that which was so much sought and needed in the working class themselves. The conclusion that the honest, purposeful object is the face of the future where all is efficient and has material integrity is also a reflection of the social construct it inhabits and sustains. Dishonest objects are therefore the corollary of this and represent the worst of all worlds. Nowhere is this better illustrated than in the case

10.5
"Honesty and Dishonesty, II. Electric Heaters," in Anthony Bertram, *Design in Daily Life*, 1937

of some electrical goods pretending to belong to another order of objects altogether. "Honesty" and "dishonesty" as attributes in electric light fittings and electric heaters imbue the object with characteristics we might see reflected in the consumer's self. Anthony Bertram, too, as early as 1937, had similarly entered the debate about the relative honesty and dishonesty of objects as exemplified in the design of electric heaters in his book *Design in Daily Life* (Figure 10.5).

Pevsner's choice of words used to describe the physical characteristics of these objects perhaps reflects some latent issues, with the terms "mongrel" and "disgusting" used in the description of an "electric fire" too easily transferred on to the owners of such items, while "*ersatz* for real" seems to sum up the absolute poverty of these objects mischievously misrepresenting themselves as real and therefore truthful.[31]

Learning to See: From the Crude Eye to the Seeing Eye

Drawing attention to objects honest and dishonest, right or wrong, good and bad, real or *ersatz* was the preoccupation of the literature of design reform. In postwar Britain and in a new climate of consumption the necessity to purchase the best possible goods was the overriding concern of this literature.

At the outset *The Things We See* series had a very clear goal. In a memorandum relating to the scope of the series the full range of titles and authors are detailed, the overall purpose of the texts is identified:

> The aim of the authors in this series is to encourage us to look at the objects of everyday life with fresh critical eyes. Thus while increasing our

> Opinions of the artistic merits of the objects illustrated here, both animate and inanimate, may vary with each reader. No special criticisms are implied in the analogies: they are an inducement to LOOK at things around us and really, conscientiously, to SEE them.
>
> 38

10.6
Alan Jarvis, *The Things We See Indoors and Out*, Penguin, 1946

own daily pleasure we also become better able to create surroundings that will give us permanent pleasure. To achieve this in the furnishing and equipment of our homes, we must buy with discrimination and so prove to the designers, who set the machines to work, that we are no longer bound by habit or indifference to accept whatever is offered.[32]

The Things We See series published by Penguin from 1946 to 1948 were essentially picture books for adults. The inside front cover of *The Things We See Indoors and Out* emphasizes this in a note "To The Reader": "This is not a book of words illustrated by pictures—it is a book of pictures with a verbal commentary. If the reader spends three quarters of his time studying the pictures and one quarter reading the accompanying text, he will fulfill the author's intentions."[33]

In the section entitled "Words and Pictures" the text points to a number of examples of furnishings illustrated by photographs juxtaposed with comparators from the natural world to deliver the message more clearly. A hippopotamus, a greyhound, a toad, a pelican, a bear, and a clipped poodle are set alongside their furnishing counterparts in order to demonstrate ornament, clumsiness, heaviness, or grace (Figure 10.6). This device of using images juxtaposed to make comparisons between forms was familiar from popular magazines of the period.[34] It is not entirely clear in all examples in *The Things We See Indoors and Out* how the comparison should be interpreted or understood despite this explanation:

> Understanding the visual arts has always been hampered by the problem of words. . . . Words are not the same as things. Understanding must be reinforced by the seeing eye. If, as a result of the combination of picture and words, our reaction is "Yes, I *see* what you mean," the book has served its purpose. We will understand design better, and make our judgments of taste more clearly if we *picture* these analogies as well as verbalize them.[35]

The analogies that the photographs were used to indicate and the critique one might imagine they implied are, somewhat confusingly, disavowed in the text. So although the illustrations form the structuring of the argument in the text, this disclaimer leaves the reader in something of a quandary.

The structured use of language as an intellectual activity is synonymous with taste here. In order to grasp the issue of taste itself then the discourses that surrounded taste needed to be introduced in such a way as to bridge the perceived intellectual gap between the working classes and those versed in aesthetics, "the philosophy of beauty."[36] The taste project necessitated the development of a language that might be useful and constructive in delineating more clearly some of the most fundamental aspects of aesthetics without actually using that nomenclature. So allusions to soccer, popular culture, and pastimes may have seemed to be a natural route to take in establishing a rapport with the reader around their culture and traditions. However, the paradox here is that those same popular cultural activities, the social and economic circumstances they represented, and the innate taste that they so clearly demonstrated were completely at odds with the design reformers' goals. How ironic that the very things that were associated with the more problematic aspects of working-class taste were used to draw them into a project dedicated to changing them. As Jarvis notes,

> Or, if the appetite is not cultivated, we will be satisfied with crude or second hand satisfactions, with a synthetic taste in visual things like a taste for soups and custards made of powder. Semiconsciously at least, we recognize that somewhere the *real thing* exists; but most of us hope to find it the easy way, failing to see that enjoyment of the things we see needs practice, work and effort, as with music or soccer or anything else that gives us pleasure.[37]

Rather interestingly, especially in postwar Britain where the effects of rationing were still felt well into the 1950s, the conjunction in the text of taste and

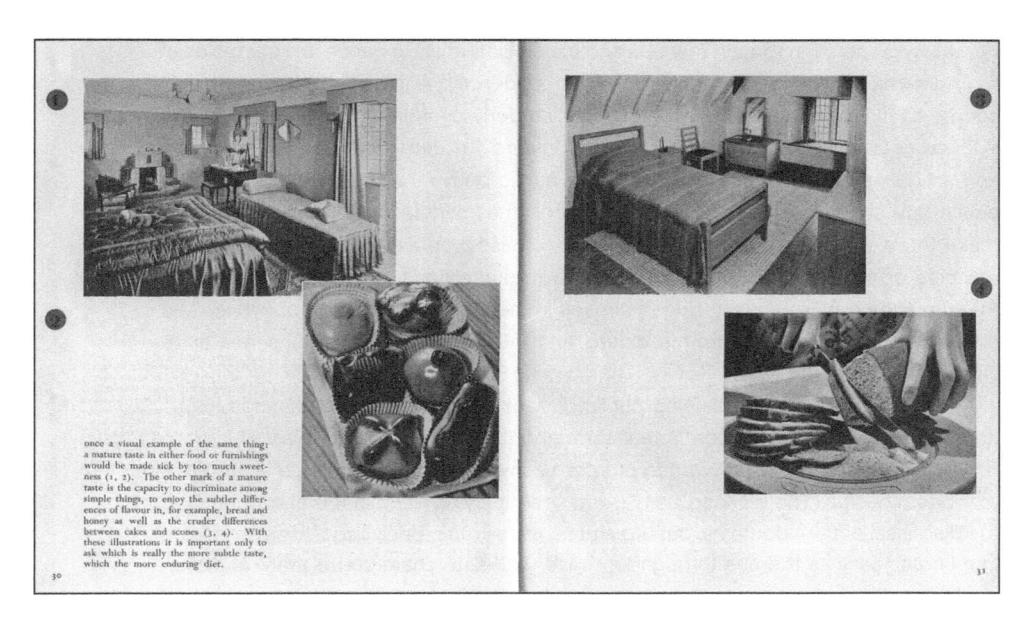

10.7
Alan Jarvis, *The Things We See Indoors and Out,* Penguin, 1946

appetite, descriptions of food and eating, wholesome and unwholesome diets and palates were viewed as a route to the most effective demonstrations of "discrimination and refinement."[38]

It seems insensitive and patronizing to make comparisons of this kind in a text directed at a population that had recently endured some very lean years and were still subject to the rationing of basic staples and restrictions on various commodities, and where "gorging on sweets" had not been possible for many years (Figure 10.7).[39]

The text beside the image reads: "We know the childish impulse to gorge on sweets and we recognize at once a visual example of the same thing: a mature taste in either food or furnishings would be made sick by too much sweetness. The other mark of a mature taste is the capacity to discriminate among simple things, to enjoy the subtler flavor in, for example, bread and honey as well as the cruder differences between cakes and scones. With these illustrations it is important only to ask which is really the more subtle taste, which the more enduring diet."[40]

Subtle taste would also recognize the place of something sweet or savory in a more mature discourse around food and consumption. Castigating consumers in this way for their willfulness and their lack of self-control reminds us once again of both Bertram's and Pevsner's prewar texts disparaging the senseless and aesthetically untrained working class. It is often difficult to see in the texts how closely linked they were with the economic constraints of the period. The nation in recovery was one of increased manufacturing and productivity drives, a new nation of renewed energy in foreign markets and export potentials, a nation in a postcolonial moment rediscovering itself and its industrial identity. And yet this literature still seems to insist on a prewar view of the disorderly consuming public. The blame is once again placed squarely on their shoulders for demanding tasteless goods and a "debasement" that was part of the public body—"with ourselves": "If the public buy shoddy, ill designed or ugly things the manufacturers will continue to make them. . . . The debasement of quality in mass-produced goods lies not in the machine or mass production process, but with ourselves." However, it is doubtful that the author, Alan Jarvis, included himself in the all-encompassing "ourselves" as the distinction made between the writers and the readers of these texts was quite clear.[41]

The theme of arousing public dissatisfaction with their existing chaotic domestic circumstances continued throughout the series and was linked to government objectives that were to promote consumption and a change in attitudes to modern design. The working classes are seemingly reduced in this literature, with the dismissal of their domestic culture and taste as crude, uncivilized, and disordered used continually as themes throughout these works, to characterize them and *their everyday things* as unsatisfactory in order to foster discontent with their surroundings.

Remaking Commodity Culture

Domestic consumer goods available in postwar Britain were severely limited of course but the revitalization of the economy through them would be of paramount importance. The *Britain Can Make It* exhibition in 1946 stood as testimony to this with its remit as a vehicle for marketing and promoting the British design industry through its products, first, abroad for their trade potential, and second, at home as a demonstration of the shape of things to come, both socio-economically and socio-culturally. The impulse to buy goods was going to be difficult to re-ignite in the wake of wartime rationing, but the urge to buy only those goods that were well designed was to be of primary importance in achieving the transformation of the postwar British home. Poor design might perpetuate unwelcome associations and anxieties about "popular" and "makeshift" working-class cultures, and reveal again the "*völkisch*" or folkloric tendencies of a formerly artisan identity.

This task was to be even more difficult when it was attached to the reinvention of the British public's taste. The postwar period offered an opportunity to permanently change the direction of taste via the perceived *tabula rasa* achieved through mass bombing, the strictures of rationing, and the willingness of new consumers to rededicate themselves to purchasing goods. If the modernist project were to be effective in the reinvented working-class home it would be in eradicating decoration and frippery entirely.

The modernist insistence on clean lines and smooth unadorned form appeared to seek to eliminate the overly ornate and decorated forms from the average working-class home and expunge along with them any trace of the residual bitter taste it had left behind. However, this particular reading of the idea of "modern" and the interpretation of modernism owes much to the very British tendency towards overdecoration in the first place. Working-class taste in the 1940s was still strongly associated with the novelty of the ornate and overembellished, the crudely decorated and grotesque in form much as it had been in the nineteenth century.

If the expectation had been that modernism would repair and reconstruct working-class sensibility and infuse order into their haphazard existence then this was never realized. Perhaps the most significant failure of the design reformers' project was in not getting rid of decoration. The use of decoration and ornament in very specific objects, and in patterns and textiles, was deeply inscribed in working-class culture and structures. Like a stain deeply ingrained, it was impossible to remove completely. If the literature promoting modernism as a panacea to the limitations of British working-class taste was to accomplish this shift in sensibility it had to rely on anxiety and concerns with taste to accelerate any changes in direction.

How was this to be achieved? All efforts to reestablish consumption shared an attitude that signaled the dominance of modernism as a philosophy of form but one also of social recuperation. The exhibitions and literature of postwar Britain concentrated on this clean interior at the expense of the now-denigrated "homely." The many styles of publications produced in this venture, from simple paperback books to more specific pamphlets, employed a diverse range of approaches in language and in textual construction and were the output of equally disparate organizations and government bodies. All in all they stand as a remarkable attempt at a cohesive expression of aesthetic clarity to an audience of widely different backgrounds and ambitions albeit one held together by one common factor, that of their class.

Notes

Acknowledgments: I would like to thank my Ph.D. supervisors and the Royal College of Art for their extraordinary support and guidance, and the staff of the Penguin Archive at Bristol University, the Design Council Archive at Brighton University, the Royal Society of Arts Library, and the Royal College of Art Library for their very generous assistance.

1. "Parvenu" describes the desire of the lower classes to achieve a position further up the social scale.
2. Anthony Bertram, *Design in Everyday Things* (London: British Broadcasting Corporation, 1937), 6.
3. Ibid., 5.
4. Bertram, *Design in Everyday Things*, 1; Alister Maynard, ed., *The Value of Good Design* (Glasgow: Council of Industrial Design Scottish Committee, 1954), 5.
5. George Orwell, *The Road to Wigan Pier* (London: Penguin, 2001), 65.
6. Gordon Russell, *How to Buy Furniture* (London: The Council of Industrial Design, 1947), 27.
7. For example, Kensal House, 1937, designed by Elizabeth Denby and Maxwell Fry.
8. Bertram, *Design in Everyday Things*, 3.
9. Ibid., 1.
10. Anthony Bertram, *Design* (London: Penguin, 1938), 52.
11. Bertram, *Design in Everyday Things*, 3.
12. Ibid., 8.
13. Ibid., 10.

14 Ibid., 5.
15 Ibid., 6.
16 Ibid.
17 Nikolaus Pevsner, *An Enquiry into Industrial Art in England* (Cambridge: Cambridge University Press, 1937), 11.
18 John Ruskin, *Lecture III. Modern Manufacture and Design: A Lecture: Delivered at Bradford, March 1859*.
19 Pevsner, *An Enquiry into Industrial Art in England*, 11.
20 Ibid., 58.
21 Ibid., 63.
22 Ibid., 64–65.
23 Ibid., 201.
24 Anthony Bertram, *Design*, 38.
25 Ibid., 76.
26 Ibid., 68.
27 Ibid., 74.
28 New Towns Bill HC Deb., 8 May 1946, *Parliamentary Debates* (Hansard), Commons, 5th series, vol. 422, cc.1072-184 1072.
29 Central Office of Information 1947, VADS record no: WM PST 16325. Part of the *Life in Britain Today* poster series. A Hebrew language version, an Arabic language version, a Persian language version and an English language version were produced.
30 Nikolaus Pevsner, *Visual Pleasures from Everyday Things* (London: Batsford, 1946), 1.
31 Ibid., 18.
32 Memo prepared by A. B. R. Fairclough, Penguin editor of the series, Penguin Archive Materials, DM1107/E0703/E1-7.
33 Alan Jarvis, *The Things We See Indoors and Out* (London: Penguin, 1946), 2.
34 For example, *Lilliput Magazine*, published from 1937, used a similar device to make humorous comparisons.
35 Jarvis, 36.
36 Ibid., 36.
37 Ibid., 27.
38 Ibid., 29.
39 David Kynaston, *Austerity Britain 1945–51* (London: Bloomsbury, 2007), 19. Items still rationed in 1945–1946 included meat, butter, lard, margarine, sugar, tea, cheese, jam, eggs, sweets, soup, and clothes.
40 Jarvis, 29; 30–31.
41 Text about the author on the inside flap of *The Things We See Indoors and Out* reads: "At present on the staff of the Council of Industrial Design, in charge of the work of educating the public in an appreciation of design."

Chapter 11

Upper West Side Stories
Race, Liberalism, and Narratives of Urban Renewal in Postwar New York

Jennifer Hock

In early 1961, Father Henry Browne, a priest working on Manhattan's Upper West Side, wrote to a prominent planning consultant asking how he could explain the city's West Side urban renewal plan to his working-class Puerto Rican parishioners, many of whom were facing displacement. The city was planning for new schools, safer streets, and modern, low- and moderate-income housing for this aging neighborhood of overcrowded brownstones. Would the renewal plan help residents, as promised? Browne supported the city's goals—indeed, he had actively supported the West Side Urban Renewal Plan throughout the early planning process—but he was worried that the plan did not provide for the return of every family that would be displaced. Judging from the extent of redevelopment that was planned, thousands of residents would need to move. Even those who were lucky enough to secure new housing in the neighborhood faced a long waiting period before they could return. Many worried they would be forced to relocate to the outer boroughs, far from family. Was it true, as rumor had it, that Puerto Ricans were being pushed from the neighborhood to make room for new development?[1]

The consultant, Roger Shafer, demurred. Puerto Ricans were not so much being pushed away, he replied, as they were being given a chance to better their lives by moving out of an increasingly crowded and dangerous neighborhood. "In answer to your question of what to say to the Puerto Rican family who accuses you of trying to push them out of the neighborhood over to Staten Island," Shafer wrote, "I would consider the following approach: Throughout the centuries people have come a long distance to America to improve the status of their living conditions. To get your wife a decent kitchen and a clean home and a good neighborhood, surely it is worth moving to Staten Island."[2]

From the aging brownstones of the Upper West Side to the new, middle-class housing on Staten Island: Shafer's narrative of social and geographical mobility represents the height of postwar liberal optimism about the social promises of urban renewal. Earlier urban renewal projects, like Boston's troubled West End project or New York's high-profile Lincoln Center, had envisioned the construction of luxury housing or institutions of high culture as ways of drawing the suburbanizing middle and upper-middle classes back into the central city. By the late 1950s and early 1960s, however, liberal politicians and planners were backing away from large-scale clearance projects, which had sparked accusations of land grabs, mismanagement of public funds, and insensitivity toward the residents they displaced by the thousands. Chastened by the experiences of these early projects and dependent on good will for continued support at the polls, planners and city officials began to scale back their renewal plans and articulate the short-term and local benefits of renewal for the specific communities affected as well as for the city as a whole. In a calculated effort to win the support of critics and community leaders like Father Browne, who were worried about the impact of displacement, they argued that federally subsidized physical planning projects, implemented with the consent of residents, might improve life for residents in the very urban neighborhoods that were being replanned and renewed, all while helping modernize the city as a whole.

On Manhattan's Upper West Side and elsewhere, planners proposed spacious new middle-income housing, rehabilitated apartments, moderate-income co-ops, and public housing projects. Rather than envisioning institutions of high culture, they planned elementary schools, community centers, and public libraries. In an effort to generate community support and convince residents to relocate or participate in rehabilitation programs, they drew residents into the planning process, created citizens' committees, and framed these urban renewal projects as participatory and democratic, an opportunity for declining neighborhoods to stabilize and transform themselves. Most significantly of all, they used the language of racial liberalism to emphasize the renewal program's commitment to racial integration and the potential for physical planning to create stable, racially and economically mixed urban neighborhoods. Public intervention in the postwar city, they argued, would do what the private housing market on its own could not: break up the ghetto, encourage the movement of black and Puerto Rican families to the new suburbs and integrate existing urban neighborhoods.

The idealism of this integrationist, participatory, and neighborhood-oriented idea of urban renewal stands in stark contrast with the evidence of the impact that renewal had on urban neighborhoods, particularly with the evidence of the impact of relocation politics on working-class residents and communities of color. Between the late 1940s and the early 1970s, when the urban renewal program was in effect, projects in hundreds of American cities displaced hundreds of thousands of urban residents, disrupting neighborhood life, damaging local and small-scale economies, and altering the social geography of the city. Even the less heavy-handed, more liberal neighborhood renewal schemes had devastating effects. In the polarizing atmosphere of the 1960s, damning critiques of the impact of renewal developed on both the right and the left, and mainstream liberal proponents faltered under the pressure of public critique, inflation, mounting construction costs, diminished federal funding, and increasingly organized community groups critical of relocation policies. Critics and subsequently historians of the program argued that it did not matter what ideas motivated the supporters of urban renewal policies in the 1960s, when their plans had so clearly gone awry.[3]

Recovering the understudied liberal idea of renewal, however, is essential to understanding how and why urban housing emerged as such a powerful and contentious site for debate in the 1960s and why there was so little protest when federal support for urban areas was withdrawn so abruptly by the Nixon administration in the early 1970s. Renewal projects brought together an unlikely coalition of liberal supporters, among them civil rights leaders, who supported the construction of integrated housing; homeowners, who were eager to participate in local decisions about their neighborhood; unions and local institutions, which supported investment in construction and in neighborhood development; and liberal members of co-op boards, who saw themselves integrating the central city, one building at a time. For a brief time in the early and mid-1960s, they were joined by tenant organizers, community activists, public housing advocates, and other allies on the left, in part because the participatory and open housing requirements of the urban renewal program made urban renewal areas natural targets for intervention and change. The vision of the stable and racially and economically mixed renewal neighborhood was the only thing that brought these groups together and made the extensive redevelopment and rehabilitation of the 1960s possible. When that liberal vision collapsed, these coalitions fell apart, and the radical reshaping of the city that had characterized the 1950s and the 1960s came to an abrupt and uncelebrated end.

This essay explores the rhetoric of urban renewal and the politics of housing in Father Browne's neighborhood, the twenty-block West Side Urban Renewal Area (WSURA), stretching from West 87th to West 97th, and from Central Park West to Amsterdam. The WSURA was New York City's first attempt at rehabilitation and renewal rather than large-scale clearance and redevelopment, the approach the city had taken under the controversial public administrator Robert Moses in the 1950s. It is also one of the best examples of the liberal neighborhood renewal projects of the 1960s, a project with broad social ambitions that brought together a coalition of residents and local leaders who hoped to use the resources of urban renewal funding to improve a deteriorating neighborhood. It drew community groups and local officials to the table to discuss modernization of the local housing stock and opened up discussions about open occupancy laws and discrimination in the housing market, absentee landlords, rent gouging, *de facto* segregation in the schools, and inadequate municipal services. It also initiated large-scale displacement of low-income and Puerto Rican and Dominican residents and ultimately sparked a powerful protest movement that was instrumental in the formation of a stronger and more politically active Spanish-speaking community in New York.

It is almost impossible to study the WSURA without realizing the extent to which housing is a cultural product, one that tells us how people understand themselves and helps them construct their social identities. Indeed, the most striking

Jennifer Hock

lesson of the WSURA is that stories matter: narratives of progress and development, community, and identity all helped shape key planning and development decisions. Especially in the 1960s, as planners came to depend more and more on renewal-area homeowners, who were in charge of rehabilitating their properties, and on community leaders, who had to rally support for city plans through the increasingly lengthy and complex approvals process, stories mattered; the idea of urban renewal needed to be made and remade, year by year, in social, political, and economic circumstances that were changing so rapidly the planners could hardly catch up. Narratives helped residents understand the complexities of urban change and adjust to new urban environments; they justified policy decisions that entailed hardship or loss; they tied housing issues to larger public debates over racial integration or social mobility. These stories were ideologically charged and often palpably biased or misleading, but they were powerful and consequential nevertheless, and by neglecting these stories, much of the complexity of the period is lost. In short, the history of the West Side Urban Renewal Area is a history of contested meaning as well as contested space.

The West Side Urban Renewal Area: The Planners' Story

A residential district of modest, nineteenth-century tenements and brownstones as well as grand elevator buildings lining the park, the once-fashionable West Side was in decline in the years after the Second World War. While the Upper East Side increasingly attracted upper-middle-class and wealthy households and new high-rise development, the Upper West Side had seen no new construction in the two decades since the Depression. Its tenements and brownstones were falling into disrepair, subdivided into smaller apartments and turned into rooming houses. Banks and lending institutions had "redlined" the neighborhood, preventing landlords and brownstone owners from borrowing money to purchase or repair properties.

Demographically diverse, the West Side was home to wealthy professionals who lived in the elevator apartment buildings along Central Park West, as well as elderly men who lived in single-room occupancy hotels along Columbus and Amsterdam Avenues. In the early 1950s, it was also one of the more racially integrated areas in Manhattan, with a significant number of African Americans and Puerto Rican families, many of whom had moved into the neighborhood since the Second World War. But with its long-time Jewish and Irish residents departing for the outer boroughs and the suburbs, many middle-class residents were afraid the neighborhood would "tip," losing its balance of upper-, middle-, and working-class residents as those who could afford to leave abandoned a troubled neighborhood.

In the mid-1950s, the city's first proposals for the area found favor in Washington, where federal officials were wary of Robert Moses' blunt, controversial approach to urban redevelopment and interested in the new "renewal" techniques city officials wanted to try on the Upper West Side. Initially, the city had ambitious plans to renew the entire West Side and devote the city's full allowance of federal low-income housing funds to the area, but by early 1956, the city had settled on a project area of twenty blocks, from West 87th to West 97th, and from Amsterdam Avenue to Central Park West (Figure 11.1). Between the summer of 1956 and the

11.1
West Side Urban Renewal Area before redevelopment, aerial photograph, c. 1960
(Photograph by Thomas Airviews)

spring of 1958, an army of planners and consultants visited the area, compiling data and sketching out options for its future. The result of their efforts, a lavish, 96-page report containing the preliminary plan for the area and entitled simply *Urban Renewal*, was published by the City Planning Commission in April 1958.[4]

Like so many planning reports of the day, *Urban Renewal* began by describing a neighborhood facing overcrowding, deteriorating housing conditions, and uncertainty about its future. Like the larger West Side, the project area was going through demographic transition. Between 1950, when Census figures were taken, and 1956, when the City Planning Commission took statistics in the area, the overall population of the neighborhood increased from 33,000 to 39,000. The Puerto Rican population, 4.9 percent of the population in 1950, had increased to 33.4 percent, and the non-white (predominantly African American) population had increased from a little more than 1 percent to 9 percent. While the overall percentage of the white population had dropped precipitously, from roughly 94 percent to roughly 58 percent, the trend in the area was not merely the flight of long-time white residents; more than half of the white families living in the project area were newcomers themselves. Many of these new white households were wealthier than the ones they replaced, since per capita income for the area was rising quickly even as more low-income families of color moved into the area.

Aging housing stock, landlord neglect, and pressure on the housing market in the area resulting in the subdivision of apartments and conversion of brownstones to rooming houses all contributed toward declining housing conditions in the neighborhood. Although the area included a number of modern elevator buildings, the twenty-block area had been selected precisely because it had some of the oldest, most densely developed housing in the area, including old-law tenements along Columbus Avenue and parts of Amsterdam Avenue and brownstones lining the east-west side-streets.[5] There had been almost no new construction in the area since before the Depression, institutional lenders were reluctant to grant mortgages in the area, and owners were less and less likely to improve their buildings.[6] A full 17 percent of the dwelling units in the area were single-room occupancy, and roughly two-thirds of the brownstones had been converted to rooming houses. Residential densities on some of the side streets reached as high as 800 persons per acre. Rents in the brownstones and old-law tenements—the most deteriorated housing in the area, where many of the Puerto Rican families lived—were excessive, roughly double what was charged in nearby, high-quality elevator apartment buildings on a square-foot basis.[7] The physical condition of neighborhood institutions was similarly varied. The area had a number of well-established, thriving institutions, including churches, synagogues, and wealthy private schools, but because the number of children living in the area had doubled, the local public elementary schools were over capacity and in some cases experiencing turnover of 50 percent during a single school year.

The case for public intervention made in *Urban Renewal* was not that different from the case made for earlier, more interventionist urban renewal projects the late 1940s and early 1950s. The West Side was in crisis, overcrowded, increasingly poor and transient, and physically deteriorating. Private landlords had a vested interest in profitable overcrowded conditions, and only public intervention would halt the decline. The solutions proposed in the report, however, differed significantly. Earlier urban renewal projects had typically targeted relatively small deteriorated areas of six to thirty acres, prescribing near-total clearance of the existing buildings on the site, the reassembly of the land into superblocks, and the construction of luxury modern high-rise housing and shopping for a new, middle- and upper-income population. The West Side project, on the other hand, had a different starting point: only some of the buildings in the 106 acres of the project area were so physically deteriorated that they required demolition. In most parts of the project area, the city could encourage stability and reinvestment by enforcing the housing code and offering federally insured, long-term, low-interest loans to owners willing to rehabilitate the older housing stock. The redevelopment of specific areas still played a crucial role in this scenario, but the plan's aim was to restore the confidence of building owners and investors in an existing neighborhood without redeveloping it entirely—working with existing owners and with the neighborhood's existing physical structure.

The renewal plan proposed in this report was, above all, concerned with increasing the amount of modern, high-quality housing in the neighborhood. It recommended the redevelopment of the major north-south avenues, Columbus and Amsterdam, with residential towers, as well as the redevelopment of the most deteriorated areas on the side streets with double-loaded corridor apartment

11.2
Above and *Below*: Brown and Guenther (architectural consultants) and Candeub and Fleissig (planning consultants), West Side Urban Renewal Plan, Renewal Plan Model and Presentation Drawing of Columbus Avenue (showing planned redevelopment), New York City Housing and Redevelopment Board, 1960

buildings (Figure 11.2). Unlike the typical project of the 1950s, however, the plan aimed to provide housing for all income levels: low-rent public housing, subsidized middle-income housing, and luxury or market-rate housing. Specific parcels had not been allocated and the proportion of low-, middle-, and high-income housing had not yet been determined, but the report explained how, with various types of financing, the city could achieve a wide range of rentals, from $14 to $18 per room per month in public housing, to $21.29 per room per month (limited-profit cooperative housing), to $44.82 (rental housing constructed with federally subsidized loans), to $45.00 to $60.00 (conventionally financed housing).[8] New construction would be supplemented by a program to finance the rehabilitation of deteriorated brownstones in the area, while most of the modern elevator buildings and almost all of the buildings fronting Central Park were left untouched.

Given what must have been an obvious and inevitable consequence of renewal in this area—the large-scale displacement of low-income Puerto Rican families, who lived in the most deteriorated housing and who would be disproportionately affected by redevelopment and rehabilitation plans—one of the most interesting and significant aspects of the report was its commitment to racial and economic integration, made explicit in a chapter entitled "Goals of Renewal." The report echoes the city's commitment to open-occupancy housing, reinforced most recently with the Sharkey-Brown-Isaacs law of 1957, which barred racial discrimination in the rental of apartment units or in the sale of homes in developments of ten or more. In principle, at least, housing in the West Side project, like housing in all Title I projects to date, would be racially integrated. But the goal of an economically "balanced" neighborhood was a more complex and elusive notion—developed specifically, it seems, for the West Side of the late 1950s. As the report pointed out, the luxury apartments facing on to Central Park, the spacious brownstones on the side streets, and the cramped tenements of Columbus and Amsterdam Avenues had always been occupied by residents of very different class backgrounds and income levels. "Although this original pattern left much to be desired from a design point of view," the report argued, "it was a balanced neighborhood in a democratic pattern with considerable character which should be maintained. An economically integrated community also must have fairly extensive provisions for middle-income families, not just for high-rental and public housing tenants."[9] In the context of the area's changing demographics, particularly the increase in low-income Puerto Rican residents, the goal of "racial and economic integration" is not as progressive as it might first seem; the emphasis on "middle-income" families suggests that the city would use redevelopment and rehabilitation to retain or attract middle- and upper-middle-class residents, who were likely to be white, at the expense of lower-income residents, who were likely to be Puerto Rican. But the inherent flexibility of the concept and its broad appeal across the ideological spectrum mean that ideas of "integration" or "balance," written into the plan from the very beginning, would become the rallying point around which future debates about the neighborhood would take place.

My House is Your House: Relocation Stories

The tension between the urban renewal plan's promise of a racially and economically integrated West Side and the displacement of the area's poor Puerto Rican community is almost palpable in *My House is Your House*, a children's picture book from 1970 that illustrates the extent to which middle-class liberals struggled to understand and justify the displacement caused by the urban renewal project. The main character, Juana, a young girl who has recently arrived from Puerto Rico, is living with her family in a single room in a tenement on the Upper West Side and has just learned that her building has been condemned by the city as overcrowded and unsafe; she and her family will have to move elsewhere. Her mother is eager to leave, but Juana enjoys her walks through this familiar part of the city and doesn't want to move (Figure 11.3). A forgotten cigarette sparks the crisis the city had warned of, and a fire breaks out in Juana's apartment. The family barely manages to escape before the building is destroyed. The family's moving date is brought foward, and Juana leaves the Upper West Side without a chance to say goodbye to her friends. The story ends with Juana's family locating a spacious, brightly lit apartment in the suburbs in Long Island, next door to another Spanish-speaking family fleeing redevelopment in the city (Figure 11.4). Presumably both families will begin to build ties again here. The story's optimistic portrayal of relocation echoes the optimism that planners and city officials had expressed, but it was hardly representative of the experience most families had.

11.3
Juana walking in her Upper West Side neighborhood. Toby Talbot, *My House is Your House*, 1970

Jennifer Hock

11.4
Above and *Below*: Juana and her father in their new apartment.
Toby Talbot, *My House is Your House*, 1970.

The sheer scale of human displacement required by the West Side Urban Renewal Plan is shocking to us today. In a neighborhood of twenty blocks and 40,000 people, some 3,200 families and individuals—or about 10,000 people altogether—lived in housing scheduled for demolition or extensive rehabilitation in the 1958 plan. In the late 1950s, the Puerto Rican community was not powerful enough to launch an effective, large-scale protest against the city's plans, and thus the liberals' views of relocation as a method to disperse low-income communities of color and integrate them into middle-class life in the outlying boroughs and suburban communities went unchallenged at community meetings and in debate in the city's major newspapers. Large-scale relocation was framed as an opportunity for families who had not yet moved out of aging older neighborhoods and a chance for the city to disperse poverty and arrest decline on the Upper West Side.

This point deserves further elaboration. No one in the late 1950s—not city officials, not community leaders, not liberal proponents of renewal—expected that rehabilitated units or new construction might accommodate all the residents who would be displaced by the plan. In fact, the very opposite was true: one of the salient attributes of a plan like this one was the likelihood that a significant minority of the residents would be relocated from the neighborhood and find new housing in other parts of the city. Conceived at the height of the postwar suburban boom, when a surprising 25 percent of the American population was estimated to be on the move, the urban renewal process assumed that urban residents were geographically mobile and had few attachments to their neighborhood. Sociologists and planners repeatedly emphasized that many of the neighborhoods that were scheduled for redevelopment or renewal had few residents with a long tenure; families who lived here, they assumed, did so only because they could not find or afford better housing. Economists theorized this aspect of the urban renewal process as the elimination of "prior suboptimality," the phenomenon of so-called slum households that, for one reason or another—racial discrimination, habit, cultural preference—had failed to move into the larger urban housing market and remained trapped in low-cost, substandard housing in the central city. In retrospect, this theory, which failed to distinguish between groups that could not move out of the slums and groups that simply had not done so, seems brutally naive. But in the late 1950s, with city officials pledging to open the city to open occupancy and the first open occupancy laws on the books, the potential for renewal to help bring about integration helped planners generate support among middle-class liberals.[10]

What liberals did not realize was that many residents, particularly families with limited English, would have enormous difficulty leaving a familiar neighborhood and finding new housing. Some displaced families were offered public housing in other parts of the city; others were offered moving expenses and assistance finding a new apartment elsewhere in the city. Relocation provisions were minimal, however, and often landlords abandoned all repairs and maintenance work on buildings that had been condemned, forcing residents to move out even before they became eligible for the few benefits and the modest compensation the city had to offer. Residents of color suffered doubly during this process because they depended most on existing social networks and had the most difficulty finding alternative housing in a racially stratified private housing market. So acute was this problem in cities like Chicago, where African Americans were displaced, that the urban renewal program acquired the nickname "Negro removal."[11]

In the late 1950s, the Puerto Rican community in New York was so politically powerless that groups were unable to launch a protest against the plan. As the city moved from the planning stages to implementation, hundreds of Upper West Side families, many of whom were poor and Puerto Rican, received eviction notices. Reluctant to leave family and friends, local schools and bodegas, they began crowding into nearby tenements and rooming houses—some in the urban renewal area, some just outside it. By the early 1960s, however, the climate of public opinion in the project area was changing. The moderate community group organized to help the city plan the renewal project, the Provisional Council, reorganized itself as the Strycker's Bay Neighborhood Council (SBNC). Headed by Father Browne, the SBNC became engaged in issues related to the local Puerto Rican community and increasingly outspoken about the problems faced by displaced residents. The local Democratic club, the FDR-Woodrow Wilson Democrats, published an analysis of the West Side plan that found the plan's provisions for low-income residents insufficient.[12] Most importantly, the area was finally developing a vocal Puerto Rican constituency led by Aramis Gomez, a resident who had recently been relocated from the nearby Lincoln Square project area and who, along with several other community members, had formed the Puerto Rican Citizens' Housing Committee (PRCHC). In a report drawn up in January 1962, the group contended that Puerto Ricans were "being 'pushed' out of so-called prime real estate in Manhattan" and that "the overall housing program seems to envision a New York without Puerto Ricans."[13] Like the Reform Democrats, they pushed for a significant increase in the number of low-income housing units as well as more meaningful Puerto Rican participation in the renewal project.

Public hearings on the final plan, held in May and June 1962, were contentious. At the first hearings on May 17, proponents of the plan emphasized the city's commitment to open housing, its attempt to provide housing for all income levels in a single neighborhood, and its innovative rehabilitation program. Speaking on behalf of the national office of the National Association for the Advancement of Colored People (NAACP) in support of the plan, civil rights leader Jack Wood argued that accommodating every low-income resident in low-income housing in the area amounted to a policy of racial "containment" and "would encourage the development of a community characterized by racial and economic imbalance." Jackie Robinson, the former baseball star, appeared at the hearing to express his support, praising the project as "the first truly integrated project the city ever attempted." Critics attacked the extent of Puerto Rican displacement, the city's poor track record with relocation, and the disparity between the number of households displaced and the number of low- and middle-income housing units, arguing that the social costs of the plan were too high. The PRCHC's Gomez attacked the plan as a "masterpiece of deception" intended to "get rid of the Negroes, Puerto Ricans, and low-income families from the area" and declared that "if you [the City Planning Commission] approve this plan, you are declaring war on the Puerto Rican community."[14] After three years of delays, the city wanted nothing more than to begin the West Side project. On May 29 the planning commission announced its approval of the final plan, urging it forward through the next round of hearings "quickly and expeditiously" and warning that changes in the plan at this late date would cause delays.

Both critics and proponents geared up for a second round of debate in June. In a series of meetings leading up to the next hearings on June 22, Father Browne pushed the SBNC to support an increase in the number of low-income units to 2500 without success. He and other opponents of the plan organized a rally at Holy Name Church in support of more low-income housing on the night of June 21. In the face of this opposition, city officials conceded defeat and phoned Browne, promising an increase in the number of low-income units in the plan from 1,000 to 2,500 and the number of middle-income units from 4,200 to 4,900. The number of luxury units was reduced, from 2,800 to 2,000.[15] In addition, the city's Bureau of Relocation would be authorized to step in and terminate private relocation contracts if at any time the Bureau believed that relocation was not being handled adequately.[16] The rally was held anyway, and the crowd sang anti-renewal songs written by an SBNC activist.

At the Board of Estimate hearing the next day, Puerto Rican leader Joseph Monserrat denounced the destruction of 5,000 existing low-income units in the WSURA and the impact that it would have on the Puerto Rican community. A representative of the local branch of the NAACP, Percy Sutton, spoke against the plan, challenging the national association's position and requesting more low-income units and minority representation on the City Planning Commission on the grounds that "members of the minority groups should participate in these decisions that affect us." Father Browne spoke about the plan's insufficient attention to low-income residents who would be displaced by the project. Defending the plan, officials cited the "very high degree of voluntary turnover" among Puerto Ricans, arguing that the effects of displacement were not as dire as the opposition made them out to be. Moreover, if the city built housing for all the low-income residents in the area, there was the danger of "permanently embedding a low-income and minority ghetto in the area."[17] As one official said, the plan's "vision is of an entire neighborhood truly integrated on a stable basis, not simply caught at the point where there is apparent integration while one group is moving in and another out."[18] Several days later, on June 26, the Board of Estimate approved final plan.

By the end of the second round of hearings, two opposing views of the West Side plan had emerged. One was optimistic about the effects of renewal and favored the use of renewal tools—particularly new middle-income housing and loans for rehabilitation—to draw new residents to the neighborhood and precipitate change. One was skeptical about the effects of renewal and wanted to use its tools—low-income housing, and to a lesser extent limited-profit middle-income housing—to secure a place for current residents who would be displaced during the process. One was consensual and used the liberal language of participation and opportunity; the other was increasingly militant and wanted the city to concentrate its resources on helping the poor. The issue of low- and middle-income housing was where they found common ground to negotiate, and the ideal of the stable, integrated neighborhood informed both approaches.

Jennifer Hock

Vertical Neighborhoods: Apartment Stories

The story of Puerto Rican displacement, however, is not the only story of the West Side Urban Renewal Area. In the early 1960s, as the civil rights movement picked up momentum, community leaders involved in the planning process began to question some of the initial assumptions of the plan. They succeeded in lobbying the city for the Manhattan's first low-rise "vest-pocket" public housing, public housing that was integrated directly into the fabric of the neighborhood. Through strategic organizing, they also pushed the city to convert much of the proposed high-rise housing along Columbus Avenue, the "Avenue of Tomorrow," from market-rate apartments to subsidized cooperatives, drastically altering the demographics and political tenor of the high rises at the very heart of the redevelopment project. Originally conceived of as luxury housing for young professionals, these high rises instead became moderate-income housing for families, often organized by politically engaged activists with social goals for the new housing.

In accordance with the city's vision of a mixed-income West Side, plans for the redevelopment areas along Amsterdam and Columbus Avenues—the areas where new construction would be concentrated—included both market-rate and subsidized middle-income housing. (For the most part, the public housing was confined to the side streets, where land prices were lower.) Of the three types of housing, the middle-income housing posed the biggest challenge. As city officials like Moses had been arguing for years, it was becoming increasingly difficult to construct anything but luxury housing in Manhattan without subsidy, and even then it was difficult to keep monthly rents (for rental apartments) or maintenance charges (for cooperatives) low enough that families of modest means could afford them.[19] In the WSURA, planners made use of legislation unique to New York State, the 1955 Mitchell-Lama Act, which offered generous financing terms for housing projects whose sponsors agreed to accept limited profits on their investment.[20]

The sponsorship requirement attracted organizations with strong social agendas that helped develop a culture of cooperative living on the avenues. The first and most active sponsors to come forward were the major community organizations that had been involved in the planning process—the Riverside Neighborhood Assembly, which had been involved in the earliest planning stages, in the 1950s; the Goddard-Riverside Community Center, a local settlement house; and the SBNC, the organization formed to represent project area organizations and residents in the planning process. Along with a fourth sponsor, a group of individuals organized specifically for the purpose of sponsoring middle-income housing in the neighborhood, they pushed forward the first middle-income housing projects in the WSURA.

All of them approached sponsorship with the idea that middle-income housing could help solve some of the neighborhood's problems. Goddard-Riverside's housing offshoot, the Goddard-Riverside Housing Corporation (G-R Housing Corporation), for example, sought middle-income residents in the so-called helping professions to live in the area and strengthen the community, while the Strycker's Bay Housing Corporation, formed out of the SBNC, wanted to provide as many units for displaced project area residents as possible. Believing that home ownership would encourage stability and investment in the area as well as a more socially minded community, these groups organized their projects as cooperatives rather than rental buildings. They set up storefront sales offices in the neighborhood, interviewed potential cooperators, and launched pre-occupancy programs aimed at introducing future residents to cooperative living. All actively sought families, rather than singles or young couples, the demographic most attractive in the larger housing market; Goddard Tower was the first cooperative in the city with a significant number of four-bedroom apartments intended for large families, and the Strycker's Bay sponsors opted to have fewer units than zoning guidelines allowed so that the units could have more rooms. They recruited families displaced by the renewal process and Spanish-speakers and favored applicants who supported racial integration within the cooperative. When they interviewed potential cooperators, they also looked for residents who supported renewal on the West Side and were interested in sending their children to the local public schools. In accordance with city and state policy, all four buildings also contained a designated number of "skewed rental" units, low-income units whose lower rents and maintenance charges were subsidized by the middle-income units, echoing the ideals of economic balance of the project as a whole.[21]

These community groups began organizing shortly after the approval of the preliminary plan, retaining architects and economic consultants, developing site plans and designs, and seeking cooperators who wanted to purchase units in the development. By early 1961, the Strycker's Bay Housing Corporation had an executive board, an architect, a *pro bono* consultant, and preliminary plans for a building with approximately 240 units on Columbus Avenue. Already approximately one hundred families, many of whom were residents of the project area, had put a deposit on their down payment.[22] The G-R Housing Corporation established a sales office in 1961, and by the end of the year it had collected down payments from 125 families for housing on the east side of Amsterdam Avenue.[23] RNA House, sponsored by the Riverside Neighborhood Assembly, and Columbus Park Towers, sponsored by a group of West Side residents, had secured sites on West 96th Street and Columbus Avenue respectively.

With these projects underway, city officials and local groups—notably the SBNC—continued to negotiate the way in which the parcels along Columbus and Amsterdam Avenue would be redeveloped.[24] Headed by Father Browne, who was increasingly active in anti-poverty work and critical of the way the city's housing and renewal programs were displacing low-income families, the SBNC was aggressive in its advocacy for more low-income units to house residents who had been relocated from the project area. The city agencies were changing direction as well, backing away from Moses-era policies that favored using redevelopment areas for market-rate housing. When the Urban Renewal Board was reorganized as the Housing and Redevelopment Board (HRB) in 1962, it was given the specific mandate to construct more middle-income housing in the city. In the WSURA, the middle-income cooperatives in the first stage of the plan became the model for subsequent housing projects, and the HRB actively sought sponsors for the second and third stages that were interested in providing housing for displaced, low-income, and minority families.[25] When market-rate projects stalled for lack of financing, the HRB

11.5
Frederick G. Frost, Jr. &
Associates, Goddard Tower
Cooperatives, 711 Amsterdam
Avenue, New York City, 1967

re-designated these sites for middle-income housing. Successive amendments to the plan added two new public housing projects and progressively altered the proportion of low-, middle-, and high-income units, so that by the end of the decade almost all of the new development was limited-profit housing, and each of these middle-income developments contained a designated number of "skewed rental" units for low-income families.[26]

The first of the high-rise housing developments—Goddard Tower, the Strycker's Bay Apartments, RNA House, and Columbus Park Towers—opened in the spring of 1967. Because of their tight budgets, carefully calculated to yield the lowest possible cost per room, they were architecturally modest. Designed to incorporate as many units as possible, they were also massive, on a completely different scale from the neighborhood's brownstones or prewar elevator buildings. The Strycker's Bay Apartments' 235 units, designed by Holden, Egan, Wilson & Corser, were located in two plain red-brick towers sited carefully to avoid the demolition of an older apartment building on the site. Columbus Park Towers, designed by Ballard, Todd Associates, had 162 units in a 27-story tower with concrete balustrades. Goddard

Tower, designed by Frederick G. Frost, Jr. and Associates, had 193 units rising 27 stories above a landscaped public plaza (Figure 11.5). RNA House, designed by Edelbaum and Webster, was a long slab with a concrete façade and 207 units. Strycker's Bay Apartments and Columbus Park Towers, both located on Columbus Avenue, and Goddard Tower, on Amsterdam, had commercial space on their ground floors, and all had community rooms and facilities like nursery schools, as well as an active and engaged group of residents, many of whom had been involved for years in pre-occupancy programs intended to build community within the co-ops. Although neither the architectural language nor the spatial organization of these first middle-income buildings was especially innovative, their sheer scale and their presence along the reconstructed avenues matched an equally new social agenda for neighborhood life on the Upper West Side.[27]

The Street of the Flower Boxes: Brownstone Stories

Brownstone rehabilitation was still an ill-defined, untested technique in the late 1950s and early 1960s, as the West Side project got underway. As a potential alternative to redevelopment, it appealed to city officials, who felt public pressure to slow down the rate of demolition in Manhattan's neighborhoods. It also appealed to the small group of residents who already lived in brownstones in the urban renewal area and who wanted to see adjacent houses fixed up and to planners who were increasingly concerned with maintaining the smaller and more intimate scale of the prewar city. New York needed "quiet, old-fashioned neighborhoods" just as much as it needed "brand-new monumental projects," said Albert Cole, the national housing administrator, expressing his approval of the West Side project in 1958.[28] Rehabilitating the brownstones on the neighborhood's side streets rather than redeveloping them meant that the area would "keep the charm of diversity—the mixture of old and new, big and small, the variety of people and material and buildings that has always attracted people to city living," the Housing and Redevelopment Board declared in its summary of the final plan in 1962.[29]

The catchphrases the city used in discussing the plan—"worth saving," "keeping the good"—obscured the extent to which the HRB hoped to use rehabilitation to change the area's side streets, where the majority of the once-grand, turn-of-the-century brownstones had been subdivided into single rooms or small, low-rent units. Almost two-thirds of the 665 brownstones in the WSURA were in use as rooming houses, many of which lacked private bathrooms and had only makeshift kitchens. Single rooms housing entire families were common. Unlike the densely developed old-law tenements, with their high lot coverage and their narrow light wells, however, the brownstones could easily be converted back into the high-quality, middle-class housing the city desired. With their high ceilings, spacious, well-lit rooms, and private back yards, they were "potentially excellent housing," as the HRB stated in its summary of the final plan.[30]

Rehabilitation thus was as much an attempt to reduce overcrowding, modernize the area's housing stock, and encourage middle-class occupancy as it was an effort to maintain the scale and physical diversity of the neighborhood or reignite interest in the area's historic architecture—a significant point in light of the emphasis on preservation often associated with rehabilitation today. The focus on modernization rather than restoration is evident in the initial study of the area in 1958, in which architectural and economic consultants made detailed studies of three types of brownstone rehabilitation: minimum, which called for very few structural changes, just the patching of plaster and floors and the addition of baths and kitchenettes; intermediate, which also involved the removal of the stoop, the resurfacing of the façade, and new heating and wiring; and extensive, which called for the merging of multiple structures, the reconstruction of the entire interior space, and the consolidation of individual rear yards into communal landscaped parks and play areas. The emphasis in all three schemes was on the viability of these buildings as modern, five- or six-unit apartment buildings, not on their restoration to an earlier, more historically authentic state. Where possible, the consultants wanted to eliminate old-fashioned features like stoops and reconfigure the units to emphasize flowing interior spaces and the open, green, park-like spaces they hoped to achieve through demolition elsewhere in the WSURA.

All three types of rehabilitation, but especially the intermediate and extensive types, were so costly that the consultants doubted individual homeowners would invest in them without some kind of city, state, or federal assistance, a point that touched on the economic challenges of rehabilitation as a way of renewing the neighborhood. What could the city do to encourage private investment in an area that was widely perceived to be declining and dangerous? What combination of financial incentives would encourage investors to purchase and modernize these buildings? While city officials had initially conceived of rehabilitation as a purely market-driven enterprise, part of an effort to involve more private capital in the renewal and redevelopment process, the HRB believed it would need to offer some form of subsidy, encouragement, or guidance to attract new owners to the area and facilitate the process. Because of their location in a designated urban renewal area, rehabilitation projects were eligible for generous FHA-insured loans. In addition, city officials convinced three West Side banks to establish a lending pool of $3 million to help with rehabilitation work—an essential form of assistance, since few institutions were willing to lend in the area—and exempted brownstone owners who improved property anywhere in the WSURA from city real estate taxes for a designated period of time. The HRB also set up a site office at 167 West 89th Street offering free consultation to prospective brownstone owners that eventually grew to house a staff of thirty, including mortgage consultants as well as architects and engineers who made preliminary studies of properties eligible for rehabilitation.[31]

Several private groups also purchased contiguous units and converted them into cooperative apartments, and the language they used to describe their endeavors echoes the language used to describe the mixed-income co-ops along Columbus Avenue—self-consciously progressive, these brownstone owners saw themselves as "racially and economically integrated," and their co-ops represented "a new kind of housing" in the city. A group of seven families, for example, purchased seven buildings on West 93rd and West 94th Streets from a private school moving to another location on the West Side. Their cooperative, Old Ridge, included 30 apartments of one to four bedrooms, many of which were duplexes and had balconies or terraces facing on to a common landscaped garden and recreation area between the buildings.[32] The 9-G Cooperative at 19–35 West 93rd Street was created from nine brownstones the city had considered too small for rehabilitation and slated for demolition and redevelopment. Brownstone owners on the adjacent south side of West 94th Street opposed the development of a mid-rise building on that site and began the fight to have it re-designated in 1963. The nine units were purchased from the city for $200,000 and the renovation was financed with a low-interest loan made possible through the 213 program for cooperatives. The architectural firm Edelman & Salzman redesigned the units, retaining the façades but reorganizing the interior space to form 34 apartments of one to five bedrooms, extending the backs of the houses to a uniform 52 feet, and creating a community garden and recreation area behind the buildings. Among the organizers of the cooperative were the former baseball star Jackie Robinson, who had publicly supported the WSURA plan during hearings in 1962, and his wife Rachel. The project was repeatedly referred to as an experiment in integrated living in the press.[33]

For the most part, however, rehabilitation of the brownstones along the side streets was carried out by young couples who bought and renovated brownstones themselves. Although the city encouraged cooperative conversions, offering three and four buildings together as "package deals" as it sold off the brownstones it had acquired, the majority of rehabilitation in the WSURA was carried out by individual owners who negotiated the purchase of individual brownstones privately. Private sales picked up quickly in the mid-1960s, particularly at the southern edge of the urban renewal area, on West 87th and West 88th Streets, where the gentrifying effects of the Lincoln Square Urban renewal project were beginning to be felt. The Kempner Corporation, a real estate firm that did property management for brownstone owners, estimated that thirty-two brownstones had been sold in the WSURA in 1963 and eighty-four in 1964. By 1968, 226 had changed hands, mostly from absentee landlords to young couples who planned to renovate them and live in them, often in duplexes on the ground and first floors. Some funded rehabilitation privately, some took advantage of the FHA-insured loans associated with the renewal project; all benefited from tax breaks offered by the city and from the HRB's assistance in relocating tenants from the buildings. These young brownstoners, as they were called, were attracted to the architectural quality of the older buildings, the cultural diversity of the West Side, and the opportunity to own a house in Manhattan. While the city certainly played a role encouraging the conversion of rooming houses and low-rent apartment houses into middle-class, owner-occupied apartments, the WSURA was only one of a dozen neighborhoods in Manhattan and Brooklyn where an influx of these home-seeking professionals—among them lawyers, bankers, architects, editors, and teachers—sparked a brownstone revival. Prices soared; available for as little as $17,000 in the early 1960s, unrenovated houses were worth $25,000 to $45,000 by 1965. By 1968, they sold for $60,000, with renovated houses going for much more.

One of the unexpected consequences of rehabilitation in the WSURA was the growth of local community organizations and the formation of new constituencies in the planning and development process. Like many of the middle-income

11.6
Above and *Below*: Carlos and friends in the neighborhood; planting a flower box. Peggy Mann, *The Street of the Flower Boxes*, 1971

cooperative owners in the high-rises along Columbus Avenue, brownstone owners were often drawn to the Upper West Side by the neighborhood's diversity and were committed to improving their houses, their blocks, and their neighborhood. Brownstone owners helped revive and carry on the work of many of the area's block associations, organizing clean-up days and tree plantings, and they formed the Little Old New York Citizens' Committee, which helped families buy and renovate brownstones and acted as a clearinghouse for information about the process.[34]

Self-help was the prevailing ethos. In the early 1960s, William Houlton and Peggy Mann Houlton purchased a brownstone along one of the Upper West Side's most crime-ridden streets, West 94th. Mann worked with several Puerto Rican children on her block to set up flowerboxes on her house and neighboring houses as a sign of investment and pride in the neighborhood and described her experiences in *The Street of the Flower Boxes,* a children's book that follows the adventures of the young Puerto Rican boy Carlos (Figure 11.6). Initially, Carlos is puzzled by all the efforts the Mitchells, a white couple, put into their house; everyone knows that West 94th is a "crummy street." He's especially curious about the flower boxes they put outside their brownstone, which are vulnerable to teenage troublemakers. But when the Mitchells engage him to help protect their flower boxes, Carlos becomes an advocate for this kind of modest beauty on his street, and he begins building and selling flower boxes himself, prompting both white and Puerto Rican residents to work together to clean up the neighborhood.[35]

Unlike the cooperators along the avenue, the brownstoners tended to have had a strong individualist ethos and described themselves as "pioneers" in a declining and dangerous part of the city. Like Peggy Mann, many brownstoners saw themselves as a civilizing influence in the neighborhood, "integrating" a neighborhood that other whites had abandoned as landlords began subdividing brownstones and renting them—often at exorbitant costs—to Puerto Rican families. "We were the first white family on the block," Peggy Mann Houlton recalled of her experience on West 94th Street in 1980. "It all sounded so great—as idealists, we considered integration the hope of the nation—and we could be part of the movement at a time when most whites were moving out of the city."[36]

Squatters: Reframing the West Side Story

Between brownstoners purchasing old rooming houses along the side streets and converting them into single-family houses and the demolition and high-rise construction taking place along the avenues, the Upper West Side was in flux for most of the 1960s. Construction proceeded more slowly than expected, and many brownstones and tenements languished, unattended, even as modern housing was constructed or rehabilitated next door. Under the inflationary pressures of the late 1960s, housing costs in the new towers soared, and the city, now a major landlord in the project area, struggled to maintain brownstones and tenements that were slated for demolition or rehabilitation.

In 1970, the death of a young boy, Jimmy Santos, in a dilapidated apartment with a faulty gas main led to organized activism amongst the Puerto Rican community. A rally at the boy's funeral was followed by intense grassroots

Jennifer Hock

11.7
Operation Move-In banner hung at Site 30 on Columbus Avenue. Photograph from *Broadway Local*, November 1–23, 1971

organizing, and late one night in the spring of 1970, activists armed with crowbars broke in to half-a-dozen unoccupied West Side tenements that had been shuttered, awaiting demolition. By morning, several dozen families had moved their furniture and belongings into the apartments. Within a week they were repairing the damaged buildings, organizing politically, and calling for the city to recognize their right to safe and decent housing. Operation Move-In, one of the largest and most sustained squatting movements in New York history, had begun (Figure 11.7).

It was no coincidence that this movement was centered on the WSURA. By 1970, more than a decade of redevelopment and rehabilitation had displaced thousands of area residents who, like the squatters themselves, were predominantly low-income and Puerto Rican. Frustrated with the renewal process and with an unresponsive housing bureaucracy, the squatters attacked the city's housing and renewal policies. They city had failed to recognize their housing needs, they argued. Some squatters, radicalized on issues of Third World oppression, offered an anti-colonialist critique of the displacement that they had endured: "From Saigon to Hanoi we have to move. From San Juan to Santiago, we have to move." Still others began to formulate the idea of a city of sweat equity—one in which decent housing was a right to all who lived or worked in the area, not simply those who could afford it. "We are the people who built this city. We work here. We work in factories, hospitals, supermarkets, subways, banks. So we are the city," one squatter said. "Why should we move?" By the spring of 1971, their numbers had swelled to several hundred, and their demands had focused on a single redevelopment parcel, Site 30, where twenty families lived and where a coffee house, a free high school, and a women's liberation center had been established.[37]

Operation Move-In boldly called in the promises the city had made more than a decade earlier—promises to reconstruct a racially and economically integrated neighborhood. With the costs of new, middle-income housing rising rapidly and the brownstone side streets gentrifying, housing activists worried that working-class and low-income families would be priced out of the area unless the city moved quickly to expand the housing stock available to them. Led by locals like Melba Bruno, a Spanish-speaking instructional aide at one of the local schools, as well as a group of local Puerto Rican and Dominican political activists, the squatters demanded that relocated families be granted the "right of return" to the Upper West Side. They wanted a moratorium on demolition and construction and a chance to rehabilitate existing structures for low-income families. The city prevaricated but ultimately granted a number of their demands, including additional low-income housing units for displaced families. Activism provoked more protests and extended discussion of the housing crisis faced by low-income families—a crisis neither renewal nor planned relocation had addressed. Twice in February 1971, welfare rights activists occupied one of the middle-income apartment buildings awaiting occupation, calling for more housing for low-income city residents. "We want priority given to poor people who live in welfare hotels," said Dr. George Wiley, executive director of the National Welfare Rights Organization. "We don't object to this building, we want welfare people to live in this building." The squatters' headquarters became a stop on the campaign of Shirley Chisholm, the first African American woman to run for the Democratic presidential nomination. She called for more government action on behalf of low-income families and called the area a "typical example of our Government's piecemeal approach to dealing with the housing problem."[38]

Brownstoners, meanwhile, began organizing against the inclusion of more public housing in the urban renewal area, arguing that the government had already done enough. The squatters' militancy stirred strong feelings among middle-class homeowners, particularly the multi-racial, middle-class brownstoners, some of whom panicked in the face of a forthright challenge to traditional property rights. "Polarization and hatred are supplanting cooperation and understanding among different economic and ethnic groups in the city," one brownstoner newsletter warned. "The middle class people, who with great effort and dedication have established their families on the West Side in response to the idea of a truly integrated community . . . are disillusioned [and] frustrated."[39] Once loosely organized around the practical problems of restoring nineteenth-century houses, the brownstoners now also banded together in an organization called CONTINUE, which opposed the squatters' movement as a sign of the immanent ghettoization of the neighborhood.[40]

The Nixon administration's 1973 moratorium on the construction of subsidized housing effectively ended both the urban renewal project and the squatters' experiment on the Upper West Side. Concessions won in the early 1970s were placed on hold as the city scaled back its ambitions for the area. Site 30, the chief point of contention in the squatters' revolt, was first cleared and then left empty for years. If the squatters lost the struggle for Site 30, however, they had other victories. The squatters' widely publicized stories of displacement and hardship challenged the dominant narratives of integration and progress, helped delegitimize the city's plans for the area, and galvanized local activism. Indeed, the occupation of Site 30 provoked other actions during those same years. In 1970, many of the same activists pressured the local elementary school to abolish the tracking system that had separated Spanish-speaking children from their peers and introduce new leadership, and in 1971, they helped launch a ground-breaking dual-language program. As activist Federico Lora recalled, "we were organized because of the housing issue. . . . The parents moved with us from one issue to the other."[41]

While conflicts around the issue of housing and neighborhood are often viewed as a struggle for turf, the history of the WSURA shows us that the battle lines were rarely sharply drawn. The participatory requirements of this generation of urban renewal projects as well as the amount of red tape involved in implementation meant that plans were not simply imposed upon a neighborhood at the beginning of the process but negotiated constantly, with different aspects of the renewal process receiving more or less attention as city and community priorities shifted. Neighborhood renewal projects often helped produce unexpected coalitions of residents brought together by varying hopes for and fears about their neighborhood. Moderate activists like Father Browne became radicalized. New coalitions, like the coalition of Spanish-speaking activists organizing the squatters' movement, emerged. Who had the right to represent the community and set the agenda during the planning and implementation process were deeply contentious issues, and the right to speak for the community could be challenged during the course of the project. Planners and city officials often began by dealing with established community leaders and ultimately found themselves negotiating with radicals. Even where residents held reservations about renewal from the outset, effective protest required a strong sense of community identity and organizing skills, and in many cases protest only gained momentum as residents learned from the social movements of the 1960s. The lessons of the West Side Urban Renewal Area belie the common perception that urban renewal is a chapter of history best forgotten. The fight for housing on New York's Upper West Side was a battle of truths and ideas as well as resources, and these ideas—about community and identity, particularly—have remained with us, even when policies were cast aside.

Notes

1 Letter from Roger Shafer to Father Henry Browne, 25 January, 1961, Henry Joseph Browne Papers, Rare Book and Manuscript Library, Columbia University, New York.

2 Ibid.

3 The best-known work of criticism of the urban renewal program from the right remains Martin Anderson, *The Federal Bulldozer* (Cambridge, MA: MIT Press, 1964). Among the most significant radical and progressive critiques focusing on the impact of renewal are Herbert Gans, "The Human Implications of Current Redevelopment and Relocation Planning," *Journal of the American Institute of Planners* 25, no. 1 (1961): 15–26 and "The Failure of Urban Renewal," *Commentary* 39 (April 1965): 29–37; Robert Goodman, *After the Planners* (New York: Simon and Schuster, 1972); and Joel Schwartz, *The New York Approach: Robert Moses, Urban Liberals, and Redevelopment of the Inner City* (Columbus, OH: Ohio State University Press, 1993). More recent scholarship has paid greater attention to liberal ideals and ambitions, notably Hilary Ballon and Kenneth T. Jackson, eds., *Robert Moses and the Modern City: The Transformation of New*

York (New York: W. W. Norton, 2007) and Samuel Zipp, *Manhattan Projects: The Rise and Fall of Urban Renewal in Cold War New York* (New York: Oxford University Press, 2010).

4   Charles Bennett, "West Side To Get Pilot Slum Study," *New York Times,* February 24, 1956.
5   As the report pointed out, much of the neighborhood to the west of the project area had been redeveloped privately and incrementally with modern elevator buildings in the 1920s, as had 86th Street to the south.
6   New York City Planning Commission, *Urban Renewal* (New York: The Commission, 1958), 28. The report also noted that building owners had "shallower roots" in the area: between 1945 and 1956, the median length of building ownership had declined from nine years to seven, from 13 to eight among brownstone owners; absentee ownership increased from 64 percent to 72 percent; and the number of absentee owners who lived outside Manhattan increased from approximately 12 percent to approximately 23 percent. New York City Planning Commission, *Urban Renewal,* 27–29.
7   Ibid., 23–26.
8   An appendix works out these monthly rentals using a single Columbus Avenue site to calculate the cost of development. See New York City Planning Commission, *Urban Renewal,* 90–91.
9   New York City Planning Commission, *Urban Renewal,* 40.
10 For a theorization of urban renewal's impact on the low-cost housing market, see Jerome Rothenberg, *Economic Evaluation of Urban Renewal* (Washington, DC: The Brookings Institution, 1967).
11 The phrase is often associated with black writer and activist James Baldwin, who famously used it to describe the urban renewal program in a televised interview with the black scholar Kenneth Clark; see Fred L. Standley and Louis H. Pratt, eds., *Conversations with James Baldwin* (Jackson: University of Mississippi Press, 1989), 42. But it was also in common usage in discussions of urban renewal and public housing programs in newspapers like the *Chicago Defender* and in the black press more generally in the 1950s.
12 On the FDR-Woodrow Wilson report analyzing the plan, see Clarence Davies, *Neighborhood Groups and Urban Renewal* (New York: Columbia University Press, 1966), 137.
13 Cited in Davies, *Neighborhood Groups and Urban Renewal,* 133. The other founding members were Roland Cintron, Josephine Nieves, Efrain Rosa, and Petra Rosa. The organization was funded and staffed by the city's powerful Commission on Intergroup Relations, COIR. On Puerto Rican involvement in city politics in the 1950s and early 1960s, see Sherrie Baver, "Puerto Rican Politics in New York City: The Post-World War II Period," in *Puerto Rican Politics in Urban America,* ed. James Jennings and Monte Rivera (Westport, CT: Greenwood Press, 1984), 43–59.
14 Martin Arnold, "Disputes Aroused by West Side Plan," *New York Times,* May 18, 1962.
15 Martin Arnold, "More Low-Cost Housing Added to Plan for West Side Renewal," *New York Times,* June 22, 1962.
16 Ibid.
17 *Journal of Proceedings of the Board of Estimate of the City of New York VIII* (May 25, 1962 to June 26, 1962): 8607; 8608.
18 Ibid., 8607.
19 On the difficulties producing low- or middle-income housing without subsidy in postwar New York, see Gordon D. McDonald and Rosalind Tough, "New York City: Changing Social Values and the New Housing," *Land Economics* 39, no. 2 (May 1963): 157–165.
20 The Limited-Profit Housing Companies or Mitchell-Lama Program was devised in 1955 to encourage the production of housing in the "middle-income range," between public housing, which rented for $8 to $14 per room per month, and privately built, market-rate housing, which rarely rented for less than $34 per room per month. (Figures are for 1955.) A combination of low-cost financing and tax exemptions—the Act authorized state or city loans covering up to 90 percent of construction costs repayable for period of up to 50 years, and the city could also

grant tax exemptions of 50 percent for thirty years—helped bring down the cost for private developers, who agreed to a maximum return of 6 percent and public oversight of design, construction, rents, and operating costs. It was a popular financing mechanism in New York; some 138,000 Mitchell-Lama units, rental and co-op, were built between 1958 and 1975. On the program, see "Mitchell-Lama Housing" in *Robert Moses and the Modern City*, 305–306; Barbara M. Woodfill, *New York City's Mitchell-Lama Program: Middle-Income Housing?* (New York: Rand Institute, 1971).

21 These buildings were the first in the city to use "skewed" rentals to create units affordable for low-income families. By adjusting the monthly rentals or maintenance charges for 80 percent of the units, the remaining 20 percent could be offered for monthly costs equivalent to those found in public housing—which, in the early 1960s, was $18 per room per month. The 80–20 formula was used throughout the WSURA until 1970, when it was revised to 70–30.

22 Some of the SBHC's success in finding tenants from the project area may have been due to its aggressive outreach program, during which the group distributed bilingual leaflets explaining the Church's approval of cooperative living. See letter from Henry Browne to Most Reverend John J. Maguire (Auxiliary Bishop of New York), 17 January 1961, Henry Joseph Browne Papers, Rare Book and Manuscript Library, Columbia University, New York.

23 On the early stages of Goddard Tower Cooperative, see Clara Fox, *Vertical Neighborhood in an Urban Renewal Community* (New York: The Goddard-Riverside Corporation, 1969), 12–15.

24 After the passage of the final plan, the SBNC had been designated the "project area committee," the organization charged with the responsibility for facilitating community involvement in the urban renewal area.

25 In 1964 the Housing and Redevelopment Board announced that fourteen sponsors of housing in the second and third stages of the project included five that were "primarily interested in expanding housing opportunities for Negroes and Puerto Ricans," including the Congress of Puerto Rican Hometowns, Harlem Neighborhoods Association, the Spanish-language newspaper *El Diario-La Prensa,* a local union, and a group associated with St. Martin's Protestant Episcopal Church. See Lawrence O'Kane, "Sponsors Named in Renewal Area," *New York Times,* June 11, 1964.

26 On the city's decision to convert sites slated for market-rate housing to middle-income, see "Commissioner Nathan Offers Program To Speed Up Construction in West Side Area," *Real Estate Record and Builders' Guide* 198 (October 1, 1966): 2. For a breakdown of the housing projects over time, see "WSURA Fact Sheet." Citizens Housing and Planning Council Archives, New York.

27 On the issue of the architectural banality of the first limited-income housing developments and the city's attempt to redress it in the second and third phase of the project, see "Individualized Architecture Is Apparent in West Side Renewal," *Real Estate Record and Builders' Guide* 202 (July 20, 1968): 2.

28 For Cole's comments, see Charles Grutzner, "US Funds May Go For Brownstones," *New York Times,* June 12, 1958.

29 Housing and Redevelopment Board, *West Side Urban Renewal Area: A Summary of the Final Plan* (New York: The Board, 1962), 16.

30 Ibid., 5. For housing conditions in the brownstones, see New York City Planning Commission, *Urban Renewal,* 25–26.

31 For financing options available to brownstone owners, see "West Side Plan Opens New Vista," *New York Times,* April 27, 1958, and "New Program Set in Area Renewal," *New York Times,* December 8, 1961. The loans, financed under Section 220 of the National Housing Act, were for thirty years at 5 percent interest for 90 percent of the value of the property plus the costs of rehabilitation. The real estate tax exemptions were also generous: owners were exempted from real estate taxes entirely for nine years, and then for an additional three years owners were required to pay taxes only on the value of the improvements, not the total value of the property.

32 See Thomas W. Ennis, "10-Year Renewal Stirs West Side," *New York Times*, October 13, 1963. The project, located at 145–149 West 93rd and 146–152 West 94th streets, between Columbus and Amsterdam Avenues, was designed by Melvin Grossgold and financed with a mortgage loan insured under Section 213 of the National Housing Act. Down payments were $1,750 a floor and monthly carrying charges were roughly $30 a room.

33 Thomas W. Ennis, "City Plans to Sell West Side Houses," *New York Times*, November 5, 1967 and "9 West Side Brownstones Converted Into Co-op," *New York Times*, January 14, 1968. See also "Whatever Happened to the Little Old New York Brownstone," *Progressive Architecture* 49 (December 1968): 46–47; "Nine-G Cooperative," *Architectural Forum* 131 (July–August 1969): 78–81. In 1969 the development was cited for excellence in civic architecture and urban design: "City Club Gives Annual Bard Award for Excellence in Civic Architecture," *New York Times*, May 24, 1969. Purchase prices ranged from $2,725 for a one-bedroom unit to $10,900 for a five-bedroom unit, with monthly carrying charges ranging from $120 to $360.

34 On the Little Old New York Citizens' Committee, see Brownstone Revival Committee, *Home-buyer's Guide to New York City Brownstone Neighborhoods* (New York: 1969), 53. In addition to saving the houses that the 9-G Cooperative would later renovate, they fought and defeated plans to widen the cross streets, a move which would have narrowed the sidewalks in the area.

35 *The Street of the Flower Boxes* became a popular children's book and was made into a film, both of which gave rise to a national program of privately funded neighborhood beautification in the 1960s and 1970s. (By the time the story was made into a short film in the early 1970s, however, West 94th Street had gentrified to the point that the producers used a street on the Lower East Side for filming.) On the movie, see Edith Evans Asbury, "A Tough Manhattan Block Stars in a Film and Then Goes Soft," *New York Times*, February 12, 1973; "TV: 'Street of the Flower Boxes,'" *New York Times*, February 19, 1973; Ruth Rejnis, "Movies Show How Neighborhoods Can Improve," *New York Times*, March 9, 1975. On the beautification campaign sparked by the book and movie, see "US Flower-box Campaign Begins," *New York Times*, June 3, 1976; "The Impact of the Flower Box," *New York Times*, March 20, 1977.

36 Mann is quoted in Laurie Johnston, "West Side Renaissance is Fanning Old Tensions," *New York Times*, January 18, 1980. See also: Thomas W. Ennis, "Buyers Compete For Brownstones," *New York Times*, March 21, 1965; "Renewal Snarl May Be Reduced," *New York Times*, March 13, 1966; "Old Houses Gain Status in Renewal," *New York Times*, August 11, 1968; Bernard Weinraub, "W. 94th St.: Microcosm of Change," *New York Times*, December 30, 1969. On the brownstone revival's goals more generally, see Brownstone Revival Committee, *Home-buyer's Guide to New York City Brownstone Neighborhoods* (New York: Brownstone Revival Committee, 1969).

37 Squatters quoted in the documentary film *Rompiendo Puertas (Break and Enter)* (New York: Newsreel, 1970). See also Cynthia A. Young, *Soul Power: Culture, Racialism, and the Making of a US Third World Left* (Durham, NC, and London: Duke University Press, 2006), 135–144.

38 Alfonso A. Navarez, "Housing Is Scored By Mrs. Chisholm," *New York Times*, June 14, 1972.

39 "What's Happening to the West Side Urban Renewal Project: A Report to the Community by CONTINUE," dated April 1971, p. 1. Citizens' Housing and Planning Council Archives.

40 Murray Schumach, "Segregated Slum 'Threat' Fought on West Side," *New York Times*, July 21, 1970.

41 Federico Lora is quoted in Rose Muzio, "Puerto Rican Radicalism in the 1970s" (Ph.D. diss., City University of New York, 2008), 135. On Puerto Rican community power and the founding of the bilingual program, see Muzio, and Norman I. Fainstein and Susan S. Fainstein, *Urban Political Movements: The Search for Power by Minority Groups in American Cities* (Englewood Cliffs, NJ: Prentice-Hall, 1974).

Chapter 12

Pawns or Prophets?
Postwar Architects and Utopian Designs for Southern Italy

Anne Parmly Toxey

Postwar Design and the Sassi Problem

Post–Second World War architects worked extensively in southern Italy—although they were not rebuilding a landscape devastated by war. The many sources of funds that were available in Italy at this time (for example, national reconstruction funds and Marshall funds) were channeled into building better housing for poverty-stricken areas as well as for areas with premodern living conditions, which described much of the South as well as many other parts of Italy.

Italian postwar modernist architects defined their mission as creating a new building form for the new society. Steering the re-forming nation away from moral and material ruin, which they associated with Fascism, Italy's political and social leaders (including architects) designed the nation s reconstruction. The peasant South presented thinkers and designers with an especially large challenge, its underdevelopment and lack of modernity being acutely felt by the nation in crisis and prostrate after the war (Figure 12.1).

The city of Matera in the region of Basilicata received a bounty of this attention. In the eyes of the postwar West, Matera was the nexus of the South's problems: poverty, disease, squalor, high infant mortality, illiteracy, primitive living conditions, stagnant economy, and lack of consumerism. Lumped together these formed what was called the Southern Question. (The term is still in use today, though it describes different conditions.) Solving these social and economic "problems" through architectural and urban design was the goal of the postwar architectural program. By finding solutions for Matera, the designers involved hoped to develop a formula that could be replicated across the South. Politicians meanwhile hoped that by finding a solution for Matera, the Southern Question would go away—or at least the nation's focus on it would dissipate.

Despite its diminutive stature—Matera is generally unknown outside Italy—this small, remote city played a surprisingly large role in national politics and

12.1
Part-constructed, part-cave houses in the ancient *Sassi* districts of Matera, c. 1950 (Photograph by Scalcione, Enzo Viti Collection)

in national architectural discourse and urban theory, especially in the twenty-five years following the Second World War. For example, the sociological, community approach to design that was forged in the Materan crucible was employed in state housing projects throughout the nation and was marginally adopted in the mid-to-late 1950s by members of the *Congrès International d'Architecture Moderne* (CIAM) and its offshoot, Team 10.[1]

So what made Matera stand out? Why was it singled out as the exemplar of the Southern Question and as the recipient of all this attention? After all, Matera was and is typical of most southern Italian towns culturally, socially, and economically. Its poverty and underdevelopment were par for the course and in fact better than many places.[2]

Matera is distinguished from other towns in being a provincial capital—making it more visible than surrounding villages—and in having cave structures as an indigenous building form. Many Italian towns and villages have cave structures, but no other provincial or regional capitals and not on this scale. Matera has a prodigious, dense network of thousands of part-cave, part-constructed homes called the *Sassi*, which are woven into the side of a cliff. Caves in this location have been inhabited more or less continuously since Paleolithic times. Through the late 1950s, the majority of Materans lived in the Sassi. Apart from the town's nobility, which lived on a high point separating the two zones of caves, the troglodyte population was socially mixed until the late seventeenth century. At this time, the elite minority

12.2
The Sassi crested by noble and elite palaces, 2004

began to move to the flat ridge above the cliff, leaving the Sassi to become the domain of the non-elite majority (mostly land-working peasants and artisans). In this act the elite established themselves physically and socially above the humbler cave residents below (Figure 12.2).

This move both socially and physically stratified the city. Ghettoizing the Sassi was the first step in a process of demonizing them, which gained momentum into the mid-twentieth century. The socio-geographic shift within the city paralleled the trajectory of modern perceptions of proper lifestyles and livelihoods. Europe's rising living standards and the qualification of these also spurred outside censure of the Sassi, as seen in travel literature. While early eighteenth-century accounts described the caves as "curious" with no negative descriptors or condemnation of living in caves, late eighteenth- and nineteenth-century accounts caustically described the residents held within as "barbarous," "delinquent," and "the least civilized of . . . Basilicata."[3]

By the early twentieth century, Matera's squalor (as perceived by modern standards) had moved beyond travelers' accounts and had entered academic and political discussions under the rubric of the Southern Question. Politicians visited Matera and promised aid beginning with Prime Minister Giuseppe Zanardelli in 1902 and continuing through King Vittorio Emanuele III and Benito Mussolini in the 1920s–1930s. Also during this time, political detractors exploited Matera's misery in sensational articles bringing negative attention to such regimes as Fascism—despite the fact that Mussolini was the first national leader to bring relief to Sassi residents in the form of an aqueduct, a paved, vehicular road, and some modern housing (part of a larger renovation and decentralization plan). However, the full-scale sacrifice of Matera for political goals began in 1946 with Carlo Levi (the famous writer, artist, physician, and left wing political activist), accelerated with Communist Party (PCI) leader Palmiro Togliatti in the 1948 election, and continued into the 1950s with Christian Democratic (DC) Prime Minister Alcide De Gasperi. Each leader promised to evacuate the Sassi (which were blamed for the residents' social strife) and to move the denizens to new, modern houses, which were the postwar panacea for social and economic distress.

Following the Second World War in 1946, Carlo Levi published a book of memoirs entitled, *Cristo si è fermato a Eboli* (Christ Stopped at Eboli). Written before the war, it documented his political exile in the South under the Fascist regime. While impressed by Matera's magnificence and the singular lifestyle maintained there, Levi expressed horror and alarm over its deplorable living conditions. His book exposed to the progressive world the peasant lifestyle of Matera perceived by modern standards as "primitive" and "backward" (to use his terms). Levi is also credited with giving Matera the title *"la Capitale della Civiltà Contadina"* ("the Capital of Peasant Civilization") due to its sizable populace.[4] Though real enough, this city's poverty, ill health, and pre-industrial lifestyle were less extreme than those of other southern Italian towns and villages.[5] While Matera's misery may have been exacerbated in the densely populated Sassi, where physical expansion was limited, its squalor was also more visible to outsiders than that of other communities due to the city's large size, its political importance as a provincial capital, and the contrasting

12.3
Typical Sassi interior with farm animals, c. 1950 (Photograph by Scalcione, Enzo Viti Collection)

opulence of its elite private and ecclesiastical architecture. Most significantly, however, the idea of Italians living in caves heightened the primitive and destitute image of the residents and shocked readers (Figure 12.3). Despite fifty years of political promises for aid and Matera's broadly published, long-lived denigration, it was the circulation of Levi's famous book during the politically fecund postwar period that finally catalyzed governmental action in Matera.

Intended to reproach Fascism by flaunting social problems manifested in the Sassi in particular and the South in general, this work disgraced the Italian nation through its broad distribution and translation into many languages. Negative exposure from the book labeled Matera as the "*vergogna nazionale*" ("national shame"), which Anglophone critics broadcast as the "shame of Italy."[6] Using this calumny and Levi's book, the Communist Party made an example of Matera during the post–Second World War state elections. PCI leader Palmiro Togliatt even visited Matera during the 1948 election to witness the infamous situation himself, censure previous political regimes, and make new promises of aid.

National interest in the South awakening at this time resulted from growing anxiety over the Southern Question. Although Matera shared the misfortunes of the South, its cave-setting gave these ills a picturesque poignancy that newspapers and politicians alike exploited. Helped by the media, the elections' particular focus on Matera shaped it into the emblem of peasant misery, of southern underdevelopment and alterity, of the third world within the first world, the stepchild spawned by unification, the embarrassment of the nation, and the *symbol* of the Southern Question.[7]

The communists lost the 1948 election; however, the winning Christian Democrats were forced to address the Materan issue in particular and the Southern Question in general. Following the example set by past national leaders, the Christian Democratic Prime Minister, Alcide De Gasperi, visited Matera in 1950. Like his predecessors, De Gasperi condemned the cave society, which by the 1950s appeared all the more backward and all the more embarrassing for the nation. The weight of scorn heaped onto the Sassi and their attendant peasant culture made living in them untenable and unacceptable for both the residents and the nation. Through the passage of the Sassi Law (*Legge 619* of 17 May 1952), Matera became the case study for the *solution* to the Southern Question.

Based on the previously devised Fascist decentralization plan for relocating Sassi residents to new rural communities, the focus of the plan was to move the residents to new housing, rather than renovate the caves. Shame was the largest but not the only obstacle to making the Sassi (even if renovated) fit the modernist vision for Matera. A key term in the critique of premodern lifestyles and living conditions was "hygiene." Decades of labeling these structures as unhygienic —due mostly to the cohabitation of people with non-domestic animals, but also due to bedrooms and beds shared by parents and children, boys and girls—prevented them from filling the prescription of "correct" housing that all Italians had a right to occupy in this period of history (Figures 12.3 and 12.4).[8] The planners did not believe that the Sassi could be adapted to modern needs. Also, decades of evacuation plans had established the closed political mindset that relocation was the only method for erasing Matera's and the nation's shame. The mere idea of a cave with its subhuman associations offended the progressive mentality of the designers and leaders of the postwar world.

International Studies and Neorealist Interventions

In addition to capturing the attention of the media, Levi's book drew scholars to Matera to study the peasant cave population. Backed by postwar funding and calling themselves the *Commissione per lo studio della città e dell'agro di Matera* (Commission for the Study of the City and Surroundings of Matera), or simply the Study Group, an illustrious roster of national and international social scientists, planners, and progressive architects converged on Matera. One such scholar, philosophy professor and Fulbright fellow Friedrich Friedmann, stated that he and others came to study this "archaic society that no one had suspected existed within the confines of Europe. For [us, Levi's] book was a sort of revelation."[9]

The group members transformed their individual interests in the cave society into a coordinated effort to analyze the social and political dimensions of architecture and urbanism, which would form the basis of postwar urban design for Matera (Figure 12.4).[10] By taking almost a participant–observer approach, they believed that they achieved a greater understanding of the objects of their study through the vehicle of sympathy, the human dimension. In fact, Friedmann used the term "encounter" instead of "study" to describe his work, finding that it defined a sociologist's rapport with a living community. This study, or encounter, was revolutionary among the many postwar southern research projects taking place at this time in that it crossed multiple disciplines and was both theoretical and practical, both technical and moral. Their work would provide precise, scientifically based yet historically informed guidance for the Materan postwar building program, and their conclusions would guide similar projects throughout the South.

Following the publication of the Study Group's in-depth research, an army of Roman architects and planners (including members of this group) convened in Matera to realize the Sassi evacuation program by transforming the Study Group's

Anne Parmly Toxey

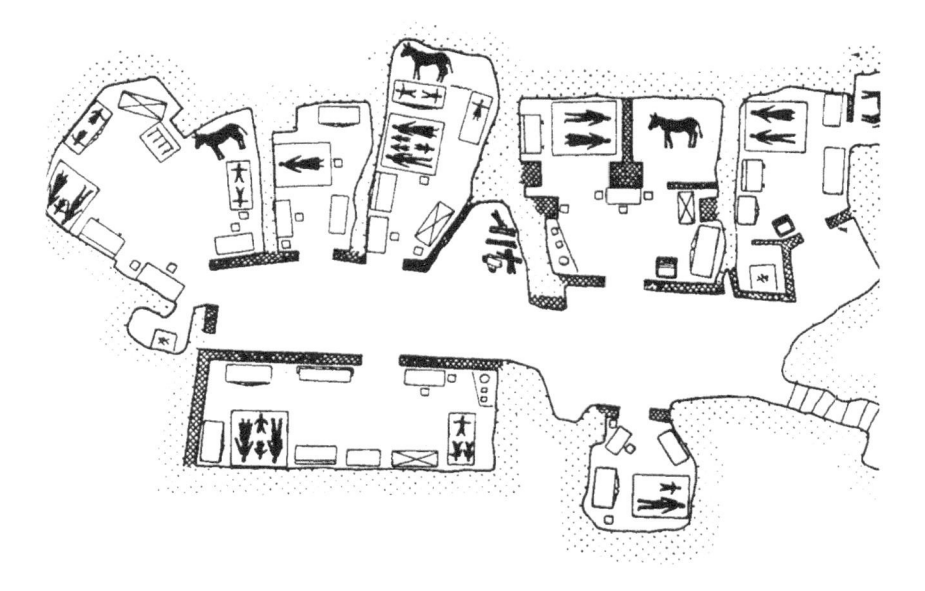

12.4
Lidia De Rita, study of the sleeping arrangements in Sassi houses surrounding a vicinato, early 1950s, published in *Casabella Continuità* 200 (February–March 1954), 33

conclusions into action. Their design objective was to create model, modern agricultural towns that kept "traditions of the historic community" intact and functioning into the future.[11] Innumerable articles were written about the Matera project in the 1950s, many of which were authored by architects and published in national architectural journals. The attention resulted in part from the fame of the architects and planners employed on the project. The cast included the Roman stars of Italian modernism: Ludovico Quaroni, Carlo Aymonino, Giancarlo De Carlo, Marcello Fabbri, and their numerous colleagues, largely belonging to the school of Neorealism. Validating the program, the nation's highly respected architectural critics, whose postwar roles were essential to the reconstruction of the nation, published regularly on the Materan project. These included: Manfredo Tafuri, Bruno Zevi, Ernesto Rogers, and the journals *Casabella*, *Metron*, *Urbanistica*, and *Comunità*.

The differing purposes of the program's participants (designers, scholars, and bureaucrats—but not the residents themselves) came together in this multi-disciplinary, multi-party, multi-institutional collaboration. They described their work in Matera as an "experiment in town-planning"[12] and a laboratory of postwar urban innovation. Matera, which had been derided as the epitome of the Southern Question, now became the model modernist city and was repeatedly described as the "Italian Utopia."[13]

The collaboration of these famous architects rescued Matera from villainy by cleansing it in the light and optimism of 1950s Italian modernism. Believing in the power of architecture to teach and to improve as well as to corrupt, they held the

Sassi responsible for residents' social and economic situations and thought that modern urbanism would remedy these problems. Planners and architects would show these peasants a "correct" and "civilized" lifestyle.[14]

The designers' intent was to attack the region's social problems by physically restructuring the entire territory.[15] The initial idea was to develop a series of satellite villages around Matera and to transfer the evacuated Sassi peasants to these rural complexes. Non-peasant Sassi residents (which were thought to be a small minority of artisans) would be moved to new housing complexes within Matera. Manfredo Tafuri described the integrated result as an "idyllic model of peasant development."[16]

The satellite villages would be designed to support Matera's traditional peasant lifestyle updated to conform to modern standards of hygiene. Each family would receive a house, garden plot, stable, and arable land. Bringing peasants close to their fields would reduce transit time (which usually ranged from four to six hours per day by foot). Transforming unfarmed land into productive land tied this project politically and economically to the agrarian reform program already in motion for the region. More importantly, however, the authors of this plan believed that repopulating the countryside with urban peasants and redistributing land to their ownership would metamorphose peasant farmers into modern agricultural entrepreneurs. From a political standpoint, the result would be to divide and conquer this politically dangerous concentration of destitute people with a history of political uprising by dispersing them over the countryside.

The political as well as social dimensions of the program are important. In their writings, for example, the designers expressed their intent to foster a democratic society through the provision of public space. The mechanism by which they hoped to accomplish this actually derived from the Sassi. It was the semi-public courtyard called the *vicinato* around which groups of four to twelve houses clustered throughout the site (Figures 12.1 and 12.4). This was the one feature of the Sassi that designers and scholars did not denigrate. In fact, they waxed poetic over it. On a practical level, the vicinato served as outdoor living space for many quotidian activities. On a social level, the system of vicinati structured the community and facilitated communication. In contrast to their harsh charges of the Sassi's "frightfully humiliating state of imbalance," the same architects described the vicinato with romanticism verging upon nostalgia and even favoring the vicinato above the work of modern designers.[17] Giancarlo De Carlo described it as "a magical equilibrium that, despite the wretched hygienic conditions of the houses, maintains human communication at a level that today seems permanently lost."[18]

Throughout the Sassi, houses are grouped around vicinati, which are connected by footpaths and staircases (the "streets" of the Sassi). These courtyards served as communal living- and workspaces: safe places for children to play, places to wash and hang laundry and to prepare food. The vicinato was credited with structuring society and systematizing village communication. In fact both design practitioners and critics appreciated this feature most for its social value. They admired the marriage of space and humanity achieved in this "ideal nucleus."[19] It was a native, vernacular example of what sociologists were advising architects at this time to use as the building block of urban design: a neighborhood unit organized around essential services. By employing this feature in modern Matera, architects would carry out what Tafuri called "a rationalization of the spontaneous tradition."[20]

Neorealist architects—like other architects at this time, including their CIAM counterparts—believed in the social reform powers of architecture and urban planning.[21] During the postwar period, architecture as social commitment and for social change became the guiding principle of the Neorealist movement. Antimonumental and anti-abstract, Neorealism was an architecture for the people. The satellite villages surrounding Matera manifest this ideal in their planned social homogeneity and were described as "town[s] for peasants."[22] Other than a few priests and shopkeepers, the residents would all belong to the peasant class, with no aristocracy or wealthy landowners among them. Also typical of Neorealists' quest to design for the lifestyles of the intended users, the villages surrounding Matera reference the Sassi in building materials, scale, and occasionally form.

The spiritual leader of the Roman school and therefore a powerful influence on the designers of new Matera was Bruno Zevi. Based on the ideas of Frank Lloyd Wright, which he studied during his training in the United States during the Second World War, Zevi was a proponent of "organic architecture." His definition of organic, however, extended beyond formal concerns to include a human dimension: "an architecture for the people, not for the architect."[23] In the words of Zevi,

> An organic architecture means . . . an organic society. . . . Architecture is organic when the spatial arrangement of room, house and city is planned for human happiness, material, psychological and spiritual. The organic is based therefore on a social idea and not on a figurative idea. We can only call architecture organic when it aims at being human before it is humanist.[24]

Carlo Aymonino explains that the social interest among Roman organic architects was "a means of approaching the reality of the country."[25]

The designers of new Matera also liberally employed the terms "picturesque" and "spontaneous" in their descriptions of the Sassi, which they explored for ideas to incorporate in their designs. One such architect, Marcello Fabbri, described modern urbanists' "discovery in the Mezzogiorno [the South] of an inexhaustible mine of so-called 'spontaneous architecture' and with this a tradition in which to situate their own activity."[26] Contrasting descriptions of stunning and frightening views reveal their nostalgic engagement with the Sassi. They could accept the Sassi as a form of habitation for the distant past, but they caustically rejected them as housing for contemporary culture.

Sergio Lenci, another designer of new Matera, writes of the

> backwardness of living conditions . . . [that] requires a drastic and immediate solution . . . [and] an invitation to a more civilized way of living. . . . This change of one's home . . . should coincide with the beginning of

new aspirations to a different standard of living, to more varied human relations. The intimacy which the small neighborhood loses should become the acquisition of a new freedom of contacts.[27]

Through descriptions reminiscent of the paternalistic liberalism espoused by Western reformers and colonizers from the mid-nineteenth through early twentieth centuries, Lenci acknowledges the loss of the Sassi's character in the new neighborhoods and villages, despite years of study and volumes written on the designers' intent to "preserve" the Sassi's "vital characteristics"[28] in the new constructions.

In fact, the new neighborhoods drew little or no formal inspiration from local vernacular urbanism. They were orderly, rational, and clean: the diametric opposite of the spontaneous, labyrinthine scene of the Sassi. Even the vicinati, so loved and lauded by the Neorealists, were translated into overscaled, exposed yards with no defensible space or into generic streets, which were labeled "linear vicinati" but did not function as the intimate, semi-public, work spaces of the Sassi.

Developed by members of the Study Group, namely Ludovico Quaroni, the first and most famous of the exurban Materan building projects was the rural village of La Martella (Figure 12.5). Its 200 houses were paired duplex-style along curved streets, described as linear vicinati. Designed to keep mules, other animals, feed, and tools *separate* from the house, the accompanying barns were also duplexes. The buildings' lime-coated local limestone block walls and red, curved-tile roofing were intended to recall Sassi constructions. Next to a small kitchen garden, an inner courtyard housed the family's cart at night. A large living room, kitchen, and bedroom composed the ground floor of each house with more bedrooms upstairs. Modern codes of hygiene dictated a separation of sleeping activities from living, a separation of food preparation from the presence of animals, and a separation of parents' beds and bedrooms from those of children (who were further segregated by gender). Explaining their design challenge, Friedmann wrote:

> Our principal problem was to construct a new settlement that would improve the living conditions of the inhabitants, in particular the hygienic conditions, without destroying that culture that had permeated the Sassi for centuries. In particular, we wanted to ensure that the people and their mules did not live in the same spaces, as they did in the Sassi. We also wanted to find a method that permitted the mule's owner to be sure that even during the night no one was stealing his animal.[29]

In addition to providing a new, more healthful physical setting that was expected to cure social problems, the new housing program provided an educational component to teach the peasants modern lifestyles. This included lessons in how to use a shower, how to clean houses and wash hands before meals, how to prepare food hygienically, and even how to eat as a family (that is, not out of one large bowl, as Materans used to do).[30] They were also taught to speak Italian—and disparage their native dialect of Materano—and to be consumers. Store-bought pasta, for example, became valued over homemade pasta.

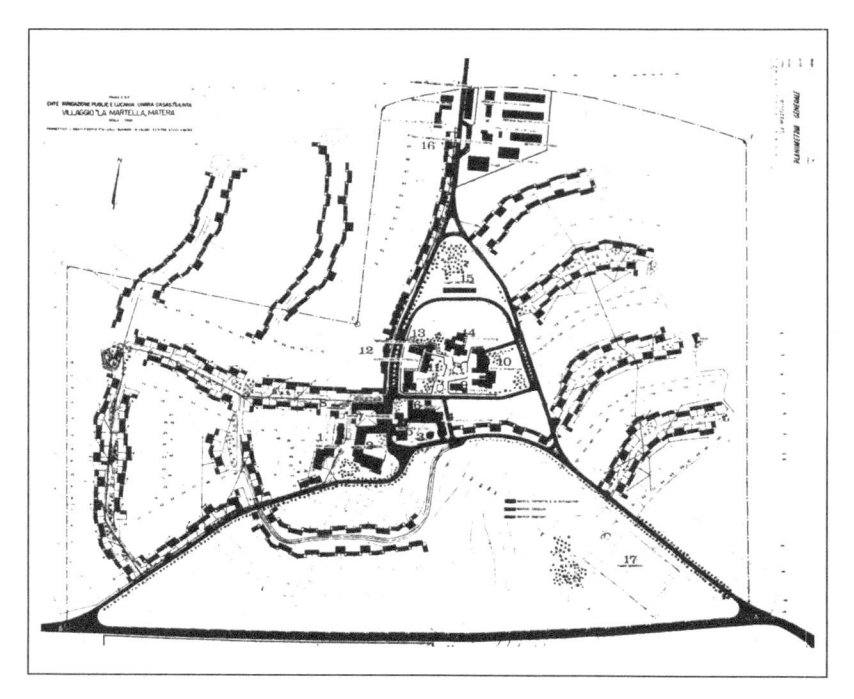

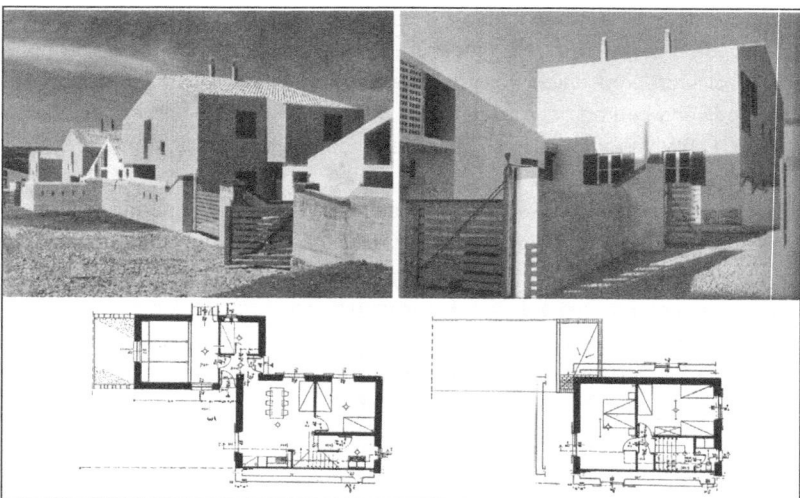

12.5
Above: Ludovico Quaroni, plan for the rural village of La Martella, 1954
Below: Ludovico Quaroni, photographs and plans (ground floor on the left; upper floor on the right) of duplex houses and adjoining duplex barns at La Martella, 1954, published in *Casabella Continuità* 200 (February–March 1954), 32, 34

Failures and Successes

The Sassi depopulation process did not proceed as planned. The salient reason for this was that the services and lands that were supposed to support the new rural villages were not forthcoming. Some families refused to move to the villages. Some moved but then returned to the Sassi. The city–country equilibrium failed to live up to urbanistic accolades and expectations. Dreams of land redistribution and rural utopias faded.

La Martella, the highest-profile project and the first to invite new residents, led to the greatest disillusionment and, along with the foundational idea of decentralization, has drawn the most criticism. Even its greatest apologist, Friedmann, denied its "success."[31] Some scholars attribute this failure to the tenets of the program's design, for example, the myth of being able to relocate a people to a different context without destroying its culture and the myth of emancipating the peasant world through design. Although these are valid criticisms that undoubtedly contributed to the program's defeat, its largest obstacle was the politicians and central government, which did not provide the essential services and public utilities necessary for the new villages' survival. Compounding the situation was the collapse of the land reform program, which did not provide land to the displaced peasants.[32] Reigning DC political interests were at odds with the program's Robin Hood ideals and therefore hindered land redistribution.[33] Friedmann even described the local political intrusion into selection of families to go to La Martella, which involved political favors as well as the local bishop's political agenda (expressing a bias against PCI members).[34]

In 1954 when it became evident that no land was forthcoming to support the agrarian community of La Martella, a study was completed showing that the land surrounding Matera already belonged almost entirely to small farming operations, not to large absentee owners as it had been assumed. The excess land that was earmarked to give to Materan peasants therefore did not exist, and the foundation of the Materan reruralization program was fatally flawed. The result of this realization was that the Sassi evacuation program became unhitched from the postwar agrarian reform initiative, which nationwide was a dying issue by this time, and rural village construction and inhabitation were more or less abandoned.

It is hard to believe that, after decades of government-sponsored research and the collaboration of multiple agencies and organizations, the land situation had not been studied in the vicinity of Matera before construction of these villages. Either these studies were not actually carried out (in a case of bureaucratic freeloading) or the program was sabotaged (in which case the government's intentions come into question). In either case, Tafuri described the result as one of "land counterreform," preventing the occupation of Sassi houses while barring the construction of rural villages.

Without land for the peasants, the evacuation and decentralization program lost its socio-economic dimension and was reduced to merely a building program. The decision was made to expand the old city by constructing new urban neighborhoods for the former Sassi residents. Matera's second phase of postwar reconstruction (1958–1965) again involved star architects and considerable visibility

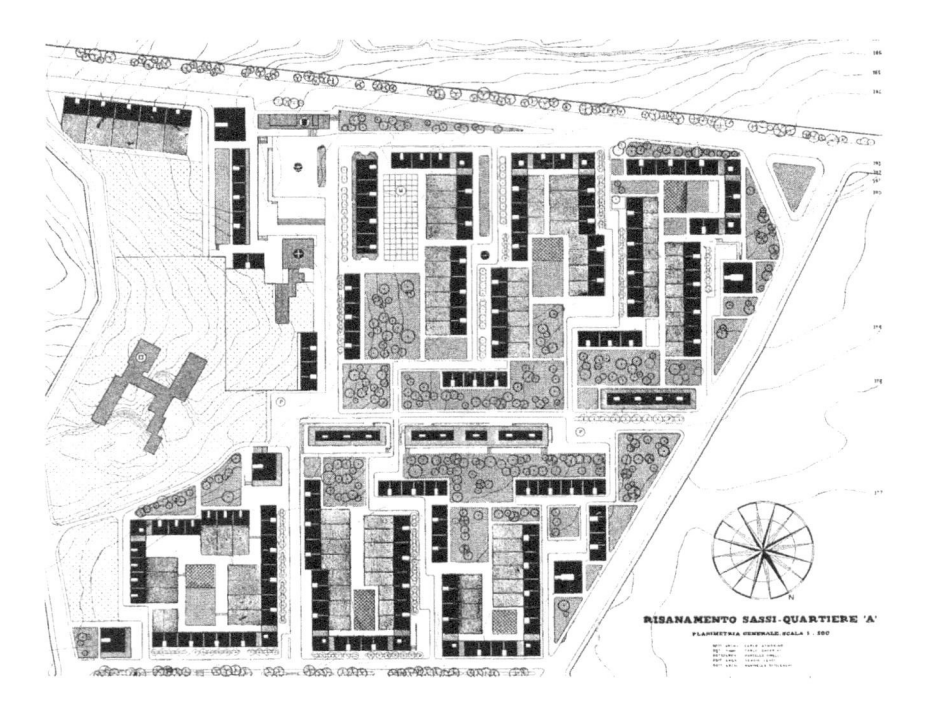

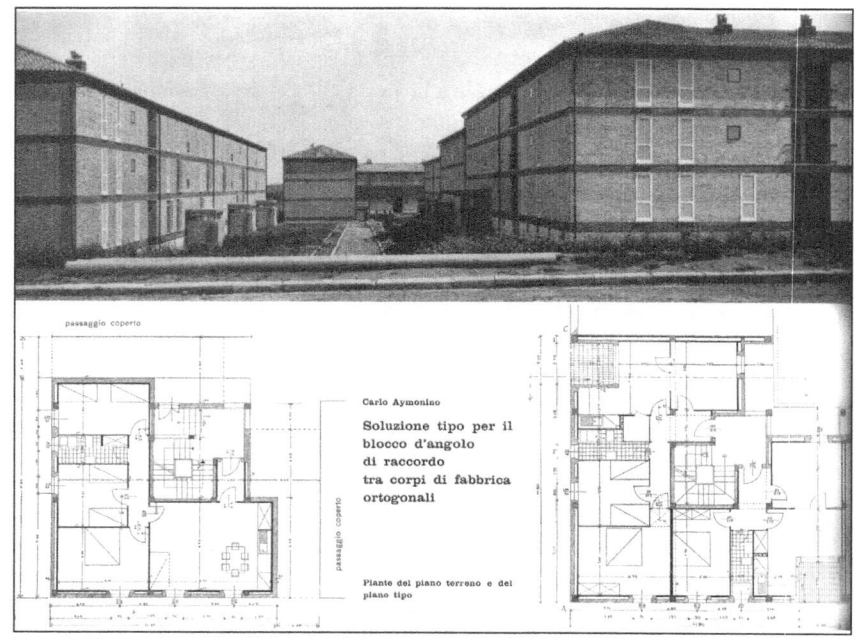

12.6
Carlo Aymonino and colleagues, site plan, photograph, and building plans for the new urban neighborhood of Spine Bianche, 1959, published in *Casabella Continuità* 231 (September 1959), 13, 16

in professional design journals (Figure 12.6).[35] Though less closely tied to the Study Group's conclusions, their work nevertheless shared the postwar ideals and objectives of the earlier designs and belonged to the Neorealist tradition.

Also like the satellite villages, these new urban neighborhoods proved disappointing. Their description as "towns within a town" may have been intended to commend the completeness of their design, which included schools, churches, artisan workshops, and public spaces, but the term also described the continued exclusion of these poorer people from the life of the elite in the center of town.[36] Their reputation as *"quartieri ghetto"* (ghetto neighborhoods) reflects this darker interpretation.[37] Contemporary observers also critiqued the projects for the lack of participation offered to future residents in the planning and design of these neighborhoods and for their generic quality that did not address the needs or lifestyles of the intended occupants.[38]

Accompanying the programmatic change from city–country reorganization of the first plan to the second plan's simple urban expansion was a new problem: the need for economic development. The building program obscured this problem by temporarily solving it through the provision of construction work for the new neighborhoods. Many having little or no land of their own and offered a paycheck as an attractive alternative to the hardscrabble lifestyle of the peasant farmer, Sassi residents flocked to fill construction jobs. Those unable to find construction work were forced to emigrate to northern and foreign factories.

When the bonanza ended in the early 1970s, the local construction force found itself unemployed. These people had lost their economic base of farming, and the new urban arrangement provided no alternative. When the postwar reconstruction plan was reduced to an urban renewal project, it economically and vocationally handicapped the Sassi society that it transferred.

Lack of provision of economic development for Matera in the revised plan, however, was not an oversight. A number of prominent voices pointed out this deficiency before the plan was approved. Fabbri, for example, published an impassioned article attempting to reverse this omission several years before the plan was accepted. He forecast that it would lead to permanent dependence upon the government.[39] The fact that the guiding plan did not provide for the future development of industries, therefore, indicates the planners' continued complicity with the economic strategy of the reigning political power.

Looking back at these events from the distance of fifteen years, Tafuri wrote:

> The Sassi have ... been a pretext for an artificial incentive of the construction economy, for an agricultural reform that was functional only as a capitalistic management of underdeveloped areas, for the preservation of territorial equilibrium (and disequilibrium), for the sake of hiding or giving very little importance to the grave and decisive decisions that are about to condition the social and economical situation of the Basilicata.[40]

He and other critics viewed the entire agrarian reform movement as a DC ploy to transform the South into a labor pool for Northern factories.

> The Matera case exemplified the role that the great industrial capital had assigned to underdevelopment: the underdeveloped area was managed as a pool of reserve labor for industrialized areas. To achieve this the agricultural vocation of the south was stressed, the service sector was artificially expanded, and a policy of public works instigated to stimulate consumerism in the south. . . . Public works and building functioned as a means of containing unemployment and providing training for agricultural groups that would later on be encouraged to migrate to developed areas. There they would form a reserve force, enabling producers to keep wages low.[41]

Historian Paul Ginsborg arrived at an analogous conclusion in his analysis of similar occurrences across the South. He observed that the agrarian reform laws gave peasants (and at that, only non-communist ones) insufficient land and of the poorest quality (much of which had already titularly been given to peasants by previous reform measures). The results only further disadvantaged the peasants through decreased returns, increased land prices, and decreased power. "Above all, the reform broke forever those attempts at aggregation and cooperation . . . [to] split irrevocably the peasant movement. . . . The agrarian reform was an important part of an overall strategy for securing Christian democratic power in the agrarian South."[42]

As Tafuri predicted, those who had not emigrated for northern and foreign factories previously did so when construction of new Matera ended. Therefore, far from economically and socially emancipating Sassi residents from their historical oppression and dependence upon others as the evacuation program was billed to do, it perpetuated the situation under modern raiment. By deracinating the population and spreading it over a much larger area, the new arrangement diffused (and divided into different communities) what strength the former Sassi residents had had in their concentrated numbers. The city was stripped of its peasant lifestyle and economy, its groundedness, and self-identity. In the space of twenty-five years, the government transformed the populace from a dialect-speaking, land-working, troglodyte peasant culture that largely existed outside the Italian nation into wage-earning, tax-paying, Italian-speaking, state employees and blue-collar consumers living in "hygienic" if mundane concrete apartment blocks, and dependent upon the government for work, wages, housing (rented from the government), and modern identity.

This feat was accomplished through humiliating the Sassi residents and making them feel shame not only for their social "problems" but also for their vernacular lifestyle, its physical setting, and even their language, Materano. By enticing people to leave their homes, which were deserted to decay, their fields, their livelihoods, and their customs, the national government was able to dictate politically sanctioned lifestyles and to transform Materans' beliefs and allegiances, their values and ideology. Using the guise of social reform and the tools of urban and architectural planning, the republican government altered allegiances to create national citizens. The result of this indoctrination was a forced forgetting of their peasant ways and deemed inferior past and an adoption of the culture and glorious history of the fledgling nation.[43] The convenient invisibility of the Sassi from the rest of the city on the ridge above them physically reinforced this policy.

From a political perspective, therefore, the program was successful. Matera's shame was forgotten. This population of premodern cave residents, which had been visible to the whole nation and world, disappeared from the radar screen when they adopted the trappings and ways of prescribed modern life. They became consumers and a ready force of labor. From a design standpoint, however, the project failed. The architects' and planners' humanitarian and social idealism was never realized, and their utopian villages were abandoned. Serving as pawns, these architects and planners unwittingly assisted the Italian state's exploitive scheme, which was veiled beneath the larger structure of social reform. Although direct government intervention did curb such problems as illiteracy, poverty, and high infant mortality, all laudable achievements, architecture had nothing to do with these changes.

In 1959 architect Carlo Aymonino expressed the postwar optimism and climate of anticipation when, playing on Levi's title, he wrote, "Christ has arrived at Matera. Let's hope that well-being also arrives." In the same article, however, he betrayed the cynicism and disappointment felt at the end of the decade when he called the whole Sassi evacuation program "a midsummer night's dream with, unfortunately, an unhappy ending."[44] Similar ambivalence fills the pages of the salient issue of *Casabella* dedicated to the Mezzogiorno (specifically, Matera and Naples). Even though politicians were largely responsible for the downfall of the plan's grand idea of urban–agricultural synthesis and its associated social and economic reforms, architects were disillusioned by the events and by the disconsolate realization that fundamental societal change was beyond the powers of architecture to achieve. The failure of the plan also shook their belief in the validity and objectivity of the hard sociological science on which it was based. They reevaluated the forms of and ideas behind postwar architecture and deemed them flawed.

Eschewing the social idealism of their Neorealist predecessors, 1960s architects designing more new neighborhoods in Matera criticized the previous decade's work as patronizing and therefore scornful of the non-elite occupants.[45] They critiqued their predecessors' romantic obsession with peasants, who turned out *not* to be the predominant Sassi dwellers of the 1950s. This position was instead filled by artisans and laborers. Even legitimate peasants, however, were leaving their fields in favor of other employment opportunities, yielding a meager and dwindling peasant population to fill the paper plans for rural villages.

Anne Parmly Toxey

12.7
Above: Construction of dense new housing in Matera, 2006
Below: A peasant museum in the Sassi, 2003

Repercussions of the 1950s Events

Life for those who moved to the new city—now just called "the city" while the Sassi continued to be marginalized as "the Sassi"—changed radically in some ways and not at all in others. Illustrating the power of modernization to control societies, this process changed the lifestyles, livelihoods, identity, values, and even the foods and language of these people; however, for many years they continued to be isolated in their enclaves and separated from the elite, older city. Published in 1955, the words of Francesco Nitti describing current changes in Matera rang true for the following two decades:

> The reforms, only partially realized, have not yet succeeded in removing the old social arrangement and instead have created a new and more complicated bureaucracy with a concentration of power. ... But the lowest levels of society are no longer estranged to the new events and to State interventions, and they become ever more conscious of proper functions.[46]

Today, the agricultural sector of the economy continues to diminish, as does the industrial sector, while the overwhelming majority of Materans hold government jobs.[47] This situation fulfills Fabbri's prophecy that without economic development, Matera and the South would be forever economically dependent upon the state. This dependence fuels current Southern Question debates.

While the elite still reside in their seventeenth-to-nineteenth-century palaces in the old city center, a new professional crowd lives in the Sassi—now elegantly renovated, listed as a UNESCO World Heritage Monument, and attracting cultural tourists. As for the evicted Sassi population, social leveling did largely occur. The second and third generations of this group compose the ever-growing middle class of civil servants, which continues to expand Matera's footprint with new apartment buildings (Figure 12.7).

Although most Materans are descended from the 20,000 people who were evacuated from the Sassi from 1950–1975, few admit their connection to the site. Their middle-class status depends upon this separation. The shame that the nation felt for the Sassi has transferred to this population, who continue to shun the site and have readily sold out to tourism. Portrayed as the bygone past, Matera's peasant culture resides only in tourist museums in the Sassi.[48] Except for a few scholars interested in saving Materano, it is essentially a dead language.

Notes

Acknowledgments: Special thanks go to Enzo Viti for the liberal access he provided me to his personal archives, which have supported the research for this article and my other work. Also essential to this study have been the following public archives and libraries: the Archivio di Stato di Matera, the Biblioteca Provinciale "T. Stigliani" di Matera, and the Environmental Design Library at the University of California, Berkeley. For further development of the research presented here and a history of the eventual preservation of the Sassi, please see Anne Parmly Toxey, *Materan Contradictions: Architecture, Preservation, and Politics* (London: Ashgate, 2011).

1. Vittorio Gregotti, *New Directions in Italian Architecture* (New York: George Braziller, 1968), 52; Eric Mumford, *The CIAM Discourse on Urbanism, 1928–1960* (Cambridge, MA: MIT Press, 2000), 7.
2. Francesco Nitti's data from June 6, 1950, demonstrate that 38 percent of Materan households (1,582 out of 4,182) had running water at this time. He also states that in 1927, the upper portion of the city (above the Sassi, known as the *Piano*), received electricity. This represented 63 percent of Materan households (2,621 homes), though Nitti does not specify whether every household on the Piano had electricity. Compare this with Paul Ginsborg's nationwide statistic that "in 1951, the elementary combination of electricity, drinking water, and an inside lavatory could be found in only 7.4 percent of Italian households." These numbers imply that Matera as a whole was far more modernized than much of Italy; however, they do not show that the caves, which supported 53 percent of the population, were largely unmodernized. Francesco Nitti, "Una Comunità in Cammino: Matera," *Basilicata: Mensile di Politica e Cronache Meridionale* 2, no. 26 (1955): 48; Paul Ginsborg, *A History of Contemporary Italy: Society and Politics 1943–1988* (New York: Penguin Books, 1990), 210, n. 1. See also note 5, below.
3. Giovanni Battista Pacichelli, *Il Regno di Napoli in Prospettiva*, vol. 1 (Naples: Michele Luigi Mutio, 1702; Sala Bolognese: Arnaldo Forni Editore, 1975), 267; Abate Alberto Fortis, *Viaggio nel Regno di Napoli* (c. 1780); John. A. Murray, *Handbook for Travellers in Southern Italy: Being a Guide for the Provinces Formerly Constituting the Continental Portion of the Kingdom of the Two Sicilies* (London: John Murray, 1868).
4. Of the total city population of 30,136 calculated on June 30, 1950, the Sassi housed 15,990, the majority of whom were identified as peasants (Nitti, "Una Comunità in Cammino: Matera," 3).
5. Manfredo Tafuri, *History of Italian Architecture, 1944–1985* (Cambridge, MA: MIT Press, 1989), 25; Graeme Barker, *A Mediterranean Valley: Landscape Archaeology and Annales History in the Biferno Valley* (New York: Leicester University Press, 1995), 298; Ginsborg, 122, describing conditions of Calabria that are obviously worse than Matera; Luigi Piccinato, "Matera: I Sassi i Nuovi borghi e il Piano regolatore," *Urbanistica* 15–16 (1955): 147; and Cid Corman, *Sun Rock Man* (New York: New Directions, 1970) whose introduction similarly describes Matera's affluence in relation to the "undisguised, unmitigated" poverty of neighboring villages.
6. Although this expression is attached to Levi and the media coverage of his book, the calumny "*vergogna nazionale*" first appeared in a 1941 government document drawn by engineer Vincenzo Corazza, a term which he credits to Professor Arcangelo Ilvento. See Vincenzo Corazza, *Abitazioni nei Rioni dei Sassi di Matera, Condizioni Igieniche, Statistiche, Proposte di Soluzione* (Matera: Comune di Matera Ufficio Tecnico, 1941); quoted in Alfonso Pontrandolfi, *La Vergogna Cancellata: Matera negli Anni dello Sfollamento dei Sassi* (Matera: Altrimedia Edizioni, 2002), 30.
7. The tropes of "shame" and "hygiene" applied to the Sassi generated from the "filth" and "promiscuity" associated with cohabitation of non-domestic animals and people. Figure 12.3 shows a typical Sassi interior dating from c. 1950. A mule stands near the bed, though the stable was often the deepest, darkest, most humid area of the cave, separated from living quarters by a wall, curtain, or furniture. Roaming chickens sought refuge under the high beds.
8. On his visit to Matera in 1948, Togliatti claimed that comfortable housing is a human necessity and that all citizens have the right to live in humane conditions. Quoted in *I Comunisti e i Sassi di Matera* (Matera: Festa de l'Unità, 1977) and in Pontrandolfi, 43.
9. Friedrich George Friedmann, *Miseria e dignità: Il Mezzogiorno nei primi anni Cinquanta* (Rome: UNRRA-Casas, 1956; San Domenico di Fiesole: Edizioni Cultura della Pace, 1996), 46. Unless otherwise noted, translations are the author's own.
10. This illustration by Lidia De Rita was developed during the Study Group's analysis of Materan peasant culture. It shows a vicinato surrounded by several cave houses and the sleeping arrangements of residents (parents sharing beds with children) and their mules, which were greatly valued.

11 Riccardo Musatti, "L'ambiente geografico," in *Saggi Introduttivi (1), Commissione per lo Studio della Citta e dell' Agro di Matera,* ed. Riccardo Musatti, Federico G. Friedmann, and Giuseppe Isnardi (Rome: UNRRA-Casas, 1956), 8. See also Carlo Aymonino, "Matera: Mito e Realtà," *Casabella Continuità* 231 (1959): 9–10.
12 Aymonino, "Matera: Mito e Realtà," 9.
13 For example, Marcello Fabbri, "Frammenti per Matera," *Rivista Italiana d'Architettura* 5, no. 21 (1999): 22.
14 For use of this terminology, see for example, Aymonino, "Matera: Mito e Realtà," 10; Cesare Valle, "Pianificazione integrata," *Casabella Continuità* 231 (1959): 8; and the authors of *Rivista Italiana d'Architettura* 5, no. 21 (1999), including Luigi Acito, "I Pionieri della Modernità," 14.
15 Federico Bellini, "Matera moderno modernità: Realtà, ideologia, e architettura nel dopoguerra Materano," *Rivista Italiana d'Architettura* 5, no. 21: 19. For a more complete description, see Fabbri, "Frammenti per Matera," 22.
16 Manfredo Tafuri, *Ludovico Quaroni e lo sviluppo dell'architettura moderna in Italia* (Milan: Edizioni di Comunità, 1964), 109 and n. 63, paraphrasing Marcello Fabbri.
17 Giancarlo De Carlo, "A proposito di La Martella," *Casabella Continuità* 200 (1954): viii.
18 De Carlo, "A proposito di La Martella," viii.
19 Federico Gorio, "Il villaggio La Martella," *Casabella Continuità* 200 (1954): 36.
20 Tafuri, *Ludovico Quaroni e lo sviluppo dell'architettura moderna in Italia,* 112.
21 In fact, Le Corbusier's urbanisitic philosophy that he brought to CIAM was that "physical design rather than political action could provide solutions to the poor living conditions of industrial cities" (Mumford, 2, 20).
22 Mauro Padula, "Matera, vicende storiche e varie fasi di sviluppo della città," in *Lamisco 2002: Studi e Documenti sulla Storia di Matera e del suo Territorio,* ed. D. Amoroso et al. (Matera: Edizioni Giannatelli, 2002), 38.
23 Panayotis Tournikiotis, *The Historiography of Modern Architecture* (Cambridge, MA: MIT Press, 1999), 56.
24 Bruno Zevi, *Towards an Organic Architecture* (London: Faber and Faber, 1949), 76.
25 Carlo Aymonino, "Storia e Cronaca del Quartiere Tiburtino," *Casabella Continuità* 215 (1957): xi (English translation of p. 19).
26 Marcello Fabbri, "La Paura degli Urbanisti," *Basilicata: Mensile di Politica e Cronache Meridionale* 2, no. 22–25 (1955): 3.
27 Sergio Lenci, "Esperienze nella progettazione del quartiere Spine Bianche a Matera," *Casabella Continuità* 231 (1959): viii (English translation of p. 21).
28 Giancarlo De Carlo, "Il risultato di un concorso," *Casabella Continuità* 231 (1959): ix (English translation of p. 24).
29 Friedmann, 70–71.
30 Personal communications: via Casalnuovo residents, Peppino Piumini, and Vincenzo Santacroce, July 2003.
31 Friedmann, 71.
32 Ibid., 71–74, 80; Aymonino, "Matera: Mito e Realtà," viii, 9–10; Tafuri, *Ludovico Quaroni e lo sviluppo dell'architettura moderna in Italia,* 109; Tafuri, *History of Italian Architecture,* 24–25; Mauro Saito, "Quaroni e La Martella," *Rivista Italiana d'Architettura* 5, no. 21 (1999): 17; Pontrandolfi, 146.
33 Pontrandolfi describes the local fight between the DC and PCI blow by blow and the impact on the renovation program in the early–mid-1950s, see in particular pages 121–125.
34 Friedmann, 69–70.
35 As illustrated in Figure 12.6, for example, the neighborhood of Spine Bianche was designed by Carlo Aymonino, Giancarlo De Carlo, Federico Gorio, Sergio Lenci, and other notables. Notice the lack of formal relationship with the Sassi.

36 Tafuri, *History of Italian Architecture,* 25; Cosimo Damiano Fonseca, Rosalba Demetrio, and Grazia Guadagno, *Matera* (Bari: Editore Latereza, 1998), 105.
37 Lorenzo Rota, "Matera: la Vicenda Urbanistica," in *Matera: Storia di una Città,* ed. Franco Conese, Lorenzo Rota, and Mario Tommaselli (Matera: BMG, 1990), 142.
38 Fabbri, "La Paura degli Urbanisti," 3 and Marcello Fabbri, *Matera: dal Sottosviluppo alla Nuova Città* (Matera: Basilicata Editrice, 1971), 63. Ironically, Olivetti makes similar criticisms of other plans in his presentation (reproduced in *Urbanistica* 15–16 (1955): 7–10) at the Urbanistica congress in 1954.
39 Fabbri, "La Paura degli Urbanisti," 3. See also Fabbri, *Matera: dal Sottosviluppo alla Nuova Città,* 63–68, and Pontrandolfi, 127.
40 Manfredo Tafuri and Amerigo Restucci, *International Competition for the Arrangement of the "Sassi" of Matera: Contribution to the Comprehension of the Events of the History of Matera* (Matera: BMG/Italian Republic Ministry of Public Works, 1974), 7.
41 Tafuri, *History of Italian Architecture,* 24–25 and n. 42. Tafuri also asserts that the reform efforts were successful in their intentions, in that they were never meant to carry out real reform but to continue "political standstill *through* reforms" (Tafuri and Restucci, 65).
42 Ginsborg, 139. Similarly, Gregotti, 52, asserts that the sociological approach to the design of La Martella was an illusion of objectivity and "was intended to preserve the social structure and underdevelopment."
43 Mia Fuller describes a comparison in Rhodes where colonization within Europe—by Italy, incidentally—has led to feelings of humiliation and forgetting in "Good as Bread: Nostalgia and Forgivability in Postcolonial Rhodes" (paper presented at the American Anthropological Association annual meeting, 1995).
44 Aymonino, "Matera: Mito e Realtà," viii (English translation of pages 9–10).
45 Massimo Locci, "Architettura Contemporanea a Matera," *Rivista Italiana d'Architettura* 5, no. 21 (1999): 32.
46 Francesco Nitti, *Una Città del Sud: Saggio Storico* (Rome: UNRRA-CASAS-Prima Giunta, 1956), 55–56.
47 According to Antonio Panetta, the heavily subsidized Italian agricultural industry has transformed farmers into state employees as well (personal communication, August 2010).
48 Figure 12.7 illustrates one of several private museums in the Sassi that preserve accoutrements of peasant culture, which the rural villages were intended to keep alive.

Coda

From Homelessness to Homelessness
David Crowley

Covering the period between the end of the Second World War and the early 1970s, the essays in this book explore subjects in the era in which modernism triumphed, or so it seems. A set of aesthetic and intellectual propositions about the nature of modern design generated after the First World War were realized around the world in the uneasy peace which followed the end of the Second World War. The dream of an "International Style" was achieved to a large extent, with, of course, "local" differences in context and timing.[1] North American and Western European industry turned to modernist designers to provide the blueprints for chic modern furniture and electronic consumer goods as the "affluent society" took shape in the 1950s; after 1956, Eastern European states set about creating the kind of mass housing schemes which had been proposed by Le Corbusier, Ludwig Hilbersheimer, and others in the 1920s; and newly independent states in Africa and the Middle East commissioned concrete and glass monuments from "First" and "Second World" architects to demonstrate their claims on modernity. *Twenty years* after the end of the Second World War, modernist architects and designers could justifiably claim to be shaping the world. Ernesto Roger's 1952 totalizing ambition for design, *dal cucchiaio alla città* (from the spoon to the city), was, it seems, being realized.[2] Thirty years after 1945, however, the modernist project seemed to be in jeopardy, threatened by economic recession and environmental anxieties, and disturbed by the critiques of rationalism and technocracy in the West and the emergence of dissidence in the Eastern Bloc.[3] In 1975, Gaetano Pesce, the subject of Jane Pavitt's essay in this book, could assert "Le Futur est peut-être passé."

The reasons for what is usually described as the historic "failure" of modernism are many and often debated. Much of the explosion of writing on post-modernism in the 1980s was largely dedicated to providing explanations of its breakdown.[4] In this coda, however, I would like focus on the midpoint of the period covered by the essays in this book, the late 1950s. Even at the moment of its greatest success, as the essays in this book demonstrate, postwar modernism in architecture and design displayed many symptoms of anxiety. But, of course, all

David Crowley

societies fret about the conditions of the age in which they live. Even those times and places which have been cast in retrospect as "golden ages" were invariably understood by their contemporaries in terms of anxiety. "Golden Age Vienna" was the birthplace of psychoanalysis and the "Swinging Sixties" produced the Counter Culture. Moreover, the home has often been claimed as either a symptom of or as an antidote to social failure, anomie or poverty. The indictment of the domestic environment as a generator of poverty and "lax" morality in the postwar discussion of the Sassi cave homes in Matera, Italy, described by Anne Parmly Toxey in her essay, for instance, shares much with characterizations of London's rookeries one-hundred years earlier.[5] So what distinguishes the anxieties of modern dwelling in the age of its accomplishment? In what follows I will reflect on this question by exploring views of the past, present and future of the modern home articulated in the late 1950s. In each "moment," the question of what constituted a *human* environment rose sharply to the fore.

Coming to Terms with the Past

Modern design in Europe after 1945 was conscripted into the project of postwar reconstruction and the creation of new, "just" societies. The view that modern design should ameliorate social problems was, of course, nothing new: what had changed in the postwar years was the sense that modern architecture and design could address *existenzfragen* (existential questions) (and, as such, formed a European counterpart to North American design psychologism). Postwar modernism could not only create the future but, in some settings, would also heal the wounds of the recent past. The recent experience of "total war" which had seen entire societies conscripted into the war effort as well as the shocking awareness of humanity's terrible potential for destruction made the heady technological futurism of the 1920s seem naive and obsolete. The challenge—widely accepted by modernist designers and architects—was to set new technologies to peaceful or "humanist" purposes. Writing about the intellectual mindset of architects and designers, Barry Curtis has described humanism as a "pervasive mood" which "responded to recent experiences of totalitarianism and scientifically planned mass destruction."[6] Similarly, Ignasi de Solà-Morales has described it "not as a strictly philosophical current but as a cultural climate."[7] The impressionistic tenor of words like "mood" and "climate" accurately capture the widespread but diffused influence of humanism in its existential and phenomenological modes in the postwar years. "Humanity" and "man" were the common platitudes, invoked at almost every important gathering of architects and designers in Europe during the reconstruction years: the German Werkbund organized the second Darmstädter Gespräch to discuss "Mensch und Raum" in 1951; the Milan Triennale in the same year took "Architettura, misura dell'uomo" as its governing theme; whilst the following year the Congrès Internationaux d'Architecture Moderne met in Hoddesdon, a town near London, and published its findings there in *The Heart of the City: Towards the Humanisation of Urban Life*.[8]

Preparing the West German pavilion at the Brussels World's Fair in 1958, Hans Schwippert represented modern architecture and design as part of this humanist crusade:

> A movement is starting in the world . . . against the dehumanizing trends of mechanization, against the threat of the new horrifying means of annihilation and of "progress" . . . a movement that seeks and achieves a new lightness, a new tenderness and a new beauty. The glass walls of the new architecture, the new lightness of offices, workshops, factories, the graceful style of new furnishings, the pleasure of living among green, growing things . . . are all wonderful experiments in a general human opposition to the threat of darkness and impending chaos.[9]

Schwippert was the secretary of the German Werkbund, a much-celebrated professional lobby that had played a key role in the development of Weimar modernism. After 1945, the Werkbund came to enjoy a significant role in West Germany, derived, in part, from its standing as a rare prewar institution which could claim some degree of autonomy from Nazism. In the first half of the 1950s the Werkbund sought to orient the material culture of the country to its cherished ideal of *gute Form* (good form), a loose formulation which claimed moral effects for modernist design. It mounted didactic exhibitions, promoted design education and the output of a few prominent manufacturers.[10] Claiming a prewar Modern Movement heritage and counting figures like the former director of the Bauhaus, Walter Gropius, amongst its alumni, the Werkbund saw an opportunity to remake the world—in material and moral terms—from the ruins of the Second World War.

The Werkbund sought to be a moral compass which would steer West Germany through reconstruction to democracy. In 1951 it invited Ortega y Gasset and Martin Heidegger to speak at the second Darmstädter Gespräch which gathered to discuss "Mensch und Raum." This event took the following words as its motto:

> Building is a fundamental activity of man
> Man builds, by joining spatial figures, thus shaping space
> Building, he responds to the spirit of the age
> Our age is the age of technology
> The plight of our age is homelessness.[11]

Heidegger famously presented his "Building Dwelling Thinking" essay at this meeting in which he reflected on homelessness as an ontological state. The solution to this existential quandary was *not* to be found in "well planned, attractively cheap, open to air housing" but in understanding "what it is to dwell."[12] It is clear that Heidegger did not directly capture the imagination of those who met in Darmstadt but he did reflect something of the existential mood of the gathering and, in fact, of Werkbund thinking in the period. Werkbund secretary Schwippert's contribution to the discussion was to claim that the existential question of dwelling in was best answered by "bright and mobile [architecture] as a light and open sequence of spaces, and this is something that for some time now and ever more insistently asserts itself in these times."[13] This was hardly Heidegger's famous home of the spirit, the Black Forest farmhouse. Glass and steel were, nevertheless, capable of metaphysical effects. They could, for Schwippert, produce light, open spaces which would counteract the darkness and monumentality of the Third Reich and of the Soviet Bloc.

The West German pavilion at Expo 58 in Brussels—orchestrated by the Werkbund (with the Rat für Formgebung)—was perhaps the most spectacular realization of Schwippert's vision of "a new lightness, a new tenderness and a new beauty."[14] Not a single structure, it was a series of two and three-story pavilions connected by a chain of walkways covered with a white polythene roof forming a circular route. The complex was entered across a footbridge suspended from a high steel pylon, the only element visible from a distance. Emphasizing the overall effect of low horizontality and transparency, the structure of each building was created by a grid of stanchions and framed by a glass wall set one meter inside the roofline. The effects of transparency were amplified by the ascetic and controlled style of display inside. The selection of exhibits tended towards modesty, a feature which was heavily laced with ideological significance in Werkbund debates. Alfons Leitl, writing in the exhibition catalogue, stressed "there is a social and democratic element . . . in the modest but dignified atmosphere of our everyday life."[15] What might have been presented as glittering commodities took the form of a display of possessions (*Persönlicher Bedarf*) which were exhibited to demonstrate the ordinary face of a nation which had once proclaimed its citizens to be *Übermenschen*.

This meant that the home was given special significance above all other social sites in the national display in Brussels. Expo visitors were presented with three different full-scale model homes in the West German pavilion. The most important of these domiciles was a six-person family, single-story apartment. It was presented as a glass-walled exhibit within the "Stadt und Wohnung" section. The family kitchen was displayed in cross-section with all the facing walls framed with glass. The viewer was offered uninhibited views of the pipework under the sink and the contents of the cupboards. Things were to reveal themselves in the most direct and unmediated fashion. The isolation of the single object—whether a cardigan, a bass violin, or a prosthetic limb—suspended in the air released it from the need to address its viewer as consumer. Such displays even aspired to what Susan Sontag was to call "transparence," the experience of "luminousness of the thing itself."[16] The model home and, in fact, the entire West German pavilion, displayed a kind of distrust of images or, more accurately, of their powers of seduction. An image which treated images with suspicion, visitors were presented with evidence of inward-looking and modest Germany to suppress recent memories of her belligerence and to demonstrate her commitment to spiritual renewal. Here was a German home without a past or even an unconscious in the sense proposed by Gaston Bachelard.[17] For the French philosopher, writing when millions of Europeans had been homeless as a result of the Second World War and the decisions made at the Yalta Conference in February 1945, the home was the place where one's most intimate dreams and anxieties could be stored. Privacy had—since 1945—been given a central role in the denazification of a militarized, corporate society. At Brussels, this order of domestic politics was publicly demonstrated to the rest of the World.

West Germany presented the most pronounced version of what were the general circumstances in which many modernist architects and designers found themselves in Western Europe in the 1950s. Substituting radical politics for a humanist rhetoric, many put themselves in an *arrière-garde* position. Exercising what artist Richard P. Lohse called their "artistic ability, moral powers of resistance and knowledge of continuing cultural and psychological conditions," architects and designers were to stave off what they saw as alienating effects of modern life.[18] New terms entered into the discourse of modern architecture. Community, to give one instance, now had to be reconciled with the needs of privacy, argued Serge Chermayeff and Christopher Alexander in 1963, in order to produce a "new architecture of humanism."[19]

Here, Now

The home was given ideological functions in Western Europe after 1945. The Marshall Plan had, for instance, put numerous model homes on display across Western Europe in the early 1950s. This technique, in Greg Castillo's words, "conflated democratic freedom with rising private consumption" and contested Soviet claims on the superiority of socialism.[20] In the early 1950s a series of exhibitions promoted American models of domesticity in West Germany, Belgium, and France, albeit in the "elevated" mode promoted by Edgar Kaufmann, curator of Industrial Design at MoMA. The designs of Eero Saarinen manufactured by Knoll and the import of the Knoll line of furniture to Belgium—the subject of Cammie McAtee and Fredie Floré's essays in this book—were turned into symbols of reassurance, democracy, affluence and liberalism by being conscripted in this fashion. Berlin was given its own venue for such exhibits, the George Marshall-Haus, which opened in 1950. *Wir bauen ein besseres Leben* (We're Building a Better Life, 1952) was a typical Marshall-Haus event. Its centerpiece was a single-family home containing a generous supply of consumer goods manufactured by Marshall Plan member nations. Here was a demonstration of the benefits of international exchange guided by the market. For many contemporaries, this was Americanization by another name.[21] Lefebvre called it "that ideological commodity imported in the name of technical progress, 'consumer society' and the mass media."[22] The building—ordinary in most respects—was rendered knowable by the fact that it was roofless. Visitors to the exhibition were led up on to an elevated gantry from which they could spy on everyday family life, performed by adult and child actors. Here, what Barthes later called the "publicity of the private" was given the ideological function of producing both envy and knowledge of the lifestyles contained therein.[23]

These techniques were almost a decade old when, in 1958, the West Germans built and furnished their pavilion in Brussels and when, in the following year, the United States put consumerism on display in Moscow at the famous American National Exhibition. Evidence of American prosperity—automobiles, kitchen appliances, color television and even a supermarket—were exhibited in order to produce the destabilizing effects of envy amongst the Soviet citizenry. The angry conversations between US vice president Richard Nixon and premier Nikita Khrushchev on the opening day became one of the best-known arguments of the

Cold War, known as the "Kitchen Debate." Nixon seized the opportunity to represent America as a land in which householders held the whip hand: manufacturers and housing developers were, he suggested, compelled by market pressures to meet their every whim such was the power of the consumer. Nothing could be better for the economy than the fact that ordinary citizens grew tired of their new homes within a few years. This kind of psychological obsolescence was, he argued, the engine of progress. Khrushchev countered by boldly claiming the minor miracles of washing machines and refrigerators were nothing new: "You think the Russian people will be dumbfounded to see these things" barked the Soviet premier, "but the fact is that newly built Russian houses have all this equipment right now."[24] The Soviet system was superior because it eschewed short-term benefits for the long-term goals of socialism. Paradoxically, however, this event came at the end of Soviet "long-termism" and was coincidental with policies designed to produce immediate effects.

At the Twenty-Second Party Congress in 1962 Khrushchev announced "For the first time in history there will a be a full and final end of the situation in which people suffer from the shortage of anything . . . [by] 1980 this country will far outstrip the United States . . . ."[25] Families in the Soviet Union and in satellite socialist nations were to enjoy new levels of domestic comfort: high-rise housing in single-family apartments was the first and most important aspect of this promise to meet the material and social needs of working men and women. After the idealized collectivism of the *domkomuna* (the experimental housing communes of the 1920s) and cramped conditions of the *komunalka* (the communal apartment shared by many families), the single-family apartment represented a much-desired atomic dwelling in which the family constituted the key social unit. It was not the only symbol of the age. The design of scooters, consumer goods like East German plastic kitchen utensils and radios, and fashionable clothing were all attempts to materialize Khrushchev's promise to make socialism a worker's paradise. Eastern Bloc authorities, as Ana Miljački explores in her contribution to this book on Czechoslovak images of "socialist lifestyle," could no longer rely on the conventional indices of industrial progress—the factory and the machine—to demonstrate their hold on modernity. By turning consumerism into a site of "peaceful competition," the East and the West had produced a state of affairs in which consumption was equated with citizenship. In fact, when faced with the American dream home implanted on Soviet soil in 1959, Khrushchev had bragged "In Russia all you have to do to get a house is to be born in the Soviet Union. You are entitled to housing."[26]

This promise was repeated and extended in the years that followed by the Soviet government and in the regimes which formed the Eastern Bloc. Material comforts which had once been offered to a narrow elite in return for their loyalty and political activism were now extended to all.[27] This was a new kind of contract based on political passivity, acquiescence, and ritualized gestures of support.[28] This was perhaps most evident in the period of "normalization" in Czechoslovakia following the suppression of the political reforms of the Prague Spring.[29] Václav Havel writing in 1978 described this uneasy contract in succinct terms when he wrote, "The post-totalitarian system has been built on foundations laid by the historical encounter between dictatorship and the consumer society."[30] For critics from the

New Left in the 1960s, the symmetries of East and West in this regard (and others) was evidence of the intellectual poverty of both worlds. In his book, *The Revolution of Everyday Life* (1967), Raoul Vaneigem wrote:

> The cultural détente between East and West is not accidental! On the one hand, *homo consomator* buys a bottle of whiskey and as a free gift the lie that accompanies it. On the other, Communist buys ideology and gets a free gift of a bottle of vodka. Paradoxically, Soviet and capitalist regimes are taking a common path, the first thanks to their economy of production, the second thanks to their economy of consumption.[31]

For contemporary critics like Vaneigem—an associate of the *Situationiste Internationale*—the idea that happiness could be measured in possessions was perhaps the most troubling illusion of the age.

Into the Future?

Even by the standards of the day, Khrushchev's futurology was rather limited. Purpose-built, single-family homes equipped with a refrigerator or washing machine may well have represented a kind of dream for the citizen-comrades of the Eastern Bloc (and for many people in the so-called First and Third Worlds too), but it was a relatively modest ambition for an utopian ideology which proclaimed its superior command of advanced technology. Even the most ambitious form of high-rise housing in the Soviet Union in the 1960s—conceived by Nathan Osterman working for Mosprojekt 3 (the Institute of Standard and Experimental Projects in Moscow) and known as *Dom Novogo Byta* (House of New Life)—offered a modest strain of futurism. In the *Dom Novogo Byta*, some 2,000 people were to occupy the 812 small apartments in the tall residential blocks served by a low complex containing a canteen, library, television rooms, hairdressing salons, launderettes, cinema, and a sports center with a swimming pool. The aim was to provide housing for young people and new families, who would exchange the privacy of the single flat for the benefits of communal life. A revival of ideas of the *domkomuna* of the 1920s, this scheme looked much like a First-World hotel.

Other experimental schemes of the era—described as "the house of tomorrow" or the "house of the future"—were more spectacular. Characteristically featuring plastic monocoque shells, electronic communication systems, and domestic robots, this was a genre of housing which claimed its place in an era of space travel, cybernetics, nuclear power, and electronic communications. The most celebrated of these schemes was British architects Alison and Peter Smithson's House of the Future, an exhibit at the annual Ideal Home exhibition in London in 1956. They built their vision of what life would be like in 1980. A series of flowing spaces organized around a central patio space, the House of the Future had no meaningful exterior. It was a cave-like space made from smooth panels, seemingly made from plastic, which formed the walls, ceiling, and floors. The living room was organized around an adjustable table which could be set at different heights or disappear into the floor. This was also a thoroughly commodified future home, full of "push-button" gadgets. The shower for instance not only regulated its own temperature, but also combined a blow drier and a sun lamp. Other celebrated schemes of the era included Ionel Schein's Plastic House of 1956, shown at the Salon des Arts Ménagers in Paris in 1956 and the Monsanto House designed by MIT engineers and exhibited at Disneyland in 1957. In the course of the 1960s others were created in Germany and the Soviet Union as well. Even Cuba participated in this global experiment with young architects designing the *Módulo Experimental de Vivienda de Asbesto-Cemento* (Experimental Asbestos Housing Module), an experimental housing type constructed from prefabricated molded sheets (1964–1968).[32]

Based on off-site prefabrication, these structures were to be light and mobile. Freestanding homes could be delivered to their plots by truck or even helicopter and living "pods" would be stacked to form high-rise structures or laid in interlocking chains on the ground. Their architects celebrated the idea that such schemes would become redundant within a generation. After all, the pace of technological invention would supply new and better homes. Such homes also assumed a kind of diagnostic function, presenting models of life in the future. Often displayed at international exhibitions and trade fairs, they invited the visitor to imagine that they too would one day enjoy life in a "smart home."[33]

Whilst this genre of domestic architecture demonstrated faith in future technology, in the early 1960s no one could assert with complete confidence that there would be a future. Periods of high tension in the Cold War—particularly at the time of the Cuban Missile Crisis of 1962—brought the prospect of war between two antagonistic systems armed with nuclear weapons terrifyingly close. In an age when apocalypse seemed one potential future for mankind, any consideration of this genre of buildings needs to be supplemented with "homes of future apocalypse." These might include the smart home in Ray Bradbury's 1950 short story, "There Will Come Soft Rains," which continues to operate even when its inhabitants have become irradiated shadows after a nuclear explosion. Other homes in this unarticulated genre might include the Underground House presented at the New York Fair of 1964 by the Underground World Corporation. Visitors descended into a kind of cave which contained a suburban home complete with artificial garden and swimming pool. In this luxury bunker, "natural" conditions could be sustained with lighting which simulated the conditions of dawn, daylight, dusk, and night. The "dial-a-view murals" could be changed at the press of a button. New York's skyline could be substituted for San Francisco's Golden Gate Bridge. In the company's own publicity, the true purpose of these structures—survival after a nuclear attack from Moscow— was almost entirely ignored in favor of soothing descriptions of the benefits of underground life. What could be better, trilled the company's publicity, than life underground in a world protected from criminals and intruders: "Greater security— peace of mind—the ultimate in true privacy."

Even those structures which loudly proclaimed their technological optimism might be understood as belonging to the category of "homes of future apocalypse." As Beatriz Colomina has shown, the Smithson's house was full of defenses.³⁴ Visitors to the house were required to walk through a draft of warm air, as if being decontaminated. Moreover, the steel door through which they passed was itself a kind of electronically operated air lock, like that required for a spacecraft or for a submarine. It implied the possibility of sealing the house from the outside world. The external threat was both invisible and deeply penetrating, not unlike the nuclear threat posed by the Cold War itself. Like a spaceship, submarine, or bunker, this was also a home without an outside. But, in a vertiginous fashion, it was also the prehistoric form of a cave. Caves are, of course, not only spaces of shelter but also the home of dark fears. They represent, as numerous films and novels depicting life after nuclear war produced during the period show, a kind of return to the primal condition of "bare life."

In the 1960s, growing interest in life in what the architect Peter Cook was to call "edge situations" like the Arctic and on the seabed—popular themes in the architectural imagination—can also be understood in terms of anxiety. In 1971, Frei Otto, the brilliant engineer, was commissioned by Farbwerke Hoechst AG to plan a new city for the Arctic that would be home to 45,000 workers exploring and developing the Arctic. Living under a transparent pneumatic dome covering 3 km², they would enjoy an artificial climate. The most challenging form of marine architecture, the underwater structure, was a recurrent dream throughout the period, shared by Archigram architects Warren Chalk (Underwater City, 1964), Peter Cook (Sea Farming Project, 1968), and Claus Jürgen (Submarine Centre, 1971). From such environments man could explore these *terrae incognitae* for mineral resources and farm the seabed. Although rarely articulated, these schemes harbored within them the fear that mankind's conventional habitat faced destruction: perhaps in the future, humanity would have no choice but to colonize hitherto uninhabited environments. The greatest threat to mankind was increasingly understood to be man himself. Critic Michel Ragon, for instance, examined the implications of overpopulation in his influential books *Où vivrons-nous demain?* (*Where Will We Live Tomorrow?* 1963) and *Les cités de l'avenir* (*Future Cities*, 1966). Combining serious-minded sociology with spectacular futurology, Ragon extrapolated from statistics predicting acute population growth, an immense expansion in car ownership, and private housing. Mankind faced asphyxiation in the "mineral desert" of urban sprawl.³⁵

It is perhaps a paradox that the futurology of the house of tomorrow or the city of the future was rather conservative on a number of counts. The social and political structures—like the nuclear family—on which these visions of the future were based, owed much to present circumstances. Robert Cottrell has argued something similar about the technologies which they claimed:

> We can see now that the golden age of blockbuster futurology in the 1960s and 1970s was caused, not by the onset of profound technological and social change, but by the absence of it. The great determining technologies—electricity, the telephone, the internal combustion engine, even manned flight—were the products of a previous century, and their applications were well understood. The geopolitical fundamentals were stable, too, thanks to the Cold War.³⁶

Future houses fashioned with plastic walls, equipped with electronic communication devices, and serviced by robots were recognizable as conventional homes, namely, spaces for dwelling in a sense that would be understood and promoted by even the most doubtful critics of modern technology.

Where were more critical or radical forms of futurology to be found in the period? What, for instance, was to be the domestic landscape of the posthuman figure of the cyborg? Manfred E. Clynes and Nathan S. Kline coined the term in 1960 to describe the enhanced human being who could survive in extraterrestrial conditions:

> Man in space, in addition to flying his vehicle, must continually be checking on things and making adjustments merely in order to keep himself alive, he becomes a slave to the machine. The purpose of the Cyborg, as well as his own homeostatic systems, is to provide an organizational system in which such robot-like problems are taken care of automatically and unconsciously, leaving man free to explore, to create, to think, and to feel.[37]

With the cyborg redefining the relationship of the human to the environment, it is not surprising that they attracted the attention of architects and designers in the West and the East in the mid-1960s. Archigram in the United Kingdom, and Haus-Rucker-Co and Walter Pichler in Austria proposed schemes in which portable homes or "living environments" were as attentive to sensory stimulation as they were with matters of shelter and sustenance. Archigram described the "Suitaloon"—a portable environment inspired by the design of space suits or what NASA called "Extravehicular Mobility Units"—as "clothing for living in. . . . If it wasn't for my Suitaloon I would have to buy a house."[38]

At a deeper or perhaps more philosophical level, the cyborg offered an image of man dissolved in technology.[39] Assuming a kind of posthuman viewpoint, the great Polish science fiction writer Stanisław Lem eschewed any kind of moral or technical limits in his conceptualization of the cyborg. In his 1964 book *Summa Technologiae* he sketched worlds populated with *various* types of genetically and biochemically modified human beings as diverse as "the various kinds of ants." His concept of "Phantomology" disturbed all the conventional metaphysics of humanism: a mind could be stimulated into the perception of being somewhere else or multiple individuals could be networked to a single brain. *Summa Technologiae* was a disavowal of the central figure of Man, the rallying symbol of the postwar reconstruction:

> I don't trust any promise, I don't believe in assurances based on the so called humanism. The only way to deal with a certain technology is another technology. Today, man knows more about his dangerous inclinations than he knew a hundred years ago, and in another hundred years his knowledge will be even more complete.[40]

Lem was not the only figure to eschew postwar humanism. By the early 1960s it was coming under attack in other fields of intellectual life. Structuralism in France represented existentialist-humanism as loose, ill-disciplined thinking which over-exaggerated individual agency and responsibility in the face of the codes, rituals and structures of language and society. As Claude Lévi-Strauss famously wrote in 1962 "I believe the ultimate goal of the human sciences is not to constitute but to dissolve man."[41] Two years later Theodor Adorno published his attack on Martin Heidegger, *Jargon der Eigenlichkeit* (*The Jargon of Authenticity*). Existential humanism, in adopting a metaphysical and sermonizing vocabulary of "shelteredness," "transcendence," "truth," and "freedom," had invented a kind of secular religion which only disguised alienation and injustice:

> The empty phrase, Man, distorts man's relation to his society as well as the content of what is thought in the concept of Man. The phrase does not bother about the real division of the subject into separated subject that cannot be undone by the voice of the mere spirit.[42]

For Adorno, this was evidenced by the deep penetration of "the jargon of authenticity" into radio, television, and advertising—arenas which produced alienation and broadcast false illusions.

The earliest signs of a kind of anti-humanist attitude in architecture and design were to be found in Europe and North America in the late 1960s. New kinds of homes were devised which eschewed principles of community, privacy, dwelling, and other humanist preoccupations. As Sean Keller explores in his essay on the formal principles adopted by Peter Eisenman in the design of his "House" series from 1967 onward and, as Mary Louise Lobsinger points out in her essay, Superstudio's adoption of the grid as the form of its "Continuous Monument" (1970–), abstraction provided the means for a kind of critical estrangement from the mythical notion of home. They were not the only critiques of this kind. We might add here Ettore Sottsass's contribution to MoMA's *Italy: The New Domestic Landscape* exhibition in 1972. Exhibiting a "home" as a series of free-standing plastic shells, each of which contained the equipment to serve a domestic function such as cooking and bathing, Sottsass presented a domestic space which sought to "decondition" its user. "The form isn't cute and even, maybe, rough," he wrote, "and the expected deconditioning process, even if it works in a negative direction, I mean in the direction of eventually eliminating the self-indulgence of possession, will certainly impose a responsibility upon whoever ventures to use these objects. Eliminating the protective layer of alibis we build around ourselves always necessitates great commitment."[43] Lacking any kind or pre-determined form or setting, Sottsass's "domestic landscape" was a de-territorialized one.

Working at the end of the modernist project, Sottsass—like other designers stirred by the Counter Culture's antagonism to the commodity and traditional social structures—sought to shake off the so called "affluent society's" attraction to property. Nomadism and communalism might produce a new kind of being, based on a deeper engagement with the world and with society. In 1951 the

Darmstädter Gespräch had gathered writers, artists and architects to debate the rejuvenation of humanity. In the aftermath of mechanized war, the organizers had announced that the "the *plight* of our age is homelessness." This was both a real and a metaphysical condition for many Europeans. Only twenty years later—after the consumer boom and the deep penetration of technologies into the home—the *promise* of the age was to be a form of homelessness.

Notes

1. For discussion of local inflections in the International Style see various essays in Hubert-Jan Henket & Hilde Heynen, ed., *Back from Utopia: The Challenge of the Modern Movement* (Rotterdam: 010 Publishers, 2002).
2. Ernesto N. Rogers, editorial in *Domus*, 20 (1946): 65.
3. See various essays in Giovanna Borasi and Mirko Zardini, ed., *Sorry, Out of Gas: Architecture's Response to the 1973 Oil Crisis* (Montreal: Canadian Centre for Architecture, 2008).
4. David Harvey, *The Condition of Postmodernity: An Enquiry into the Origins of Cultural Change* (Oxford: Blackwell, 1989).
5. See Robin Evans, "Rookeries and Model Dwellings: English Housing Reform and the Moralities of Private Space," in *Translations from Drawing to Building and Other Essays* (London: Architectural Association, 1997), 93–117, and Alain Corbin, *The Foul and the Fragrant: Odor and the French Social Imagination* (Cambridge, MA: Harvard University Press, 1986).
6. Barry Curtis, "The Heart of the City," in *Non-Plan: Essays on Freedom, Participation and Change in Modern Architecture and Urbanism*, ed. Jonathan Hughes and Simon Sadler (Oxford: Architectural Press, 2000), 52.
7. Ignasi de Solà-Morales, *Differences: Topographies of Contemporary Architecture,* trans. Graham Thompson (Cambridge, MA: MIT Press, 1997), 42.
8. Congrès Internationaux d'Architecture Moderne, *The Heart of the City: Towards the Humanisation of Urban Life*, ed. J. L. Sert and E. N. Rogers, trans. J. Tyrwhitt (New York: Pellegrini and Cudahy, 1952).
9. Hans Schwippert, "Ein Vorschlag zur Gestaltung der deutschen Beteiligung der Weltausstellung Brüssel 1958" in *Hans Schwippert* (Cologne: Akademie der Architektenkammer Nordrhein Westfalen, 1984), 102. Unless otherwise noted, translations are the author's own.
10. Its highest achievement was the organization of the famous Interbau exhibition in the Hansa district of Berlin in 1957. This living exhibition of model housing was a conscious reiteration of many of the themes of the Weissenhof Exhibition in Stuttgart of 1927 and a rebuttal of the socialist realist aesthetic being promoted in East Berlin. See the special issue of *Bauwelt* 24 (1957): 561–600.
11. Otto Bartning, ed., *Mensch und Raum: Darmstädter Gespräche 1951* (Darmstadt: Neue Darmstädter Verlagsanstalt, 1952), 33.
12. Martin Heidegger, "Building, Dwelling, Thinking" (1951) in *Rethinking Architecture: A Reader in Cultural Theory*, ed. Neil Leach (London: Routledge, 1997), 100.
13. Hans Schwippert in Bartning, ed., *Mensch und Raum*, 87.
14. Hans Schwippert, "Ein Vorschlag zur Gestaltung der deutschen Beteiligung . . .," 102.
15. Alfons Leitl, "Towns and Homes," in *World Exhibition of Brussels 1958 Germany,* eds., Wend Fischer and Gustav B. von Hartmann (Düsseldorf: Generalkommissar der Bundesrepublik Deutschland bei der Weltausstellung Brüssel 1958, 1958), 117.
16. Susan Sontag, "Against Interpretation," in *A Susan Sontag Reader*, ed. Elizabeth Hardwick (Harmondsworth: Penguin Books, 1983), 103–104.
17. Gaston Bachelard, *La Terre et les rêveries du repos: Essai sur les images de l'intimité* (Paris: J. Corti, 1948). As Bruno Zevi noted: "Germany pretends to have forgotten the gas chambers and

shows us a distinguished face as if to say that technology justifies everything, whether tanks or electric razors." *L'Architettura*, 4, (May 1958): 4.
18   Richard P. Lohse, "Zur soziologischen Situation des Grafikers," *Neue Grafik* 3 (October 1959): 58.
19   Serge Chermayeff and Christopher Alexander, *Community and Privacy: Toward a New Architecture of Humanism* (Garden City, NY: Doubleday, 1963).
20   Greg Castillo, "Domesticating the Cold War: Household Consumption as Propaganda in Marshall Plan Germany" *Journal of Contemporary History* 40, no. 2 (April 2005): 263.
21   Richard F. Kuisel, *Seducing the French: The Dilemma of Americanization* (Berkeley, CA: University of California Press, 1993).
22   Henri Lefebvre, *Critique of Everyday Life*, trans. John Moore (London: Verso, 1991), 245.
23   Roland Barthes, *Camera Lucida: Reflections on Photography*, trans. Richard Howard (New York: Hill and Wang, 1981), 98.
24   For a transcription of the "Kitchen Debate" in English see http://teachingamericanhistory.org/library/index.asp?document=176
25   Nikita Khrushchev, cited by Zsuzsanna Varga, "Questioning the Soviet economic model in the 1960s," in János M. Rainer and György Péteri, ed., *Muddling Through in the Long 1960s: Ideas and Everyday Life in High Politics and the Lower Classes of Communist Hungary* (Trondheim: Programme on East European Cultures and Societies, 2005), 110.
26   The "Kitchen Debate," 1959.
27   Vera Dunham, *In Stalin's Time: Middleclass Values in Soviet Fiction* (Durham, NC: Duke University Press, 1990), 17.
28   James Millar, with reference to Vera Dunham, calls this phenomenon in Brezhnev-era Soviet Union the "little deal." James R. Millar, "The Little Deal: Brezhnev's Contribution to Acquisitive Socialism," *Slavic Review* 44, no. 4 (1985): 694–706.
29   Milan Simecka, *The Restoration of Order: The Normalization of Czechoslovakia, 1969–1976*, trans. A. G. Brain (London: Verso, 1984), especially chapter fifteen, "Corruption."
30   Václav Havel, *The Power of the Powerless* (1978), ed. John Keane (London: Hutchinson, 1985), 37–40.
31   Raoul Vaneigem, *The Revolution of Everyday Life*, trans. John Fullerton and Paul Sieveking (London: Rising Free Collective, 1979), 36.
32   See Barry Bergdoll, Peter Christensen and Ron Broadhurst, ed., *Home Delivery: Fabricating the Modern Dwelling, Part 1* (New York: Museum of Modern Art, 2008), 128.
33   Davin Heckman, *A Small World: Smart Houses and the Dream of the Perfect Day* (Durham, NC: Duke University Press, 2008).
34   Beatriz Colomina, "Unbreathed Air 1956," *Grey Room* 15 (Spring 2004), 28–59.
35   Michel Ragon, *Les cités de l'avenir* (Paris: Encyclopédie Planète, 1966), 119.
36   Robert Cottrell, "The Future of Futurology," in *The World in 2008* (London: The Economist Publications, 2007), 110.
37   Manfred E. Clynes and Nathan S. Kline, "Cyborgs and Space," *Astronautics*, September 1960: 31.
38   Peter Cook, ed., *Archigram* (London: Archigram Group, 1970; repr., New York: Princeton Architectural Press, 1999), 80.
39   Michael Kandel, "Stanisław Lem on Men and Robots," *Extrapolation* 14 (1972–73), 19.
40   Stanisław Lem, *Summa Technologiae* (Kraków: Wydawnictwo Literackie, 1964), 12.
41   Kristin Ross, *Fast Cars, Clean Bodies: Decolonization and the Reordering of French Culture* (Cambridge, MA: MIT Press, 1995), 162.
42   Theodor Adorno, *The Jargon of Authenticity* (London: Routledge & Kegan Paul, 1973), 55
43   Ettore Sottsass in the exhibition catalogue *Italy: The New Domestic Landscape, Achievements and Problems of Italian Design*, ed. Emilio Ambasz (New York: The Museum of Modern Art, New York, in collaboration with Centro Di, Florence, 1972), 162.

Illustration Credits

Cover   Stefan Zwicky, Stuhlobjekt "Grand confort, Sans confor, Dommage a Corbu," 1980
1.1   Eero Saarinen Collection, Manuscripts & Archives, Yale University Library. © Knoll, Inc.
1.2   Courtesy Cranbrook Archives
1.3   Courtesy Cranbrook Archives
1.4   Courtesy Cranbrook Archives
1.5   Works by Norman Rockwell printed by permission of the Norman Rockwell Family Agency Book Rights Copyright © 2011 The Norman Rockwell Family Entities
1.6   © The Estate of William M. Gaines
1.7   © The Freud Museum, London (*left*)
      Courtesy of the National Library of Medicine (*right*)
2.1   © Gaetano Pesce. Image supplied courtesy of Gaetano Pesce
2.2   © Gaetano Pesce. Image supplied courtesy of Gaetano Pesce
2.3   © Gaetano Pesce. Image supplied courtesy of Gaetano Pesce
2.4   © Gaetano Pesce. Image supplied courtesy of Gaetano Pesce
2.5   © Gaetano Pesce. Image supplied courtesy of Gaetano Pesce
2.6   © Gaetano Pesce. Image supplied courtesy of Gaetano Pesce
2.7   © Gaetano Pesce. Image supplied courtesy of Gaetano Pesce
2.8   © Gaetano Pesce. Image supplied courtesy of Gaetano Pesce
3.1   Image courtesy of Dave Travers
3.2   *Architectural Forum* (August 1949)
3.3   © J. Paul Getty Trust. Used with permission. Julius Shulman Photography Archive, Research Library at the Getty Research Institute (2004.R.10)
3.4   Image courtesy of Anton Maix Fabrics LLC
3.5   Image courtesy of Dave Travers
3.6   © J. Paul Getty Trust. Used with permission. Julius Shulman Photography Archive, Research Library at the Getty Research Institute (2004.R.10)
3.7   Image courtesy of Dave Travers
4.1   Associated Press
4.2   *Architectural Review*, London
4.3   National Archive, Prague, Czech Republic

Illustration Credits

4.4 National Archive, Prague, Czech Republic (*above*)
　　 Jindřich Santar, *Světová výstava v Bruselu Expo 1958* (Prague: SNKLU, 1961) (*below*)
4.5 National Archive, Prague, Czech Republic (*above*)
　　 Photograph by Alexander Paul courtesy of Prokop Paul (*below*)
4.6 Photograph by Allan Hallstone (*above*)
　　 Photograph by Alexander Paul courtesy of Prokop Paul (*below*)
4.7 Photograph by Allan Hallstone (*above*)
　　 National Technical Museum Archive, Prague (*below*)
5.1 IIT Archives (Chicago)
5.2 IIT Archives (Chicago) (*above*)
　　 László Moholy-Nagy, *Vision in Motion*, 1956 edition (*below*)
5.3 Bauhaus-Archiv Berlin (*above*)
　　 IIT Archives (Chicago) (*below*)
5.4 Bauhaus-Archiv Berlin
5.5 IIT Archives (Chicago)
5.6 © 2011 Artists Rights Society (ARS), New York / VG Bild-Kunst, Bonn
5.7 Institute of Design Collection, [photo ID# IDC_0003_0084_cover1], University of Illinois at Chicago Library, Special Collections (*above*)
　　 © 2011 Artists Rights Society (ARS), New York / VG Bild-Kunst, Bonn (*below*)
6.1 Courtesy of Peter Eisenman
6.2 Courtesy of Peter Eisenman
6.3 © Norman McGrath All rights reserved
6.4 © 2011 The LeWitt Estate / Artists Rights Society (ARS), New York.
6.5 Courtesy of Peter Eisenman
6.6 © Norman McGrath All rights reserved
6.7 © Norman McGrath All rights reserved (*above*)
　　 Photo Dick Frank. Courtesy Eisenman Architects (*below*)
7.1 *Besser leben—schöner wohnen! Raum und Möbel* (Berlin: Deutsche Bauakademie & Ministerium für Leichtindustrie, 1954): 85 (*above*)
　　 Besser leben—schöner wohnen! Raum und Möbel (Berlin: Deutsche Bauakademie & Ministerium für Leichtindustrie, 1954): 45 (*below*)
7.2 *Besser leben—schöner wohnen! Raum und Möbel* (Berlin: Deutsche Bauakademie & Ministerium für Leichtindustrie, 1954): 15
7.3 *form+zweck* 3 (1986): 33, fig. 18
7.4 *Hubert Petras Design: Eigene Arbeiten und Arbeiten der Schüler* (Halle/Saale: Freundes- und Förderkreis der Burg Giebichenstein—Hochschule für Kunst und Design Halle e.V., 1995), 19 (*above*)
　　 V. Deutsche Kunstausstellung Dresden 1962 (Dresden: Komitee der Fünften Deutschen Kunstausstellung, 1962) (*below*)
7.5 *Bildende Kunst* 1 (1963): 37, courtesy of Stiftung Haus der Geschichte der Bundesrepublik Deutschland, Sammlung Industrielle Gestaltung, Berlin (*above*)

Illustration Credits

form+zweck 2 (1966): 39, fig. 10, courtesy of Stiftung Haus der Geschichte der Bundesrepublik Deutschland, Sammlung Industrielle Gestaltung, Berlin (*below*)

7.6 Courtesy of Stiftung Haus der Geschichte der Bundesrepublik Deutschland, Sammlung Industrielle Gestaltung, Berlin
7.7 *Kultur im Heim* 4 (1964): title page
8.1 *Architecture* 14 (1955). © Knoll Archive
8.2 Stichting De Coene Archive, Kortrijk
8.3 *Bouwen en Wonen* 12 (1958)
8.4 Stichting De Coene Archive, Kortrijk
8.5 Stichting Jenny en Luc Peire, Knokke, Belgium. © Atelier Luc Peire—Stichting Jenny en Luc Peire
8.6 Vlees & Beton Archives, Department of Architecture and Urban Planning, Ghent University
8.7 Geert Bekaert and Ronny De Meyer, *Paul Felix, 1913–1981: Architectuur* (Lannoo: Tielt, 1981)
9.1 Courtesy of Marirosa Toscani Ballo
9.2 *Domus*, copyright Editoriale Domus S.p.A., Rozzano Milano, Italy
9.3 © The Museum of Modern Art / Licensed by SCALA / Art Resource, NY
9.4 Riccardo Dalisi. *Untitled Photograph*, 1974, published in *Architettura d'animazione* (Editore Beniamino Carucci, 1974), 72
9.5 Ugo La Pietra, *Modello di comprensione*, published in *Casabella* 366 (June 1972): 47
9.6 *Domus*, copyright Editoriale Domus S.p.A., Rozzano Milano, Italy
9.7 *Domus*, copyright Editoriale Domus S.p.A., Rozzano Milano, Italy
9.8 *Domus*, copyright Editoriale Domus S.p.A., Rozzano Milano, Italy
10.1 Anthony Bertram, *Design in Everyday Things*, London: British Broadcasting Corporation, 1937 (*above*) Nikolaus Pevsner, *Visual Pleasures from Everyday Things,* London: Batsford, 1946 (*below*)
10.2 Gordon Russell, *How to Buy Furniture*, Council of Industrial Design, 1947, p. 27 (Upper Bedroom). Film Producers' Guild.
10.3 Nikolaus Pevsner, *An Enquiry into Industrial Art in England*, Cambridge: Cambridge University Press, 1937
10.4 VADS Record no: WM PST 16322
10.5 Anthony Bertram, *Design in Daily Life,* London: Methuen, 1937, p. 67
10.6 Alan Jarvis, *The Things We See Indoors and Out,* London: Penguin, 1946, p. 38. Credits for Figure 1: H. Gohler; Figure 2: W. Suschitsky; Figure 3: V&A Museum; Figure 4: Eric Freeborn
10.7 Alan Jarvis, *The Things We See Indoors and Out,* London: Penguin, 1946, pp. 30, 31. Credits for Figure 1: Fox Photo; Figure 2: Denes Studio; Figure 3: Gordon Russell; Figure 4: Studio Briggs
11.1 City of New York Housing and Redevelopment Board, *West Side Urban Renewal Area: A Summary of the Final Plan* (New York: The Board, c. 1962), 3

Illustration Credits

11.2 Courtesy of the Marian Sameth and Ruth Dickler Archival Library, Citizens Housing and Planning Council, New York
11.3 Estate of Robert Weaver
11.4 Estate of Robert Weaver
11.5 Goddard-Riverside Community Center
11.6 Peggy Mann, *The Street of the Flower Boxes,* New York: Coward-McCann, 1971, pp. 25, 22
11.7 Henry Joseph Browne Papers, Rare Book and Manuscript Library, Columbia University, New York
12.2 Anne Parmly Toxey, 2004
12.7 Anne Parmly Toxey, 2006, 2003

Index

A

Aalto, Alvar 5, 20n; Paimio Chair 15, 20n
Adorno, Theodor 91
aesthetic withdrawal 190
Age of Anxiety (Auden) 11, 22n
Alexander, Christopher 50, 127
All-Union Builders' Conference 69, 83–4n, 155–6
Alton, John 56
Ambasz, Emilio 30, 31
America: anxiety, national phenomenon 11, 15, *16*; civil defense and designers 90, 91, 104, 108–9; domestic sphere, threats to 12; émigré assimilation 87, 90–1; Kitchen Debate 67, *68*, 279–80; suburban interiors and "good living" 46, 52, *53*, 55–60
America, the Haven 91
anti-humanism 285
architectural photography 46, 52, 54, 58, *59*
Archizoom: "No-Stop City," Capitalism's demise 199–202, *200, 201*; "*The New Domestic Landscape*" 31; "The Theater of Power" 198
Argan, Guilio Carlo 197
Art Deco 5
Arte Programmata 39–40
Arts and Architecture 52, 59, *60*
Aulenti, Gae 31
Aymonino, Carlo 262, *266*, 269

B

Barthes, Roland 9, 10
Baudrillard, Jean 40, 42

Bauhaus (German): ideas adopted by GDR designers 154; *Kunstgewerbe* influence 93; principles adopted in US 113–15; rejected by GDR consumers 151
Bayer, Herbert 91, 102, 117n
"B" (Bartemeier), Dr. 14, 23n
BBC (British Broadcasting Corporation): aesthetic education 208; *Design in Everyday Things* 212–13
Belgium: domestic interiors and Knoll 169, 176–7; postwar furniture showcased 177–9, *178*
Bellini, Mario 31
Benelux, Knoll's presence 169, 171, 176
Bertoia, Harry 21n, 24n, 171, *172*
Bertram, Anthony: *Design in Daily Life* 220, 220; *Design in Everyday Things* 208, *209*, 212–14; disorder and uncleanliness 216–17
Black Mountain College 94, 97
Blake, Martha Howard 17
Blake, Peter 17
Branzi, Andrea 191–2, 195
Brecht, Bertolt 91
Breuer, Marcel 91, 181
Britain: aesthetic education 208, 210, 224–5; modernist design, clean home 212; new towns, civilized living 218–19, *219*; politics and design reform 208, 210, 217–18; working class "crippled" taste 207–8, 213–17
Browne, Father Henry 227, 238, 239, 241
Brussels Expo (1958): Czechoslovak pavilion 69–70, 77, *78–9*; site map *70*; Soviet pavilion 77, *78–9*; West German pavilion 278

295

Index

C

C&B Italia 32, 37
Calder, Alexander 5
Cambridge University 127–8
camouflage 97, 104
Case Study Houses 52, 54, 62n
Cassina 32, 37–8
Celant, Germano 30
Chomsky, Noam 129, 135
"Church of Solitude" 33, *34*
CIAM (Congrès International d'Architecture Moderne) 91, 255
cinematography 56, 59
Cold War: American propaganda through business 175–6, *177*, 279–80; Soviet dominance in Eastern Bloc 69; Soviet dominance of Czechoslovakia 77
Colombo, Joe 31
Colomina, Beatriz 35–6, 45
Communist Party (PCI) 257–8
constructivism 128, 134
Container Corporation of America (CCA) 91, *101*, 102
Cranbrook Academy of Art 8, 97
Cubr, František 71
curtains 50, *51*
cyborgs 284
Czech architects: socialist lifestyle, interpretation of 68–70, 82–3
Czechoslovak pavilion, Expo 1958: contradictory ambitions 72, 74; Czech Politburo assessment 80–1; exhibit manifesto 70–1; Gold Medal entry *73*; pavilion design 77, *78–9*; political allegory 80, 81; socialist achievement, presentation of 74, *75–6*, 82; theater and film technology, success of 74, *75*, 82; "total social synthesis," aim of 69, 80

D

Dalisi, Riccardo 191–2, *192*
De Coene: America lifestyle promoted 176; Brussels Expo (1958) product showcase 179; building products 171, *172*; economic war collaborator 171; Knoll license obtained 169, 171; luxury products 170

design methods movement 127–8
design reform, British literature: *Design in Daily Life* (Bertram) 220, *220*; *Design in Everyday Things* (Bertram) 208, *209*, 212–14; *How to Buy Furniture* (Russell) *211*; *An Inquiry into Industrial Art* 214–15, *215*; *The Things We See* (Jarvis) 220–4, *221*, *223*; *Visual Pleasure From Everyday Things* (Pevsner) 208, *209*, 219–20
Deutsche Werkstätten Hellerau 151, *152*, 155, 157, *157*
Dietel, Clauss 160, *161*
displacement (relocation): Matera, Italy 261, 263, 265; New York Puerto Ricans 228–9, 234; stylized account of 235, *235–6*
domestic space: British working class "crippled" taste 207–8, 213–17; curtain as protective screen 50, *51*; electric lighting, role of 55–6, 58; glass walls and interior exposure 45–6, *47–9*, 48, 54–5; "House of the future" 35–6, 281–2, *283*; indoor outdoor living, promotion of 52, *53*; object design and social conformity 195, 219–20; perfection under pressure 57–60; transparency and privacy 278

E

Eames, Charles: "Organic Design in Home Furnishings" 5, *5*, 22n
Eames, Charles and Ray: "dream home," Pacific Palisades, CA 14, 24n; "La Chaise" 22n; Lounge Chair 17; Lounge Chair and Ottoman 6; materials paramount 9; Side Chair 20n; wartime design 97
Eco, Umberto 188, 197–8
Ehrlich, Franz 157, *157*
Eisenman, Peter: 285; anxiety for autonomy 135–6; conceptual architecture 134; critique of design methods 127–8; existential anxiety 131, 144; form and function, contradiction of 137–9; form, logic of 128–9, *130*, 131; Hiroshima and Holocaust, view on 144; House II *132*, 133, 134, *135*, 138; House III 138,

139, 139–40; house series 131; House VI *140*, 140–1, *142*, 143; Milan Triennale (1973) 133–4; post-functionalism approach 143–5
electric lighting, domestic 55–6, 58
émigrés, assimilation 87, 113
environment: aesthetic experience 197–8; human behavior, shaped by 28–9, 31; personalizing surroundings 191–3, 195; pro-design and counter-design 31–2
excavation 26, 27, 28
existentialism 127, 131, 144, 285
existenzfragen (existential questions) 276

F

Farnsworth House 57–8
Fascism 257
F.B.I., émigré surveillance 90–1
Felix, Paul 179, *181*, 181
Ferrari-Hardoy, Jorge 8, 21n
Fiberglas 8, 9, 21n
film noir 45–6, *49*, 56
formalism: Formalism Debate 151, 155; rejection by GDR officials 150
Freud, Sigmund: *Civilization and Its Discontents* 18; consulting room couch 16–17, *17*; "looking" as sexual deviation 51; theories adopted in U.S. 15, 18
La Futur est peut-etre passé 36, 36–7
futuristic housing 281–4

G

General Motors 8
George Marshall-Haus 279
German Art Expo: Fifth 158; Fourth 158
German Democratic Republic (GDR): adoption of socialist realism 150, 164; aesthetic preferences of public 151, 153, 160; designers' defiant functionalism 153–4, 157–8, 160, *161–2*, 162–3, *163*; formalism, campaign against 155–6; *Form und Zweck* 158; modernism rejected 149–51
Gestalt psychology 128, 129
glass walls, interior exposure 45–6, *47–9*, 48, 54–5, 59

Golgotha Chair *38*, 38–9, *39*
Grosz, George 91
Group de Recherche d'Art Visuelle (GRAV) 39, 40
Groupe EGAU 179, *180*
Groupius, Walter: American Defense Committee 90; émigré assimilation 87, 91, 118n; German Bauhaus 93, 119n; New Bauhaus supporter 120n
Gruppo N (Padua) 39
Gruppo Strum 31, 199
Gruppo T (Milan) 39
Gruppo Zero 39

H

Hagen, Karl-Heinz 158, 160
Les Halles (Paris) 35
Harvard University 94, 97
Haskelite Manufacturing Corporation 6
Heisig, Walter 153, 164
Heywood-Wakefield Company 6
Hilberseimer, Ludwig 91
Hoffmann, Josef 15
homelessness 286
Horkheimer, Max 91
Houlton, Peggy Mann *246*, 247
Hrubý, Josef 71
humanism: 276, 279, 284–285; Colin Rowe and 143–4; Peter Eisenman and 137

I

Illinois Institute of Technology 116n
Institute for Applied Art, Berlin 158, 160, 164
"International Style" 169, 174, 176, 275
Italy: contemporary design 30; culture and neo-avant garde design 192–8; Southern Question 254–5, 258–9, 271

J

Jahny, Margarete 162, *162*
Jarvis, Alan *221*, 222, *223*, 224
Johnson, Philip 91

Index

K

Kelm, Martin 158, 164
Kepes, Gyorgy *101*, 102, 104, 106
Khrushchev, Nikita 69, 155–6, 280
Kiesler, Frederick 5
Kitchen Debate 67, *68*, 279–80
Knoll: Butterfly Chair 8; Federal Building Operation 175; Grasshopper Chair (no.61) *6*, 6; international identity 169, 173–4; international style 176–9, 182; Knoll Planning Unit 174; New York showroom 12, *13*; Pedestal furniture series 9, 10; Rapson series 20n; Womb Chair (no.70) 3–5, *7*, 17–18
Knoll, Florence Schust: Cranbrook Academy of Art student 8; design vision 6; Eero Saarinen project 8–9; Illinois Institute of Technology student 21n; Knoll (no.70) launched 17–18; Knoll Planning Unit 15, 173; marriage to Hans Knoll 14, 24n
Knoll, Hans 6, 8, 14, 18, 21n, 24n, 173
Kölbel, Sigrid *159*, 160
Krauss, Rosalind 134–5

L

Lacan, Jacques 57
Laterna Magika 74, 82
Le Corbusier 3
Levi, Carlo 257–8
LeWitt, Sol 134–5, *136*
Liebknecht, Kurt 151, 155
lucite 95, 122n

M

Marcek, George 95
March, Lionel 128
Marcuse, Herbert 198, 201–2
Mari, Enzo 31
Marshall Plan 175, 176, 279
Matera: pawn in economic strategy 267–9, *270*; political sparring 257–8; premodern living in Sassi 254–5, *255–6*, *258*; relocation plans, failure of 265, *266*, 267; Sassi ties denied 271; social studies and urban design 259–63, *260*, *264*
Mathsson, Bruno 20n
Matter, Herbert 18
May, Rollo, *The Meaning of Anxiety* 11
Mead, Margaret 11
Mendelsohn, Erich 91
Mendini, Alessandro 36–7
Michel, Horst 156–7
Mies van der Rohe, Ludwig: Barcelona Chair 20n; émigré assimilation 91, 118–19n; Farnsworth House 57; Illinois Institute of Technology 21n, 94
Miller, J. Irwin 18
Miltown, tranquilizer 12
Miró, Joan 5
Modernica 20n
Moholy-Nagy, László: American CIAM 91; Bauhaus principles, adoption of 113–15; Civil Defense Commission (Chicago) 90, 108–9; "constructive rehabilitation" programs 102–4; émigré assimilation 87, 89, 90–1; integrated humanitarian design 92, 111; Office of Civilian Defense (Washington) 90, 104; problem-driven design 93–4, 96, 99–100; social responsibility 115–16; "war industry" projects 94
Moholy-Nagy, Sibyl 118n, 119n, 120n
MoMA *see* Museum of Modern Art
mono-space 77, 81
Moses, Robert 228, 230
Müller, Erich *162*, 162
Mulvey, Laura 54
Museum of Modern Art: émigré assimilation 91; *The New Domestic Landscape* exhibition 26–33; "Organic Design in Home Furnishings" 5–6; wartime exhibitions 117n, 121n, 123n, 125n
Mussolini, Benito 257

N

neighborhood planning 228–9, 232, 234, 239
Nekimken, Elic 95
Nelson, George 18
neo-avant garde 186
Neorealism 262

Index

Neutra, Richard 19, *49*, 52, *59*
New Bauhaus: Chicago building *88*; financial and cultural links 91; integrated humanitarian design 92; problem-driven design 93–4; renamed as School of Design 94; wartime design and beyond 89–90
The New Domestic Landscape exhibition: environments, pro and counter-design 30–1; "The Period of Great Contaminations" 26–9, 32
New York City: Housing and Redevelopment Board (HRB) 241–2, 243–4; public housing, demand for 240, 242; *see also* West Side Urban Renewal Area (WSURA); urban renewal and community integration 227–9, 249–50; *Urban Renewal*, planning report 231–4, *233*

O

Office of Civilian Defense (Washington) 90, 104
organic architecture 262
"Organic Design in Home Furnishings" 5, 6
Orwell, George 210

P

Paepcke, Walter 91, 97–8, 102, 119n
Paessagio Domestico (film) 28, 32
Pahlavi National Library (Iran) 35
participatory planning 228
participatory practices 191–2
"Period of Great Contaminations" 26, *27*, *28*, *29*
Pesce, Gaetano: "Church of Solitude" 33, *34*; emotional and material stability 32–3, 35, 36–7; La Futur est peut-etre passé *36*, 36–7; Golgotha Chair *38*, 38–9, *39*; objects, symbolic function of 40–2; plastics, properties of 40–1; Pratt Chair *41*; subterranean buildings of 35; "The Period of Great Contaminations" 26–9, *27*, *28*, *29*, 31, 32; UP series 37, 40
Peters, Jürgen, 158, *161*, 162
Petras, Hubert 158, *159*, 163

Pevsner, Nikolaus: *An Inquiry into Industrial Art* 214–15, *215*; Moholy-Nagy report 96; *Visual Pleasure From Everyday Things* 208, *209*, 219–20
photography: School of Design, Chicago 106; as therapy 103
La Pietra, Ugo 31, 192–3, *194*
Pioneer modernism 153
plastics 8–9, 40–1
plywood 6, 10, 96, 99, 171
Pokorný, Zdeněk 71
Polyecran 74, *75*, 82
polyurethane 27–8
posthumanism: humans and cyborgs 284–5; Peter Eisenman and 143–4
post-utopia 31
postwar architecture: Cold War anxiety and militarized design 33–6; humanism, influence of 276, 279; West German design 277–8; window walls and exposed interiors 46, *47*, 48
psychoanalysis 15

R

Rapson, Ralph 20n, 21n
Rawlings, John 18
Reik, Theodor 50, 52
Rhoades, Nolan 95–6
Risom, Jens 20n, 21n
Rockwell, Norman: *Easter Morning* 12, *13*; studio, Stockbridge, Mass. 12
Rosselli, Alberto 31
Rowe, Colin 128, 143–4
Rudolph, Lutz *161*, 162
Rush, Benjamin, Dr.: "tranquilizer" chair 15–16, *17*

S

Saarinen, Aline (Bernstein) Louchheim 12, 18
Saarinen, Eames 18
Saarinen, Eero: Bloomfield Hills, MI, home *7*; David S. Ingalls Hockey Rink, Yale University 3, 19; dream home 14, 24n; Grasshopper Chair (Knoll no.61) 6, *6*; Jefferson National Expansion Memorial, St. Louis 3, 19; Knoll Pedestal furniture series 9, 10;

Index

plastics, advocate of 8, 9; psychoanalysis of 14, 23n; Trans World Airlines Terminal, J.F.K. Airport 3, 18, 19, 25n; Womb Chair (Knoll no.70) 3–6, *4*, *7*, 8–9, 15, 16–19
Saarinen, Eliel 6, 14, 19, 25n
Saarinen, Lily Swann 22n, 25n; marriage to Eero Saarinen 14, 23n; psychoanalysis of 14, 15, 23n
Santar, Jindřich 74
Sapper, Richard 31
Schlesinger, Arthur Jr.: "Politics in the Age of Anxiety" 11
School for Applied Art, Berlin-Weißensee 155, 158
School for Industrial Design Halle-Burg Giebichenstein 158
School of Design, Chicago *see also* New Bauhaus; the Army, working with 101, 102, 106; camouflaging Chicago project 108–9; *Design Workshops* (1944) 106, *107*; *Exhibition Work of Camouflage Class* (1943) 106, 109, *110*; guerrilla supply bomb 96; Industrial Camouflage course 104, *105*, 106, *107*; integration of disciplines 111–14; mobile machine gun unit 95–6; the Navy, working with 102; occupational therapy and rehabilitation 102–4; plastic balloon skin 96; postwar production, designing for *98*, 99; rubberized-cloth units *95*, 95; social responsibility 115–16; *War Art* exhibition 109, *110*, 111; war courses 100–2; "war industry" projects 94–7
Schwippert, Hans 276–8
scopophilia 50, 52, 54, 57
scopophobia 54–5
Scott, Robert *13*
Selye, Hans 11, 23n
Seng Company 96
shelter-homes 34, 35–6
Shklovsky, Viktor 138–9
Sleeping International Systems Italia 32
Slutzky, Robert 134
Smithson, Alison and Peter 35–6, 281–2, 283
Socialist Lifestyle 68
socialist realism: arts to reflect national values 150; communication of themes 68, 150; domestic interior styles 151, *152*, 153; Khrushchev's interpretation 69, 155–6, 230
Society of Plastics Industry 8
Sottsass, Ettore 31, 285
Soviet Union: Brussels Expo (1958) 77, *78–9*; housing schemes (1960's) 281; Kitchen Debate 67, *68*, 279–80; socialist realism, revision of 69, 155–6, 280
springs, wooden *95*, 96
Stam, Mart 153, 154, 155, *156*
Stern, Robert A. M. 143
Strycker's Bay Neighborhood Council (SBNC) 238, 239, 240–1
Superstudio: "A Place to Eat," 195, *196*; *Continuous Monument* 189; Istogrammi di architettura, grid design 188, *189*, 195, *196*; *Quaderna* tables 186, *187*, 188; supersurface, interpretation of function 188–91; "*The New Domestic Landscape*" 31

T

Tafuri, Manfredo 261, 262, 267
Terragni, Giuseppe 128
tranquilizers 11–12, 58
Tronti, Mario: "The Factory and Society" 199–201
Tupper, Earl 9

U

UFO 193, 195
Ulbricht, Walter 151, 160
underground buildings: defensive spaces 34–6; domestic space 282–3
underwater housing 283
University of Pennsylvania 97
utopia 31

V

veneer 96

W

Waldheim, Jack 99
War Production Board 97–8

300

West Side Urban Renewal Area (WSURA):
brownstones, life in 232, 243–5, 247;
brownstones, rehabilitation 231–2,
233, 234, 243–4; cooperative housing
240–3, *242*, 244–5; displacement not
integration 234, 237; geography and
demographics 230–1, *231*; Operation
Move-in, squatter action 247–9, *248*;
opponents denounce plan 238–9;
urban renewal plans 228–9

Whiting, Sarah 143

Wilson, Christopher 55

Winner Manufacturing Company 9, 22n

Wittkower, Rudolf 128, 144

Womb Chair (Knoll no.70): construction,
origins of *4*, 4–6, 8–10; cultural icon
3–4; *Easter Morning* (Rockwell) 12, *13*;
feature in *Easter Morning* (Rockwell)
14; function of 16–17; launch and
promotion 17–18; signature piece 19

working class, British: aesthetic education,
anxiety over 210, 218–19; bad taste
and crude vision 212–14; good taste,
learning to see 220–4, *221*, *223*;
homes of, critical description 212;
indiscriminating public 207–8;
meretricious goods, inherited traits
214–15

World War II: computing and design methods
128; German émigré assimilation 89;
School of Design, Chicago 94–7,
100–2; wartime design and beyond
92–3, 117–18n

Y

Yale University 94

Z

Zanardelli, Giuseppe 257

Zanuso, Marco 31

Zaugg, Klaus 28

Zinns, Robert 99